Ore ...

The Magazine of Westminster Cathedral

THE SODALITY OF THE BLESSED SACRAMENT

A Confraternity dedicated to Jesus Christ, Truly Present in the Most Holy Sacrament of the Eucharist

Patron: His Eminence, Vincent Cardinal Nichols

Solemn Sung Mass, Adoration & Benediction every month with a different guest preacher at the *Diocesan Shrine of the Blessed Sacrament*

Members receive a monthly newsletter and a Sodality lapel badge.

Monthly Mass offered for the intentions of members around the world. Music by the *Schola Corpus Christi.*

SODALITY 2023 MASSES	SOLEMNITY OF CORPUS CHRISTI 2023 ANNUAL QUARANT'ORE AT THE SHRINE
5th January	
2nd February	**Thursday 8th June, 7pm**
2nd March	Sung Mass, opening *Quarant'Ore*. Exposition
6th April	until Midnight
4th May	
1st June	**Friday 9th June, 7am – Midnight**
6th July	Exposition and continuation of Forty Hours
7th September	
5th October	**Saturday 10th June, 7am – 6pm**
2nd November	Exposition and continuation of Forty Hours
7th December	**6pm** – Solemn Mass closing *Quarant'Ore*
Mass at 6:30pm	**Sunday 11th June, 11am**
	Solemn Mass, followed by Procession of the Blessed Sacrament around Covent Garden

JOIN TODAY!

sodality.co.uk
Live stream at maidenlane.org.uk/live

CORPUS CHRISTI SHRINE, MAIDEN LANE, LONDON, WC2E 7NB | 0207 836 4700
Corpus Christi is part of the Westminster Roman Catholic Diocesan Trust.
Registered Charity Number 233699

Westminster Year Book 2023

71st Edition

Patrons of the Diocese

Our Blessed Lady Immaculate, 8 December;
St Joseph, 19 March; St Peter, Prince of the Apostles, 29 June;
and St Edward the Confessor, 13 October.
Consecration to the Sacred Heart of Jesus 17 June 1873.

The Westminster Year Book
Communications Office
Vaughan House
46 Francis Street
London SW1P 1QN
Editor: Fr John Scott
Paul Moynihan KSG *(from 1/11/2022)*
Tel: 020 7798 9178
Email: wyb@rcdow.org.uk

The Diocese of Westminster
comprises the London Boroughs
north of the River Thames
and west of Waltham Forest and Newham,
the Borough of Spelthorne, and the County of Hertfordshire

Unless stated otherwise,
all email addresses in this publication
are formed as follows:
Individuals: firstname+surname@rcdow.org.uk,
e.g. francesmurphy@rcdow.org.uk
Parishes: parish@rcdow.org.uk,
e.g. abbotslangley@rcdow.org.uk

Front cover:
The piazza in front of the Cathedral enabled our reponsibility
towards God's good creation to be revealed before our eyes.
© Photo: Diocese of Westminster

Perfect-bound: 978-1-7398141-1-3
Ring-bound: 978-1-7398141-2-0

CONTENTS

Printed on paper
from responsible sources

Dear Brothers and Sisters in Christ

What an autumn it has been so far, as I write these words in mid-September.

My autumn began with a meeting of Cardinals in Rome at the very end of August. Much of it concerned reforms to the Roman Curia. One aspect of the reform caught my imagination. While all Dicasteries are said to be equal in prestige, there are three taking prime spot, in a kind of triangular interdependence. They are the Dicastery for Evangelisation, the Dicastery for the Doctrine of the Faith and the Dicastery for the Service of Charity. Announcing the Gospel of Jesus Christ, ensuring and deepening the soundness of faith, and the action of charity seem to me to take us to the heart of our mission.

There is no doubt that the service of charity provided for those in need by parishes, schools and so many individuals during the time of the pandemic has been a great contribution to our society. I thank all those who have played a part in this. I thank all who work through Caritas and so many other organisations in helping to fashion and develop this service of charity. It has given so many people a fresh or renewed perspective on our Church and a respect, too.

Many will have recognised the link between this sustained and developing commitment to those in need and the life of faith. Food banks and faith go well together, for we are all people of more than one hunger. Recognising the spiritual emptiness that can come with distress or despair is precisely part of what we do. Often this shared spiritual struggle lies at the heart of many conversations which frequently begin with a tin of soup or a packet of toiletries. Through this service of charity we seek to express the love and mercy of God for every one of his children.

The love of God was evident in a special way in the Cathedral at the beginning of September. Over three days, more than 20,000 people passed through the doors to venerate the relics of St Bernadette. The experience was truly remarkable. I found it most moving to be there during the endless procession of people coming to present themselves to Mary and Bernadette, with their prayers, their gestures, their movement, their invariable, spontaneous gracefulness.

And now, as I write, we are in the time of mourning for Her Majesty The Queen. So much has already been said and written about her. For me, her joy in life, her faithfulness, her kindness, and her steadfastness are four key qualities, four central reasons why she was so loved and now mourned so sincerely by so many. She will always remain a shining light in the history of our nation. May she rest in peace. And may God save the King.

+ Vincent Nichols

Section 1

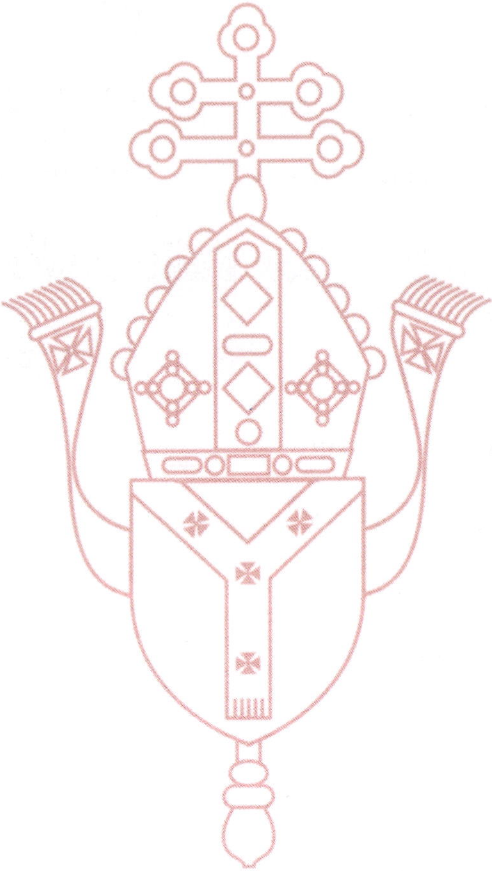

FRANCIS

BISHOP OF ROME
Historic Titles:
Vicar of Jesus Christ
Successor of the Prince of the
Apostles
Supreme Pastor of the Universal
Church
Primate of Italy
Archbishop and Metropolitan of the
Province of Rome
Sovereign of the State of the Vatican
City
Servant of the Servants of God

© Photo: Fr Alexander Balzanella

His Holiness Pope Francis (Jorge Mario
Bergoglio SJ)
Born in Buenos Aires, Argentina 17
December 1936.
Ordained Priest 13 December 1969.
Ordained Titular Bishop of Auca and
Auxiliary Bishop of Buenos Aires 27 June
1992.
Appointed Co-adjutor Archbishop of
Buenos Aires 3 June 1997.
Installed as Archbishop of Buenos Aires 28
February 1998.
Created Cardinal Priest of San Roberto
Bellarmino 21 February 2001.
Elected Pope 13 March 2013.
Inaugurated 19 March 2013.

THE HIERARCHY IN ENGLAND AND WALES

Dates shown below are of Episcopal Ordination and Translation.
The Cardinal is addressed as **His Eminence**; Archbishops as **The Most Reverend**; and Bishops as **The Right Reverend**.

THE PROVINCE OF WESTMINSTER

WESTMINSTER H.E. Cardinal Vincent Nichols (1992; 2009)
Archbishop's House, Ambrosden Avenue SW1P 1QJ
Auxiliary Bishops John Sherrington (2011), Nicholas Hudson (2014), Paul McAleenan (2016)
BRENTWOOD Alan Williams SM (2014)
Cathedral House, Ingrave Road, Brentwood, Essex CM15 8AT
Bishop Emeritus Thomas McMahon (1980)
EAST ANGLIA Peter Collins (2022)
The White House, 21 Upgate, Poringland, Norwich NR14 7SH
Bishop Emeritus Alan Hopes (2003; 2013)
NORTHAMPTON David Oakley (2020)
Bishop's House, Marriott Street, Northampton NN2 6AW
Bishop Emeritus Peter Doyle (2005)
NOTTINGHAM Patrick McKinney (2015)
Bishop's House, 27 Cavendish Road East, The Park, Nottingham NG7 1BB

THE PROVINCE OF BIRMINGHAM

BIRMINGHAM Bernard Longley (2003; 2009)
Archbishop's House, 8 Shadwell Street, Birmingham B4 6EY
Auxiliary Bishops David Evans (2020), Stephen Wright (2020)
Retired Auxiliary Bishops William Kenney CP (1987; 2006), Philip Pargeter (1990), David McGough (2005)
CLIFTON Declan Lang (2001)
St Ambrose, North Road, Leigh Woods, Bristol BS8 3PW
SHREWSBURY Mark Davies (2010; 2011)
Bishop's House, Laburnum Cottage, 97 Barnston Road, Barnston, Wirral L61 1BW

THE PROVINCE OF CARDIFF

CARDIFF Mark O'Toole (2014; 2022)
Archbishop's House, 43 Cathedral Road, Cardiff CF11 9HD
Archbishop Emeritus George Stack (2001; 2011)
MENEVIA Mark O'Toole (2014; 2022)
Convent Street, Swansea SA1 2BX
Bishops Emeriti Mark Jabalé OSB (2000; 2001), Tom M Burns SM (2002; 2008)
WREXHAM Peter Brignall (2012)
Bishop's House, Sontley Road, Wrexham, Clywd LL13 7EW
Bishop Emeritus Edwin Regan (1994)

THE PROVINCE OF LIVERPOOL

LIVERPOOL Malcolm McMahon OP (2000, 2014)

Archbishop's House, 19 Salisbury Road, Cressington Park, Liverpool L19 0PQ

Archbishop Emeritus Patrick Kelly (1984; 1986)

Auxiliary Bishops Tom Williams (2003), Thomas Neylon (2021)

HALLAM Ralph Heskett CSsR (2010; 2014)

75 Norfolk Road, Sheffield S2 2SZ

Bishop Emeritus John Rawsthorne (1981; 1997)

HEXHAM & NEWCASTLE Robert Byrne (2014; 2019)

Bishop's House, 26 West Avenue, Gosforth, Newcastle-upon-Tyne NE3 4ES

Bishop Emeritus Seamus Cunningham (2009)

LANCASTER Paul Swarbrick (2018)

Cathedral House, Balmoral Road, Lancaster LA13BT

Bishop Emeritus Michael Campbell OSA (2008)

LEEDS Marcus Stock (2014)

Bishop's House, 13 North Grange Road, Leeds LS6 2BR

Bishop Emeritus H. E. Cardinal Arthur Roche (2001; 2004)

MIDDLESBROUGH Terry Drainey (2008)

Bishop's House, 16 Cambridge Road, Middlesbrough, Cleveland TS5 5NN

Bishop Emeritus John Crowley (1992)

SALFORD John Arnold (2006; 2014)

Wardley Hall, Worsley, Manchester M28 5ND

Bishop Emeritus Terence Brain (1991; 1997)

THE PROVINCE OF SOUTHWARK

SOUTHWARK John Wilson (2016; 2019)

Archbishop's House, 150 St George's Road SE1 6HX

Archbishop Emeritus Kevin McDonald (2001; 2003)

Auxiliary Bishop Paul Hendricks (2006)

Retired Auxiliary Bishops John Hine (2001), Patrick Lynch SS.CC (2006)

ARUNDEL & BRIGHTON Richard Moth (2009; 2015)

High Oaks, Old Brighton Road North, Pease Pottage, West Sussex RH11 9AJ

PLYMOUTH Awaiting appointment

Bishop's House, 31 Wyndham Street West, Plymouth, Devon PL1 5RZ

Bishop Emeritus Christopher Budd (1986)

PORTSMOUTH Philip Egan (2012)

Bishop's House, Bishop Crispian Way, Portsmouth PO1 3HG

Bishop Emeritus Crispian Hollis (1987; 1988)

THE BISHOPRIC OF THE FORCES

BISHOP OF THE FORCES Paul Mason (2016; 2018)

Wellington House, St Omer Barracks, Thornhill Road, Aldershot, Hants GU11 2BG

THE APOSTOLIC NUNCIATURE

APOSTOLIC NUNCIO His Excellency Archbishop Claudio Gugerotti (2002, 2020)
54 Parkside SW19 5NE Tel: 020 8944 7189

THE BISHOPS' CONFERENCE OF ENGLAND AND WALES

General Secretary Canon Christopher Thomas
Catholic Bishops' Conference of England and Wales, 39 Eccleston Square SW1V 1BX
Tel: 020 7901 4815 Email: christopher.thomas@cbcew.org.uk
Web: www.cbcew.org.uk
Registered in England and Wales
Company Number: 4734592 Registered Charity Number: 109748239
The Secretariat of the Conference consists of the office of the General Secretary and a
number of departments whose work focuses on the work of the Bishops of England and
Wales. These are Christian Life and Worship, Christian Responsibility and Citizenship,
Catholic Education and Formation, Dialogue and Unity, Evangelisation and Catechesis, and
International Affairs. Further information on their work, and contact details, can be found
on the website.

The Bishops' Conference also has a number of agencies and offices, for which entries can
be found in Section 6, under Catholic Societies and Organisations, and Other Useful
Addresses:
Catholic Agency for Overseas Development
Catholic Association for Racial Justice
Catholic Communications Network
Catholic Education Service
Catholic Safeguarding Advisory Service
Catholic Social Action Network
**Mission Directorate, comprising the Department of Dialogue and Unity and the
Department for Evangelisation and Discipleship, including the National Office for
Vocation**
Stella Maris (Apostleship of the Sea)

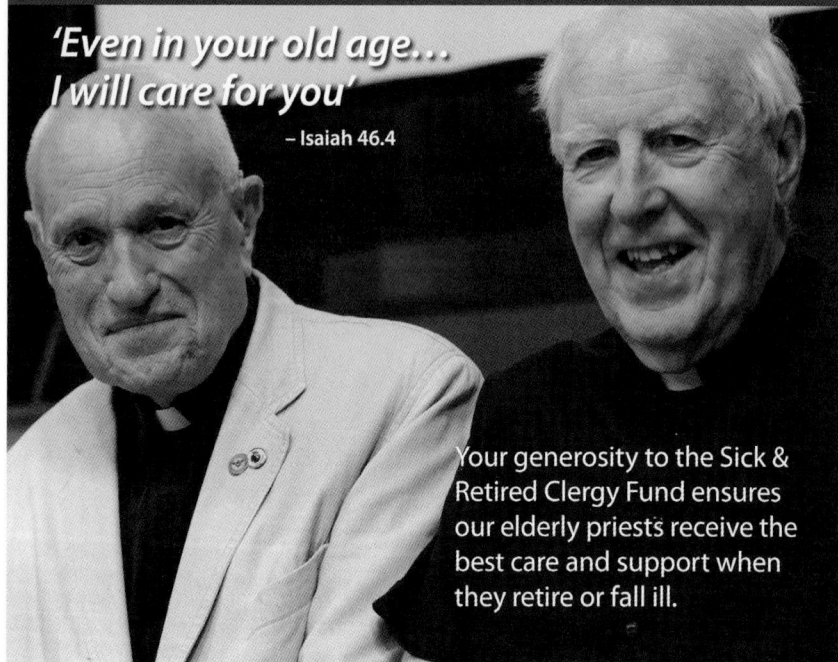

Section 2

PATRONS, SAINTS AND BLESSED

Here are listed the Diocesan Patrons and other Saints and Blessed associated with Westminster. The Liturgical Calendar can be found on page 299.

PATRONS

19 March
St Joseph
On 10 December 1898, at the request of Cardinal Vaughan, St Joseph was added as a patron of the diocese. Blessed Pius IX had already declared him to be Patron of the Universal Church (1870) and Cardinal Vaughan himself had a great devotion to him. As a young priest he had founded St Joseph's Society for the Foreign Missions and established a National Shrine of St Joseph at Mill Hill (now at St Michael's Abbey, Farnborough). This patronage of St Joseph was thought appropriate since, as Vaughan noted, 'the Church itself is the expansion of the Holy Family'.

29 June
St Peter, Prince of the Apostles
The inclusion of St Peter among our diocesan patrons testifies to the age-old devotion shown by English men and women to the 'Prince of the Apostles'. From an early date English pilgrims flocked to Rome to visit his tomb and it was King Ine of Wessex who is thought to have initiated the Peter's Pence collection to support the papacy. Many churches were dedicated to the chief of the apostles, including Westminster Abbey. On 29 June 1893 England was re-consecrated to St Peter.

13 October
St Edward the Confessor, King (1003-66)
King of England from 1042, St Edward was famed for his piety, alms-giving and the building of Westminster Abbey. He died on 5 January 1066 and the resulting Norman and Saxon claims to the succession were fought out on the battlefield of Hastings. Canonised in 1161, St Edward's incorrupt body was translated to a new shrine on 13 October 1163 (the origin of his present feast day). His cult flourished in the Middle Ages and he was considered one of the patrons of England. Pope Benedict XVI prayed before his shrine on 17 September 2010, alongside the Archbishop of Canterbury, and called St Edward 'a model of Christian witness and an example of that true grandeur to which the Lord summons his disciples'.

8 December
Our Blessed Lady Immaculate
Our Blessed Lady Immaculate was the original primary patron of the diocese. There are several local Marian shrines within the diocese, including Our Lady of Graces at Tower Hill, Our Lady of Muswell Hill, Our Lady of Warwick Street and Our Lady of Westminster. Our Lady of Willesden in particular was an important Marian shrine for Londoners on the eve of the Protestant Reformation. Although the statue of Our Lady was destroyed in 1538, the shrine was restored in 1892. Since then, Our Lady of Willesden has become the focus of Marian devotion in the diocese and during the Marian Year Rally at Wembley Stadium on 3 October 1954 Cardinal Griffin solemnly crowned the statue before a crowd of over 90,000. Moreover, the shrine is unusual in having been visited by two canonised saints: St Thomas More and (in the 1950s) St Josemaria Escriva, the founder of Opus Dei.

SAINTS

15 February
St Claude la Colombière, Priest (1641-82)
St Claude was a Jesuit chaplain to Mary of Modena, then Duchess of York and wife of the future James II, at St James' Palace between 1676 and 1679. Before coming to London he was the spiritual director of St Margaret Mary at Paray-le-Monial. He became a great proponent of modern devotion to the Sacred Heart of Jesus and the Catholics of London were one of the first to receive it. Nearly two hundred years later, on 17 June 1873, the diocese was consecrated to the Sacred Heart. St Claude was banished to France at the time of the 'Popish Plot' and died on 15 February 1682. He was canonised by St John Paul II on 31 May 1992.

19 April
St Alphege, Bishop & Martyr (c.953-1012)
St Alphege started life as a monk in Gloucestershire and Somerset, but despite trying to live a solitary life his talents were soon recognised and he became successively Abbot of Bath, Bishop of Winchester and (in 1005) Archbishop of Canterbury. In 1011 he was captured and imprisoned by the Danish invaders ('Vikings'). When he refused to let his ransom be paid, he was killed at Greenwich; according to tradition, the Danes threw bones at him from their table during a banquet and then one of them struck him on the head with an axe. He was buried at St Paul's Cathedral, where his shrine was visited by many pilgrims, before being moved to Canterbury in 1023. St Thomas Becket prayed to St Alphege just before his own martyrdom in Canterbury Cathedral.

24 April
St Erconwald, Bishop (d. 693)
Born to a rich family, St Erconwald founded the Abbeys of Chertsey (where he was Abbot) and Barking (where his sister, St Ethelburga, was Abbess). In 675 he became Bishop of London - a medieval hymn calls him *Lux Lundoniae* ('light of London'). His final years were plagued by poor health, but he was transported around his diocese in a wooden litter or cart. He was buried at St Paul's Cathedral. In the present diocesan calendar, St Erconwald is kept with the first Bishop of London, St Mellitus, on 24 April.

24 April
St Mellitus, Bishop (d. 624)
St Mellitus was sent to England by St Gregory the Great in 601 to assist the mission of St Augustine. In 604 he was consecrated first Bishop of London. However, he was expelled under St Ethelbert's pagan son, King Saeberht, and eventually became third Archbishop of Canterbury (619). He died on 24 April 624 and was buried at Canterbury. In the present diocesan calendar, St Mellitus is kept with St Erconwald on 24 April.

22 June (celebrated 20 June)
St Alban, Protomartyr (d. *circa* 209)
St Alban is the earliest British Christian whom we know by name. He was a prominent citizen of Verulamium (a town later renamed St Albans), who hid a priest fleeing from persecution. So impressed was he by the priest's example that he took instruction and was baptised. When the soldiers came to search for the priest, Alban put on the fugitive's cloak and was arrested and beheaded – the punishment reserved for Roman citizens. A cult quickly grew up around the martyr – St Germanus, Bishop of Auxerre, visited his shrine in 429 and spread his cult on the continent. Pilgrims visited his shrine in St Albans Abbey until the Reformation. Perhaps the most astonishing thing about St Alban is that he may have suffered as early as 209, testifying to the early existence of Christianity in Britain.

9 October
St John Henry Newman, Priest (1801-90)
Cardinal Newman is normally associated with the West Midlands but it is often forgotten that he was born a Londoner. He was born at 88 Old Broad Street (in the City) on 21 February 1801 and moved the following year to 17 Southampton Street (now Southampton Place). The Newman family lived there until 1816. St John Henry went to school in Ealing before entering Trinity College, Oxford as an undergraduate. Newman was a leading force in the Oxford Movement within the Church of England until his search for truth led him to the Catholic Church. He was received into the Church by Blessed Dominic Barberi at Littlemore on 9 October 1845. He set up the Oratory of St Philip Neri in England and spent most of the remainder of his life in Birmingham. After many disappointments and trials, he was created a Cardinal by Leo XIII in 1879 in recognition of his theological work and personal witness. Newman died on 11 August 1890.

16 November
St Edmund of Abingdon, Bishop (c.1175-1240)
Educated at Oxford and Paris, St Edmund started off as an academic and pioneer of scholasticism. In 1222 he became Treasurer of Salisbury and, in 1233, Archbishop of Canterbury. As Metropolitan, he became known as a defender of the Church's rights, which often brought him into conflict with the king. He died on his way to see the Pope on 16 November 1240 and was buried at Pontigny. He is the patron of St Edmund's College, Ware, which was for many years the location of the diocesan seminary. Several other Archbishops of Canterbury are remembered in our diocesan calendar – Ss Laurence (d.619), Dunstan (909-88) and Theodore (d.690) (3 February) – stressing the links between Canterbury and Westminster. Indeed, the arms of the See of Westminster are similar to those of Canterbury, although there is a red instead of blue background (or 'field') and there is no cross above the pallium.

29 December
St Thomas of Canterbury, Bishop and Martyr (1118-70)
St Thomas Becket was born in Cheapside and entered the service of the Archbishop of Canterbury. He was soon noticed by Henry II, who became a close friend and appointed him Chancellor (1155). St Thomas lived a worldly life, like many in his station, until becoming Archbishop of Canterbury in 1162 when, in the saint's own words, he went from being 'a patron of play-actors and a follower of hounds to being a shepherd of souls'. Taking his responsibilities seriously and living an austere life, he was careful to defend the rights and prerogatives of the Church. Inevitably his relationship with the king began to suffer and for six years he lived as an exile in the French towns of Pontigny and Sens. Returning to England at the end of 1170, he was murdered in his own Cathedral by four of Henry's knights on 29 December (his feast day). The king did penance and Canterbury soon became one of the most popular shrines in Europe. St Thomas was quickly canonised by Alexander III in 1173 and, in more recent times, was proclaimed Patron of the English Secular Clergy.

THE MARTYRS OF THE SIXTEENTH AND SEVENTEENTH CENTURIES

Many of these men and women had London connections – some ministered in the diocese, others were brought to the capital for trial and execution. Among the sites of martyrdom in London are Tyburn, Clerkenwell, Fleet Street, Gray's Inn, Isleworth, Lincoln's Inn Fields, Mile End Green, St Paul's Churchyard, Shoreditch, Smithfield and Tower Hill. Of special importance are the following martyrs:

4 May
St Richard Reynolds (c.1492-1535)
Born in Devon and educated at Cambridge, St Richard joined the Bridgettine community at Syon Abbey, Isleworth in 1513. Famed for his holiness and learning, Ss Thomas More and John Fisher consulted him over Henry VIII's divorce. He was arrested in the spring of 1535 and, refusing to take the Oath of Supremacy, was taken to the Tower together with the three Carthusian Priors. He suffered with them at Tyburn on 4 May.

11 May
The Carthusian Martyrs (1535)
The London Charterhouse (founded 1371) was one of the great religious houses of pre-Reformation London. At the break with Rome, the monks remained loyal to the Pope. The three English Carthusian Priors (including St John Houghton of London) suffered on 4 May 1535. Some other members of the Charterhouse (Bl Sebastian Newdigate, Humphrey Middlemore and William Exmew) were martyred on 25 May; others died in prison. Traditionally the diocese kept their feast on 11 May.

27 June
St John Southworth (d.1654)
St John Southworth's significance for our diocese lies in the discovery of his body at Douai in 1927 and his subsequent translation to Westminster Cathedral in 1930. He acts as a representative figure for the many priests who courageously worked in London in the sixteenth and seventeenth centuries, at the risk of imprisonment and execution. Southworth was trained at Douai and worked in Lancashire and London. Together with the Jesuit St Henry Morse (1595-1645), Southworth cared for the victims of the 1636 plague at great personal risk. Spending many years in prison, he was finally hung, drawn and quartered at Tyburn on 28 June 1654, together with two counterfeiters. Westminster has traditionally kept his feast on 27 June because 28 June (the day of his martyrdom) is already occupied by St Irenaeus and the Vigil of Ss Peter and Paul.

6 July (celebrated 22 June)
St Thomas More (1478-1535)
Born in Milk Street in Cheapside (near the birthplace of St Thomas Becket), he studied at Oxford and Lincoln's Inn and followed a successful career as lawyer, politician and humanist scholar. Henry VIII appointed him Lord Chancellor in 1529 but More resigned three years later as pressure was put on him to support the king's divorce. His refusal to take the Oath of Supremacy led to his imprisonment and execution on Tower Hill on 6 July 1535, a few weeks after the martyrdom of his friend St John Fisher, Bishop of Rochester. He was a devoted family man, twice-married and father of four. His beloved 'great house' in Chelsea was situated near Allen Hall. St Thomas More was canonised by Pius XI in 1935 and has since been proclaimed Patron of Politicians.

BLESSED

10 October
Blessed Carlo Acutis (1991-2006)
Born in London on 3 May 1991, Blessed Carlo was baptised 15 days later at the church of Our Lady of Dolours, Fulham Road. In September 1991 the family returned to Milan. The young boy loved computers, football, and Pokémon. He also attended Mass and prayed the Rosary every day, and once declared: 'to always be close to Jesus, that's my life plan.' Using his great talent for computing, he produced a website cataloguing the world's Eucharistic Miracles, which was also turned into a travelling exhibition. He was diagnosed with leukaemia, dealing with his sufferings cheerfully and offering them up for the Church. He died on 12 October 2006, aged 15, and was buried in Assisi, where he was beatified on 10 October 2020.

29 October
The Blessed Martyrs of Douai College (1577-1679)
Cardinal Allen founded the English College, Douai, in 1568 to train new recruits for the priesthood. This was crucial to the survival of English Catholicism. Over 160 of the priests trained at Douai are now recognised as martyrs, led by the proto-martyr, St Cuthbert Mayne (1577). This is of special significance to the diocese, since St Edmund's, Ware and Allen Hall claim continuity with Douai.

Pact

'I WAS IN PRISON AND YOU VISITED ME'

"We are all loved by God and are called to be sharers in His kingdom. I commend to you the work of Pact, who do so much to support those in need of hope and a fresh start."

- Cardinal Vincent Nichols, President of Pact

Pact is a national Catholic charity that provides support to prisoners, people with convictions, their children and families.

We keep families together. We reduce crime. We make a real difference.

Whether you are a priest, deacon, parishioner, member of a religious community; whether you've been coming to church your whole life or are recently discovering what life as a faithful Catholic means.

This invitation is for you.

Our work is inspired by Catholic Social Teaching, giving hope to women and men in prison, to their loved ones in our communities and to their children.

- We welcome volunteers for our children and family services across England & Wales. We offer full training and support

- We need 'Parish Links', people who will share about our work in parishes, in the deaneries and the diocese.

- And of course, we need funds, to help us continue our life-changing work. Please consider setting up a regular donation with us or find out about leaving us a legacy or memorial donation.

CONTACT US
Please support the work of Pact, the Catholic charity for prisoners and their families.
E: parish.action@prisonadvice.org.uk
T: 0207 735 9535

Pact is a registered charity - number: 219278.
Registered office: 29 Peckham Road, London SE5 8UA

THE ARCHBISHOP

His Eminence Cardinal Vincent Nichols
Born Crosby, Liverpool 8 November 1945. Ordained Priest in Rome on 21 December 1969 for the Archdiocese of Liverpool. Appointed Assistant Priest in St Mary's Parish, Wigan and Chaplain to the Sixth Form College and St Peter's High School in 1971. Ordained Bishop of the titular see of Othona and Auxiliary Bishop of Westminster on 24 January 1992. Translated to Birmingham as Archbishop on 29 March 2000, and to Westminster on 21 May 2009. Created Cardinal Priest of the Most Holy Redeemer and St Alphonsus Liguori on 22 February 2014.

Archbishop's House, Ambrosden Avenue SW1P 1QJ
Tel: 020 7798 9033
Email: cardinalnichols@rcdow.org.uk Web: www.rcdow.org.uk/cardinal

Private Office of the Cardinal Archbishop

Private Secretary to the Cardinal Fr Alexander Master
Tel: 020 7798 9041 Email: privatesecretary@rcdow.org.uk

PA to the Cardinal Ellen Dunleavy
Tel: 020 7798 9039 Email: ellendunleavy@rcdow.org.uk

Press Enquiries

Press Secretary to the Cardinal Alexander Des Forges
Tel: 07983 704097 Email: adesforges@rcdow.org.uk

Archbishop's House Reception

Receptionist Marie Haggerty
Tel: 020 7798 9033 Email: abhreception@rcdow.org.uk

Sisters responsible for the Cardinal's Household

La Sagesse
Tel: 020 7798 9398

THE AUXILIARY BISHOPS, EPISCOPAL VICARS AND VICAR GENERAL

The Right Rev John Sherrington Titular Bishop of Hilta
Born Leicester 5 January 1958. Ordained Priest 13 June 1987.
Ordained Bishop 14 September 2011 by Archbishop Vincent Nichols.
Archbishop's House, Ambrosden Avenue SW1P 1QJ Tel: 020 7798 9060
PA Sue Davies **Tel: 020 7798 9831**
Email: pabishopjsherrington@rcdow.org.uk

The Right Rev Nicholas Hudson Titular Bishop of St Germans
Born Hammersmith 14 February 1959. Ordained Priest 19 July 1986.
Ordained Bishop 4 June 2014 by Cardinal Vincent Nichols.
Archbishop's House, Ambrosden Avenue SW1P 1QJ Tel: 020 7931 6061
PA Sue Davies **Tel: 020 7798 9381 Email: suedavies@rcdow.org.uk**

The Right Rev Paul McAleenan Titular Bishop of Mercia
Born Belfast 15 July 1951. Ordained Priest 8 June 1985.
Ordained Bishop 25 January 2016 by Cardinal Vincent Nichols.
Archbishop's House, Ambrosden Avenue SW1P 1QJ Tel: 020 7931 6062
PA Maura McBride **Tel: 020 7798 9023**
Email:mauramcbride@rcdow.org.uk

Fr Gerard Quinn Episcopal Vicar
44 Boston Park Road, Brentford TW8 9JF
Tel: 020 8560 1671 Email: gerardquinn@rcdow.org.uk

Canon Paschal Ryan Episcopal Vicar
7 Cheyne Row SW3 5HS
Tel: 020 7352 0777 Email: paschalryan@rcdow.org.uk

Mgr Martin Hayes Vicar General
Archbishop's House, Ambrosden Avenue SW1P 1QJ
Tel: 020 7931 6076 Email: martinhayes@rcdow.org.uk
PA Paola Greco **Tel: 020 7798 9151 Email: pgreco@rcdow.org.uk**

THE DIOCESE OF WESTMINSTER AND CATHEDRAL CHAPTER

ARCHBISHOP'S COUNCIL

The Cardinal Archbishop, Auxiliary Bishops, Vicar General, Judicial Vicar, Chair of the Council of Priests, Private Secretary, Chief Operating Officer/Financial Secretary (attends for non-clergy matters).

THE WESTMINSTER ROMAN CATHOLIC DIOCESAN TRUST is the charitable trust through which the activities of the Diocese are conducted. Established by a trust deed dated 1 November 1940, it is registered under the Charities Act 2011 with Charity Registration Number 233699. The Trustees are also the **FINANCE COMMITTEE** (Canon 492, CIC) **Trustees** The Cardinal Archbishop and Auxiliary Bishops; Mgr Séamus O'Boyle; Mgr Martin Hayes; Dame Colette Bowe; Mr Edmund Craston; Mr Kevin Ingram; Mr Andrew Ndoca and Baroness Nuala O'Loan. **Secretary** Mr Paolo Camoletto.

FINANCE BOARD (with responsibilities delegated from the Trustees)
Chair Bishop John Sherrington; Bishop Nicholas Hudson; Bishop Paul McAleenan; Mgr Martin Hayes; Mr Simon Bunce; Mrs Valerie Diad; Mr John Gibney; Mr Andrew Ndoca. **In attendance** Mr Paolo Camoletto, Mr Nicholas Seed

METROPOLITAN CATHEDRAL CHAPTER (est. 19 June 1852)

(Canons 377, 463, 503-10, CIC)

The Chapter assembles at Archbishop's House for a meeting once a month, generally on the first Tuesday, after which Vespers and Capitular Mass are celebrated in the Cathedral for the intentions of the Diocese.

Provost Canon Shaun Lennard; **Secretary** Canon Patrick Browne; **Treasurer** Canon Colin Davies; **Theologian** Canon John O'Leary; **Penitentiary** Canon Anthony Dwyer; **M.C.** Canon Daniel Cronin; Canon Michael Munnelly; Canon Robert Plourde; Canon Stuart Wilson; Canon Paschal Ryan; Canon Peter Newby; Canon Terence Phipps; Canon Roger Taylor; Canon Alexander Sherbrooke; Canon Gerard King; Canon Michael Dunne; Canon Mehall Lowry.

Provost Emeritus Canon Michael Brockie; **Canons Emeriti** Canon Bernard Scholes; Mgr Canon Henry Turner; Mgr Canon Thomas Egan, Mgr Canon Paul McGinn.

SECTION 2

CONSULTATIVE BODIES

COLLEGE OF CONSULTORS (Canon 502, CIC)
Functions are entrusted to the Cathedral Chapter.

COUNCIL OF DEANS
Chair The Cardinal Archbishop; Auxiliary Bishops; Vicar General; Deans; Chair of Council of Priests; Private Secretary

COUNCIL OF PRIESTS (Canons 495-501, CIC)
President The Cardinal Archbishop
Chair Mgr James Curry **Secretary** Fr Daniel Humphreys

HISTORIC CHURCHES COMMITTEE
Particular Pastoral Responsibility Mgr James Curry

Under the Ecclesiastical Exemption provision of the Town and Country Planning Act, listed churches are exempt from the requirement to obtain from their local authority Listed Building Consent for works of repair and refurbishment, providing they obtain approval from the local Historic Churches Committee. These regulations have been confirmed by the Bishops' Conference of England and Wales in its 1999 'Directory on the Ecclesiastical Exemption from Listed Building Control'.

Chair Fr Peter Harris **St Joseph's, 3 Windhill, Bishop's Stortford CM23 2ND**
Tel: 01279 654063
Secretary Barry Lawrence **Historic Churches Committee, c/o Property Services Office, St Joseph's Grove NW4 4TY Tel: 020 8457 6542 / 07711 590317**
Administrator Lesley McNealis **Tel: 020 8457 6532 / 07706348876** and Roz Freeland
Tel: 020 8457 6539
Committee Members
Fr Peter Harris (Chair), Mgr James Curry (Vice-Chair), Fr Andrew Cameron-Mowat SJ, Paolo Camoletto, Andrew Derrick, Clive Horscroft, Bruce Kirk, Paul Moynihan, Canon Peter Newby, Mark Price, Paul Velluet, Barry Lawrence (Secretary), Lesley McNealis (Administrator), Roz Freeland (Administrator)

LITURGY COMMISSION
Particular Pastoral Responsibility Mgr James Curry

The Commission is charged by the Cardinal Archbishop to assist him in promoting liturgical renewal and on-going liturgical formation in the Diocese. It is to establish policy for the ordering of churches and to approve such. It also has oversight of principal diocesan liturgies.
Chair Fr Allen Morris **Email: allenmorris@rcdow.org.uk Web: www.rcdow.org.uk/liturgy**
Chair of Art and Architecture Committee Canon Peter Newby **Tel: 020 8892 3902**

MASTER OF CEREMONIES for the Cardinal Archbishop Paul Moynihan

AGENCY FOR EVANGELISATION

Particular Pastoral Responsibility Bishop Nicholas Hudson

Serving the new Evangelisation

Working under the banner of 'Proclaim; Forming Missionary Disciples, Building Missionary Parishes', the Agency for Evangelisation resources and accompanies parish communities in forming evangelisation teams, local evangelising initiatives, small faith-sharing communities, programmes of Adult Faith Formation and lifelong learning, Sacramental Catechesis, Marriage and Family Life ministry, and the liturgical ministries of Lector and Extraordinary Minister of Holy Communion.

Director Fr Christopher Vipers **Tel: 020 7798 9157 Email:** chrisvipers@rcdow.org.uk
Vaughan House, 46 Francis Street SW1P 1QN
Deputy Director and Evangelisation Co-ordinator Awaiting appointment
Team Administrator Warren Brown **General Enquiries Tel: 020 7798 9152**
Email: evangelisation@rcdow.org.uk **Web:** www.rcdow.org.uk/evangelisation
Facebook: facebook.com/westminstercatechists.evangelisation
Twitter: twitter.com/evangelisationw

Adult Faith Formation and Small Communities
Enquiries: catadmin@rcdow.org.uk

Catechesis
The Catechesis Support Team oversees the provision of ongoing formation and accreditation for parish catechists for Baptism Preparation, First Reconciliation, Holy Communion, Confirmation, RCIA, parish-based Religious Education for Children, Children's Liturgy, and helps parishes develop programmes of Family Catechesis.
Catechesis Advisers for Deaneries and Parishes
Mary Crowley **Tel: 020 7931 6090 Email:** marycrowley@rcdow.org.uk
Anna Dupelycz **Tel: 020 7798 9026 Email:** annadupelycz@rcdow.org.uk
Enquiries: catadmin@rcdow.org.uk

Learn From Me
A formation programme for all involved in parish ministry, offering a variety of formation opportunities including the Catholic Certificate in Religious Studies (CCRS).
Anna Dupelycz **Tel: 020 7798 9026 Email:** annadupelycz@rcdow.org.uk

Marriage and Family Life
MFL Ministry works alongside existing groups to proclaim and grow the Gospel of Life within parishes, schools and the wider community. It seeks to support the single, married couples and families to deepen their understanding of the beauty of Catholic teaching through guidance and resources on the formation of couples for the Sacrament of Holy Matrimony, for the provision of on-going enrichment, healing and counselling, and accompaniment for the divorced and separated. Working alongside the Catechesis Support Team by helping parishes develop programmes of Family Catechesis, MFL seeks to enable

SECTION 2

families to grow in an awareness that God is present in the ordinary everyday events of family life and that they are 'the domestic church', where the Word of God is first proclaimed, received, and lived.

Co-ordinator Rev Roger Carr-Jones (Deacon) **Tel: 020 7798 9363**
Email: rogercarrjones@rcdow.org.uk **Web: www.rcdow.org.uk/marriage-and-family-life**

ARCHIVES

Particular Pastoral Responsibility Bishop John Sherrington

Archivist Fr Nicholas Schofield (Uxbridge)
Administrative Archivist Susannah Rayner
Archives Assistant Judi McGinley
16a Abingdon Road W8 6AF
Tel: 020 7938 3580 Email: archivist@rcdow.org.uk
Open by appointment (Mon, Fri 10-12.30pm, 1.30-5pm)

CARITAS WESTMINSTER

Particular Pastoral Responsibility Bishop Paul McAleenan

Caritas Board Bishop Paul McAleenan (Chair), Jasdeep Brar, Ruth Cairns, Paolo Camoletto, John Coleby, Alba de Souza, Pat Fernandes, Mick McAteer, Andrew Ndoca, Fr Mark Woodruff

Vaughan House, 46 Francis Street SW1P 1QN		**Tel: 020 7931 6077**
Email: caritaswestminster@rcdow.org.uk **Web: www.caritaswestminster.org.uk**		
Director	John Coleby	**Tel: 020 7798 9357**
PA	Susannah Marcot	**Tel: 07803 634240**
Assistant Director	Meriel Woodward	**Tel: 020 7798 9078**
Information Officer	Caitlin Boyle	**Tel: 07874 861064**
Communications Officer	Louise Cook	**Tel: 07522 229438**

CARITAS DEVELOPMENT TEAM

Caritas Westminster accompanies parishes and schools in their mission of charity and community, informed by Catholic Social Teaching. This is met by expert leads in five key areas across the whole Diocese. Each Development Worker also has responsibility for direct contact in the different geographical regions, shown in italics.

Catholic Social Teaching	Sr Silvana Dallanegra RSCJ	*Inner West London*
Tel: 07921 471506		
1. Caritas Food Collective	Niki Psarias	*Outer West London*
Tel: 07525 812511		
2. Shelter	Elizabeth Wills	*N Herts & Central London*
Tel: 07877 902313		
3. Financial Resilience	Sr Silvana Dallanegra RSCJ	*as above*

4. Dignified Work Tel: 07525 812513	Minet Masho	*East London*
5. Social Isolation Asylum Seekers & Refugee Response Tel: 07719 563125	Rosa Lewis	*North London*
Youth Tel: 07919 812735	Frances Moore	*South Hertfordshire*

SECTION 2

THE ST JOHN SOUTHWORTH FUND

Through the Fund, Caritas Westminster provides grants to individuals in crisis and to social action projects in the Diocese.

Vaughan House, 46 Francis Street SW1P 1QN Tel: 020 7798 9063

Administrator Sandra G Joao

Email: caritasgrants@rcdow.org.uk Web: www.caritaswestminster.org.uk/grants

CARITAS BAKHITA HOUSE

Accommodation and support for women escaping human trafficking and modern slavery, under the patronage of St Josephine Bakhita.

Email: bakhitahouse@rcdow.org.uk

Web: www.caritaswestminster.org.uk/bakhitahouse

Service Manager	Karen Anstiss	**Tel: 020 7931 6045**

CARITAS DEAF SERVICE

Working with Deaf, Deafblind and Hard of Hearing people of all ages to enable them to participate fully in the life of the Church and share their gifts.

St Joseph's Pastoral Centre, St Joseph's Grove NW4 4TY

Email: michelleroca@rcdow.org.uk Web:
www.caritaswestminster.org.uk/deafservice

Director	Shell (Michelle) Roca	**Tel: 07779 341136**
Assistant	Sarah Metcalfe	**Tel: 07936 939523**

Signs of Hope – Deaf Counselling Service

Offers counselling to Deaf and Hard of Hearing people and their relatives in sign language or English. Mini-loop system available.

Tel/SMS: 07936 939522 Email: signsofhope@rcdow.org.uk

CARITAS ST JOSEPH'S

Supporting people with intellectual disabilities, their families and friends.

St Joseph's Pastoral Centre, St Joseph's Grove NW4 4TY

Email: enquiries@stjoseph.org.uk Web: www.stjoseph.org.uk

Centre Manager	Gail Williams	**Tel: 020 8202 3999**
Chaplain	Fr David Knight	**Tel: 020 89591971**

CARITAS VOLUNTEER SERVICE

Supporting engagement in social action volunteering within the Diocese and Greater London.

Email: cvs@rcdow.org.uk Web: www.caritasvs.org.uk

Volunteer Co-ordinator	Elke Springett	Tel: 07738 183833
Volunteer Service Administrator	Juliet Chiosso	Tel: 07525 812508

SEIDS Social Innovation and Enterprise Hub

The Hub is a social enterprise community centre offering a unique ecosystem of resources, inspiration and collaboration opportunities for those who have a credible enterprise idea.

SEIDS Hub, Empire Way, Wembley HA9 0RJ

Tel: 020 3026 2504 Email: hello@seids.org.uk Web: www.seids.org.uk

Head of Programmes	Kathy Margerison
Programme Officer	Vanessa Egberedu

CHANCERY

Archbishop's House, Ambrosden Avenue SW1P 1QJ

For Chancery matters please email: chancery@rcdow.org.uk

For *Celebrets* please email: celebret@rcdow.org.uk

Chancellor Fr Jeremy Trood MA, JCL		
Vice-Chancellor Brenda Roberts MA (Canon Law)		Tel: 020 7798 9037
Chancery Adminstrator Laura Dale BA (Hons), MTh		Tel: 020 7931 6042

CLERGY AND CONSECRATED LIFE

ALLEN HALL SEMINARY (Douai 1568; Old Hall Green 1793; Chelsea 1975)

Particular Pastoral Responsibility Bishop John Sherrington

28 Beaufort Street SW3 5AA Tel: 020 7349 5600

PA to the Rector Mrs Helena Duckett Tel: 020 7349 5786

Email: allenhall@rcdow.org.uk Web: www. allenhall.org.uk

Formation Staff:

Rector (resident)	Canon John O'Leary	Tel: 020 7349 5627
		Email: ahrector@rcdow.org.uk
Vice-Rector / Dean of Studies (resident)	Rev Dr Javier Ruiz-Ortiz	Tel: 020 7349 5608
Formation Advisor	Fr Lorenzo Andreini	Tel: 020 7724 8643
Formation Advisor	Sr Helen Costigane SHCJ	
		Tel: 020 7349 5786
Formation Advisor (resident)	Rev Dr Michael Doyle	Tel: 020 7349 5610
Formation Advisor (resident)	Fr John Hemer MHM	Tel: 020 7349 5618
Formation Advisor	Sr Bernadette Hunston SCSJA	
		Tel: 020 7349 5786
Pastoral Director / Formation Advisor (resident)	Fr Antonio Ritaccio	Tel: 020 7349 5617

Spiritual Director (resident) Rev Dr Anthony Doe **Tel: 020 7349 5600**

See page 188 for a list of those currently training for priesthood in the Diocese of Westminster.

COMMITTEE FOR THE WELFARE OF SICK AND RETIRED PRIESTS
Particular Pastoral Responsibility Bishop Paul McAleenan

Chair Canon Gerard King
Healthcare Visitor Sr Clement Doran RGN, RMN **Tel: 020 7798 9154 / 07817 143353**

DECEASED CLERGY ASSOCIATION
Vaughan House, 46 Francis Street SW1P 1QN
Registrar Mgr John Conneely **Tel: 020 7798 9003**

EASTERN CATHOLIC CHURCHES
Episcopal Vicar Mgr John Conneely **Tel: 020 7798 9003**

ETHNIC CHAPLAINCIES
Particular Pastoral Responsibility Bishop Paul McAleenan

Co-ordinator Fr Philip Miller **Tel: 020 7387 6370**
(Co-ordinator for Westminster, Brentwood and Southwark)

ONGOING FORMATION OF CLERGY
Director for Ongoing Formation of Clergy Fr Gerard Skinner
Support for Newly Ordained Priests Fr Peter-Michael Scott

PERMANENT DIACONATE
Particular Pastoral Responsibility Bishop Paul McAleenan

Vaughan House, 46 Francis Street SW1P 1QN Tel: 020 7798 9360
Director of Diaconate Programme
Rev Adrian Cullen **Tel: 01920 462140 Email: adriancullen@rcdow.org.uk**
Assistant Directors
Rev Tony Barter **Tel: 07711 894244 Email: tonybarter@rcdow.org.uk**
Rev Colin Macken **Tel: 020 8890 2367 Email: colinmacken@rcdow.org.uk**

VICAR FOR RELIGIOUS
Episcopal Vicar Fr John Hemer MHM **Allen Hall Seminary, 28 Beaufort Street SW3 5AA**
Tel: 020 7349 5618 Email: vfr@rcdow.org.uk
Team members Sr Brigid Collins RSM, Sr Rachel Harrington SND, Sr Monica O'Brien SM,
Sr Margaret Barrett DC

VOCATION TO PRIESTHOOD IN THE DIOCESE OF WESTMINSTER
See page 40 below for full information and contact details.

COUNCIL OF CENSORSHIP
Secretary Fr Terry Tastard **Email: terrytastard@rcdow.org.uk**
For applications and information concerning the *Nihil obstat* and *Imprimatur.*
Please allow two months.

SECTION 2

DIOCESAN CURIA

Moderator of the Curia Bishop John Sherrington
Chief Operating Officer Paolo Camoletto

PRINT ROOM, Archbishop's House, Ambrosden Avenue SW1P 1QW
Tel: 020 7798 9380 Email: printroom@rcdow.org.uk
Manager   Rochelle Fernandes
Assistant   Matthew Fernandez

Based in VAUGHAN HOUSE
46 Francis Street SW1P 1QN Tel: 020 7798 9009
Curia Reception Supervisor   Milena Moniz
Receptionist   Judith Brightwell

COMMUNICATIONS

Communications Officer	Marie Saba	Tel: 020 7798 9031
Communications Assistant	Simeon Elderfield	Tel: 020 7798 9030
Diocesan Website		Tel: 020 7798 9030

Email: communications@rcdow.org.uk
Westminster Information (published in the middle of each month, except in August)
Email: communications@rcdow.org.uk

Westminster Year Book	Paul Moynihan	Tel: 020 7798 9178

Email: wyb@rcdow.org.uk

DATA PROTECTION OFFICER	Mathew D'Souza	Tel: 020 7798 9015

Email: dpo@rcdow.org.uk

	Awaiting appointment	Tel: 020 7798 9174

FINANCIAL SECRETARY and		
CHIEF OPERATING OFFICER	Paolo Camoletto	Tel: 020 7798 9036
Executive Assistant	Nicola Atkinson	Tel: 020 7798 9160

FINANCE

Director of Finance	Nicholas Seed	Tel: 020 7931 6031
PA	Mary Ann D'Cruz	Tel: 020 7798 9170
Head of Finance	Awaiting appointment	Tel:
Management Accountant	Abiola Seweje	Tel: 020 7798 9360
Management Accountant	Gabriela Szkolnik	Tel: 020 7988 9169
Management Accountant	Eimear Keegan	Tel: 020 7931 6006
Financial Accounting Manager	Gisele Mantsounga	Tel: 020 7798 9161
Financial Accountant	Wei Pang	Tel: 0207798 9163
Accounts Assistant	Kanchan Merai	Tel: 020 7798 9089
Accounts Assistant	Anita Lobo	Tel: 020 7798 9171
Accounts Assistant	Eileen Devlin	Tel: 020 7798 9388

| Parish Finance Officer | Margaret Brady | Tel: 020 7798 9197 |
| Interim Finance Support | George Kulasingham | Tel: 020 7931 6096 |

SCHOOL BUILDING PROJECTS

Fundraising Manager	John Lee	Tel: 020 7798 9168
Project Manager	Marisa Borgerth	Tel: 020 7798 9176
Project Assistant	Loan Tran	Tel: 020 7798 9016

FUNDRAISING AND STEWARDSHIP

Director of Development	Matt Parkes	Tel: 020 7798 9375
PA to the Director	Jessica Rose	Tel: 07715 209 931
Assistant Director of Development	Helen Bright	Tel: 020 7798 9353
Trusts Fundraising Manager	Jamie Holyland	Tel: 020 7798 9087
Caritas Fundraising Manager	Julie Christie-Webb	Tel: 07725 938 304
Parish & Digital Fundraising Manager	Rachel Mars	Tel: 07568 108 879
Legacies Officer legacies@rcdow.org.uk	Petra Gomersall	Tel: 07739 937 852
Supporter Care Manager Email: supportercare@rcdow.org.uk (Secretary to Stewardship Committee)	Eszter Croitor-Tifan	Tel: 020 7798 9025
Senior Supporter Care Officer Email: giftaid@rcdow.org.uk	Charlotte Bellotti	Tel: 020 7798 9351
Cathedral Fundraising Manager	Marie-Louise Van Spyk	Tel: 020 7798 9058

HUMAN RESOURCES

Director	Robert Walker	Tel: 020 7798 9166
Head of HR	Julie Dauncey	Tel: 020 7798 9167
HR Business Partner (Parishes)	Amandeep Jaswal	Tel: 020 7798 9162
HR Business Partner (Curia & Central Services)	Clarissa Kononczuk	Tel: 020 7931 6079
HR Advisor	Awaiting appointment	Tel: 020 7798 9158
HR System Administrator Email: payroll@rcdow.org.uk / humanresources@rcdow.org.uk	Carolina Iniguez	Tel: 020 7798 9172
Pensions Administrator Email: anthony williams@rcdow.org.uk	Tony Williams (Tue, Thu)	

INFORMATION & COMMUNICATION TECHNOLOGY

(Diocese of Westminster in association with the Archdiocese of Southwark)
Email: ictsupportdesk@rcdow.org.uk

Interim Director	Daniel Prasanna	Tel: 020 7798 9164
Systems Administrator	Aaron Dennis	Tel: 020 7798 9165
ICT Support Technician	Andrew Baptista	Tel: 020 7798 9050

Please remember your Parish when making your Will

Remember God's Will in yours

Diocese of Westminster

To find out how to become a regular supporter, or make a one-off donation, please contact our Supporter Care Manager on **020 7798 9025** or email **supportercare@rcdow.org.uk**. You can donate online at **www.rcdow.org.uk/donations**

| ICT Support Technician | Hin Lau | Tel: 020 7798 9050 |
| ICT Support Technician | Edward Mukasa | Tel: 020 7798 9050 |

Based in ST JOSEPH'S, HENDON
St Joseph's Centre, St Joseph's Grove NW4 4TY

PARISH SUPPORT TEAM
General Enquiries Tel: 020 8457 6531 Email: pstsupport@rcdow.org.uk
Manager Beverley Meakes
Deanery Support
Nicole Brandwood (**Enfield,Harrow, Stevenage**) Email: nicolebrandwood@rcdow.org.uk
Rev Adrian Cullen (**Ethnic Chaplaincies**) Email: adriancullen@rcdow.org.uk
Alison Gartlan (**Barnet, Brent, Camden**) Email: alisongartlan@rcdow.org.uk
Donna Hyde (**Islington, Lea Valley, Marylebone,Westminster**)
Email: donnahyde@rcdow.org.uk
Lynne Kelly (**Ealing, Hammersmith and Fulham, Kensington and Chelsea,
North Kensington**) Email: lynnekelly@rcdow.org.uk
Diana Morain (**Hillingdon, Hounslow, Upper Thames**) Email: dianamorain@rcdow.org.uk
Boguslawa Psiuch (**Hackney, Haringey, Tower Hamlets**)
Email: boguslawapsiuch@rcdow.org.uk
Marie Ryan (**St Albans,Watford**) Email: marieryan@rcdow.org.uk

PROPERTY
Director	Clive Horscroft	Tel: 020 8457 6538
Assistant to the Director	Sarah Nagle	Tel: 020 8457 6533 / 07395 798559
Health and Safety Manager	Louise Mahon	Tel: 020 8457 6543 / 07720 590909
Health and Safety Administrator	Awaiting appointment	Tel: 020 8457 6546
Estates Surveyor	Carol Haigh	Tel: 020 8457 6534 / 07515 065695
Parish Buildings Surveyor and Secretary, Historic Churches Committee	Barry Lawrence	Tel: 020 8457 6542 / 07711 590317
Parish Building Surveyor	Awaiting appointment	Tel: 020 8457 6537 / 07874 878705
Parish Building Surveyor	Awaiting appointment	Tel: 020 8457 6540 /07885 768889
Project Manager (Education)	Owen Davis	Tel: 07851 248703
Administrative Officer / HCC Admin / Property Archives	Lesley McNealis	Tel: 020 8457 6532 / 07706 348876

Administration Project Manager		
(Parishes) / HCC Admin	Roz Freedland	Tel: 020 8457 6539
Technical Administrator	Anthony Williams	Tel: 020 8457 6541

ECUMENISM

Particular Pastoral Responsibility Awaiting appointment

Ecumenical activity in the Diocese is very much rooted at the local level, with numerous clergy and laity involved in a variety of ecumenical bodies and projects that are too many to list here. In addition to this local ecumenical engagement:
Cardinal Vincent Nichols attends London Church Leaders;
Bishop John Sherrington (North London), **Bishop Nicholas Hudson** (Central and East London), **Bishop Paul McAleenan** (Hertfordshire) all support the Church Leaders' groups in their areas. West London awaits an appointment.
Mgr Canon Henry Turner is Ecumenical Chaplain at St. Albans Abbey.

EDUCATION AND FORMATION

Particular Pastoral Responsibility Bishop John Sherrington *ad interim*

THE DIOCESAN EDUCATION COMMISSION
is appointed by the Cardinal Archbishop as a decision-making body which acts in his name. It is responsible to him in all areas relating to education in schools and colleges set out in Canon law and English law. It is responsible to the Diocesan Trustees for the financial aspects of providing and maintaining Catholic education in the Diocese. Through its Chair, the Education Commission liaises with the Cardinal Archbishop, his Auxiliary Bishops and the Diocesan Trustees. It liaises with schools and colleges mainly through the Director of Education and the staff of the Education Service.

Members of the Commission
Chair Canon Michael Dunne, Mr John Asgian, Mr Paolo Camoletto, Mr Edward Conway, Mrs Kate Griffin, Mrs Juliette Jackson
In attendance Director of Education, Deputy Director

THE EDUCATION SERVICE
works to the Diocesan Education Commission in providing professional support for Catholic Schools and Colleges, Head Teachers, Principals and Governing Bodies.
Vaughan House, 46 Francis Street SW1P 1QN Tel: 020 7798 9005
Email: education@rcdow.org.uk Web: https://education.rcdow.org.uk

Director of Education	Peter Sweeney	
(Diocesan Schools Commissioner)	Email: petersweeney@rcdow.org.uk	
PA to the Director	Susannah Marcot	Tel: 07803 634240
	Email: susannahmarcot@rcdow.org.uk	

Deputy Director of Education (Religious Education and Catholic Life)	Amanda Crowley Email: amandacrowley@rcdow.org.uk
Deputy Director of Education (Leadership and Governance)	Awaiting appointment Email:
Chief Inspector	Nancy Conoboy Email: nancyconoboy@rcdow.org.uk
Assistant Director (Capital Strategy and Pupil Placement)	Nigel Spears Email:nigelspears@rcdow.org.uk
Governance Co-ordinator	Carol Campbell **Tel: 020 7931 6050** Email: carolc@rcdow.org.uk
Events and Marketing Co-ordinator	Linette Blackmore **Tel: 020 7798 9189** Email: eduemc@rcdow.org.uk
Co-ordinator of School Chaplains	Fr David Reilly Email: davidreilly@rcdow.org.uk

Advisers for Catholic Education
Regional Hub East:

Primary Adviser	Elaine Arundell Email: elainearundell@rcdow.org.uk
Secondary Adviser	Claire O'Neill Email: claireoneill@rcdow.org.uk

Regional Hub West:

Primary Adviser	Awaiting appointment Email:
Secondary Adviser	Claire O'Neil Email: claireoneill@rcdow.org.uk

Regional Hub Central:

Primary Adviser	Tony Gorton Email: tonygorton@rcdow.org.uk
Secondary Adviser	Trisha Hedley Email: trishahedley@rcdow.org.uk

Regional Hub Hertfordshire:

Primary Adviser	Patrick Murphy Email: patrickmurphy@rcdow.org.uk
Secondary Adviser	Trisha Hedley Email: trishahedley@rcdow.org.uk

INTERFAITH

Particular Pastoral Responsibility Bishop Nicholas Hudson

Vaughan House, 46 Francis Street SW1P 1QN Tel: 020 7931 6028
Email: westminsterinterfaith@rcdow.org.uk
Director Awaiting appointment

JUSTICE AND PEACE

Particular Pastoral Responsibility Bishop Nicholas Hudson

JUSTICE & PEACE COMMISSION
The Commission exists to promote action and reflection on peace and social justice in the diocese of Westminster, in the light of the Gospel and Catholic Social Teaching.

Vaughan House, 46 Francis Street SW1P 1QN Tel: 07593 434905
Email: justiceandpeace@rcdow.org.uk   Web: https://westminsterjusticeandpeace.org
Chair Fr Dominic Robinson SJ
Co-ordinator Colette Joyce
Commission Members John Coleby (Caritas), Tony Sheen (CAFOD), Sr Carolyn Morrison, Positions vacant
Parish Contacts for details of parish Justice and Peace contacts, see page 163.

METROPOLITAN TRIBUNAL
Vaughan House, 46 Francis Street SW1P 1QN Tel: 020 7798 9003

Judicial Vicar Mgr John Conneely JCL
Assistant Judicial Vicar Canon Michael Brockie JCL
Canonical Assistant Alicia Sloan JCL
Judges Sr Rachel Harrington SND JCD, Fr Gerard Quinn STL, Alicia Sloan JCL
Defenders of the Bond Sr Isabel MacPherson SND JCD, Paul Robbins JCL
Advocates Fr Noel Barber SJ, Dr Francesca Bugliani-Knox
Tribunal Assistant Matthew Gillespie
Auditors Mr Nathan Paine-Davey, Mrs Margaret Dixon, Mrs Jo O'Neill, Fr Dennis F P Touw Tempelmans-Plat

PILGRIMAGES
HOLY LAND
Director Fr Paul McDermott
St Edward the Confessor, 700 Finchley Road NW11 7NE Tel: 020 8455 1300

LOURDES
Director Fr Dennis F P Touw Tempelmans-Plat
60 Rylston Road SW6 7HW Tel: 020 7835 4040 Email: lourdes@rcdow.org.uk
For volunteer helpers aged 16+ interested in the diocesan pilgrimage to Lourdes contact Katrina Lavery, Youth Director Tel: 07921 409402

WALSINGHAM
DIRECTOR Fr John McKenna
82 Union Street, Barnet EN5 4HZ Tel: 020 8449 3338

Pilgrimage Co-ordinator Elizabeth Uwalaka **Vaughan House, 46 Francis Street
SWIP IQN Tel: 020 7798 9173 Email: elizabethuwalaka@rcdow.org.uk**

SAFEGUARDING SERVICE

If you have information of a safeguarding nature where a child or an adult is in immediate danger or requires immediate medical attention call the emergency services on 999. If you wish to report any safeguarding concerns, past or present, please email us at safeguarding@rcdow.org.uk. We will ensure that any concerns are dealt with in a timely and appropriate manner. Otherwise, please contact RCDOW Safeguarding Team.
Vaughan House, 46 Francis Street SWIP IQN Email: safeguarding@rcdow.org.uk

Episcopal Vicar for Safeguarding Mgr Séamus O'Boyle **Tel: 020 7226 3277**
Email: seamusoboyle@rcdow.org.uk
Safeguarding Co-ordinator Geraldine Allen **Tel: 020 7798 9196 / 07803 634236**
Email: geraldineallen@rcdow.org.uk
Team Administrator Stephanie Uwalaka **Tel: 020 7798 9356 / 07394 560926**
Email: stephanieuwalaka@rcdow.org.uk
Safeguarding Office Manager Rika Pfaff **Tel: 020 7798 9359 / 07936 935707**
Email: rikapfaff@rcdow.org.uk
Administration and Online Training Tel: 020 7798 9356
Email: safeguardingadmin@rcdow.org.uk

Reporting Concerns
Deputy Safeguarding Co-ordinator Monawara Bakht **Tel: 020 7798 9096 / 07738 183832**
Email: monaware bakhet@rcdow.org.uk
Safeguarding Officer Freddie Coombs **Tel: 020 7798 9186 / 07851 250897**
Email: frederickcoombs@rcdow.org.uk
Safeguarding Officer Eithne Atterbury **Tel: 020 7798 9096 / 07851 250899**
Email: eithneatterbury@rcdow.org.uk

PSR Support and Creating a Safe Environment
Email: safeguardingsupport@rcdow.org.uk
Safeguarding Support Officer Arianna Sommariva **Tel: 020 7798 9358 / 07719 563119**
Email: ariannasommariva@rcdow.org.uk
Parish Safeguarding Support Officer Maria Eid **Tel: 020 7798 9358 / 07874 878710**
Email: mariaeid@rcdow.org.uk

Safer Recruitment
DBS Enquiries Tel: 020 7798 9352 Email: dbsadmin@rcdow.org.uk
Senior DBS Administrator Veronica Officer **Tel: 020 7798 9352 / 07803 634239**
Email: veronicaofficer@rcdow.org.uk
DBS Administrator Johanna Ashley **Tel: 07874 861060**
Email: johannaashley@rcdow.org.uk
DBS Administrator Alexander Dance **Tel: 07874 878712**
Email: alexanderdance@rcdow.org.uk

SECTION 2

VOCATION TO PRIESTHOOD IN THE DIOCESE OF WESTMINSTER

Particular Pastoral Responsibility Bishop John Sherrington

GENERAL CONTACT INFORMATION ABOUT VOCATIONS
Web: www.rcdow.org.uk/vocations
Initial contact Canon Roger Taylor **Tel: 07515 065696**

VOCATIONS PROMOTER
Canon Roger Taylor **St James, Spanish Place, 22 George Street W1U 3QY**
Tel: 07515 065696 Email: vocationspromoter@rcdow.org.uk

ASSISTANT VOCATIONS PROMOTER
Fr Mike Maguire **Cathedral Clergy House, 42 Francis Street SW1P 1QW**
Tel: 020 7798 9098 Email: vocations@rcdow.org.uk

VOCATIONS DIRECTOR
Fr Andrew Connick **The Presbytery, Dundee Street E1W 2PH**
Tel: 020 7481 2202 Email: vocationsdirector@rcdow.org.uk
The Vocations Director is responsible for helping men in the later stages of discernment, as they consider applying to the Diocese and as they prepare for the Selection Conference.

PRIEST TRAINING FUND (PTF)
Chair Bishop John Sherrington
The Fund **(Registration No 233699-13, formerly 312528)** supports the work of vocations to the priesthood, formation of priests and on-going clergy formation.

WESTMINSTER YOUTH MINISTRY

Particular Pastoral Responsibility Bishop Nicholas Hudson

Director of Youth Ministry
Andrzej Wdowiak   **Tel: 020 3757 2502 Email: andrzejwdowiak@rcdow.org.uk**
Diocesan Youth Chaplain
Fr Michael Guthrie   **Tel: 020 3757 2519 Email: michaelguthrie@rcdow.org.uk**

1. Westminster Youth Ministry Outreach, Waxwell House, 125 Waxwell Lane, Pinner
HA5 3EP Tel: 020 3757 2516   Email: youth@rcdow.org.uk Web: http://dowym.com

Manager
Phoebe Prendergast   Email: phoebeprendergast@rcdow.org.uk
Acting Outreach Manager
Holly Cook   Email: hollycook@rcdow.org.uk
Development Worker
Hannah Phoenix   Email: hannahphoenix@rcdow.org.uk

DIOCESE OF
WESTMINSTER
YOUTH MINISTRY

We're looking forward to welcoming you!

Through the retreat experience, we aim to create opportunities for young people from **Year 4 to Sixth Form** to have a *spiritual and personal encounter with Christ*, being accompanied on the path to vocational awareness and thereby equipping them to live out the mission entrusted to them by the Lord.

Contact Us
020 3757 2500 | https://dowym.com/retreat-centre | spec@rcdow.org.uk
Waxwell House, 125 Waxwell Lane, Pinner HA5 3EP

Diocese of Westminster

Registered Charity No. 233699

2. SPEC Retreat Centre, Waxwell House, 125 Waxwell Lane, Pinner HA5 3EP
Tel: 020 3757 2500 Email: spec@rcdow.org.uk Web: http://dowym.com/spec
SPEC stands for *Spiritual and Personal Encounter with Christ*

Retreat Team   Tel: 020 3757 2503   Email: spec@rcdow.org.uk
Enquiries and Bookings   Tel: 020 3757 2500   Email: spec@rcdow.org.uk

CATHOLIC CHILDRENS SOCIETY (CRUSADE OF RESCUE, FOUNDED 1859)

73 St Charles Square W10 6EJ Tel: 020 8969 5305
Email: info@cathchild.org.uk Web: www.cathchild.org.uk
Chief Executive Officer Gregory Brister BA, MSc

The Catholic Children's Society (CCS) works across the diocese to support disadvantaged
children and families. Services include:

SCHOOL COUNSELLING & THERAPY
CCS's ConnectEd counselling and therapy service supports the mental health and
emotional wellbeing of thousands of children each year. Qualified and experienced
counsellors/therapists work on-site in over 80 primary, secondary and special schools.
Contact Michelle Hegarty, **Head of School Services and Safeguarding**
Email: michelleh@cathchild.org.uk

MENTAL HEALTH TRAINING
Expert training delivered to school staff, clergy and other members of the children's
workforce, helping enhance their skills to identify and support children experiencing mental
health issues. Examples of topics covered include: mental health awareness and promoting
positive mental health; introduction to attachment theory; working with challenging and
hard-to-reach children. Bespoke training is also available.
Contact Michelle Hegarty, **Head of School Services and Safeguarding**
Email: michelleh@cathchild.org.uk

RAINBOWS BEREAVEMENT SUPPORT PROGRAMME
Training for school staff so they can deliver support groups for pupils who have
experienced separation, bereavement and loss.
Contact Suzanne Wintz **Rainbows Registered Director**
Email: suzannew@cathchild.org.uk

CRISIS FUND
A special fund providing emergency financial assistance for families in immediate need.
Applications can be made by Headteachers and Parish Priests.
Contact Duty Manager **Email: reception@cathchild.org.uk**

GRENFELL CRISIS FUND
A fund to deliver material and therapeutic help to all those affected by the Grenfell Tower
fire. Applications can be made by Headteachers and Parish Priests.
Contact Duty Manager **Email: reception@cathchild.org.uk**

FAMILY CENTRE BASED SERVICES

Qualified Early Years staff operate in two centres to help disadvantaged families. Services include an Ofsted-rated 'Outstanding' nursery, drop-in, after school groups, holiday play-schemes and trips, a toy library, welfare advice and information.

St Francis Family Centre 34 Wades Place E14 0DE
Contact Margaret Wilkinson **Centre Co-ordinator**
Tel: 020 7987 8257 Email: margaretw@cathchild.org.uk
St Mark's Stay & Play, St Mark's Road W10 6BZ
Contact Maria McKenzie **Drop-in Worker** Tel: 020 8960 2970 (12-4pm)

POST ADOPTION & AFTERCARE

Although no longer an Adoption Agency, we offer support, counselling and advice to former adoptees, their adopters and birth families. We also provide information to those formerly in our care.

Contact Irena Lyczkowska **Post-Adoption Manager** Email: irenal@cathchild.org.uk

SECTION 2

OTHER RESOURCES

MINISTRY TO ALIENATED CATHOLICS

The purpose of the apostolate is to be a practical sign that the Church is reaching out to alienated Catholics and to allow them to voice any hurt or grievance.

Fr Francis Wahle **Tel: 020 7487 5956 Email: franciswahle@yahoo.com**

PARLIAMENTARY ROMAN CATHOLIC DUTY PRIEST

Canon Pat Browne is, by kind permission of the Speaker, available for the celebration of the Sacraments and pastoral care of Peers, MPs and Staff of the Palace of Westminster.

Holy Apostles Church, 47 Cumberland Street SW1V 4LY

Tel: 07988 441691 Email: patbrowne@rcdow.org.uk

CARDINAL HUME CENTRE

The Centre welcomes homeless young people, individuals, and vulnerable families in need. Our front-line teams help them access the support, and gain the skills they need to overcome poverty and possible homelessness. A range of specialist services are on-site in Westminster: advice and assessment; family and young people's services; housing and welfare rights advice and advocacy; learning and employment services; immigration advice and representation; and residential services for homeless young people aged 16-25. There is also a GP surgery, and a charity shop on Horseferry Road. The Centre is supported by regular volunteers who play an integral part in all that we do. We also regularly visit schools and parishes across the Diocese to talk about these issues and how our work aligns with Catholic Social Teaching – please contact us if you would like to arrange a speaker.

Chair of Trustees Robert Arnott **Chief Executive** George O'Neill **Fundraising Relationship Manager** Stephen Currid **Volunteer Co-ordinator** Flora Swartland **Director of Services** Louise Davies **Surgery** Sr Dr Mary Hickey MBE **3-7 Arneway Street SW1P 2BG**

Tel: 020 7222 1602 Email: info@cardinalhumecentre.org.uk

Web: www.cardinalhumecentre.org.uk

PROVIDENCE ROW

For homeless or vulnerably housed people, finding employment and housing opportunities can feel like an uphill battle, even more so if affected by health, mental health or substance misuse issues. Providence Row works with around 1,200 people a year in East London, offering an integrated service of crisis support, advice, recovery and learning and training programmes. It helps those who are so often excluded from mainstream services gain the support and opportunities they need to help create a safer, healthier life off the streets.

Chief Executive Tom O'Connor **The Dellow Centre, 82 Wentworth Street E1 7SA**

Tel: 020 7375 0020 Email: getinvolved@providencerow.org.uk

Web: www.providencerow.org.uk

THE PASSAGE

We provide resources which encourage, inspire and challenge homeless people to transform their lives, and undertake street outreach work, including the area around the Cathedral and Victoria stations, which has the UK's highest incidence of people sleeping outside. The Resource Centre provides food, showers, laundry and clothing store facilities, as well as addressing health, education, employment, housing and welfare rights issues. The hostels help give people additional support when they first move from the streets, including some of the longest-term rough sleepers. The Passage's Home for Good project enables volunteers to support former rough sleepers across London. In summary, the Passage helps people to stop living on the streets and supports them as they move into places of their own, and helps many to return to employment. We welcome support from parishes and schools and are happy to deliver talks and provide information about our work.

Chief Executive Mick Clarke **Community Fundraiser** Max Elgot **Tel: 020 7592 1856**
St Vincent's, Carlisle Place SW1P 1NL Tel: 020 7592 1850 Email: info@passage.org.uk
Web: www.passage.org.uk

Section 3

DEANERIES

The name of the Auxiliary Bishop or Episcopal Vicar with particular pastoral responsibility is given in brackets.

1. **BARNET** (Bishop John Sherrington)
Barnet, Burnt Oak, Cricklewood, Edgware, Finchley Church End, Finchley East, Finchley North, Golders Green, Grahame Park, Hendon, Hendon West, Mill Hill, New Barnet, Whetstone
Dean Fr Eugene Curran CM **(Mill Hill)**   Tel: 020 8959 1021

2. **BRENT** (Bishop John Sherrington)
Dollis Hill, Kensal Rise, Kingsbury Green, Neasden, Stonebridge, Wembley 1, Wembley 2, Wembley 3, Willesden, Willesden Green
Dean Fr Stephen Willis **(Willesden)**   Tel: 020 8965 4935

3. **CAMDEN** (Bishop Nicholas Hudson)
Camden Town, Hampstead, Haverstock Hill, Kentish Town, Kilburn, Kilburn West, Lebanese Church, Somers Town, Swiss Cottage
Dean Fr John Deehan **(Kentish Town)**   Tel: 020 7485 4023

4. **EALING** (Fr Gerard Quinn)
Acton, Acton East, Acton West, Ealing, Greenford, Hanwell, Northfields, Perivale, Polish Church 3, Southall
Dean Fr Jim Duffy **(Northfields)**   Tel: 020 8567 5421

5. **ENFIELD** (Bishop John Sherrington)
Cockfosters, Cuffley, Edmonton, Enfield, New Southgate, Palmers Green, Ponders End, Potters Bar
Dean Fr David Reilly **(New Southgate)**   Tel: 020 8368 1638

6. **HACKNEY** (Bishop Nicholas Hudson)
Clapton, Clapton Park, Hackney, Homerton, Hoxton, Kingsland, Manor House, Stoke Newington
Dean Fr David Evans **(Hackney)**   Tel: 020 8985 2496

7. **HAMMERSMITH & FULHAM** (Canon Paschal Ryan)
Brook Green, Fulham1, Fulham 2, Hammersmith, Parsons Green, Polish Church 2, Shepherd's Bush, White City
Dean Fr Richard Andrew **(Brook Green)**   Tel: 020 7603 3832

8. **HARINGEY** (Bishop John Sherrington)
Muswell Hill, Stamford Hill, Stroud Green, Tottenham, West Green, Wood Green
Dean Fr Perry Sykes **(Wood Green)**   Tel: 020 8888 2390

SECTION 3

9. HARROW (Bishop John Sherrington)
Harrow-on-the-Hill, Harrow North, Harrow South & Northolt, Headstone Lane, Kenton, Pinner, Stanmore, Sudbury, Wealdstone
Dean Mgr Jeremy Fairhead **(Sudbury)**   Tel: 020 8904 2552

10. HILLINGDON (Fr Gerard Quinn)
Eastcote, Harefield, Hayes, Hillingdon, Northwood, Ruislip, Ruislip South, Uxbridge, West Drayton, Yeading
Dean Fr Nicholas Schofield **(Uxbridge)**   Tel: 01895 233193

11. HOUNSLOW (Fr Gerard Quinn)
Brentford, Chiswick, Cranford, Feltham, Grove Park, Heathrow Airport, Heston, Hounslow, Isleworth, Osterley
Dean Fr Gerard Quinn **(Brentford)**   Tel: 020 8560 1671

12. ISLINGTON (Bishop Nicholas Hudson)
Archway, Bunhill Row, Clerkenwell, Copenhagen Street, Highbury, Highgate, Holloway, Islington, Polish Church 1, Tollington Park
Dean Mgr Séamus O'Boyle **(Islington)**   Tel: 020 7226 3277

13. KENSINGTON AND CHELSEA (Canon Paschal Ryan)
Chelsea 1, Chelsea 2, Fulham Road, Kensington 1, Kensington 2, Oratory
Dean Fr Shaun Middleton **(Chelsea 1)**   Tel: 020 7589 5487

14. LEA VALLEY (Bishop Paul McAleenan)
Bishop's Stortford, Buntingford, Cheshunt, Hertford, Hoddesdon, Old Hall Green & Puckeridge, Waltham Cross, Ware
Dean Fr Peter Harris **(Bishop's Stortford)**   Tel: 01279 654063

15. MARYLEBONE (Bishop Nicholas Hudson)
Farm Street, Marylebone, Ogle Street, St John's Wood, Spanish Place, Ukrainian Cathedral, University Chaplaincy
Dean Fr Kevin Jordan **(St John's Wood)** Tel: 020 7286 3214)

16. NORTH KENSINGTON (Canon Paschal Ryan)
Bayswater, Harrow Road, Kensal New Town, Notting Hill, Paddington, Queensway, St Charles Square
Dean Fr Gerard Skinner **(Notting Hill)**   Tel: 020 7727 7968

17. ST ALBANS (Bishop Paul McAleenan)
Berkhamsted, Borehamwood, Borehamwood North, Harpenden, Hemel Hempstead East, Hemel Hempstead West, London Colney, Radlett, Redbourn, St Albans, St Albans South, Shenley, Tring, Wheathampstead
Dean Canon Anthony Dwyer **(Harpenden)**   Tel: 01582 712245

18. STEVENAGE (Bishop Paul McAleenan)
Baldock, Hatfield, Hatfield South, Hitchin, Knebworth, Letchworth, Royston, Stevenage Bedwell, Stevenage Old Town, Stevenage Shephall, Welwyn Garden City, Welwyn Garden City Digswell and Welwyn Garden City East
Dean Fr Norbert Fernandes **(Welwyn Garden City)** Tel: 01707 323234

19. TOWER HAMLETS (Bishop Nicholas Hudson)
Bethnal Green, Bow, Bow Common, Commercial Road, German Church, Limehouse, Lithuanian Church, Mile End, Millwall, Poplar, Tower Hill, Underwood Road, Wapping
Dean Fr William Skehan **(Commercial Road)**   Tel: 020 7790 5911

20. UPPER THAMES (Canon Paschal Ryan)
Ashford, Hampton Hill, Hampton-on-Thames, St Margarets-on-Thames, Shepperton, Staines-upon-Thames, Stanwell, Sunbury-on-Thames, Teddington, Twickenham, Whitton
Dean Canon Peter Newby **(St Margarets-on-Thames)** Tel: 020 8892 3902

21. WATFORD (Bishop Paul McAleenan)
Abbots Langley, Bushey, Carpenders Park, Chipperfield, Chorleywood, Croxley Green, Garston, Mill End & Maple Cross, Rickmansworth, Watford, Watford North
Dean Fr Andrew Gallagher **(Rickmansworth, Chorleywood & Mill End)**
Tel: 01923 773387

22. WESTMINSTER (Bishop Nicholas Hudson)
(City) Ely Place, Italian Church, Lincoln's Inn Fields, Moorfields;
(West End) Cathedral, Covent Garden, French Church, Pimlico, Soho Square, Warwick Street
Dean Canon Alexander Sherbrooke **(Soho Square)**   Tel: 020 7437 2010

23. ETHNIC CHAPLAINCIES (Fr Philip Miller)
Dean Fr John Mudereri **(Zimbabwean Chaplaincy)**   Tel: 020 3802 2911

PARISH MAP

The diocesan website features an interactive map-based search facility on which you can search for Catholic parishes and schools, and explore the geography of the Diocese on Google Maps.

Royston

Baldock
Letchworth
Hitchin
Buntingford

Stevenage
Shephall
Bedwell
Puckeridge
Knebworth
Old Hall Green
Bis Sto.

(Much Hadham)

Harpenden
Welwyn Garden City Digswell
Wheathampstead
Ware
(Sawbridgew
Tring
Redbourn
Welwyn Garden City (East)
Welwyn Garden City
Hertford
Berkhamsted
Hemel Hempstead N.
St. Albans
Hatfield
Hemel Hempstead West/Boxmoor
Hemel Hempstead E.
St. Albans S.
Hatfield S.
Hoddesdon
Abbots Langley
London Colney
Chipperfield
Radlett
Cuffley
Garston
Shenley
Potters Bar
Cheshunt
Watford N.
Borehamwood
Chorleywood
Croxley Green
Watford
(North)
Barnet
Waltham Cross
Bushey
Ponders End
Rickmansworth
Carpenders Park
Borehamwood
Enfield
Mill End
Cockfosters
New Barnet
Harefield
Northwood
Stanmore
Pinner
Headstone Lane
Eastcote
Wealdstone
SEE
Uxbridge
Ruislip
Kenton
INSET
Northolt
Harrow S.
Harrow
MAPS
S. Ruislip
Sudbury
Hillingdon
Yeading
Perivale
CENTRAL LONDON
West Drayton
Cranford
Greenford
Heathrow
Polish Church 3
Ealing
Hayes
Northfields
Stanwell
Southall
Hanwell
Brentford
Heston
Hounslow
Osterley
Staines-upon-Thames
Isleworth
River Thames
Whitton
St. Margarets
Ashford
Feltham
Twickenham
MILES
Hampton
Sunbury-on-Thames
Hill
Teddington
0   5   10
Shepperton
Hampton-on-Thames

HERTFORDSHIRE

ESSEX

MIDDLESEX

Harrow N.

Parishes in the Diocese of Westminster

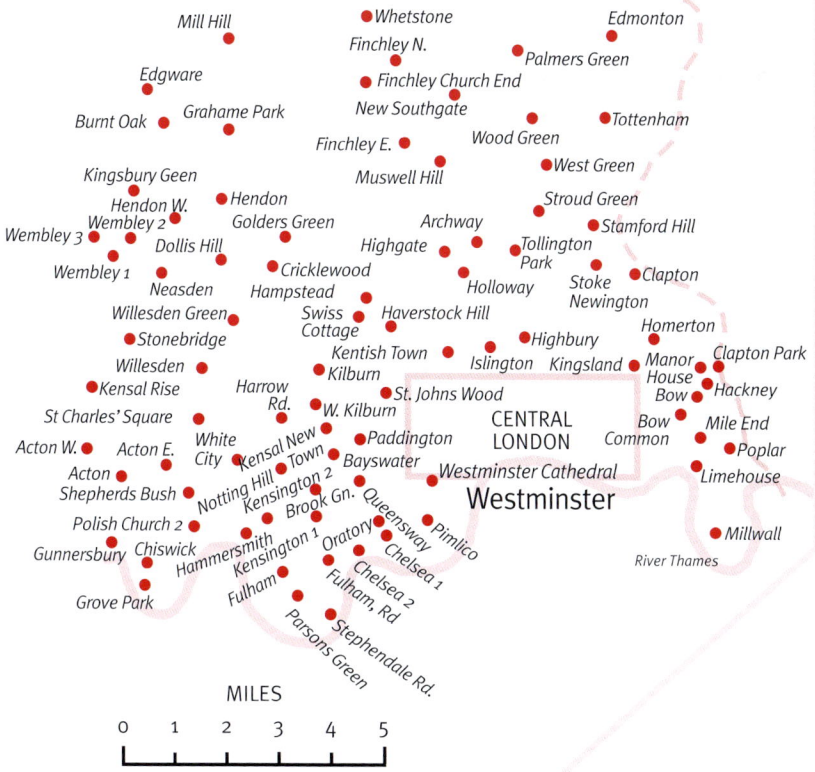

Parishes in London

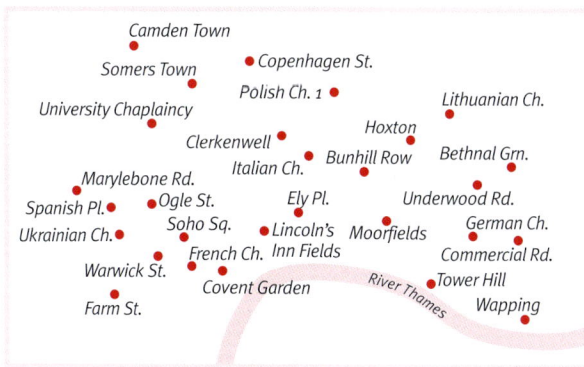

Mill Hill
Whetstone
Edmonton
Finchley N.
Edgware
Palmers Green
Finchley Church End
Grahame Park
New Southgate
Burnt Oak
Tottenham
Finchley E.
Wood Green
Kingsbury Geen
Muswell Hill
West Green
Hendon W.
Hendon
Stroud Green
Wembley 2
Golders Green
Wembley 3
Archway
Stamford Hill
Dollis Hill
Highgate
Tollington Park
Wembley 1
Cricklewood
Clapton
Neasden
Hampstead
Holloway
Stoke Newington
Willesden Green
Swiss Cottage
Haverstock Hill
Homerton
Stonebridge
Kentish Town
Highbury
Manor House
Clapton Park
Willesden
Kilburn
Islington
Kingsland
Hackney
Kensal Rise
Harrow Rd.
St. Johns Wood
Bow
Mile End
St Charles' Square
W. Kilburn
Bow Common
Acton W.
White City
Acton E.
Paddington
Poplar
Acton
Kensal New Town
Bayswater
Limehouse
Shepherds Bush
Notting Hill
Kensington 2
Westminster Cathedral
Polish Church 2
Brook Gn.
Queensway
CENTRAL LONDON
Gunnersbury
Chiswick
Hammersmith
Kensington 1
Oratory
Pimlico
Millwall
Grove Park
Fulham
Chelsea 2
Chelsea 1
Fulham, Rd
River Thames
Parsons Green
Stephendale Rd.

Westminster

MILES

0   1   2   3   4   5

Parishes in Central London

Camden Town
Somers Town
Copenhagen St.
University Chaplaincy
Polish Ch. 1
Lithuanian Ch.
Hoxton
Clerkenwell
Bunhill Row
Bethnal Grn.
Italian Ch.
Marylebone Rd.
Ely Pl.
Underwood Rd.
Spanish Pl.
Ogle St.
German Ch.
Ukrainian Ch.
Soho Sq.
Lincoln's Inn Fields
Moorfields
Warwick St.
French Ch.
Commercial Rd.
Farm St.
Covent Garden
Tower Hill
River Thames
Wapping

Parish Directory

1. Within the Diocese the parishes are grouped in deaneries. The deaneries, with their component parishes, are listed on the preceding pages.

2. + Indicates a church registered for marriages.

3. Each parish entry gives the name of the parish, the title of the church, the postal address, telephone number, email address and website, the road in which it is situated, and its deanery reference (*in italic bold type*). Dates in parentheses refer to its founding, the building of the church and its consecration. London postal addresses indicate the name of the road and postcode. Hertfordshire and Middlesex addresses include the name of the nearest town. Details of all parishes can be found at **parish.rcdow.org.uk/parishname**.

4. The name highlighted in red is that of the Parish Priest. Priests are listed by name only; degrees etc. can be found in the alphabetical list of clergy in Section 4.

5. Diocesan email addresses are formed thus: **firstname+surname@rcdow.org.uk**.

6. The first Mass of Sunday celebrated on Saturday evening, or the first Mass of a Holy Day celebrated on the evening of the preceding day, is indicated thus:
Sunday Mass (Sat 6pm), 8, 9, ... **Holy Day Mass** (Vigil 8pm), 10, 11 .....
Different timetables will apply at Christmas, Easter and on Public Holidays; enquire at the church.

7. Times of services shown are a.m. (i.e. 11.15), unless specifically indicated as p.m. (i.e. 6pm).

8. For Ecumenical or Justice and Peace contacts, ring the parish office. A list of Justice and Peace contacts is also given at the end of this Section.

9. Parish details are followed by relevant mission institutions, houses of female and male religious, then other public institutions (e.g. hospitals). These are served by priests of the parish unless otherwise stated.

10. Facilities for physically disabled and/or hearing impaired people are indicated after the name of the church by the following symbols:
    A   Access only (ramps, etc)
    ♿   Full facilities (access, plus disabled access lavatory)
    ∂   Loop System for hearing-aid users
    S   Mass celebrated regularly in Word and Sign, and/or Confession in Sign Language; enquire for details and times.

WESTMINSTER CATHEDRAL + METROPOLITAN CATHEDRAL OF THE MOST PRECIOUS BLOOD ♿ ♫

Sunday Mass (6pm Sung) 8, 10 (Sung), 12noon (Solemn, Choir), 5.30pm (Sung), 7pm;
Holy Day Mass (Vigil 5.30pm, Choir), 8, 10.30 (Latin), 12.30pm, 5.30pm (Choir);
Weekday Mass Mon-Fri 8, 10.30 (Latin), 12.30pm, 5.30pm (Choir);
Saturday Mass 8, 10.30 (Latin, Choir), 12.30pm; **Public Holidays** Mass 10.30, 12.30pm, 5.30pm

Divine Office: Morning Prayer Sun 9.30 Mon-Sat 7.35, **Vespers** Sun 4pm with
Benediction (Solemn, Choir), Mon-Fri 5pm (Choir, except Tue), Sat 5.30pm (Sung);
Public Holidays Morning Prayer 7.35; *No Vespers*

Confession Sat 11.30-12.30pm, 5-6pm Sun 10-12.30pm, 5-6.30pm; Mon-Fri 11.30-12.30pm, 4.30-5.30pm; **Public Holidays** 11.30-12.30pm

Opening times Mon-Sat 7.30-7pm; Sat 7.30 -7.15pm, Sun 7.30-7.45pm;
Public Holidays 7.30-6pm

Victoria Street SW1P 1LT; Clergy House is at 42 Francis Street SW1P 1QW
Clergy House Reception open Mon-Fri 9-4.30pm, Sat, Sun 10-1pm
Enquiries Tel: 020 7798 9055
Email: chreception@rcdow.org.uk Web: www.westminstercathedral.org.uk
Victoria Station (BR/TfL)
Westminster Deanery (1903; cons 28 June 1910)

Administrator Fr Sławomir Witoń Tel: 020 7798 9374
PA Elizabeth Arnot Tel: 020 7798 9062

Cathedral Chaplains
Fr Brian O'Mahony (**Sub-Administrator**) Tel: 020 7798 9180
Fr Michael Donaghy Tel: 020 7798 9048
Fr Hugh MacKenzie Tel: 020 7798 9055
Fr Michael Maguire (**Precentor**) Tel: 020 7798 9098
Fr Vincent Mbu'i SVD Tel: 020 7798 9055
Fr John Scott (**Registrar**) Tel: 020 7931 6041

Music Department:
Email: music@westminstercathedral.org.uk
Master of Music Simon Johnson Tel: 020 7798 9066
Assistant Master of Music Peter Stevens Obl OSB Tel: 020 7931 6091
Organ Scholar Carolyn Craig Tel: 020 7798 9378
Music and Liturgy Administrator William Waine Tel: 020 7798 9057
Email: musicadmin@rcdow.org.uk
Cathedral Choir School, Ambrosden Avenue SW1P 1QH Tel: 020 7798 9081
Head Neil McLaughlan **Chaplain** Fr Brian O'Mahony

Cathedral Manager Peter McNulty Tel: 020 7798 9064
Finance Manager Awaiting appointment Tel: 020 7798 9073
Fundraising Manager Marie-Louise Van Spyk Tel: 020 7798 9058
Head of Security Andrew Grange Tel: 020 7798 9014 / 07801 572433
Works Manager Neil Fairbairn Tel: 020 7798 9054
Works Assistant Caroline Keogh Tel: 020 7798 9053

Franciscan Sisters of Our Lady of Victories, Cathedral Clergy House Tel: 020 7798 9067

Friends of Westminster Cathedral
Co-ordinator Joe Allen Tel: 020 7798 9059 Email: josephdavidallen@rcdow.org.uk

Oremus, the Magazine of Westminster Cathedral
Editor Fr John Scott Tel: 020 7798 9052

Registry Tel: 020 7798 9376 Email: registrar@rcdow.org.uk

Sacred Heart Church, Horseferry Road SW1P 2EF (Parochial Chapel of Ease)
Enquiries Fr John Scott Tel: 020 7931 6041
Ukrainian Divine Liturgy (English) Sun 10
Croatian Chaplaincy Mass Sun 4pm

• Daughters of Charity, St Vincent's Centre, Carlisle Place SW1P 1NL
Tel: 020 7828 7841 Email: carlisleplace2016@gmail.com
Web: www.daughtersofcharity.org.uk
also 94a Horseferry Road SW1P 2EE Tel: 020 7222 6485
Email: horseferryroaddc@gmail.com
• Vincentian Care Plus (Care of Elderly in Own Home)
• Cardinal Hume Centre, 3-7 Arneway Street SW1P 2BG Tel: 020 7222 1602
Web: www.cardinalhumecentre.org.uk
Director George O'Neill
• The Passage, St Vincent's, Carlisle Place SW1P 1NL Tel: 020 7592 1850
Web: www.passage.org.uk
Chief Executive Mick Clarke
• The Gordon Hospital Tel: 020 8746 8733
• St Paul's Bookshop Managing Director Fr Francy Kochupaliathil SSP
Morpeth Terrace SW1P 1EP Tel: 020 7828 5582

ABBOTS LANGLEY + ST SAVIOUR &.♪

Sunday Mass (Sat 5pm), 8.30, 11.30; **Holy Day Mass** 10, 7pm; **Weekday Mass** Mon-Fri 10;
Exposition *Ist Fri only* 10.30-12noon; **Holy Hour** and **Benediction** *Ist Sunday only*
4 pm, with **Confession** available; **Confession** Sat 4.15-4.45pm & on request

Salvatorians (SDS) Fr Richard Mway-Zeng, Fr Dieudonne Zeng (clergy also serve
Chipperfield)
The Presbytery, 96 The Crescent, Abbots Langley, Watford WD5 0DS
Tel: 01923 266177 (Presbytery)
Email: abbotslangley@rcdow.org.uk Web: parish.rcdow.org.uk/abbotslangley
Watford Deanery (1928; 1963)

ACTON + OUR LADY OF LOURDES &.♪

Sunday Mass (Sat 7pm), 9, 10.30, 12noon, 6pm; **Holy Day Mass** 10, 7pm; **Weekday Mass**
Mon-Sat 10, Fri 10, 7pm; **Confession** Sat 10.30, 6-7pm & on request

Fr Patrick Adusei-Poku CSSp,.Fr Jude Kurumeh, Rev Tito Pereira (Deacon)
5 Berrymead Gardens W3 8AA Tel: 020 8992 2014
Email: acton@rcdow.org.uk Web: parish.rcdow.org.uk/acton
On High Street, between Town Hall and Horn Lane.
Ealing Deanery (1878; 1902; cons 17 May 1961)

• Medical Mission Sisters (Generalate) (SCMM), 41 Chatsworth Gardens W3 9LP
Tel: 020 8992 6444 Email: generalate@medicalmissionsisters.org.uk
Web: www.medicalmissionsisters.org.uk
• Religious Sisters of Charity, Caritas, 4 Buxton Gardens W3 9LQ Tel: 020 8992 8550
also 9 Rosemont Road W3 9LU Tel: 020 8992 4461
Email: rsocacton@gmail.com Web: www.religioussistersofcharity.org
• Damien Centre (Acton Homeless Concern), 3-5 Church Road W3 8BU
Tel: 020 8993 6096
• Emmaus House (Acton Homeless Concern), 1 Berrymead Gardens W3 8AA
Tel: 020 8992 5768

ACTON EAST + ST AIDAN OF LINDISFARNE ♪

Sunday Mass (Sat 6.30pm), 10 1pm (Gheez Rite); **Holy Day Mass** 10, 7.30pm; **Weekday
Mass** 10; **Exposition** Sat 5.30-6.15pm, with **Benediction** 6.15pm; **Confession** Sat 5.30-
6.15pm

Fr Mark Walker
85 Old Oak Common Lane W3 7DD Tel: 020 8743 5732
Email: actoneast@rcdow.org.uk Web: parish.rcdow.org.uk/actoneast
On Old Oak Common Lane just off Western Avenue (A40) at Savoy Circus, 1 min East Acton Stn
Ealing Deanery (1922; 1961; cons 31 October 1972)
Parish Office Mon, Wed, Fri 10.30-12noon

• Infant Jesus Sisters, 16 East Acton Lane W3 7EG Tel: 020 8248 9458,

SECTION 3

also at **30 Sunningdale Avenue W3 7NS** Tel: 020 8743 0116

• HMP Wormwood Scrubs Chaplain Fr Chima Ibekwe **(See HM Prison Service)**

• Hammersmith, Queen Charlotte's & Chelsea Hospitals

Sunday Mass 11.30; Weekday Mass Tue 12.30pm

Chaplains Fr Giles Pinnock, Fr Benedict Abuo, Fr Blaise Amadi CM, Veronica Burns **Tel 020 3313 4574**

ACTON WEST + THE HOLY FAMILY &♿

Sunday Mass (Sat 6pm), 8.45, 10 (Polish), 11.15, 1pm (Iraqi, Chaldean Rite); **Holy Day Mass** 10, 7.30pm; **Weekday Mass** as announced, *Bank Holidays* 12 noon; **Exposition** and **Benediction** *First Fri only* after 10 Mass; **Confession** Sat 9.45-10, 5.30-5.45pm

Fr Neil Reynolds

The Presbytery, Vale Lane W3 0DY Tel: 020 8992 1308

Email: actonwest@rcdow.org.uk Web: parish.rcdow.org.uk/actonwest

Closest Stns: North Ealing or West Acton

Ealing Deanery (1967; cons 1 April 2017)

• IBVM, 21 Twyford Avenue W3 9PY Tel: 020 8993 6931

Email: magdalenibvm@gmail.com

• Congregation of the Sacred Hearts of Jesus and Mary (SS.CC), 372 Uxbridge Road W5 3LH Tel: 020 8992 5941 Web: www. ssccpicpus.com

Frs Kenneth Barnes, Chris McAneny

• Focolare Movement, 57 Twyford Avenue W3 9PZ

ARCHWAY + ST GABRIEL OF OUR LADY OF SORROWS A ♿

Sunday Mass (Sat 6.30pm), 9, 11.30 (with Children's Liturgy), 6.30pm; **Meditative Rosary** precedes each Sunday Mass, with **Exposition** Sun 11; **Holy Day Mass** 12noon, 7pm; **Weekday Mass** Mon-Sat 12noon; **Healing Mass, Holy Hour** and **Benediction** *First Fri only* 12 noon; **Confession** Sat 11.30, 6pm & on request

Spiritans (CSSp) Fr Moses Enehizena, Fr Ignatius Quan, Fr Oliver Ugwu (in residence, Hospital Chaplain)

15 St John's Villas N19 3EE Tel: 020 7272 8195

Email: archway@rcdow.org.uk Web: www.stgabes.uk

Between Upper Holloway Stn (BR) and Archway Stn (TfL)

Islington Deanery (1928; cons 1967)

Parish Administrator Patricia Essien-Oku

• Marist Sisters, 17 St John's Villas N19 3EE Tel: 020 7272 1079

Email: marist.sisters@btinternet.com

ARNOS GROVE, N11: *SEE NEW SOUTHGATE*

ASHFORD + ST MICHAEL &♿ S

Sunday Mass (Sat 6pm), 9.15, 11.30, 6pm; **Holy Day Mass** 9.15, 7pm; **Weekday Mass** Mon, Tue, 9.15, Wed 6pm, Fri, Sat 9.15; **Exposition** Sat 9.45-10.15; **Confession** Sat 10.15-10.45

The Sons of Divine Providence (FDP) Fr Sidon Sagar, Fr Carlo Mazzotta, Fr Henryk Halman (in residence) (clergy also serve Stanwell)
112 Clarendon Road, Ashford TW15 2QD Tel: 01784 252230
Email: ashford@rcdow.org.uk Web: parish.rcdow.org.uk/ashford
Corner of Fordbridge Road & Clarendon Road, close to the War Memorial
Upper Thames Deanery (1906; 1928; cons 19 November 2006)

• HMP Bronzefield Chaplain Karen Connaughton (See HM Prison Service)

BALDOCK + HOLY TRINITY AND ST AUGUSTINE OF CANTERBURY A 🎵

Sunday Mass (Sat 6.30pm), 8.30, 10.30 (Sung), 3pm (1962 Missal, *First Sun only*); Holy Day Mass 10, 7.30pm; Weekday Mass Mon-Thu 10; Holy Hour Sat 5.15-6.15pm; Confession Sat 5.45-6.15pm

Fr Denis Sarsfield
Holy Trinity Church, London Road, Baldock SG7 6LQ Tel: 01462 893127
Email: baldock@rcdow.org.uk Web: parish.rcdow.org.uk/baldock
Stevenage Deanery (1913; 1926; cons 17 December 1977)

BARNET + MARY IMMACULATE AND ST GREGORY THE GREAT A 🎵

Sunday Mass (Sat 6pm), 8.30, 10.30, 6pm; Holy Day Mass 10, 7.30pm; Weekday Mass Mon 6pm, Tue, Thu, Fri 10; Mass for Healing *First Fri only* 7.30pm; Confession by appointment

Fr John McKenna
82 Union Street, Barnet EN5 4HZ Tel: 020 8449 3338
Email: barnet@rcdow.org.uk Web: parish/rcdow.org.uk/barnet
Barnet Deanery (1849; 1860; cons 15 December 1931; new church cons 8 December 1977; renewed church cons 3 September 2017)
Pastoral Assistant Anita Hammond
Parish Administrator Georgina Awan
Evangelisation Co-ordinator Jonathan Stephens

• Barnet Hospital
Chaplain Awaiting appointment Tel: 0845 111 4000
• Poor Clares, Poor Clare Monastery, 102 Galley Lane, Arkley, Barnet EN5 4AN
Tel: 020 8449 8815 Email: stclaresarkley@yahoo.co.uk
Web: www.arkleypoorclares.weebly.com
Chaplain Awaiting appointment
• Sisters of Christian Instruction, Summerhill, Leecroft Road, Barnet EN5 2TH
Tel: 020 8440 1853 Email: stgildasbarnet@yahoo.co.uk

BAYSWATER + ST MARY OF THE ANGELS A 🎵

Sunday Mass (Sat 4.30 (Portuguese), 6pm), 9 (Portuguese), 11, 6pm; Holy Day Mass 12noon, 6pm; Weekday Mass 12 noon; Exposition 8-6.30pm daily; Confession before Mass & on request

Mgr Keith Barltrop, Fr Richard Price (in residence)
The Presbytery, Moorhouse Road W2 5DJ Tel: 020 7229 0487

SECTION 3

Email: bayswater@rcdow.org.uk Web: www.humilitas.org
West of junction of Westbourne Grove & Chepstow Road, via Artesian Road
North Kensington Deanery (1857; cons 4 November 2007)

• Convent of the Assumption, St Catherine's, 7 Pembridge Square W2 4EQ
Tel: 020 7792 0623 Email: Stcatherines@assumptionreligious.org
• Sisters of Our Lady of Sion, 34 Chepstow Villas W11 2QZ
Tel: 020 7229 6266 Email: sionbayswater@gmail.com
Sion Centre for Dialogue and Encounter, Conference Centre and Jewish/Christian
Library Study Days and Reading/Library Resources Tel: 020 7313 8286
Email: sioncentrefordialogue@gmail.com Web: sioncentre.org
• Comboni Missionaries (MCCJ), 16 Dawson Place W2 4TJ
Tel: 020 7229 7059 Email: benitodemarchi@hotmail.com, anzioli47@hotmail.com
Web: www.comboni.org.uk
Frs Angelo Anzioli (Superior), Carmine Curci, Benito De Marchi, Pasquino Panato
• **Pembridge House, 29 Pembridge Square W2 4DS Tel: 020 7221 0588**
Pastoral care entrusted to the Prelature of Opus Dei
• **Courage** Support group for those experiencing same-sex attraction and who wish to
live a chaste life in accordance with the Church's teaching. **Contact** the Parish Priest or
london.courage@gmail.com

BERKHAMSTED + SACRED HEART CHURCH ♿ ♪

Sunday Mass (Sat 5pm), 8.30, 10; **Holy Day Mass** as announced; **Weekday Mass**
Mon, Tue 10, Thu 12noon, Fri, Sat 10; **Exposition** Sat 9 with **Benediction** 9.45;
Confession Sat 9-9.45

Fr Joseph Okoro
Sacred Heart Church, Park Street, Berkhamsted HP4 1HX Tel: 01442 863845
Email: berkhamsted@rcdow.org.uk Web: www.sacredheart.org.uk
Off Berkhamsted High Street (north side)
St Albans Deanery (1909; 1967)
Parish Administrator Laura Etson

BETHNAL GREEN + OUR LADY OF THE ASSUMPTION ♿ ♪

Sunday Mass (Sat 6.30pm), 9.30, 11.30 (all with Children's Liturgy), 2.15pm (Chinese);
Holy Day Mass 7.30 (Priory Chapel), 12.15pm, 6.30pm; **Weekday Mass** Mon-Fri
12.15pm; Sat 9.30; **Exposition** Wed 11-12noon; **Confession** Sat 5.45-6.15pm

Assumptionists (a.a.) Fr Justin Kasereka, Fr Antigon Claude Bahati; Fr Joseph Quoc
Cuong Tran;
Fr Joseph Liang (in residence, Chinese Chaplain)
Assumption Priory, Victoria Park Square E2 9PB Tel: 020 8980 1968
Email: bethnalgreen@rcdow.org.uk Web: parish.rcdow.org.uk/bethnalgreen
Just off main road, close to Bethnal Green Stn (TfL)
Tower Hamlets Deanery (1901; 1912)

• Sisters of La Sainte Union, 36 Gawber Street E2 0JH
• Chinese Community Fr Joseph Liang **Tel: 020 8709 5281 / 07753 471611**
Email: josephliang1998@gmail.com; Amy Lou (Mandarin & Cantonese-speaking)
Tel: 07878 582111 Email: amyfclou@hotmail.com

BISHOP'S STORTFORD + ST JOSEPH AND THE ENGLISH MARTYRS ♿☂

Bishop's Stortford, + St Joseph and the English Martyrs: **Sunday Mass** (Sat 6pm), 9, 11, 6pm;
Holy Day Mass 9.30, 7.30pm; **Weekday Mass** Mon-Fri 9.30, **Confession** (also **Exposition**)
Sat 3-4pm
Much Hadham, + Shared Church of St Andrew and Holy Cross: **Sunday Mass** 11.30
Sawbridgeworth, Most Holy Redeemer: **Sunday Mass** 9
Live streaming from St Joseph's at **www.churchservices.tv/bishopsstortford**

Fr Peter Harris, Fr Antonio Pineda
St Joseph's, 3 Windhill, Bishop's Stortford CM23 2ND Tel: 01279 654063
Email: bishopsstortford@rcdow.org.uk Web: www.rcstortford.org.uk.
St Andrew and Holy Cross, Church Lane, Much Hadham SG10 6DH; Most Holy Redeemer,
Sayesbury Road, Sawbridgeworth CM21 0ED
Lea Valley Deanery (St Joseph's: 1900; 1906; cons 19 June 1906; Much Hadham 1939;
Sawbridgeworth 1940)
Parish Administrator Debbie Jackson

• St Elizabeth's Centre, South End, Much Hadham SG10 6EW Tel: 01279 843451
Email: enquiries@stelizabeths.org.uk Web: www.stelizabeths.org.uk
52 week residential Special School and FE College for those with severe epilepsy, autism
and other complex medical needs. St Elizabeth's also has a 5-bedded Respite Care Unit for
people aged 18+ with epilepsy.
Chaplain Fr Paul Arnold **Tel: 01279 842145**
• Herts and Essex Community Hospital
• Rivers Hospital

BOREHAMWOOD + ST TERESA OF THE CHILD JESUS ♿☂

Sunday Mass 10, 12noon; **Holy Day Mass** 7, 9.15; **Weekday Mass** Mon, Tue, Thu, Fri 9.15;
Rosary Thu after 9.15 Mass, Fri 6.30pm; **Confession** Sat 11-11.40
Live streaming from St Teresa's at **www.churchservices.tv/borehamwood**

Fr Dominic McKenna (also serves Borehamwood North)
291 Shenley Road, Borehamwood WD6 1TG Tel: 020 8953 1294
Email: borehamwood@rcdow.org.uk
Web: www.catholicparishesofborehamwood.org
Opposite Hertsmere Civic Offices
St Albans Deanery (1925; 1962; cons 27 September 1978)
Parish Administrator Sue Partington

SECTION 3

BOREHAMWOOD NORTH + SS JOHN FISHER AND THOMAS MORE ♿ ♪

Sunday Mass (Sat 6pm), 8.30; **Holy Day Mass** 7.30pm; **Weekday Mass** see times for Borehamwood **Confession** Sat 5-5.40pm

Fr Dominic McKenna, (also serves Borehamwood and resident at **291 Shenley Road, Borehamwood WD6 1TG**, which is also the office for both Borehamwood parishes) Ss John Fisher and Thomas More, Rossington Avenue, Borehamwood WD6 4LA
Email: borehamwood@rcdow.org.uk
Web: www.catholicparishesofborehamwood.org
St Albans Deanery (1955; 1958; cons 27 October 1992)

• Daughters of Divine Love, Villa Scalabrini, Green Street, Shenley WD7 9BB
• Scalabrini Fathers, Villa Scalabrini, Green Street, Shenley WD7 9BB
Tel: 020 8207 5713 Fr Alberto Vico CS

BOW + OUR LADY REFUGE OF SINNERS AND ST CATHERINE OF SIENA A

Sunday Mass (Sat 6pm), 9.30 (Sung), 11.30 (Family), 6pm; **Holy Day Mass** 10, 7pm; **Weekday Mass** Mon-Wed 10, Fri 12noon; **Exposition** Fri 11, with **Benediction** 11.45; **Confession** Sat 5-5.45pm

Fr Howard James
177 Bow Road E3 2SG Tel: 020 8980 3961
Email: bow@rcdow.org.uk Web: parish.rcdow.org.uk/bow
Tower Hamlets Deanery (1869; 1870)

• Columban Sisters, 6/8 Ridgdale Street E3 2TW
Tel: 020 8980 3017 Web: www.columbansisters.org

BOW COMMON + THE HOLY NAME AND OUR LADY OF THE SACRED HEART

English: **Sunday Mass** 9.15; **Holy Day Mass** as announced; **Weekday Mass** Thu 9.15; *Vietnamese:* **Sunday Mass** 12noon; **Holy Day Mass** as announced; **Weekday Mass** Mon, Tue 10, Thu, Fri 8pm, Sat 10; **Confession** before Mass or by arrangement

Fr John Hai Pham, Fr Tri Nguyen Van
117 Bow Common Lane E3 4AU Tel: 020 7987 3477
Email: bowcommon@rcdow.org.uk Web: parish.rcdow.org.uk/bowcommon
Tower Hamlets Deanery (1892; 1894; cons 30 June 1894)

• Vietnamese Chaplaincy Tel: 020 7987 3477 Chaplains Fr John Hai Pham (**Tel: 07878 818561**), Fr Tri Nguyen Van, Rev Paul Song Trong Ly (Deacon)

BRENTFORD + ST JOHN THE EVANGELIST A ♪

Sunday Mass (Sat 6.30pm), 9.30, 11.30; **Holy Day Mass** 9, 7.30pm; **Weekday Mass** as announced; **Confession** Sat 5.30-6.15pm

Fr Gerard Quinn
44 Boston Park Road, Brentford TW8 9JF Tel: 020 8560 1671

Email: brentford@rcdow.org.uk Web: parish.rcdow.org.uk/brentford
North side of Great West Road (A4); approach via Windmill Road
Hounslow Deanery (1856; cons 1866)

• Poor Servants of the Mother of God, St Mary's Convent, 10 The Butts, Brentford
TW8 8BQ Tel: 020 8847 4800 Email: kathleen.coleman@psmgs.org.uk
Chaplain Fr Hilary Crewe
Maryville Care Home Tel: 020 8560 7124
• Missionaries of Africa (MAfr) (White Fathers), 64 Little Ealing Lane W5 4XF
Tel: 020 8799 5010 Email: lelsuperior@mafrgb.org.uk
Frs Donald Anderson, Richard Calcutt, David Cullen, Joseph Cummins, Thomas Cummins,
Francis Nolan, Hugh Seenan (Provincial **Tel: 020 8799 5012**), Aylward Shorter, Peter Smith,
Denis Starkey (Treasurer **Tel: 020 8799 5011**), Christopher Wallbank (Superior **Tel: 020
8799 5037**), Edward Wildsmith, Edward Woo; Br Patrick O'Reilly
• Hungarian Chaplaincy, 62 Little Ealing Lane W5 4EA Tel: 020 8566 0271
Fr János Csicsó
• Clayponds Hospital

BROOK GREEN + HOLY TRINITY ♿ ♪

Sunday Mass (Sat 6pm), 8.30, 10, (Family, with Children's Liturgy), 11.30 (Solemn), 1.30pm
(Syriac Rite), 6.30pm; **Holy Day Mass** 9, 6pm; **Weekday Mass** Mon-Wed 6pm, Thu, Fri 9, Sat
9.30; **Divine Mercy Prayers** Fri 9.30; **Rosary** Tue 6.30pm, Thu 9.30; **Exposition** and
Benediction Mon 6.30-7pm; **Confession** after Sat Vigil Mass and Sun 11.30 Mass, and on
request.
Times are subject to alteration; please check the website.

Fr Richard Andrew, Fr Rajiv Michael, Fr Benedict Abuo (in residence, Hospital Chaplain)
41 Brook Green W6 7BL Tel: 020 7603 3832
Email: brookgreen@rcdow.org.uk Web: www.holytrinityw6.org
Off Hammersmith Road (north side) between Hammersmith Broadway & Olympia.
Hammersmith & Fulham Deanery (1851;1853; cons 2 June 1866)
Catechetical Co-ordinator Sr Jenefer Glencross OSU
Parish Administrator Mrs Anja Huynh
Safeguarding Laurice Sanderson

• Sisters of Nazareth, Nazareth House, 169-175 Hammersmith Road W6 8DB
Tel: 020 8748 3549 Web: www.sistersofnazareth.com
Chaplain Fr John Cullen
• Society of the Holy Child Jesus, 42 Batoum Gardens W6 7QD Tel: 020 7602 9265
• Society of the Sacred Heart (Paris), 3 Bute Gardens W6 7DR (Provincial House)
Tel: 020 8748 9353 Email: sshprovincial@btopenworld.com
Web: www.societysacredheart.org.uk
11 Bute Gardens W6 7DR Tel: 020 8748 9887
35b Bute Gardens W6 7DR Email: silvanadallanegra@rcdow.org.uk
• St Joseph's House, 42 Brook Green W6 7BW Tel: 020 7603 9817

SECTION 3

BUNHILL ROW + ST JOSEPH ♿ ♪

Sunday Mass 11.30; **Holy Day Mass** 12.05pm, 7pm; **Weekday Mass** Wed 12.05pm; **Confession** Sun 11.15-11.30

Moorfields: **Sunday Mass** 9.30; **Holy Day Mass** (Vigil 7pm) 8.05, 12noon, 1.05pm, 5.30pm; **Weekday Mass** Mon-Fri 8.05, 1.05pm; **Exposition** as announced; **Confession** Mon-Fri 12.30-12.50pm, 1.30-1.50pm

Priest in Charge Fr Christopher Vipers, Canon Stuart Wilson (in residence) (clergy also serve Moorfields and are resident at **4/5 Eldon Street EC2M 7LS Tel: 020 7247 8390**) 15 Lamb's Passage, off Bunhill Row EC1Y 8LE
Email: bunhillrow@rcdow.org.uk Web: parish.rcdow.org.uk/bunhillrow
In small street linking Bunhill Row to Errol Street; 3 mins from entrance to Barbican Centre, beside City University Business School; nearest TfL Stns Barbican, Moorgate, Old Street
Islington Deanery (1856; 1901)
Quiet Garden Mon-Fri 8-6pm (Open Easter-Sept)

• Moorfields Eye Hospital

BUNTINGFORD + ST RICHARD OF CHICHESTER ♿ ♪

Sunday Mass 9.15 (with term time Children's Liturgy, *2nd & 4th Sun only*) ; **Holy Day Mass** 7pm; **Weekday Mass** Tue, Thu 9.30, Fri 10.30, with **Exposition** and **Benediction** 11-11.30, Sat 9.30; **Confession** Sat 10-11

Old Hall Green and Puckeridge **Sunday Mass** (Sat 6pm, Puckeridge); 11.30 (Old Hall Green); **Holy Day Mass** 10.30 (Puckeridge); **Weekday Mass** Wed 10.30 (Puckeridge); **Confession** Sat 5.15-5.45pm (Puckeridge)

Fr Cyril Chiaha, Rev Paul O'Connor (Deacon) (clergy also serve Old Hall Green and Puckeridge)
3 Station Road, Buntingford SG9 9HT Tel: 01763 271471
Email: buntingford@rcdow.org.uk Web: parish.rcdow.org.uk/buntingford
Lea Valley Deanery (1912; 1914; cons 5 June 1940)

BURNT OAK + THE ANNUNCIATION A ♪

Sunday Mass (Sat 6.30pm), 9, 10.30, 12noon; **Holy Day Mass** 9, 2pm (Annunciation Junior School), 7.30pm; **Weekday Mass** Mon 7.30, 12noon, Tue-Fri 9, Sat 10; **Confession** Sat 10.30-11, 5.45-6.15pm

Canon Colin Davies, Fr David Knight
4 Thirleby Road, Burnt Oak, Edgware HA8 0HQ Tel: 020 8959 1971
Email: burntoak@rcdow.org.uk Web: parish.rcdow.org.uk/burntoak
Off Gervase Road, close to Burnt Oak Stn (TfL)
Barnet Deanery (1928)
Administrator Susan Whelan

• Edgware Community Hospital
Chaplain Awaiting appointment **Tel: 020 8952 2381**

BUSHEY AND OXHEY + SACRED HEART OF JESUS AND ST JOHN THE EVANGELIST A ♫

Sunday Mass (Sat 6pm), 8.30, 10.30 (Sung), 6pm; **Holy Day Mass** 9.15, 7.30pm; **Weekday Mass** Tue 7.30pm, Wed-Fri 9.15; **Holy Hour** Mon 7pm; **Confession** Sat 11-11.30, 5-5.30pm & on request

Fr James McNicholas

Sacred Heart Presbytery, London Road, Bushey WD23 1BA Tel: 020 8950 2077
Email: busheyandoxhey@rcdow.org.uk Web: parish.rcdow.org.uk/bushey/.
Ten minutes walk up Chalk Hill from Bushey BR Stn
Watford Deanery (1863; 1959; cons 20 September 1977)
Sacred Heart Parish Centre Tel: 07925 979414

• Dominican Sisters' Generalate, Congregation of St Catherine of Siena of Newcastle, Natal, Rosary Priory, 93 Elstree Road, Bushey Heath WD23 4EE
Tel: 020 8950 1148 (Convent) 020 8950 6065 (Generalate) 07746 707 247 (Niland Conference Centre) Email: congsecretary@rosarypriory.co.uk
Web: www.dominicansisters.co.uk / www.nilandconferencecentre.co.uk
• Heath House, Birchville Court

CAMDEN TOWN + OUR LADY OF HAL ♿ ♫

Sunday Mass (Sat 6pm), 10 (Family), 12noon (Solemn), 5pm (Portuguese); **Holy Day Mass** 9.30, 12noon (subject to change); **Weekday Mass** Mon, Tue 12noon, Wed, Thu 9.30, Fri 12 noon, Sat 9.30; **Holy Hour and Benediction** Fri 12.30-1.30pm; **Confession** Fri 12.30-1pm, Sat 11-11.30, 5-5.40pm and on request

Fr Mark Dunglinson, Fr Christopher Connor (in residence, School Chaplain), Fr Colin McLean (in residence, retired), Fr Aneesh Thomas (in residence, Syro-Malabar Chaplaincy)
165 Arlington Road NW1 7EX Tel: 020 7485 2727
Email: camdentown@rcdow.org.uk Web: www.ourladyofhal.org.uk
Camden Deanery (1933; cons 1984)
Parish Administrator Judith Murphy

CANARY WHARF CATHOLIC CHAPLAINCY: *SEE MILLWALL*

CARPENDERS PARK AND SOUTH OXHEY + ST JOSEPH A ♫

Sunday Mass (Sat 6pm), 8.30, 10.30; **Weekday Mass** as announced; **Confession** Sat 5.30pm

Fr John Warnaby

St Joseph's Church, Oxhey Drive, South Oxhey, Watford WD19 7SW
Tel: 020 8428 0088
Email: carpenderspark@rcdow.org.uk Web: https://carpenderspark.org.uk/
Off Prestwick Road, close to Carpenders Park Stn - on South Oxhey side of railway line
Watford Deanery (1952; 1960; cons 1981)
Parish Administrator Linda Grimes
Children & Family Worker Donna Osborne

• The Fairways Care Home, Pinewood Lodge Care Home

CHELSEA 1 + ST MARY CADOGAN STREET A

Sunday Mass (Sat 6.30pm), 10.30, 6.30pm; **Holy Day Mass** 12noon, 7pm; **Weekday Mass** Mon, Tue 12noon, Thu 6pm, Fri 12noon; **Exposition** Fri 11-11.45; **Confession** Sat 5.45-6.15pm

Fr Shaun Middleton, Mgr Martin Hayes, Vicar General (in residence)
Presbytery & Communication address: St Mary's Rectory, Draycott Terrace SW3 2BG
Tel: **020 7589 5487**
(Church address: Cadogan Street SW3 2QR)
Email: chelsea1@rcdow.org.uk Web: www.stmaryscadoganstreet.co.uk
Corner of Cadogan Street and Draycott Terrace
Kensington & Chelsea Deanery (1798; 1811; 1879; cons 12 June 1882)
Administrator and Lead Catechist Muriel Akahi

• Dawliffe Hall, 2 Chelsea Embankment SW3 4LG Tel: **020 7351 0719**
Pastoral care entrusted to the prelature of Opus Dei
• Lister Hospital
• Royal Hospital, Chelsea **Chaplain** Mgr Phelim Rowland

CHELSEA 2 + OUR MOST HOLY REDEEMER AND ST THOMAS MORE

Sunday Mass (Sat 6.30pm), 10 (Family), 11 (Sung Latin), 12.15pm, 6.30pm; **Holy Day Mass** 8, 6.30pm; **Weekday Mass** Mon-Fri 8, Sat and Public Holidays 10; **Morning Prayer** Sun 9.30, Mon-Fri 7.45, Sat 9.45; **Evening Prayer** Sat and Sun 6pm; **Confession** Sat 5.30-6pm

Canon Paschal Ryan
7 Cheyne Row SW3 5HS Tel: **020 7352 0777**
Email: chelsea2@rcdow.org.uk Web: www.holyredeemerchelsea.com
North of Albert Bridge, off Oakley Street
Kensington & Chelsea Deanery (1892; 1895; cons 21 June 1905)

• **Diocesan Seminary:** see entry for Allen Hall in Section 2
• Chelsea Court Place Residential and Day Memory Care

CHESHUNT + ST PAUL A

Sunday Mass (Sat 5pm) 9, 11; **Holy Day Mass** 9.30, 8pm; **Weekday Mass** Mon-Wed, Fri 9.30 ; **Mass for parents bereaved of children** 9.30 *17th of every month*; **Mass for Carers** 9.30 *First Fri*; **Exposition** Fri 9; **Confession** Sat 4.15-4.45pm

Priest in Charge Fr Clement Nyarko
17 Churchfield Path, off Church Lane, Cheshunt EN8 9EG Tel: **01992 629878**
Email: cheshunt@rcdow.org.uk Web: parish.rcdow.org.uk/cheshunt
Lea Valley Deanery (1998)

CHIPPERFIELD + OUR LADY MOTHER OF THE SAVIOUR A ♫

Sunday Mass (Sat 6.30pm), 10; **Holy Day Mass** 12 noon; **Weekday Mass** Tue, Fri 10 (subject to change); **Confession** before any Mass & on request

Salvatorians (SDS) Fr Richard Mway-Zeng, Fr Dieudonne Zeng (clergy also serve Abbots Langley, Bovingdon and Sarratt)
Catholic Church, Dunny Lane, Chipperfield WD4 9DB (Clergy resident at **The Presbytery, 96 The Crescent, Abbots Langley, Watford WD5 0DS Tel: 01923 266177)**
Email: chipperfield@rcdow.org.uk Web: parish.rcdow.org.uk/chipperfield
Watford Deanery (1978; 1988; cons 15 July 2018)

• **Bovingdon, HM Prison The Mount Chaplains** Fr Neil Scott, Rev William Lo (Deacon) **(See HM Prison Service)**

CHISWICK + OUR LADY OF GRACE AND ST EDWARD ♿♫

Our Lady of Grace and St Edward: Sunday Mass (Sat 6.30pm), 8.30, 9.45 (Family), 11 (Sung), 12.15pm, 6.30pm; **Holy Day Mass** 10, 12.30pm, 7.30pm, **Weekday Mass** 10; **Exposition** and **Benediction** as announced; **Confession** Sat 11-11.45, 5-5.45pm & on request
St Dunstan: Sunday Mass 10; **Weekday Mass** as announced; **Confession** as announced

Canon Michael Dunne, Fr Daniel Daley, Fr Erasmus Egenonu CSSp (clergy also serve Grove Park)
247 High Road W4 4PU Tel: 020 8994 2877 Fax: 020 8987 8332
Email: chiswick@rcdow.org.uk Web: www.ourladyofgracechiswick.org
Hounslow Deanery
Administrator Sharon Bowden

+ Our Lady of Grace and St Edward
247 High Road W4 4PU
Main road, corner of Chiswick High Road and Duke's Avenue
(1852; 1886; cons 10 October 1904)

+ St Dunstan
141 Gunnersbury Avenue W3 8LE
On North Circular Road (A406), 300 yards north of Chiswick roundabout
(1931)

• Comboni Missionary Sisters (Community), 2 Chiswick Lane W4 2JF
Tel: 020 8994 0449 Email: chiswickcommunity@gmail.com
Comboni Centre for Spirituality and Mission, 2 Chiswick Lane W4 2JF
Tel: 020 8994 1220 Email: combonicentre16@gmail.com
• Little Company of Mary (Provincialate), 93 Gunnersbury Avenue W5 4LR
Tel: 020 8993 6129
• Missionary Sisters of the Immaculate (PIME), Regina Pacis Convent, 10 Chiswick Lane
W4 2JE Tel: 020 8994 2053 Email: msilondon@aol.com Web: www.mdipime.org

CHORLEYWOOD + ST JOHN FISHER &

Sunday Mass 9; Holy Day Mass as announced; Weekday Mass Tue 9.30; Confession on request & by appointment

Mill End: Sunday Mass (Sat 6pm), 10.30; Holy Day Mass as announced; Weekday Mass Wed 9.30; Exposition and Confession Sat 5-5.45pm

Rickmansworth: Sunday Mass 8.30, 11, 6pm; Holy Day Mass 9.30, 7.30pm; Weekday Mass Mon-Sat 9.30; Exposition and Confession Sun 5-5.45pm

Fr Andrew Gallagher, Fr Matteo Di Giuseppe (clergy also serve Mill End and Rickmansworth and are resident at 5 Park Road, Rickmansworth WD3 1HU Tel: 01923 773387)
Hill Cottage, Shire Lane, Chorleywood, Rickmansworth WD3 5NH
Email: rickmansworth@rcdow.org.uk Web: parish.rcdow.org.uk/chorleywood
Close to shopping centre & Stn
Watford Deanery (1955)

CLAPTON + ST SCHOLASTICA A

Sunday Mass 10, 11.45, 6pm; Holy Day Mass 9.30, 7pm; Weekday Mass as announced and Sat 10; Confession Sat 9-9.50 or on request

Fr Stewart Hasker, Rev Kingsley Izundu (Deacon)
17 Kenninghall Road E5 8BS Tel: 020 8985 2178
Email: clapton@rcdow.org.uk Web: parish.rcdow.org.uk/clapton
Hackney Deanery (1862; 1962; cons 15 February 1987)

• Servite Sisters, 12 Cleveleys Road E5 9JN Tel: 020 8880 0257
• Servite Sisters, 1 Brownsea Court, 160 Clarence Road E5 8EF
Tel: 020 8533 6628 Web: www.servites.org

CLAPTON PARK + ST JUDE

Sunday Mass (Sat 6pm), 9.30 (Sung), 11.30 (Sung); Holy Day Mass 9.30; Weekday Mass Tue-Sat 9.30; Legion of Mary Thu 5.30pm; Prayer Group Thu 7-8pm, Confession Sat 5.30-5.45pm and on request

Priest in Charge Fr Neil Hannigan
131 Glenarm Road E5 0NB (Church is at 76 Blurton Road E5 0NH)
Tel: 020 8525 1929
Email: claptonpark@rcdow.org.uk Web: parish.rcdow.org.uk/claptonpark
Off Chatsworth Road
Hackney Deanery (1964)

• Sisters of Mercy, 4 Hilsea Street E5 0SG Tel: 020 8986 3196
• Homerton University Hospital NHS Trust Tel: 020 8510 5555

CLERKENWELL + ST PETER AND ST PAUL A ♿♿

Sunday Mass 9.45 (Sung), 12noon (Sung); **Holy Day Mass** 12.30pm; **Weekday Mass** Mon 12.30pm, Tue, Wed 8, Fri 12.30pm; **Confession** Mon 11.30-12.15pm, & on request

Fr Ivano Millico
5 Amwell Street EC1R 1UL Tel: 020 7837 2094
Email: clerkenwell@rcdow.org.uk Web: parish.rcdow.org.uk/clerkenwell
Islington Deanery (1842; 1847)
Secretary Helen Lebab

• Pallottine Missionary Sisters, 35 Wilmington Square WC1X 0EG Tel: 020 7837 3010
Email: nancylogue@talktalk.net Web: http://www.pallottinemissionarysisters.co.uk/
• Royal National Throat, Nose & Ear Hospital

CLERKENWELL + ST PETER'S: *SEE ITALIAN CHURCH*

COCKFOSTERS + CHRIST THE KING ♿♿

Sunday Mass (Sat 5.30pm), 9, 11; **Holy Day Mass** 11; **Weekday Mass** 11
Ecumenical Prayer Group Mon 8pm, Thu 11.30; **Confession** Sat 11.30, 5pm

Chemin Neuf (CCN) Fr Christophe Brunet, Fr Pascal Sullivan
29 Bramley Road N14 4HE Tel: 020 8449 6648
Email: cockfosters@rcdow.org.uk Web: www.christthekingcockfosters.co.uk/
On main road, a few yards west of Oakwood Stn (TfL), junction with Peace Close
Enfield Deanery (1936; 1940)
Community Frs Christophe Brunet, Pascal Sullivan; Rev Ted Wood (Deacon)
Parish Secretary Suzanne Clarke **Catechetical Co-ordinator** Awaiting appointment

• Net for God Prayer Group Tue 8pm
• Cockfosters Centre for Spirituality Tel: 020 8449 6648
Web: www.cockfosterscs.org.uk
• Homes for the Aged: Servite House, Elizabeth Lodge

COMMERCIAL ROAD + ST MARY AND ST MICHAEL ♿♿

Sunday Mass (Sat 6pm), 8,10.30; **Holy Day Mass** as announced; **Weekday Mass** Mon-Sat10; **Confession** Sat 5-5.30pm

Fr William Skehan, Fr Crescent Iloka (in residence, Royal London Hospital Chaplaincy), Fr Julien Matondo Mboko (in residence, Congolese Chaplaincy, contact details below)
2 Lukin Street E1 0AA Tel: 020 7790 5911
Email: commercialroad@rcdow.org.uk Web: parish.rcdow.org.uk/commercialroad
200 yards east of Watney Market
Tower Hamlets Deanery (1856; cons 4 December 1929)
(Congolese Chaplaincy **Tel: 020 7790 2211 / 07452 772111**
Email julienmboko@rcdow.org.uk / julienmboko@hotmail.fr)

• Royal London Hospital (Whitechapel) Tel: 020 7377 7000
Chaplaincy Tel: 020 3594 2070

COPENHAGEN STREET + THE BLESSED SACRAMENT A ♪

Sunday Mass 8.30, 11 (Family, Sung); **Holy Day Mass** 10.30, 7.30pm; **Weekday Mass** Mon-Wed, Sat 10.30; **Confession** Sun 8-8.25, 10.30-10.55

Islington: **Sunday Mass** (Sat 6pm), 9, 10.30 (Sung, with Children's Liturgy), 12noon (Sung), 6pm; **Holy Day Mass** 10, 12.30pm, 7.30pm; **Weekday Mass** 10; **Exposition** Sat 10.30-11.30; **Confession** Sat 10.30-11, 5.15-5.45pm

Mgr Séamus O'Boyle, Fr Jakub Joszko (clergy also serve Islington and are resident at **39 Duncan Terrace N1 8AL Tel: 020 7226 3277)**
157 Copenhagen Street N1 0SR
Email: copenhagenstreet@rcdow.org.uk Web: parish.rcdow.org.uk/copenhagenstreet
Off Caledonian Road, half mile north of Kings Cross Stn (BR/TfL)
Islington Deanery (1916)

• School Sisters of Notre Dame, 41 Havelock Street N1 0DA Tel: 020 7837 8378
Email: ssnd27@yahoo.co.uk Web: www.ssnd.org and www.gerhardinger.org

COVENT GARDEN (MAIDEN LANE) + CORPUS CHRISTI A ♪

The Church is the Diocesan Shrine of the Most Blessed Sacrament (2018)
Sunday Mass (Sat 6pm), 9.30, 11.30 (Sung Latin); **Holy Day Mass** 1.05pm, 6.30pm (Sung Latin); **Weekday Mass** Mon 1.05pm), Wed-Fri 1.05pm, Bank Holidays 10; **Sodality of the Blessed Sacrament** *First Thu* 6.30pm; **Eucharistic Prayer Group** Wed 7pm; **Exposition** Mon, Wed-Fri 12-1pm; **Holy Hour** (includes **Vespers, Rosary, Exposition** and **Benediction**) Sat-Mon, Wed-Fri 5-6pm; **Confession** 30 mins before each Mass & on request

Fr Alan Robinson
Corpus Christi Presbytery, Maiden Lane WC2E 7NB Tel: 020 7836 4700
Email: coventgarden@rcdow.org.uk Web: www.corpuschristimaidenlane.org.uk
Off Southampton Street, north of Strand; near Covent Garden
Westminster Deanery (1873; cons 18 October 1956)

CRANFORD + OUR LADY AND ST CHRISTOPHER ♿♪

Sunday Mass (Sat 5pm), 9, 11; **Holy Day Mass** as announced; **Weekday Mass** as announced; **Confession** Sat 4.15-4.45 & on request

Fr John Tabor
32 High Street, Cranford, Hounslow TW5 9RG Tel: 020 8759 9136
Email: cranford@rcdow.org.uk Web: parish.rcdow.org.uk/cranford
Next to Holy Angels Church, opposite The Avenue
Hounslow Deanery (1967; 1970, cons 1979)
Parish Secretary Awaiting appointment

CRICKLEWOOD + ST AGNES ♿

Sunday Mass (Sat 6.30pm), 9, 10.30, 12noon, 6.30pm; **Holy Day Mass** as announced; **Weekday Mass** Mon-Fri 9.15, Sat 10; **Confession** Sat 10.30-11, 5.30-6pm & on request

Fr John Buckley, Fr Maricel-Irinel Mititelu (in residence, Romanian Chaplain, contact details below)

35 Cricklewood Lane NW2 1HR Tel: 020 8452 2475

Email: cricklewood@rcdow.org.uk Web: parish.rcdow.org.uk/cricklewood

On A407, midway between A41 and Cricklewood Broadway (A5)

Barnet Deanery (1883; 1930)

(Fr Mititelu **Tel: 07721 867280** Email: romanianchaplaincy@rcdow.org.uk)

Catechetical Co-ordinator Samantha Greene

• Dominican Sisters of St Catherine of Siena of Newcastle, Natal, St Rose's Convent, (St Rose's Chapel, Prayer Garden and Poustinia), 160 Anson Road NW2 6BH
Tel: 020 8830 7465 Email: raymundaop72@gmail.com
• Sisters of Mercy, 149 Walm Lane NW2 3AU Tel: 020 8450 7472
• Sisters of St Joseph of Peace, 157 Walm Lane NW2 3AY Tel: 020 8450 8859
Web: www.csjp.org

CROXLEY GREEN + ST BEDE ♿ ♪

Sunday Mass (Sat 6pm), 10, 4pm *1st Sun only* Sri Lankan (Sinhalese); **Holy Day Mass** as announced; **Weekday Mass** Thu 10, other days as announced; **Confession** as announced and on request

Fr John Wiley

185 Baldwins Lane, Croxley Green, Rickmansworth WD3 3LL Tel: 01923 231969

Email: croxleygreen@rcdow.org.uk Web: parish.rcdow.org.uk/croxleygreen

Watford Deanery (1958; cons 1975)

CUFFLEY + ST MARTIN DE PORRES A ♪

Sunday Mass (Sat 5.30pm) 9, 11; **Holy Day Mass** 9.30, 8pm; **Weekday Mass** as announced; **Confession** Sat 10.30

Priest in Charge Fr Patrick Carroll

4 Church Close, Cuffley EN6 4LS Tel: 01707 873308

Email: cuffley@rcdow.org.uk Web: parish.rcdow.org.uk/cuffley

Enfield Deanery

DOLLIS HILL + ST MARY AND ST ANDREW ♿ ♪

Sunday Mass (Sat 7pm), 8.30, 10.30 (Family), 12noon (sung), (in summer (7pm), 9,11); **Holy Day Mass** as announced; **Weekday Mass** Mon-Wed 9.30; **Confession** Sat 12.30pm & on request

Fr Michael O'Doherty

216 Dollis Hill Lane NW2 6HE Tel: 020 8452 6158

Email: dollishill@rcdow.org.uk Web: parish.rcdow.org.uk/dollishill

Brent Deanery (1915; 1933)

SECTION 3

EALING + ABBEY CHURCH OF ST BENEDICT ♿ ♪

Sunday Mass (Sat 6pm, 8.30pm with Neocatechumenate Community in Chapel), 9, 10.15 (Family, in Parish Centre), 10.30 (Sung), 12noon, 7pm; **Holy Day Mass** 7, 9.15, 6pm, 8pm; **Weekday Mass** 7, 9.15, 6pm; **Exposition** Thu 7.45-8.30pm, Fri 9.45-12.30pm; **Confession** Sat 10-11, 4-5pm, Thu 7.45-8.15pm.
Divine Office: Matins 6, but Sat 6.30, (Sun Vigil on Sat 7.30pm); **Lauds** 7.35; **Conventual Mass** 7 (Sat 9.15, Sun 10.30); **Vespers** Sat 5.15pm; Sun 6pm, Mon-Fri 6.35pm; **Compline** 8pm (except Thu, Sat and Sun)

Benedictines of the English Congregation (OSB) Dom Ambrose McCambridge, Dom Timothy Gorham (Sub Prior);
Rev Alex Burke (Deacon), Rev Ian Edwards (Deacon)
Ealing Abbey, Charlbury Grove W5 2DY
Parish Tel: 020 8194 2301
Email: ealingabbey@rcdow.org.uk Web: www.ealingabbeyparish.org.uk
1/4 mile north of station and shops; local bus via Eaton Rise to Marchwood Crescent
Ealing Deanery (1897; 1899)
Trust of St Benedict's Abbey and all Trust Operations Tel: 020 8194 2300
Email: ealingmonk@ealingabbey.org.uk
Other priests OSB in the community: Abbot Dominic Taylor, Dom Alexander Bevan (Prior), Abbot Martin Shipperlee, Doms Peter Burns, Alban Nunn, Thomas Stapleford

• **The Benedictine Institute, 74 Castlebar Road W5 2DD**
Tel: 020 8194 2320 Email: info@benedictine-institute.org
• **Little Company of Mary, Flat 10, Berkeley Court, 33 Gordon Road W5 2AE**
Tel: 020 8810 4432 Email: jbugeja@aol.com
• **Missionary Sisters of Our Lady of Africa, Flat 13 Montpelier Court, Montpelier Road W5 2QN Tel: 020 8998 6731** (Office), 020 8997 3166, 020 8810 7619
Regional Superior Email: ukmsolareg@btinternet.com Web: www.msolafrica.org
• **Sisters of Charity of St Jeanne Antide, 6/8 Woodfield Road W5 1SJ**
Tel: 020 8998 9549 Email: srstrion16@btinternet.com
• **Sisters of the Resurrection, 18 Carlton Road W5 2AW**
Tel: 020 8810 6241 Email: csr.englishregion@yahoo.co.uk
also **84 Gordon Road W5 2AR Tel: 020 8998 8954**
• **Columban Fathers (SSC), 12 Blakesley Avenue W5 2DW**
Tel: 020 8997 0587 Email: columbanlondon12@gmail.com
Web: www.columbans.co.uk
Frs Gerard Markey, Daniel O'Malley (Superior), Thomas Ryan
• **Congregation of Marian Fathers, Divine Mercy Apostolate, 1 Courtfield Gardens W13 0EY**
Tel: 020 8998 0925 Email: info@divinemercy.org.uk
Web: www.divinemercyapostolate.co.uk
Sunday Mass (Polish) 10; **Daily Mass** and **Divine Mercy Chaplet** (English) Mon-Fri 2.30pm
except First Fri
Community Fr Andrzej Gowkielewicz, Fr Dariusz Mazewski

• Missionaries of Africa (White Fathers) (MAfr), 15 Corfton Road W5 2HP
Tel: 020 8601 7900 Email: corftonsuperior@mafrgb.org.uk
Frs Matthew Banseh, Michael Heap, Hugh Seenan (Superior); Br Nicholas Murphy

EASTCOTE + ST THOMAS MORE ♿⌕

Sunday Mass (Sat 6pm), 9.30 (Family), 11.30; **Holy Day Mass** (Vigil 7.30pm), 9.30;
Weekday Mass 9.30; **Confession** with **Exposition** and **Benediction** Sat 10-11

Fr Martin Plunkett
32 Field End Road, Eastcote, Pinner HA5 2QT Tel: 020 8866 6581 Fax: 020 8429 2346
Email: eastcote@rcdow.org.uk Web: parish.rcdow.org.uk/eastcote
On main road, north of station and shops, just beyond Bridle Road junction
Hillingdon Deanery (1935; 1977; cons 6 February 1978)

• St Vincent's Nursing Home, Wiltshire Lane, Eastcote HA5 2NB
Tel: 020 8872 4900 Web: www. svnh.co.uk
Chaplain Fr Bernard Boylan **Tel: 020 8429 4778**

EDGWARE + ST ANTHONY OF PADUA ♿⌕

Sunday Mass (Sat 6.30pm), 10, 12noon, 6pm; **Holy Day Mass** 9, 7.30pm; **Weekday Mass**
Mon-Fri 9, Tue 7.30pm (followed by **Devotions to St Anthony** and **Benediction**), Sat 10;
Exposition Mon-Fri 8(am)-9pm, Sat, Sun 9(am)-church closes after evening Mass;
Confession Sat 9.30-9.50, 5.30-6pm

Fr Robert Pachuta
5 Garratt Road, Edgware HA8 9AN Tel: 020 8952 0663
Email: edgware@rcdow.org.uk Web: parish.rcdow.org.uk/edgware
Off the A5 mid-way between the junctions with Station Road and Deansbrook Road
Barnet Deanery (1913;1931;1958)

• Daughters of Mary, Mother of Mercy, 16 St Margaret's Road, Edgware HA8 9UP
Tel: 020 8958 8316
• Dominican Sisters of St Catherine of Siena of Newcastle, Natal, St Albert's, 267 Hale
Lane, Edgware HA8 8NW Tel: 020 8958 5622

EDMONTON + THE MOST PRECIOUS BLOOD AND ST EDMUND, KM ♿⌕

Sunday Mass (Sat 6pm), 8, 10, 12noon, 2pm *in Igbo, 2nd Sun only*, 5.30pm; **Holy Day
Mass** 9.15, 12noon, 7pm; **Weekday Mass** 9.15 preceded by **Morning Prayer** 8.55;
Exposition Mon-Fri 10-11, Sat 11-12noon; **Confession** Sat 11-11.45, 5-5.45pm

Missionary Society of St Paul (MSP) Fr Noel Chukwudike Ugoagwu, Fr Walter Nnaemeka
Ezenwosu
115 Hertford Road N9 7EN Tel: 020 8803 6631 Fax: 020 8345 6495
Email: edmonton@rcdow.org.uk Web: www.stedmundsedmonton.co.uk
Corner of Croyland Road, 1/4 mile north of Edmonton Green
Enfield Deanery (1903; cons 17 May 1907)

SECTION 3

Catechetical Co-ordinator Mike Boggis
Parish Secretary Susan Phagoo

• Handmaids of the Holy Child Jesus, Trinity House, 48 Cavendish Road N18 2LS
Tel: 020 8803 3839 Email: trinityconventhouse@yahoo.com
and Ancilla Convent, 4 Woodstock Crescent N9 7LY 020 8804 4070
• North Middlesex Hospital

ELY PLACE + ST ETHELDREDA

Sunday Mass 9, 11 (Sung Latin); **Holy Day Mass** 1pm; **Weekday Mass** Mon-Fri 1pm;
Confession Weekdays 1.20pm and on request

Institute of Charity (IC) Fr Tom Thomas
14 Ely Place EC1N 6RY Tel: 020 7405 1061 Fax: 020 7405 7440
Email: elyplace@rcdow.org.uk Web: www.stetheldreda.com
Westminster Deanery (1252-1290; 1297; crypt re-opened 1876; upper church re-opened 1879)

ENFIELD + OUR LADY OF MOUNT CARMEL AND ST GEORGE S

Our Lady of Mount Carmel and St George: Sunday Mass (Sat 6pm), 8, 9 (with Children's
Liturgy), 10.30, 12noon, 6pm; **Holy Day Mass** 12noon, 7pm; **Weekday Mass** Mon-Thu
12noon, Fri 10, 12noon, Sat 9.30; **Exposition** Sat 10-10.45, 5-5.45pm, *First Fri* 6-6.45pm;
Rosary Mon-Fri 11.30; **Confession** Sat 10-10.45, 5-5.45pm, *First Fri* 6-6.45pm;
Chapel of Ease: Sunday Mass (Sat 6.30pm (Polish)), 8.30 (Polish), 10 (English), 12noon
(Polish), 3.30pm (Polish); **Weekday Mass** Wed-Fri 6.30pm (Polish)
Holy Family Convent: Sunday Mass 10.30 (Maronite); **Weekday Mass** Mon-Wed 8

Fr Daniel Humphreys, Fr Timothy Mangatal, Fr Vincent Nnatuanya CSSp, Rev Peter Jones
(Deacon)
45 London Road, Enfield EN2 6DS Tel: 020 8363 2569
Email: enfield@rcdow.org.uk Web: www.catholicenfield.org
Main road, near Enfield Town Stn (Overground)
Enfield Deanery (1862; 1958; cons 16 July 1967)
Chapel of Ease: Our Lady of Walsingham and the English Martyrs, Holtwhites Hill, Enfield
EN2 8HG
Catechetical Co-ordinator Georgina Simmons Email: enfieldcat@rcdow.org.uk
Parish Secretary Susi Thompson (Mon-Thu) Email: enfield@rcdow.org.uk

• Sisters of the Holy Family of Nazareth, 52 London Road, Enfield EN2 6EN
Tel: 020 8363 4483 Web: www.nazarethfamily.org
Polish Chaplain Fr Maciej Michałek Email: jeszuam@interia.pl Web: parafiaenfield.org
• Chase Farm Hospital, Enfield Community Care Centre at St Michael's Hospital, BMI
Cavell Hospital, BMI King's Oak Hospital

EUSTON, NW1: *SEE SOMERS TOWN*

FARM STREET + THE IMMACULATE CONCEPTION A ♪

Sunday Mass (Sat 6pm), 8, 9.30 (Family), 11 (Sung Latin), 12.30pm, 5.30pm, Young Adults Mass 7pm; **Holy Day Mass** (Vigil 6pm), 8, 1.05pm, 6pm; **Weekday Mass** Mon-Fri 8, 1.05pm, 6pm, Sat 8 only, Bank Holiday 1.05pm only; **Exposition** Mon-Fri 12noon-1pm; **Confession** Mon-Fri 12 noon-1pm; Sat 10-12 noon, Sun 15mins before each Mass.

Society of Jesus (SJ) Fr Dominic Robinson, Fr Nicholas King
114 Mount Street W1K 3AH Tel: 020 7493 7811
Email: farmstreet@rcdow.org.uk   Web: www.farmstreet.org.uk
Opposite Carlos Place (south side, Grosvenor Square); and at Farm Street (off Berkeley Square)
Marylebone Deanery (1849, cons 1993)
Parish Secretary George McCombe
Jesuits (SJ) Provincial Curia, 114 Mount Street W1K 3AH Tel: 020 7499 0285
Other members of Community: Frs Damian Howard (Provincial), Michael Bossy, Paul Nicholson, Ladislav Sulik

• **LGBT Catholics Westminster** meet on the 2nd and 4th Sunday evenings at Farm Street Church; email: lgbtcatholicswestminster@gmail.com, or Mgr Keith Barltrop (**Chaplain**; *see Bayswater* entry).

FELTHAM + ST LAWRENCE ♿ ♪

Sunday Mass (Sat 5pm), 8, 9.30, 11, 1pm (Polish); **Holy Day Mass** as announced; **Weekday Mass** Mon-Fri 9.30, Sat 11; **Exposition** Sat 10-10.45; **Confession** Sat 10-10.45 & on request
Ethnic & Eastern Catholic Chaplaincy Masses: Polish Sun 1pm; **Ukrainian Liturgy** 7pm *4th Sat only*, 2.30pm *2nd Sun only*; **Malayalam** 2.30pm *3rd Sun only*; **Filipino** 3pm *4th Sat only*; **African Liturgy** 2.30pm *4th Sun only*

Fr John Byrne (**Tel: 07879 058732**), Fr David Cherry, Rev Rolly Leon (Deacon), Rev Colin Macken (Deacon)
St Lawrence's Presbytery, The Green, Feltham TW13 4AF Tel: 020 8890 2367
Email: feltham@rcdow.org.uk   Web: www.saintlawrences.org.uk
Set back on east side of High Street, not far from Feltham Stn
Hounslow Deanery (1910; 1934)
• Sisters of Mercy, 35 Ruscombe Way, Feltham TW14 9NY Tel: 020 8751 0862
• HMYOI and Remand Centre **Chaplain** Bridget Brinkley (**See HM Prison Service**)

FINCHLEY CHURCH END + ST PHILIP THE APOSTLE ♿ ♪

Sunday Mass (Sat 6.30pm), 9.30 (Sung), 11.30 (Family), 6.30pm (Polish); **Holy Day Mass** 12 noon, 7.30pm; **Weekday Mass** Mon, Tue, Thu-Sat 10; **Confession** Sat 10.30-11

Fr John P. Dermody, Fr Marek Gałuszka (in residence)
Priests House, Gravel Hill N3 3RJ Tel: 020 8346 2459
Email: finchleychurchend@rcdow.org.uk   Web: parish.rcdow.org.uk/finchleychurchend
Regent's Park Road near Finchley Central Stn, junction with Gravel Hill
Barnet Deanery (1918; 1933; cons 3 May 1975)

• Consolata Fathers (IMC), 3 Salisbury Avenue N3 3AJ
Tel: 020 8346 5498 Email: consolatafathers.uk@consolata.net
Frs Luis Tomas (Superior), Carlo Bonelli
• Finchley Memorial Hospital, Dell Field Court Nursing Home

FINCHLEY EAST + ST MARY &♿♪

Sunday Mass (Sat 5pm), 8.30, 10 (Family), 12noon; **Holy Day Mass** 10, 7.30pm; **Weekday Mass** Mon, Tue, Thu, Fri 10; **Exposition** Sat 10-11, 4.30-5pm; **Confession** Sat 10-11, 4.30-5pm

Fr Peter-Michael Scott, Rev Domagoj Matokovic (Deacon)
279 High Road N2 8HG Tel: 020 8883 4234
Email: finchleyeast@rcdow.org.uk Web: www.stmaryseastfinchley.org
10 minutes walk from East Finchley Stn (TfL), heading north
Barnet Deanery (1898; 1953)
Administrator Yvonne Tomei Email: finchleyeast@rcdow.org.uk
Director of Christian Education and Youth Holly Graham
Email: finchleyeastcatechist@rcdow.org.uk

• Sisters of Nazareth, Nazareth House, 162 East End Road N2 0RU Tel: 020 8883 1104
Email: superior.finchleyuk@nazarethcare.com
Nazareth House is a Residential Care Home
Email for enquiries: gm.finchleyuk@nazarethcare.com
Larmenier Centre, Nazareth Care (Regional Office) Tel: 020 8444 4427
Chaplain Fr John Boland
• Sisters of the Sacred Heart of Jesus (St Jacut), Nazareth House, 162 East End Road N2 0RU Email: dbissonnette1942@gmail.com

FINCHLEY NORTH + ST ALBAN &♿♪

Sunday Mass (Sat 6pm), 9.30, 11.30; **Holy Day Mass** as announced; **Weekday Mass** Mon-Fri 9.30; **Confession** Sat from 5.15pm & on request

Fr Dermot O'Neill
51 Nether Street N12 7NN Tel: 020 8446 0224
Email: finchleynorth@rcdow.org.uk Web: parish.rcdow.org.uk/finchleynorth
200 yds from Tally Ho Corner
Barnet Deanery (1903; 1909; cons 24 February 1995)
Key Catechist Ursula Morrissey

• Belarusian Catholic Mission: see under *Eastern Catholic Churches* at the end of this Section
• North London Hospice

FRENCH CHURCH + NOTRE DAME DE FRANCE A ♪

Sunday Mass - *all French* - (Sat 6pm), 11, 6pm *Summer Sunday Mass* (Sat 6pm), 11; **Holy Day Mass** 6pm *English*, 7.30pm *French*; **Weekday Mass** Mon, Wed-Fri 6pm; **Confession** before & after Mass & by arrangement

Marists (SM) Fr Pascal Boidin
5 Leicester Place WC2H 7BX Tel: 020 7437 9363
Email: frenchchurch@rcdow.org.uk   Web: www.ndfchurch.org
Off north side of Leicester Square
Westminster Deanery (1865; 1868; 1955)
Community: Frs Pascal Boidin, Hubert Bonnet-Eymard, (Superior), Damien Diouf
Parish Administrator Philippine de Beauregard **Tel: 020 7440 2642**

• Missionary Sisters of the Society of Mary SMSM, 34 Lisle Street WC2H 7BD
Tel: 020 3659 7836
• Chaplaincy to the French Schools, 23 Cromwell Mews SW7 2JY
Bénédicte Collet & Capucine Vassel **Tel: 020 7584 3006**

FULHAM 1 + ST THOMAS OF CANTERBURY ♿♪

Sunday Mass (Sat 5.30pm), 9, 10.30 (Family), 12noonSung) 3pm (Portuguese), 6pm; **Holy Day Mass** 9.30, 8pm; **Weekday Mass** Mon-Fri 9.30, Sat 10; **Exposition** Sat 10.30-11.30; **Confession** Sat 10.30-11.30, 6.15-6.45pm

Fr Dennis F P Touw Tempelmans-Plat, Fr Linford Fernandes, Rev Wayne O'Reilly (Deacon)
60 Rylston Road SW6 7HW Tel: 020 7385 4040
Email: fulham@rcdow.org.uk Web: www.stocf.wordpress.com
Hammersmith & Fulham Deanery (1847; cons 5 December 1969; recons 2006)
Parish Administrator Gerald Daly
Catechetical Co-ordinator Rev Wayne O'Reilly (Deacon)

FULHAM 2 STEPHENDALE ROAD + OUR LADY OF PERPETUAL HELP A ♪

Sunday Mass (Sat 6pm), 9, 11; **Holy Day Mass** as announced; **Weekday Mass** Mon, Wed, Fri 9.30; **Exposition** as announced; **Confession** Sat 5-5.45pm & on request

Fr Fortunato Pantisano
Parish House, 2 Tynemouth Street SW6 2QT Tel: 020 7736 4864
Email: stephendaleroad@rcdow.org.uk Web: parish.rcdow.org.uk/stephendaleroad
Sand's End: east of Wandsworth Bridge Road, south of New King's Road, southwest of Imperial Wharf
Hammersmith & Fulham Deanery (1922)
Parish Administrator Susan Keogh **Catechetical Co-ordinator** Jackie Charles

FULHAM ROAD + OUR LADY OF DOLOURS A ♪

Sunday Mass (Sat 6.30pm), 8.30, 10 (Family), 11.15 (Spanish), 12.15pm, 7pm; **Holy Day Mass** (Vigil 6.30pm), 10, 6.30pm; **Weekday Mass** 10, 6.30pm; **Exposition** Mon-Fri 10.30-11.15; **Rosary** Wed 10.30-10.45; **Legion of Mary** Tue 7.15pm; **Confession** daily 6.15-6.30pm & on request, Sat 10.45-11.15, 6-6.30pm

SECTION 3

Servites (OSM) Fr Allan Satur
St Mary's Priory, 264 Fulham Road SW10 9EL Tel: 020 7352 6965
Email: fulhamroad@rcdow.org.uk Web: www.servitechurch.org
In Fulham Road, east of Redcliffe Gardens/Edith Grove traffic lights
Kensington & Chelsea Deanery (1864; 1875; cons 4 November 1953)
Community: Frs Paul Addison, Chris O'Brien (Formation Master), Patrick Ryall, Allan Satur
(Parish Priest), Fulgensio Ssuuna; Br Patrick Gethins

• Sisters of the Cross and Passion (CP), 7 Stadium Street SW10 0PU
• Sisters Hospitallers of the Sacred Heart (Spanish), St Teresa's Residential Care Home
40-46 Roland Gardens SW7 3PW Tel: 020 7373 5820, Provincialate Tel: 020 7373 3054
Email: provincial@hsc-uk.org Web: www.sisterhospitallers.org
• Chelsea & Westminster Hospital

GARSTON + OUR LADY AND ST MICHAEL &♪

Sunday Mass (Sat 6pm), 8.30, 10, 12noon; **Holy Day Mass** 9.30, 7pm; **Weekday Mass**
Mon, Tue 9.30, Wed 7pm, Fri 9.30; **Exposition** before Wed 7pm Mass, *First Fri only* 10-
12noon; **Confession** Sat 5.15-5.45pm & by appointment

Fr Paul Antwi-Boasiako CSSp, Fr Benedict Baka CSSp (in residence, School Chaplain), Fr
Fidelis Ifeanyi CSSp (in residence, School Chaplain), Rev Paul Quinn (Deacon)
Catholic Church, Crown Rise, Garston, Watford WD25 0NE Tel: 01923 673239
Email: garston@rcdow.org.uk Web: parish.rcdow.org.uk/garston
On A405 North Orbital Road, just south of St Albans Road junction
Watford Deanery (1954)
Parish Administrator Veronika Clark Tel: 01923 673239 (Mon, Wed 9-3pm, Fri 9-1pm)

• Langley House, Tenterden House, Allington Court

GERMAN CHURCH + ST BONIFACE

Sunday Mass (Sat 5pm, 1st & 3rd Sun), 11 (2nd, 4th & 5th Sun); **Confession** (German)
by appointment

Fr Andreas Blum
47 Adler Street E1 1EE Tel: 020 7247 9529
Email: germanchurch@rcdow.org.uk Web: www.dkg-london.org
Tower Hamlets Deanery (1809; 1875; cons 4 October 1925; recons 2 October 1960)

• Wynfrid House, 20 Mulberry Street E1 1EH
Tel: 020 7247 6110 Email: info@wynfridhouse.com
German Community Centre and Bed and Breakfast Hostel
Manager Anthony Perera
• St Boniface Secular Institute (English Region) & Lioba House German Hostel for Young
People 42-44 Exeter Road NW2 4SB Tel: 020 8438 9628
Email: hostel@institut-st-bonifatius.de Web: www.hostel-lioba-house.de
(see also *Willesden Green* entry)

GOLDERS GREEN + ST EDWARD THE CONFESSOR ♿ ⚲

Sunday Mass 9, 10.30, 6pm; Holy Day Mass as announced; Weekday Mass Mon-Wed 10, Fri, Sat 10; Confession Sat 10.30-11 and by arrangement

Fr Paul McDermott, Rev Anthony Clark (Deacon), Rev David Lawrence (Deacon)
700 Finchley Road NW11 7NE Tel: 020 8455 1300
Email: goldersgreen@rcdow.org.uk Web: www.stedwardgg.uk
On main road just north of Golders Green Stn (TfL)
Barnet Deanery (1909; 1915; cons 30 September 1931)
Parish Administrator Kasonde Konie Music Director Mary Whittle Jones
Chief Catechist Alvaro Scrivano

GRAHAME PARK + ST MARGARET CLITHEROW A

Sunday Mass (Sat 6.30pm), 9, 12noon; Holy Day Mass 9.15, 7pm; Weekday Mass Mon, Fri 7pm, Tue, Wed, Thu 9.15, Sat 12noon; Exposition Sat 5-6pm; Novena Mon after Mass; Confession Sat 10-12noon, 5-6pm

Fr Brian Griffiths
The Presbytery, Everglade Strand NW9 5PX Tel: 020 8205 6830
Email: grahamepark@rcdow.org.uk Web: parish.rcdow.org.uk/grahamepark
Off Great Strand (near RAF Museum)
Barnet Deanery (1970; 1973; cons 14 November 1998)

• Metropolitan Police Training School

GREENFORD + OUR LADY OF THE VISITATION ♿ ⚲

Sunday Mass (Sat 7pm), 8, 9, 10.30, 12noon, 7pm; Holy Day Mass 8.30, 12noon, 7.30pm; Weekday Mass Mon-Sat 12noon; Confession Sat 11-12noon, 6.15-6.45pm

Pallottine Fathers (SAC) Fr Thomas Daly, Fr Joseph McLoughlin, Fr Liam O'Donovan, Fr Marcellus Ochola;
Rev Jayson Wingrove (Deacon)
358 Greenford Road, Greenford UB6 9AN Tel: 020 8578 1363 Fax: 020 8813 2230
Email: greenford@rcdow.org.uk Web: parish.rcdow.org.uk/greenford
Main Road (A4127) south of Ruislip Road junction
Ealing Deanery (1928; 1937)
Catechetical Co-ordinator Awaiting appointment

GROVE PARK + ST JOSEPH ♿ ⚲

Sunday Mass (Sat 6.30pm); Holy Day Mass as announced; Weekday Mass as announced

Canon Michael Dunne, Fr Daniel Daley, Fr Erasmus Egenonu CSSp (served from Chiswick, clergy resident at 247 High Road W4 4PU)
1 Bolton Road W4 3TE Tel: 020 8994 2877
Email: chiswick@rcdow.org.uk Web: www.ourladyofgracechiswick.org.uk
South A4, close to Chiswick Stn (BR), corner of Devonshire Gardens
Hounslow Deanery (1964; cons 23 February 1973)

HACKNEY + ST JOHN THE BAPTIST ♿ ♪

Sunday Mass (Sat 6pm), 9.30, 11.30; **Holy Day Mass** 9.30, 5.30pm (Latin), 7pm;
Weekday Mass Mon 12noon (Hospice), Tue-Fri 12noon, Sat 10; **Confession** Sat 10.30

Fr David Evans

3 King Edward's Road E9 7SF Tel: 020 8985 2496
Email: hackney@rcdow.org.uk Web: parish.rcdow.org.uk/hackney
King Edward's Road, off Mare Street, north of St Joseph's Hospice
Hackney Deanery (1847; 1956; cons 14 June 1972)

• Religious Sisters of Charity, St Joseph's Convent, 36 Mare Street E8 4AD
Tel: 020 8525 4242 Email: rschackney@yahoo.co.uk
Web: www.religioussistersofcharity.org
• Sisters of Charity of St Paul, 28 Warneford Street E9 7NG
Tel: 020 8986 2346 Email: b.devine@btinternet.com
• St Joseph's Hospice
Chaplain Awaiting appointment Tel: 020 8525 6000

HAMMERSMITH + ST AUGUSTINE ♪

Sunday Mass (Sat 6pm), 9, 10.30, 12.15pm, 6.30pm; **Holy Day Mass** 8, 12.15pm, 7pm;
Weekday Mass 8 (not Sat), 12.15pm; **Exposition** Sat 10.30-11.45; **Confession** Sat 10.30-
11.45 or by appointment

Augustinians (OSA) **Fr Tomas Banayag**
55 Fulham Palace Road W6 8AU Tel: 020 8748 3788
Email: hammersmith@rcdow.org.uk Web: parish.rcdow.org.uk/hammersmith
South Hammersmith Broadway, just beyond flyover
Hammersmith & Fulham Deanery (1903; 1916; cons 1933)
Community Bishop Michael G Campbell (in residence); Frs Barry Clifford (Prior), Tomas
Banayag, Arthur Bolivar, Br David Tan, Br Michael McLaren
Fr Robert Marsh (Provincial), **15 Dorville Crescent W6 OHH**
Parish Administrator Monica Hamilton

• St Augustine's Centre Manager Helen Murphy
Contact for all hiring and Centre matters Email: helen@staugustinescentrelondon.org
• Charing Cross Hospital, Chapel of the Holy Cross
Sunday Mass 10; **Weekday Mass** Mon 1pm
Chaplains Fr Giles Pinnock, Fr Benedict Abuo, Fr Blaise Amadi CM, Veronica Burns
Tel 020 3311 1056

HAMPSTEAD + ST MARY ♿ ♪

Sunday Mass (Sat 6.30pm), 8.30, 10, 11.30, 6.30pm; **Holy Day Mass** 10, 7.30pm;
Weekday Mass as announced; **Confession** Sat 6-6.30pm & on request

Mgr Phelim Rowland

4 Holly Place NW3 6QU Tel: 020 7435 6678
Email: hampstead@rcdow.org.uk Web: parish.rcdow.org.uk/hampstead
Near Hampstead Stn (TfL); via Church Row, lower end of Heath Street
Camden Deanery (1796; 1816; cons 1977)
Parish Administrator / Pastoral Assistant Mary Stanier Email: marystanier@rcdow.org.uk

• Sisters of St Dorothy 99 Frognal NW3 6XR
International Students' Residence Tel: 020 7794 6893
Email: stdorothylondon@gmail.com Web: www.st.dorothys.talktalk.net
• Sisters of St Marcellina, Hampstead Towers, 6 Ellerdale Road NW3 6BD
Tel: 020 7435 0181 Email: sisters@stmarcellina.org.uk Web: stmarcellina.org.uk

HAMPTON HILL (AND UPPER TEDDINGTON) + ST FRANCIS DE SALES

Sunday Mass (Sat 6pm), 9, 11; **Holy Day Mass** (Vigil 7.30pm), 9.30; **Weekday Mass** Mon-Wed, Fri, Sat 9.30; **Exposition** and **Confession** Sat 10-11

Fr Shaun Church
16 Wellington Road, Hampton Hill TW12 1JR Tel: 020 8977 1415
Email: hamptonhill@rcdow.org.uk Web: parish.rcdow.org.uk/hamptonhill
Upper Thames Deanery (1920; 1928; 1966; cons 18 December 1976)
Parish Secretary Mrs Annie D'Souza (Wed, Fri all day)

• Laurel Dene Care Home, Hampton

HAMPTON-ON-THAMES + ST THEODORE OF CANTERBURY ♿♿

Sunday Mass (Sat 6pm), 8.30, 10.30; **Holy Day Mass** 9.30, 7.30pm; **Weekday Mass** as announced; **Confession** Sat 5.45-6.15pm & on request

Fr Philip Baptiste
110 Station Road, Hampton-on-Thames TW12 2AS Tel: 020 8979 3596
Email: hamptononthames@rcdow.org.uk Web: parish.rcdow.org.uk/hamptononthames
Upper Thames Deanery (1977; 1986; cons 22 March 1987)
Pastoral assistant Sr Marian Ward SMG Tel: 020 8255 1106
Email: marian.ward@virginmedia.com

• Poor Servants of the Mother of God (PSMG), 112 Station Road, Hampton-on-Thames
TW12 2AS Tel: 020 8255 1106

HANWELL + OUR LADY AND ST JOSEPH A ♿

Sunday Mass (Sat 6pm), 8, 10 (Sung Family), 12noon; **Holy Day Mass** 10, 7pm; **Weekday Mass** Mon-Wed, Fri 10; **Exposition** Sat 5-6pm; **Confession** Sat 5-5.30pm & on request

Fr Cristiano Braz, Fr Julio Albornoz
52 Uxbridge Road W7 3SU Tel: 020 8567 4056
Email: hanwell@rcdow.org.uk Web: parish.rcdow.org.uk/hanwell
On main road, corner of St George's Road (traffic lights)
Ealing Deanery (1853; 1967)

SECTION 3

Parish Administrators Pamela Sheridan, Marlene Wakim
Catechetical Co-ordinator Awaiting appointment

• Medical Mission Sisters, 8 Springfield Road W7 3JP
Email: mmsspringfield@gmail.com Web: www.medicalmissionsisters-uk.org
• Sisters of St Joseph of Peace, St Mary's Convent, 50 Uxbridge Road W7 3PP
Tel: 020 8567 8635
• Ealing Hospital, Southall: General Wing
Mass as announced (see Hospital and Hospice Chaplains in this Section)
St Bernard's Wing

HAREFIELD + ST PAUL, MERLE AVENUE A ♪

Sunday Mass (Sat 6.30pm), 9, 11, 5pm *2nd Sun only, Syro-Malabar Rite*; **Holy Day Mass** 9.15, 7pm; **Weekday Mass** Mon-Sat 9.15; **Confession** Sat after morning Mass & 6pm

Fr James Mulligan
St Paul's House, 2 Merle Avenue, Harefield UB9 6DG Tel: 01895 822365
Email: harefield@rcdow.org.uk Web: parish.rcdow.org.uk/harefield
Bus 331 Uxbridge, U9 Northwood; church in Merle Avenue off High Street at south end of shopping parade
Hillingdon Deanery (1963; 1965; ext 1983)

• Harefield Hospital, Courtfield, Rylstone, Bardom Court, Harefield Nursing Home, Cedar House, Coppermill Care Home

HARPENDEN + OUR LADY OF LOURDES ♿♪

Sunday Mass (Sat 6pm), 8.30, 9.45 (Family), 11.30 (sung); **Holy Day Mass** 9.15, 6pm; **Weekday Mass** Mon, Tue, Wed, 9.15, Thu 11, Fri Liturgy of the Word & Holy Communion 9.15, **Novena** after Wed Mass; **Confession** Sat 10.30-11, 7-7.30pm

Canon Anthony Dwyer
Presbytery & Communication address: 1 Kirkwick Avenue, Harpenden AL5 2QH
Tel: 01582 712245
(Church address: Rothamsted Avenue AL5 2DB)
Email: harpenden@rcdow.org.uk Web: www.catholicchurchharpenden.org.uk
Rothamsted Avenue; off High Street, up from Church Green
St Albans Deanery (1905; 1929; cons 28 May 1936)
Office Administrator Melanie Armitage Mon-Thu 9.30-12.30pm Tel: 01582 712245
Email: harpenden@rcdow.org.uk
Parish Safeguarding Rep Brigid Brennan Email: harpendensg@safeguardrcdow.org.uk

• Dominican Sisters of St Catherine of Siena of Newcastle, Natal, St Michael's, 18 Kirkdale Road, Harpenden AL5 2PT Tel: 01582 712814
• Spire Hospital

HARROW NORTH + ST JOHN FISHER A ♪

Sunday Mass (Sat 6pm), 8.30, 10, 11.30; Holy Day Mass 10, 7pm; Weekday Mass Mon-Wed
10, Thu 7pm, Fri, Sat 10; Exposition Mon 9-9.45, *First Fri only*, with Benediction 10.30-11.30,
Sat 10.30-11.30; Confession Sat 10.30-11.30, 5.15-5.45pm & by appointment

Fr Graham Stokes, Fr Axcel Soriano
80 Imperial Close, Harrow HA2 7LW Tel: 020 8868 7531
Email: harrownorth@rcdow.org.uk Web: www.stjohnfisheronline.org.uk
Between North Harrow & Rayners Lane Stns, just south of The Ridgeway junction
Harrow Deanery (1939; cons 2014)
Parish Administrator Nuala Rodger
Catechist Jan Bennett Email: harrownorthcat@rcdow.org.uk

HARROW-ON-THE-HILL + OUR LADY AND ST THOMAS OF CANTERBURY ♿♪

Sunday Mass (Sat 6pm), 8.30, 10 (Family), 11.30 (Sung); Holy Day Mass 9.30, 7pm;
Weekday Mass Tue 7pm, Wed-Fri 9.30; Exposition 1 hour before weekday Masses;
Confession Sat 11-11.30

Fr Derek McGuire, Rev Eric Chelvarayan (Deacon)
22 Roxborough Park, Harrow-on-the-Hill HA1 3BE Tel: 020 8422 2513
Email: harrowonthehill@rcdow.org.uk Web: parish.rcdow.org.uk/harrowonthehill /
harrowcatholicchurch.org
Harrow Deanery (1873; 1894)
Parish Safeguarding Officer Desmond Gaynor Tel: 07936 912880
Parish Secretary Anna Byrne Mon-Wed, Fri 9.30-12.30pm

• Sisters of St Mary of Namur, 1 Grafton Road, Harrow HA1 4QS Tel: 020 8424 8185

HARROW ROAD + OUR LADY OF LOURDES AND ST VINCENT DE PAUL ♿♪

Sunday Mass (Sat 6pm), 11.30; Holy Day Mass as Weekday Mass, also 7pm; Weekday
Mass Mon, Fri 10 (Tue, Thu 10 at Paddington); Exposition and Benediction Mon, Fri 9-
10, Sat 5-6pm; Confession Sat 5-6pm

Fr Michael Jarmulowicz (also serves Paddington), Fr Daniel Isah (in residence)
337 Harrow Road W9 3RB Tel: 020 7286 2170
Email: harrowroad@rcdow.org.uk Web: parish.rcdow.org.uk/harrowroad
East of Great Western Road junction; near Westbourne Park Stn
North Kensington Deanery (1876; 1912; 1975)
Parish Administrator Mrs Jennifer Ellis Mon, Fri 9-3pm

HARROW SOUTH + ST GABRIEL & NORTHOLT + ST BERNARD ♿♪

St Gabriel: Sunday Mass (Sat 6pm), 8.30, 10, 12noon; Holy Day Mass 10; Weekday Mass
Mon, Wed, Fri 10; Exposition Mon 10.30-11; Confession Sat 5-5.40pm
St Bernard: Sunday Mass 9, 11, 5pm (Polish); Holy Day Mass 7.30pm; Weekday Mass
Tue 10, Thu 7pm Sat 10; Exposition Sat 10.30-11.45, Thu 6-6.45pm; Confession Sat
10.30-11.40, Thu 6-6.40pm

SECTION 3

Fr James Neal (resident at St Bernard's), Fr Carlos Quito (resident at St Gabriel's)
The Presbytery, 17 Mandeville Road, Northolt UB5 5HE
Parish Office: 390b Northolt Road, South Harrow HA2 8EX Tel: 020 8864 5455
Email: harrowsouth@rcdow.org.uk Web: parish.rcdow.org.uk/harrowsouth

+ St Gabriel's Church
390b Northolt Road, South Harrow HA2 8EX
On main road, south of South Harrow Stn, near junction with Park Lane
Harrow Deanery (1933; 2002; cons 2003)

+ St Bernard's Church
17 Mandeville Road, Northolt UB5 5HE
 On main road, between Target Roundabout & Northolt Stn
Harrow Deanery (1965; cons 2010)

HARROW WEALD: *SEE WEALDSTONE*

HATCH END: *SEE HEADSTONE LANE*

HATFIELD + MARYCHURCH A ♪

Sunday Mass (Sat 6pm), 11 (with Children's Liturgy), 6 (Polish); **Holy Day Mass** 9.30, 7.30pm; **Weekday Mass** Mon, Tue 9.30, Wed 7.30pm, Thu, Fri 9.30; **Divine Office** 20 mins before Weekday Mass; **Novenas** Tue: after Mass - Our Lady of Perpetual Succour, Thu after Mass - Most Sacred Heart of Jesus; **Exposition** Fri after Mass, *First Fri only* with **Benediction** 11; **Confession** Sat 5.15-5.45pm & on request

Missionary Society of St Paul (MSP) **Fr Agbor Isek,** Fr Innocent Odiaka (clergy also serve Hatfield South and are resident at **St Peter's Presbytery, Bishop's Rise, Hatfield AL10 9HN** Tel: 01707 262121)
26 Salisbury Square, Hatfield AL9 5JD Tel: 01707 262439
Email: hatfield@rcdow.org.uk Web: parish.rcdow.org.uk/hatfield
Just off Great North Road (A1000), near BR Stn & Hatfield House
Stevenage Deanery (1930, 1971)

Chapel of Ease: St Thomas More, Station Road, Welham Green
Sunday Mass 9.30; **Holy Day Mass** (Vigil 7.30pm)

HATFIELD SOUTH + ST PETER ♿ ♪

Sunday Mass 9, 11 (with Children's Liturgy), Travellers Mass 2pm, Student Mass 6pm; **Holy Day Mass** 9.30, 7pm; **Weekday Mass** Mon, Tue, Wed, Fri 9.30, preceded by **Morning Prayer** 9.10, Thu 7pm, Sat 10.30; *First Sat only* **Exposition** with **Benediction** 10.30-12noon, then **Mass** with **Anointing of the Sick**; **Exposition** Sat 11-12noon, with **Benediction** 12noon; **Novenas** Tue after Mass - Our Lady of Perpetual Help, Fri after Mass - Most Sacred Heart of Jesus; **Rosary** Wed after Mass; **Confession** Sat 11-12noon, 5-5.30pm & on request

Missionary Society of St Paul (MSP) Fr Agbor Isek, Fr Innocent Odiaka (also Chaplain to the University of Hertfordshire) (clergy also serve Hatfield Marychurch)
St Peter's Presbytery, Bishop's Rise, Hatfield AL10 9HN Tel: 01707 262121
Email: hatfieldsouth@rcdow.org.uk Web: www.stpetershatfield.org
Half-mile from Comet Roundabout, via Cavendish Way
Stevenage Deanery (1959; 1961)

HAVERSTOCK HILL + OUR LADY OF THE ROSARY AND ST DOMINIC A 🛈

The Church is the Diocesan Shrine of the Most Holy Rosary (2016)
Sunday Mass (Sat 6pm), 8.30, 10 (Family), 12noon (Solemn Shrine Mass), 6pm; **Holy Day Mass** (Vigil 6pm), 7.30, 10, 6pm; **Weekday Mass** Mon-Fri 7.30, 6pm (Thu 6pm with **Vespers**), Sat 7.30, 10; **Morning Prayer** Mon-Fri 7, Sat, Sun 8; **Evening Prayer** Mon, Tu, Fri 6.45pm, Sun 5.30pm; **Exposition** Mon-Fri 5-5.45pm, also **Benediction** Thu 5.45pm, **Exposition** and **Rosary Procession** Sat 10.30; **Confession** Sat 10.30-11, 5.30-6.15pm, Sun 9.45-10.15, 11.45-12.15pm

Dominicans (OP) Fr Lawrence Lew (Tel: 020 7482 9224)
St Dominic's Priory, Southampton Road NW5 4LB
Tel: 020 7482 9210 Fax: 020 7482 9239
Email: haverstockhill@rcdow.org.uk Web: www.rosaryshrine.co.uk
Top of Malden Road, nearest TfL Stns Chalk Farm & Belsize Park
Camden Deanery (1867; 1874; cons 1 August 1923)
Community: Frs Joseph Bailham, Michael Dunn, Leo Edgar, Martin Ganeri (Provincial **Email: provincial@english.op.org**), Peter Harries, Lawrence Lew, Rudolf Löwenstein, Thomas Skeats

• **Hospital Chaplain to UCLH NHS Trust** Fr Peter Harries OP **Tel: 020 7482 9216** (Elizabeth Garrett Anderson Wing, Heart, National for Neurology & Neurosurgery and University College Hospitals)
Sunday Mass 9.45
• **Royal Free Hospital Tel: 020 7794 0500**

HAYES + THE IMMACULATE HEART OF MARY A 🛈

Sunday Mass (Sat 6.30pm), 8.30, 10, 12noon, 7pm; **Holy Day Mass** 9.30, 12noon, 7pm; **Weekday Mass** Mon, Tue, Thu 8.10, Mon-Sat 12noon, Wed, Fri 7pm; **Bank Holidays** 10; **Confession** (Spanish available) Sat 5.45-6.15pm & by appointment

Claretian Missionaries (CMF) Fr Paul Smyth
Botwell House, Botwell Lane, Hayes UB3 2AB Tel: 020 8573 2544
Email: hayes@rcdow.org.uk Web: www.botwell.org.uk
In town centre, just off Coldharbour Lane/Station Road; near Hayes and Harlington Stn (BR)
Hillingdon Deanery (1912; 1954; 1961; cons 24 October 1972)
Community: Frs Joseph Katthula, Chris Newman, John O'Byrne, Paul Smyth (Superior)
Pastoral Assistant Daniel Ortiz **Administrator** Jackie Morris **General Parish Assistant** Bridget Fahy **Tel: 020 8573 2544**

SECTION 3

The Claretian Oasis (Pastoral Centre) Botwell Lane, Hayes UB3 2AB
Tel: 07553 911317

• Hayes Cottage Nursing Home

HEADSTONE LANE + ST THERESA OF THE CHILD JESUS &♿

Sunday Mass (Sat 5pm), 10, 6pm; **Holy Day Mass** 9.30, 7.30pm; **Weekday Mass** Mon-Thu 9.30, Fri, Sat 10; **Exposition** and **Benediction** *First Fri only* 8.50-9.45; **Confession** Sat 10.30, with **Exposition** and **Benediction** *First Sat only* 4-4.30pm

Fr Richard Parsons   (Tel: 020 8864 8021)
22 Boniface Walk, Harrow HA3 6PU Tel: 020 8428 3260
Email: headstonelane@rcdow.org.uk Web: parish.rcdow.org.uk/headstonelane
Uxbridge Road, Hatch End, junction Headstone Lane; near Headstone Lane/Hatch End Stns
Harrow Deanery (1953)

HEATHROW AIRPORT + ST GEORGE'S CHAPEL

Sunday Mass 12.30pm - Chapel of St George; **Weekday Mass** Mon, Wed, Fri 12.30pm

Fr Damian-Mary Moneke CSSp (resident at Hounslow parish)
Chapel of St George, Heathrow Airport, Central Terminal Area, Hounslow TW6 1BP
Tel: 020 8745 4261 Email: heathrowairport@rcdow.org.uk
Web: parish.rcdow.org.uk/heathrow
Hounslow Deanery (1968)
Pastoral Assistants Susan Badua, Helen Baly, Hertiberto Demelo, Fiona Gonsalves, Elisangela Rivera
The Chapel is located in the central area of Heathrow Airport. It can be accessed by the Piccadilly Line Underground (Terminals 1, 2, 3); the train from Paddington (Terminals 2, 3) and the Central Bus Station. From any point, go towards the Central Bus Station. The way to Chapel is designated along all the pathways leading to the bus and train stations. It is about three minutes from the Central Bus Station. Contact the Chapel office for details of services during the week. Priests and groups who wish to celebrate Mass at the airport should contact the Chaplain directly. Multi-faith prayer rooms are to be found in all the Terminals, either airside or landside, and are available for prayer and quiet times.

HEMEL HEMPSTEAD EAST + A &♿

Our Lady, Queen of All Creation: **Sunday Mass** (Sat 5pm), 10.30, 12noon; **Holy Day Mass** as announced; **Weekday Mass** Mon, Tue 10, Fri 7pm, Sat10; **Exposition** Sat 10.30-11; **Confession** Sat 10.30-11
The Resurrection: **Sunday Mass** 9; **Holy Day Mass** as announced; **Weekday Mass** Thu 10; **Confession** before Mass
Weekday Mass times are subject to change. Please check the parish newsletter at
parish.rcdow.org.uk/hemelhempsteadeast/

Fr Kim Addison

The Presbytery, Rant Meadow, Hemel Hempstead HP3 8PG Tel: 01442 210610

+ Our Lady, Queen of All Creation
The Presbytery, Rant Meadow, Hemel Hempstead HP3 8PG Tel: 01442 210610
Email: hemeleast@rcdow.org.uk Web: parish.rcdow.org.uk/hemelhempsteadeast/
On dual carriageway A414 between M1 (exit 8) & town centre
St Albans Deanery (1955; 1987; cons 13 November 1987)

+ The Church of the Resurrection, Grovehill
9 Henry Wells Square, Grovehill, Hemel Hempstead HP2 6BJ (Postal address:
The Presbytery, Rant Meadow, Hemel Hempstead HP3 8PG) Tel: 01442 210610
Email: hemeleast@rcdow.org.uk Web: parish.rcdow.org.uk/hemelhempsteadeast/
Access from Washington Avenue into Turnpike Green
St Albans Deanery (Shared church, 1977)

• Hemel Hempstead Hospital Tel: 01442 213141 Chaplain: Rev Anthony Curran
(Deacon) Tel: 01923 217994

HEMEL HEMPSTEAD WEST   A ♿ ♬

+ *Ss Mary and Joseph:* Sunday Mass (Sat 6pm), 8.30, 10.15; Holy Day Mass 10, 7.30pm;
Weekday Mass Mon-Wed, Fri 10; Exposition *1st Fri only* 10.30-11.30; Confession Sat 5-
5.30pm, *1st Fri only* 10.45-11.15
+ *St Mark:* Sunday Mass 12noon
For Weekday Mass times, please check the parish newsletter at
parish.rcdow.org.uk/hemelhempsteadwest/

Fr Brian McMahon
186 St Johns Road, Hemel Hempstead HP1 1NR Tel: 01442 391759

+ Ss Mary and Joseph
186 St John's Road, Hemel Hempstead HP1 1NR Tel: 01422 391759
Email: hemelhempsteadwest@rcdow.org.uk
Web: parish.rcdow.org.uk/hemelhempsteadwest/
St Albans Deanery (1890; 1938; 1951)

+ St Mark
Hollybush Lane, Warners End, in the grounds of John F Kennedy Catholic School, Hemel
Hempstead HP1 2PH
(Postal address: 186 St John's Road, Hemel Hempstead HP1 1NR)
Email: hemel@rcdow.org.uk Web: parish.rcdow.org.uk/hemelhempsteadwest/
St Albans Deanery (1977)

HENDON + OUR LADY OF DOLOURS A ♪

Sunday Mass (Sat 6pm), 10, 12noon; **Holy Day Mass** as announced; **Weekday Mass** Mon-Wed 10, Thu 8, Fri, Sat 10; *First Fri only* Exposition and **Benediction** after Mass; **Confession** Sat 9-10, 5.15-5.45pm and on request

Fr Tim Edgar
4 Egerton Gardens NW4 4BA Tel: 020 8202 0560
Email: hendon@rcdow.org.uk Web: www.ourladyofdolours.org.uk
Off The Burroughs (opp. Town Hall), close to Watford Way (A41) & Hendon Central Stn (TfL)
Barnet Deanery (1849; 1863; cons 1927; recons 25 March 1966)

• Poor Handmaids of Jesus Christ, St Joseph's Convent, Westminster House, Watford Way NW4 4TY Tel: 020 8202 7626 Email: winifred.orourke@btinternet.com
Web: www.poorhandmaidsofjesuschrist.org.uk
• Hendon Hospital

HENDON WEST + ST PATRICK ♿ ♪

Sunday Mass 10, 12noon (Polish), *Last Sun of month only* 6pm (Filipino); **Holy Day Mass** as announced; **Weekday Mass** Mon, Wed 7pm with **Exposition** from 6pm (other weekday Masses at Hendon)

Fr Tim Edgar (resident at **4 Egerton Gardens NW4 4BA Tel: 020 8202 0560**), Fr Bartosz Rajewski (in residence)
167 West Hendon Broadway NW9 7EB Tel: 020 8202 5143
Email: hendonwest@rcdow.org.uk Web: parish.rcdow.org.uk/hendonwest
Hendon Broadway on main road (A5), 800 yds north of Staples Corner
Barnet Deanery (1964)

HERTFORD + THE IMMACULATE CONCEPTION AND ST JOSEPH ♿ ♪

Sunday Mass (Sat 6pm), 8.30, 10.30 (Sung), 6pm; **Holy Day Mass** 7.30, 10 (at school in term time), 8pm; **Weekday Mass** Mon, Wed, 10, Tue, Fri, 12.15pm, Thu 7.30 *(only on Holy Days)*; **Exposition** Sat 5-5.45pm (*Stations of the Cross replace Exposition on Saturdays in Lent*); **Confession** Sat 10-10.30, 5-5.40pm

Canon Terence Phipps
23 St John's Street, Hertford SG14 1RX Tel: 01992 582109
Email: hertford@rcdow.org.uk Web: parish.rcdow.org.uk/hertford
Off Railway Sreet, close to Hertford East Stn (BR)
Lea Valley Deanery (Priory 1087-1539; 1848; 1858; cons 16 October 1866)

HESTON + OUR LADY QUEEN OF APOSTLES ♿ ♪

Sunday Mass (Sat 7pm), 8, 9.30, 11.30, 5.30pm; **Holy Day Mass** (Vigil 7pm), 9.30, 7pm; **Weekday Mass** 9.30, 7pm; **Exposition** Sat 10-10.45; **Novena** during Wed 7pm Mass; **Confession** Sat 10-10.45 & on request

Society of Divine Vocations (SDV) Fr Luigi Morrone, Fr Ritche Podador

15 The Green, Heston Road, Heston TW5 0RL Tel: 020 8570 1818
Email: heston@rcdow.org.uk Web: parish.rcdow.org.uk/heston
Set back from main road, just south of motorway bridge
Hounslow Deanery (1928; 1929; 1964; cons 19 May 1974)
(Fr Paul Rout OFM **2a Eton Avenue**;
Mgr Vladimir Felzmann **2b Eton Avenue**)
Parish Secretary Sandra Duarte **Mon-Fri 9-1pm**
Heston Catholic Social Club (Pope John Centre) Tel: 020 8574 5411
Parish Halls (Parish Secretary) Tel: 020 8570 1818

HIGHBURY + ST JOAN OF ARC A 🎵

Sunday Mass (Sat 6pm), 9, 11, 2pm (Congolese Community); **Holy Day Mass** 9.15, 7.30pm; **Weekday Mass** Mon-Fri 9.15, Sat 10; **Confession** Sat 5.15-5.45pm

Canon Gerard King
60 Highbury Park N5 2XH Tel: 020 7226 0257
Email: highbury@rcdow.org.uk Web: www.stjoanofarcparish.co.uk
Islington Deanery (1920; 1962; cons 14 June 2001)

• Our Lady of Mercy Sisters, 40 Aberdeen Road N5 2XD Tel: 020 7359 3897
• Sisters of St Paul de Chartres, 30 Aberdeen Park N5 2BL Tel: 020 7359 1712
Email: ndf_2003@yahoo.fr

HIGHGATE + ST JOSEPH ♿🎵

Sunday Mass (Sat 7pm), 8, 10, 12noon, 1.30pm (Polish), 7pm; **Holy Day Mass** (Vigil 6.30pm), 9.30, 6.30pm; **Weekday Mass** Mon-Fri 9.30, 6.30pm, Sat & Bank Holidays 9.30; **Confession** Sat 10-10.30, 6.30-6.45pm

Passionists (CP) Fr George Koloth
St Joseph's Retreat, Highgate Hill N19 5NE Tel: 020 7272 2320
Email: highgate@rcdow.org.uk Web: www.stjosephshighgate.org.uk
Corner Dartmouth Park Hill; Archway Stn (TfL)
Islington Deanery (1858; 1888; cons 28 April 1932)
Community: Frs Tiernan Doherty (Rector), Edwin Jenish George Koloth, Thomas Rockey
St Joseph's Parish Centre, Highgate Hill N19 5NE Tel: 020 7272 4571

• Whittington Hospital & Hornsey Central Hospital
Chaplain Fr Oliver Ugwu **Tel: 020 7288 5337**

HILLINGDON + ST BERNADETTE ♿🎵

Sunday Mass (Sat 6pm), 9, 11; **Holy Day Mass** 10, 7pm; **Weekday Mass** Mon, Wed-Fri 10; **Exposition** with **Benediction** Fri after Mass; **Rosary** after weekday Mass; **Confession** Sat 10.30-11

Fr Matthew J Heslin, Rev Reg Abrahams (Deacon)
160 Long Lane, Hillingdon UB10 0EH Tel: 01895 234577
Email: hillingdon@rcdow.org.uk Web: parish.rcdow.org.uk/hillingdon

South Long Lane (half mile up from Uxbridge Road)
Hillingdon Deanery (1937; 1961; cons 7 October 1978)

• Sisters of Mercy, St Raphael's Convent, Court Drive, Hillingdon UB10 0BW
Tel: 01895 233771
• Hillingdon Hospital
Sunday and **Holy Day Mass** 2pm

HITCHIN + OUR LADY IMMACULATE AND ST ANDREW ♿ ♪

Sunday Mass (Sat 6pm) 8.30, 10.30; **Holy Day Mass** 7.30, 10, 7.30pm; **Weekday Mass** 10; **Confession** (French available) with **Exposition** and **Benediction** Sat 10.30-11.15

Assumptionists (a.a.) Fr Tom O'Brien, Fr Andrew O'Dell (in residence), Fr Adams Tatsidjodoung
16 Nightingale Road, Hitchin SG5 1QS Tel: 01462 459126
Email: hitchin@rcdow.org.uk Web: parish.rcdow.org.uk/hitchin
Junction with Grove Road, opposite Bancroft Recreation Ground
Stevenage Deanery (1890; 1902; cons 18 December 1977)
Assistant Trish Bonnett (Pastoral) **Email:** trishbonnett@rcdow.org.uk
Administrator Cheryl Saunders (Mon-Thu)
Sacramental Co-ordinator / Youth Worker Rob Hitchcock

• Cheshire Home

HODDESDON + ST AUGUSTINE ♿ ♪

Sunday Mass (Sat 4pm (Italian), 6.30pm), 9.15 (with Children's Liturgy), 11.15; **Holy Day Mass** 9.15, 2pm, 8pm; **Weekday Mass** Mon-Thu 9.15 (preceded by **Exposition** 8.30), Fri 12noon (preceded by **Exposition** with **Benediction** 11), Sat 10 (preceded by **Exposition** 9.30); **Exposition** Mon-Wed, Fri 7-8pm; **Confession** Sat 10.30-11, 5.30-6.15pm, Sun 8.45-9, 10.45-11

Fr Julian Davies, Fr Mathews Valiyaputhenpura Joy (in residence, Knanaya Chaplaincy)
The Presbytery, Esdaile Lane, Hoddesdon EN11 8DS Tel: 01992 440986
Email: hoddesdon@rcdow.org.uk Web: parish.rcdow.org.uk/hoddesdon
Junction of High Street with Charlton Way
Lea Valley Deanery (1932; 1962; cons 1971)
Parish Secretary Dawn Bates

HOLBORN (CIRCUS), EC1: *SEE ELY PLACE*; (HIGH), WC1: *SEE LINCOLN'S INN FIELDS*

HOLLOWAY + SACRED HEART OF JESUS A ♪

Sunday Mass (Sat 6pm), 8.30, 11 (Sung, with choir); **Holy Day Mass** 10; **Weekday Mass** (**Morning Prayer** precedes by 15 mins) Mon, Wed, Thu, Fri 9.15, Public Holidays 10; **Confession** Sat 11-12noon & on request

Fr Gideon Wagay, Fr Henry Mobela (in residence, Zambian Chaplaincy, contact details below)
62 Eden Grove N7 8EN Tel: 020 7607 3594

Email: holloway@rcdow.org.uk Web: www.sacredheartchurchholloway.org.uk
Off Holloway Road, opposite Metropolitan University and Emirates (Arsenal FC) Stadium
Islington Deanery (1855; 1870; cons 29 May 1928)
(Fr Henry Mobela **Tel: 07495 866069 Email:** kalusamobela@gmail.com)
Parish Administrator Elizabeth Ocampo

• Sisters of La Sainte Union, 51 Freegrove Road N7 9RG Tel: 020 7609 7160
• Pentonville Prison **Chaplains** Valentine Ambe, Mary Ebbasi **(See HM Prison Service)**

HOMERTON + IMMACULATE HEART OF MARY AND ST DOMINIC

Sunday Mass (Sat 6.30pm), 9, 11; **Holy Day Mass** 9.30, 7pm; **Weekday Mass** 9.30;
Exposition for Priests / Vocations Tue 10-10.30; **Confession** Sat 10-10.45

Fr Patrick Allsop
Presbytery, Ballance Road E9 5SS Tel: 020 8985 1495
Email: homerton@rcdow.org.uk Web: www.heartofmary.weebly.com
Ballance Road
Hackney Deanery (1873; cons 30 June 1884)
Parish Administrator Marie Edgar

HOUNSLOW + SS MICHAEL AND MARTIN

Sunday Mass (Sat 6.15pm), 7.30, 9, 10.30, 12noon, 6pm; **Holy Day Mass** (Vigil 6pm), 7.30,
9, 6pm 7.30pm; **Weekday Mass** Mon–Sat 9, Mon–Thu 6pm, Fri 7pm.; **Exposition**, followed by
Benediction Sat 4.30-5.30pm; **Confession** Fri 6-6.30pm, Sat 9.30-10.15, 4.30-5.15pm
Ethnic Chaplaincy Masses 3pm Syro-Malabar Mass *1st Sun only*, 4pm Sinhalese Mass *2nd
Sun only*, 4pm Goan Mass *3rd Sun only*

Spiritans (CSSp) Fr Daniel Adayi, Fr David Atunaya, Fr Damian-Mary Moneke (Chaplain at
Heathrow Airport)
94 Bath Road, Hounslow TW3 3EH Tel: 020 8570 1693
Email: hounslow@rcdow.org.uk Web: parish.rcdow.org.uk/hounslow
Hounslow Deanery (1804; 1929; cons 12 October 1938)
Parish Administrator Priya Joseph
Parish Catechist Lionel Pereira
Youth Worker Ivan Cižmárik

HOXTON + ST MONICA'S PRIORY A

Sunday Mass (Sat 6.30pm), 9, (followed by **Legion of Mary**) 11, 6.30pm; **Holy Day Mass**
(Vigil 7pm), 9.30, 7pm; **Weekday Mass** Mon-Fri 9.30, preceded by **Morning Prayer** 9.10,
Sat 11; **Bank Holiday Mass** 11; **Exposition** Sat 5-6pm, followed by **Vespers** 6pm;
Confession Sat 5-6pm and on request

Augustinians (OSA) Fr Gabriel Hassan, Fr Jacob Choi, Fr Anthony Zabbey (Prior)
19 Hoxton Square N1 6NT Tel: 020 7739 5006
Email: hoxton@rcdow.org.uk Web: parish.rcdow.org.uk/hoxton
Off Old Street, at Shoreditch Town Hall
Hackney Deanery (1864)

Parish Administrator Michelle Tchimou

• Little Sisters of Jesus, 148 Fellows Court, Weymouth Terrace E2 8LW
Tel: 020 7729 3605 Email: lsj.hackney@virgin.net Web: www.jesuscaritas.info/lsj
• Shalom Catholic Community 150 Kingsland Road E2 8EB Tel: 07432 501250
Email: london@comshalom.org Web: http://www.comshalom.org/en
• Ashwell House, Shepherdess Walk N1 7NA Tel: 020 7490 3296
Hall of residence for women university students
Pastoral care entrusted to Prelature of Opus Dei
• Mildmay Mission Hospital

ISLE OF DOGS: *SEE MILLWALL*

ISLEWORTH + OUR LADY OF SORROWS AND ST BRIDGET OF SWEDEN &

Sunday Mass (Sat 6pm), 8, 10, 12noon; **Holy Day Mass** 9, 7pm; **Bank Holiday Mass** 10; **Weekday Mass** Mon-Thu 9, Mon, Fri 7pm, Sat 10; **Exposition** Mon-Thu half hour before Mass, Fri, Sat half hour after Mass, with **Benediction** Fri; **Confession** Sat 10.30-11, 5-5.30pm

Divine Word Missionaries (SVD) Fr Nicodemus Lobo Ratu, Fr Clement Narcher
Memorial Square, 112 Twickenham Road, Isleworth TW7 6DL Tel/Fax: 020 8560 1431
Email: isleworth@rcdow.org.uk Web: parish.rcdow.org.uk/isleworth /
www.stbridgets.org.uk
Corner of South Street (traffic lights); opposite Gumley House
Hounslow Deanery (1675; 1910; cons 6 October 1910)

• Faithful Companions of Jesus, Gumley House Convent, 251 Twickenham Road,
Isleworth TW7 6DN Tel: 020 8232 9570 Email: generalatesecretary@fcjgeneralate.org /
MFitzpatrick@FCJGeneralate.org Web: www.fcjsisters.org
The Generalate, central administration of the Community, is based here.

ISLINGTON + ST JOHN THE EVANGELIST &

Sunday Mass (Sat 6pm), 9.30, 11 (Sung); **Holy Day Mass** 10, 7.30pm; **Weekday Mass** 10; **Confession** Sat 10.30-11

Mgr Séamus O'Boyle, Fr Jakub Joszko (clergy also serve Copenhagen Street)
39 Duncan Terrace N1 8AL Tel: 020 7226 3277
Email: islington@rcdow.org.uk Web: www.st-johns-islington-org
2 mins from Angel TfL Stn, via Islington High Street, right into Duncan Street, left into Duncan Terrace Islington Deanery (1839; 1843; cons 26 June 1873)

• Sisters of the Cross and Passion, 40 Duncan Terrace N1 8AL Tel: 020 7359 8719

ITALIAN CHURCH + ST PETER'S

Sunday Mass (Sat 7pm), 9.30, 11 (Sung), 12.30pm, 6pm GMT / 7pm BST; **Holy Day Mass** 10, 12.15pm, 7.30pm; **Weekday Mass** Mon-Fri 12.15pm; **Confession** (Italian, English, Sunday during Mass & on request)

Pallottine Fathers (SAC) Fr Andrea Fulco, Fr Giuseppe De Caro
St Peter's Italian Church, 136 Clerkenwell Road EC1R 5DL
(Correspondence etc. to 4 Back Hill EC1R 5EN)
Tel: 020 7837 1528 Fax: 020 7837 9071
Email: italianchurch@rcdow.org.uk Web: www.italianchurch.org.uk
Opposite the top end of Hatton Garden
Westminster Deanery (1863)

KENSAL NEW TOWN + OUR LADY OF THE HOLY SOULS ৬

Sunday Mass (Sat 6pm), 9, 11 (Family); **Holy Day Mass** 9.30, 7.30pm; **Weekday Mass** Tue-Fri 9.30; **Confession** Sat 5.15-5.45pm & on request

Fr Damian Ryan
68 Hazlewood Crescent W10 5DJ Tel: 020 8969 2660
Email: kensalnewtown@rcdow.org.uk Web: parish.rcdow.org.uk/kensalnewtown
In Bosworth Road, off Kensal Road (near Halfpenny Bridge)
North Kensington Deanery (1862; 1882; cons 10 Nov 2012)
Parish Administrator Stephanie Mackay

- Missionaries of Charity, 177 Bravington Road W9 3AR Tel: 020 8960 2644
- Sisters of Mercy, 76 Fifth Avenue W10 4DP Tel: 020 8960 2505

KENSAL RISE + CHURCH OF THE TRANSFIGURATION A ♪

Sunday Mass (Sat 5pm), 8, 10 (Sung, with Children's Liturgy), 11.30pm (Italian); **Holy Day Mass** 10, 7pm; **Weekday Mass** Tue-Fri 10, with **Exposition** one hour before each Mass; **Confession** Sat 1pm & on request

Mgr Roger Reader, (resident at Clergy House, Peter Avenue NW10 2DD Tel: 020 8451 4677), Fr Allan Alvarado Gil
Presbytery, 1 Wrentham Avenue NW10 3HT Tel: 020 4542 3716
Email: kensalrise@rcdow.org.uk Web: www.transfigparishkensalrise.org.uk
Corner of Wrentham Avenue and Chamberlayne Road, near Kensal Rise BR Stn
Brent Deanery (1977)
Parish Administrator Chelsea Bottomley (9:30-2:30pm, Mon-Thu)

- Sisters of Jesus and Mary, 200 Chamberlayne Road NW10 3JX
Tel: 020 8451 1957
- Stigmatine Fathers (CSS), 2 Leigh Gardens NW10 5HP
Tel: 020 8969 1414 Email: donnatalino@btinternet.com Fr Natalino Mignolli
- St Mary's Cemetery, 679-681 Harrow Road NW10 5NU Tel: 020 8969 1145

KENSINGTON 1 + OUR LADY OF VICTORIES ♿

Sunday Mass (Sat 6pm), 9, 10.30, 12noon, 6pm; **Holy Day Mass** as announced; **Weekday Mass** Mon-Fri 10; **Exposition** Wed 10.30-12noon; **Confession** Sat 5-5.45pm, Wed 10.45-11.45 and as announced

Mgr Jim Curry, Fr Marco Salvagnini
The Clergy House, 16 Abingdon Road W8 6AF Tel: 020 7937 4778
Email: kensington1@rcdow.org.uk Web: parish.rcdow.org.uk/kensington1
235a High Street; south side of High Street, between Abingdon Road & Earls Court Road; not far from Kensington High Street Stn (TfL)
Kensington & Chelsea Deanery (1794; 1812; 1869; 1958)
Co-ordinator for Sacramental Programmes Sr Maureen McNamara RSM

• Augustinian Recollects (OAR), 18 Cheniston Gardens W8 6TQ Tel: 020 7937 7681
Fr Robert Riezu

KENSINGTON 2 + OUR LADY OF MOUNT CARMEL & ST SIMON STOCK ♿

Sunday Mass (Sat 6pm), 8.30, 10 (Family), 11 (Choir), 12.15pm, 6pm (Folk); **Holy Day Mass** (Vigil 6pm), 8, 12.15pm, 6pm; **Weekday Mass** 8, 12.15pm, 6pm; **Confession** Mon-Fri 5.40-6pm, Sat 10.30-11.30, 5-6pm

Discalced Carmelites (OCD) Fr Taddeus Ekuma
Carmelite Priory, 41 Kensington Church Street W8 4BB
Tel: 020 7937 9866 Fax 020 7938 1470
Email: kensington2@rcdow.org.uk Web: www.carmelitechurch.org
500 yards north of Kensington High Street
Kensington & Chelsea Deanery (1862; 1959)
Community: Frs Taddeus Ekuma (Prior & Parish Priest), Mathew Blake, John McGowan, Theophilus Nyamali, Tijo Xavier

• Adoratrices, Handmaids of the Blessed Sacrament and of Charity, 38/39 Kensington Square W8 5HP Tel: 020 7937 5237 Email: adorlonuk@hotmail.com
Web: www.adoratrices.com Hostel for Working Women & Students Tel: 020 7937 5237
• Religious of the Assumption, Convent of the Assumption, 20 Kensington Square W8 5HH Tel: 020 7361 4720 Email: enquiries@assumptionreligious.org
Web: www.assumptionreligious.org
Assumption Volunteers: Anne Marie Salgo
Email: vc@assumptionvolunteers.org.uk Web: www.assumptionvolunteers.org.uk
Milleret House Retreat centre
Administrator Pam Charlton Tel: 020 7361 4756
Email: enquiries@assumptionreligious.org
Web: www.assumptionreligious.org/Milleret-House
• Religious of Mary Immaculate, 15-16 Southwell Gardens SW7 4RN
Tel: 020 7373 2738 Email: rmilondon@btconnect.com
Hostel for working girls and students of all nationalities
Email: book@rmilondonhostel.org Web: www.rmilondonhostel.org

Social services for *au pairs*
Tel: 020 7373 3869 Email: socialservices@rmilondonhostel.org
Spanish Social Centre Tel: 020 7373 3869
• Cromwell Hospital
Chaplains Fr Giles Pinnock, Fr Benedict Abuo, Fr Blaise Amadi CM, Veronica Burns
Tel 020 3312 1508

KENTISH TOWN + OUR LADY HELP OF CHRISTIANS

Sunday Mass (Sat 6pm), 9 (Sung), 11 (Family); **Holy Day Mass** 10, 7pm; **Weekday Mass** Wed-Sat 10; **Confession** Sat 10.30-11

Fr John Deehan
4 Lady Margaret Road NW5 2XT Tel: 020 7485 4023
Email: kentishtown@rcdow.org.uk Web: parish.rcdow.org.uk/kentishtown
Corner of Falkland Road; 3 mins from Kentish Town Stn (TfL)
Camden Deanery (1859; cons 2 June 1925; new church 1970; cons 20 September 1979)
Parish Welfare Project Co-ordinator Richard Mallon **Tel: 07951 600451**

• Sisters of La Sainte Union, Croft Lodge, Highgate Road NW5 1RP
LSU Provincialate, 53 Croftdown Road NW5 1EL Tel: 020 7482 7225

KENTON + ALL SAINTS

Sunday Mass (Sat 6.30pm), 9, 11; **Holy Day Mass** as announced; **Weekday Mass** Mon-Wed, Fri 9.15; **Confession** Sat 10.30-11

Fr Hector Rouco Gutierrez
The Presbytery, 2a Salehurst Close, Harrow HA3 0UG Tel: 020 8204 3550
(Church address 531 Kenton Road HA3 0UL)
Email: kenton@rcdow.org.uk Web: parish.rcdow.org.uk/kenton
Corner of Claremont Avenue; 600 yards west of Kingsbury Circus/Kingsbury Stn (TfL); bus 183
Harrow Deanery (1932; 1963)
Parish Administrator Mrs Onitha Ratnam

KILBURN + SACRED HEART OF JESUS

Sunday Mass (Sat 6pm), 10, 12noon, 6pm; **Holy Day Mass** 10, 7pm; **Weekday Mass** Mon-Sat 10; **Filipino Mass** *3rd Sun* 3pm; **Adoration** Fri 10.30-1pm; **Divine Mercy** Sat 10.30; **Repository** Wed-Sun 9.30-1.30pm; **Confession** Sat 10.30-11.30, 5.30-6pm
Live streaming at **www.churchservices.tv/kilburn**

Oblates of Mary Immaculate (OMI) **Fr Terence Murray,** Fr Thomas Devereux, Fr Johnson Susairaj
New Priory, Sacred Heart Church, Quex Road NW6 4PS Tel: 020 7624 1701
Email: kilburn@rcdow.org.uk Web: parish.rcdow.org.uk/kilburn
Camden Deanery (1864; 1879; cons 18 June 1909)
Community: Frs Thomas Devereux (Superior), Paschal Dillon, Brian Maher, Terence Murray, Michael Phelan, Johnson Susairaj

SECTION 3

• The Missionary Association of Mary Immaculate (MAMI), 237 Goldhurst Terrace NW6 3EP Fr Paschal Dillon OMI **Tel: 020 7328 8610**
Catechetical Co-ordinator Awaiting appointment
Mazenod Centre Manager Anna Redmond **Tel: 020 7624 5517**
• Oblate Partners in Mission Office, Denis Hurley House, 14 Quex Road NW6 4PL Tel: 020 7624 7296 Fr Brian Maher
• Oblate Youth Service, Denis Hurley House, 14 Quex Road NW6 4PL Tel: 020 7624 7296
• Sisters of the Holy Family of Bordeaux, 2 Aberdare Gardens NW6 3PX Tel: 020 7624 7573
• Jesuits (SJ) Copleston House, 221 Goldhurst Terrace NW6 3EP Tel: 07816 872592
Community: Frs Michael Holman (Superior), Heinrich Angga Indraswara, Michael Barnes, Inos Chimire, Keith McMillan, Clarence Mutimutema, Christophere Ngolele, Paul O'Reilly, Luis Orlando Pérez Jiménez, Charles Nopparat Ruankool, Chester Yacub

KILBURN WEST + IMMACULATE HEART OF MARY

Sunday Mass 9, 11; **Weekday Mass** Tue, Fri 10; **Confession** before & after each Mass; **Repository** before & after each Mass

Oblates of Mary Immaculate (OMI) Fr Terence Murray, Fr Thomas Devereux, Fr Johnson Susairaj (all in residence at **New Priory, Sacred Heart Church, Quex Road NW6 4PS**)
Immaculate Heart of Mary Presbytery, 1 Stafford Road NW6 5RS Tel: 020 7624 1701
Email: kilburn@rcdow.org.uk Web: parish.rcdow.org.uk/kilburn
Off Kilburn Park Road
Camden Deanery (1948)

KINGSBURY GREEN + ST SEBASTIAN AND ST PANCRAS A ♪

Sunday Mass (Sat 5pm), 8, 9.30, 11, 12.30 (Romanian); **Holy Day Mass** 9.15, 7.30pm; **Weekday Mass** Mon 9.15, Tue 9.15, 7.30pm (Romanian), Wed-Sat 9.15, *First Fri only* 7.30pm (Romanian); **Confession** on request, 30 mins before each Mass (Romanian)

Fr Stewart Keeley
The Presbytery, 22 Hay Lane NW9 0NG Tel: 020 8204 2834 / 2117
Email: kingsburygreen@rcdow.org.uk Web: parish.rcdow.org.uk/kingsburygreen
Off Edgware Road, Colindale
Brent Deanery (1926; 2001)

KING'S CROSS, EAST: *SEE COPENHAGEN STREET*; WEST: *SEE SOMERS TOWN*

KINGSLAND + OUR LADY AND ST JOSEPH A ♪

Sunday Mass (Sat 5.30pm), 8, 10 (Contemporary sung), 12noon (Sung); **Holy Day Mass** (Vigil 7pm), 10, 12noon, 7pm; **Weekday Mass** Mon 6pm, Tue-Fri 10, Sat 12noon; **Exposition** Sat 10.30-11.40 with **Benediction** 11.45, Tue-Fri 9-9.45; **Confession** Sat 10.30-11.30 & as advertised at other times

Fr Derek Hyett
Presbytery, 100a Balls Pond Road N1 4AG Tel: 020 7254 4378

Email: kingsland@rcdow.org.uk Web: www.olsj.org
Off Kingsland High Street; at top end of Essex Road
Hackney Deanery (1854; 1964)

• Nigerian National Chaplaincy, 8 King Henry's Walk N1 4PB Tel: 020 7249 3618 / 07368 201008
Chaplains Fr Peter Tochukwu Egboo, Fr Alexander Izang Atu, Fr Michael Ogunyinka
• St Martin of Tours House, 162 New North Road N1 7BH
Rehabilitation Centre Tel: 020 7226 7516
• St Vincent's (SVP shop and counselling centre) 484/486 Kingsland Road E8 4AE
Tel: 020 7272 1263

KNEBWORTH + ST THOMAS MORE A ♪

Sunday Mass (Sat 6pm), 8, 10 (Sung); **Holy Day Mass** 9.30, 8pm; **Weekday Mass** Mon 7.15 pm, Tue-Fri 9.30, Sat 10; **Exposition** Fri after Mass-12noon; **Confession** Sat 5.15-5.45pm

Canon Daniel Cronin
72 London Road, Knebworth SG3 6HB Tel: 01438 813303
Email: knebworth@rcdow.org.uk Web: www.knebworthcatholicchurch.org
Stevenage Deanery (1929; 1936)
Office Manager / PA to Parish Priest Diana O'Donnell

LEBANESE MARONITE CHURCH: *SEE EASTERN CATHOLIC CHURCHES*

LEICESTER SQUARE, WC2: *SEE FRENCH CHURCH*

LETCHWORTH GARDEN CITY+ ST HUGH OF LINCOLN ♿♪

Sunday Mass (Sat 6pm), 9.30 (Family Mass with Children's Liturgy), 11.30 Sung), 1pm (Polish); **Holy Day Mass** 9.30, 6.15pm (Polish), 7.30pm; **Weekday Mass** Mon-Sat 9.30, Tue 6.30pm (Polish), **Morning Prayer** Mon-Sat 9.10; **Exposition** with **Confession** and **Benediction** Wed, Sat 10; **Confession** also on request

Fr James Garvey
Fortescue House, 84 Pixmore Way, Letchworth Garden City SG6 3TP
Tel: 01462 510015
Email: letchworth@rcdow.org.uk Web: parish.rcdow.org.uk/letchworth
Stevenage Deanery (1907; 1963; cons 2007)
Parish Administrator Emma Dunsire Mon, Tue, Thu 9-2.30pm

• Sisters of Charity of Jesus and Mary, Provincial House, 108 Spring Road, Letchworth Garden City SG6 3SL Tel: 01462 682153 Email: elizabeth@scjm.org
Web: www. scjmangloirishprovince.co.uk
• Garden House Hospice

LIMEHOUSE + OUR LADY IMMACULATE AND ST FREDERICK A ♪

Sunday Mass 12 noon; **Holy Day Mass** 7.15; **Confession** on request

SECTION 3

Fr Keith Stoakes (also serves Poplar and is resident at **Clergy House, 9 Pekin Street E14 6EZ** Tel: 020 7987 4523)
Island Row, 636 Commercial Road E14 7HS
Email: limehouse@rcdow.org.uk Web: parish.rcdow.org.uk/limehouse
(A13), between Limehouse DLR Stn and Burdett Road
Tower Hamlets Deanery (1881; 1934; cons 17 October 1945)

LINCOLN'S INN FIELDS + ST ANSELM AND ST CECILIA

Sunday Mass (Sat 6pm), 8.30 (Latin), 10 (Sung), 4pm (Filipino, *2nd Sun only*), 6pm; **Holy Day Mass** (Vigil 6pm), 12.30pm, 6pm (Sung); **Weekday Mass** Mon-Fri 6pm; **Exposition** Mon-Sat 5-5.50pm; **Confession** Mon-Fri 5.30-5.50pm, Sat 5-5.40pm

Fr David Barnes, Mgr John Conneely (in residence)
70 Lincoln's Inn Fields WC2A 3JA Tel: 020 7405 0376
Email: lincolnsinnfields@rcdow.org.uk Web: parish.rcdow.org.uk/lincolnsinnfields
On east side of Kingsway, a few steps south of Holborn Stn (TfL)
Westminster Deanery (1687; 1909; cons November 1959)
Parish Administrator / Bookkeeper Mrs Mandy O'Sullivan-Whiting

• Hospital for Sick Children, Great Ormond Street
Chaplains Kate Kakande, Colette Lennon Tel: 020 7813 8232
• National Hospital for Neurology & Neurosurgery
Chaplains Fr Peter Harries OP, Fr Serge Stasievich Tel: 020 3447 3007

LITHUANIAN CHURCH + ST CASIMIR A

Sunday Mass 10 (Lithuanian/English), 12noon (Lithuanian), 6pm (Lithuanian); **Holy Day Mass** 7pm; **Weekday Mass** 7pm; **Confession** (Lithuanian, Russian) daily before Mass & on request

Fr Petras Tverijonas, Fr Petras Gucevicius
21 The Oval, Hackney Road E2 9DT Tel: 020 7739 8735
Email: lithuanianchurch@rcdow.org.uk Web: www.katalikai.org.uk
Tower Hamlets Deanery (1901; 1912)

LONDON COLNEY + OUR LADY, ST MARY OF WALSINGHAM A

Sunday Mass 11.30; **Holy Day Mass** as announced; **Weekday Mass** Mon, Thu 10; **Filipino Adorers** as announced; **Confession** Sun 11.10-11.25

Fr Kevin Moule, Rev Tony Barter (Deacon), Rev Anthony Curran (Deacon) (clergy also serve Radlett and Shenley, Parish Priest is resident at **22 The Crosspath, Radlett WD7 8HN** Tel: 01923 635541)
Haseldine Road, London Colney AL2 1RP
Email: radlett@rcdow.org.uk Web: parish.rcdow.org.uk/londoncolney
At junction of Haseldine Road and High Street
St Albans Deanery (1959)
Parish Administrator Mrs Maria Crossland Tel: 01923 635541

MAIDEN LANE: *SEE COVENT GARDEN*

MANOR HOUSE + ST THOMAS MORE ♪

Sunday Mass (Sat 6pm), 10 (Sung), 12noon (Sung), 5pm (Portuguese); **Holy Day Mass** 12.30pm; **Weekday Mass** Mon, Wed 9.30, Thu 12.30pm, Fri 9.30; **Confession** On request

Fr Clive Lee, Rev Kassa Tsegaye (Deacon)
9 Henry Road N4 2LH Tel: 020 8802 9910
Email: manorhouse@rcdow.org.uk Web: parish.rcdow.org.uk/manorhouse
Off Portland Rise, south of Finsbury Park (near Manor House TfL Stn)
Hackney Deanery (1969; 1975)
Parish Administrator Ingrid Bowie

MARYLEBONE + OUR LADY OF THE ROSARY A ♪

Sunday Mass (Sat 6pm), 8.30, 11 (Family), 6pm (Folk); **Holy Day Mass** 12.30pm; **Weekday Mass** Mon-Sat 12.30pm; **Exposition** and **Benediction** Sat 5-5.30pm; **Confession** Sat 11-11.30, 5-5.30pm

Fr Michael Johnston
211 Old Marylebone Road NW1 5QT Tel: 020 7723 5101
Email: marylebone@rcdow.org.uk Web: parish.rcdow.org.uk/marylebone
South side of Old Marylebone Road, by junction with Marylebone Road
Marylebone Deanery (1855; 1963; cons 18 February 2006)
Parish Administrator Lorraine Etienne

• Tyburn Convent (Adorers of the Sacred Heart OSB), 8 Hyde Park Place W2 2LJ
Tel: 020 7723 7262 Email: admin@tyburnconvent.org.uk
Web: www.tyburnconvent.org.uk
Perpetual Exposition of the Blessed Sacrament; chapel open daily 6.15(am)-8.30 pm
Sunday Mass 9, **Weekday Mass** Mon-Fri 7.30, Sat 9;
Benediction Sun and Solemnities 3.30pm
Chaplain Fr Barry Braum
• St Mary's (Praed Street), Western Eye Hospital
Sunday Mass 11; **Weekday Mass** Thu 12.30pm
Chaplains Fr Giles Pinnock, Fr Benedict Abuo, Fr Blaise Amadi CM, Veronica Burns **Tel 020 3312 1508**
• Charter Nightingale Hospital

MILE END + THE GUARDIAN ANGELS ♪

Sunday Mass (Sat 7.30pm), 9, 11, 6pm; **Holy Day Mass** (Vigil as announced), as on weekdays; **Weekday Mass** Tue-Thu 9.30, Fri 7pm, Sat 12.30pm; **Confession** Sat 11.30-12.15pm & on request

Fr John D A Elliott, Rev Jeremy Yates (Deacon)
377 Mile End Road E3 4QS Tel: 020 8980 1845
Email: mileend@rcdow.org.uk Web: parish.rcdow.org.uk/mileend
Near Grove Road/Burdett Road junction; 2 mins from Mile End Stn (TfL)
Tower Hamlets Deanery (1868; 1901; cons 20 October 1927)

SECTION 3

- Neo-Catechumenate Communities Paul Dennis Tel: 07855 826086
- Mile End Hospital & The Bancroft Unit, Pat Shaw House

MILL END (& MAPLE CROSS) + ST JOHN THE EVANGELIST ♿✠

Sunday Mass (Sat 6pm), 10.30; Holy Day Mass as announced; Weekday Mass Wed 9.30; Exposition and Confession Sat 5-5.45pm
Chorleywood: Sunday Mass 9; Holy Day Mass as announced; Weekday Mass Tue 9.30; Confession on request & by appointment
Rickmansworth: Sunday Mass 8.30, 11, 6pm; Holy Day Mass 9.30, 7.30pm; Weekday Mass Mon-Sat 9.30; Exposition and Confession Sun 5-5.45pm

Fr Andrew Gallagher, Fr Matteo Di Giuseppe (clergy also serve Chorleywood and Rickmansworth and are resident at 5 Park Road, Rickmansworth WD3 1HU
Tel: 01923 773387)
Berry Lane, Rickmansworth WD3 7HG
Email: rickmansworth@rcdow.org.uk Web: parish.rcdow.org.uk/millend
Watford Deanery (1969; cons 30 April 2016))

MILL HILL + SACRED HEART AND MARY IMMACULATE ♿✠

Sunday Mass (Sat 6pm), 8.30, 10 (Family), 11.30, 6pm; Holy Day Mass 10, 12.15pm, 7.30pm; Weekday Mass daily 10, also Mon 7.30pm; Exposition Mon 8-9pm, Wed, Thu 10.30-12noon, Sat 10.30-11.30; Confession Sat 10.30-11.30

Vincentians (CM) Fr Eugene Curran
2 Flower Lane NW7 2JB Tel: 020 8959 1021
Email: millhill@rcdow.org.uk Web: www.shmi.info
The Broadway, just off Watford Way (A4) at Mill Hill Circus
Barnet Deanery (1889; 1922; cons 6 December 1923; 1995; cons 25 September 1996)
Community: Frs Eugene Curran (Superior), Akobundu Anywanwu, Raymond Armstrong, John Ashu, Chinedu Enuh, Noel Travers
Parish Administrator Melanie Gibbons

- Daughters of Charity, Provincial House, The Ridgeway NW7 1RE Tel: 020 8906 3777
Email: secretariat@dcmillhill.org Web: www.daughtersofcharity.org.uk
- Franciscan Sisters of Mill Hill, St Mary's Convent, 118 Chalet Estate, Hammers Lane NW7 4DN Tel: 020 8959 1364 Email: osfsistersmillhill@gmail.com

MILLWALL + ST EDMUND ♿✠

Sunday Mass (Sat 6pm), 9, 11; Holy Day Mass 9.15, 8pm; Weekday Mass Mon-Wed, Fri 9.15; Holy Hour with Exposition Sat 5pm; Confession Sat 5-5.45pm.

Priest in Charge Fr Christopher Silva
297 Westferry Road E14 3RS Tel: 020 7987 4114
Email: millwall@rcdow.org.uk Web: parish.rcdow.org.uk/millwall
Westferry Road
Tower Hamlets Deanery (1846; 1874; 2000; cons 22 September 2000)
Parish Secretary Katherine Woznicka

• Canary Wharf Multi Faith Chaplaincy, The Prayer Room, Unit 11, 2 Churchill Place E14 5RB
Catholic Chaplain (p/t) Rev Wayne O'Reilly (Deacon)

MOORFIELDS + ST MARY MOORFIELDS ♪

Sunday Mass 9.30; **Holy Day Mass** (Vigil 7pm) 8.05, 12noon, 1.05pm, 5.30pm; **Weekday Mass** Mon-Fri 8.05, 1.05pm; **Exposition** as announced; **Confession** Mon-Fri 12.30-12.50pm, 1.30-1.50pm

Fr Christopher Vipers, Canon Stuart Wilson (in residence) (clergy also serve Bunhill Row)
4/5 Eldon Street EC2M 7LS Tel: 020 7247 8390
Email: moorfields@rcdow.org.uk Web: parish.rcdow.org.uk/moorfields
100 yards west of Liverpool Street Stn (BR/TfL); just before the Red Lion
Westminster Deanery (1710; 1903)

• St Bartholomew's Hospital Tel: 020 7377 7000
Chaplains Fr Antigon Bahati AA, Fr Raphael Mose **Tel: 020 3465 7220**

MUCH HADHAM: *SEE BISHOP'S STORTFORD*

MUSWELL HILL + OUR LADY OF MUSWELL A ♪

Sunday Mass (Sat 6.30pm), 10, 11.45; **Holy Day Mass** 10, 7.30pm; **Weekday Mass** Mon-Thu, Sat 10, Fri 7.30pm; **Exposition** Sat 10.45-11.45; **Confession** Sat 10.45-11.45

Fr Mark Anwyll
1 Colney Hatch Lane N10 1PN Tel: 020 8883 5607
Email: muswellhill@rcdow.org.uk Web: parish.rcdow.org.uk/muswellhill
Haringey Deanery (1917; 1938; cons 23 September 1959)

• Sisters of Marie Auxiliatrice, 20 Elgin Road N22 7UE Tel: 020 8881 8547
and **Flats 8** and 15 The Paddock, Meadow Drive N10 1PL
• St Luke's Woodside Hospital

NEASDEN + ST PATRICK A ♪

Sunday Mass (Sat 6.30pm), 9.30, 11.30; **Holy Day Mass** 9.30, 7.30pm; **Weekday Mass** 9.30 or as announced; **Confession** Sat 5.45-6.15pm

Fr Patrick McLoughlin
The Presbytery, Hardie Close NW10 0UH Tel: 020 8451 0367
Email: neasden@rcdow.org.uk Web: parish.rcdow.org.uk/neasden
Just off North Circular Road (A406), west side, adjacent to IKEA main entrance off Drury Way
Brent Deanery (1981)
Parish Administrator Georgette Del Rosario (Mon, Tue, Fri 9-3pm)
Email: neasden@rcdow.org.uk
Catechetical Co-ordinator John Roche **Tel: 07307 897383**
Email: neasden@rcdow.org.uk
Safeguarding Officer Alero Orimoloye **Tel: 07903 757232**
Parish Food Bank in partnership with **SUFRA** (come to the table) **Tel: 020 3441 1335**

St Raphael's Edible Garden Project Tel: 020 3441 1335

• Little Aisha Nursery Tel: 020 8423 6353

NEW BARNET + MARY IMMACULATE AND ST PETER ♿🎵

Sunday Mass (Sat 6pm), 9.30, 11, 6pm; **Holy Day Mass** 7pm; **Weekday Mass** Mon-Wed 10, Thu 7pm, Fri, Sat 10, preceded by **Morning Prayer** 9.40 & followed by **Rosary**; **Exposition** Fri 10.30; **Confession** Sat 10.30-11 & on request

Spiritans (CSSp) Fr David Pember, Fr Jean Pascal Diame (in residence, School Chaplain)
63 Somerset Road, New Barnet EN5 1RF Tel: 020 8449 1961
Email: newbarnet@rcdow.org.uk Web: www.stpetersnewbarnet.org.uk
Barnet Deanery (1912; 1938)
Parish Secretary Paula Lefevre
Catechetical Co-ordinator Diana Niefiodow

NEW SOUTHGATE + OUR LADY OF LOURDES A 🎵

Sunday Mass (Sat 4, 6pm), 8.45, 10, 11.15, 12.30pm; **Holy Day Mass** 8, 10, 7.30pm; **Weekday Mass** Mon-Fri 8, 10; **Exposition** Fri 10.30-11; **Confession** Sat 3-3.45pm

Fr David Reilly, Fr Jerome Dukiya CSSp, Fr Johnson Alexander (in residence, Keralan Chaplaincy), Rev Ian Coleman (Deacon)
373 Bowes Road N11 1AA Tel: 020 8368 1638
Email: newsouthgate@rcdow.org.uk Web: www.ourladynewsouthgate.org.uk
200 yards right from Arnos Grove Stn (TfL)
Enfield Deanery (1923; 1935; 1990)

• Congregation of Our Lady of the Missions, 2 Brookdale N11 1BL Tel: 020 8361 6848
• Sisters of St Louis, 16 Chaucer Close N11 1AU Tel: 020 8617 0529

NORTHFIELDS (WEST EALING) + SS PETER AND PAUL A 🎵

Sunday Mass (Sat 6pm), 8.30, 10 (Family/Children's Liturgy), 11.30 (Sung), 6pm; **Holy Day Mass** 9.30, 8pm; **Weekday Mass** Mon 9.30, Tue 6pm, Wed, Fri 9.30; **Weekday Morning Prayer** *(Advent & Lent only)* 9.15; **Holy Hour** as announced; **Confession** Sat 5.30-6pm or by appointment

Fr Jim Duffy, Rev Andrew Goodall (Deacon)
38 Camborne Avenue W13 9QZ Tel: 020 8567 5421
Email: northfields@rcdow.org.uk Web: parish.rcdow.org.uk/northfields
Off Northfield Avenue, 1/4 mile north of Northfields Stn
Ealing Deanery (1926; 1931; cons 29 October 1959)
Parish Administrator Rosa Bambury
Pastoral Assistant Anna Dupelycz Email: northfieldscat@rcdow.org.uk

• Medical Mission Sisters, 109 Clitherow Avenue W7 2BL Tel: 020 8567 1504
Email: unit.uk.office@gmail.com Web: www.medicalmissionsisters-uk.org

• Religious of the Sacred Heart of Mary, Provincial House, 54 Grange Road W5 5BX
Tel: 020 8567 7228 Web: www.rshm-nep.org
also **44 The Park W5 5NP Tel: 020 8567 4722**

NORTHOLT: *SEE HARROW SOUTH*

NORTHWOOD + ST MATTHEW &♿

Sunday Mass (Sat 6pm), 9, 11.15, 6pm; **Holy Day Mass** Weekday Mass time and 7.30pm as announced; **Weekday Mass** Mon, Tue 10.30, Thu 7, Fri, Sat 10.30; **Exposition** Weekdays as announced, Sat 11, with **Benediction** 11.50, 5-5.45pm; **Confession** Sat 11-11.50, 5-5.45pm & by appointment

Fr Tom Montgomery
32 Hallowell Road, Northwood HA6 1DW Tel: **01923 840736**
Email: northwood@rcdow.org.uk Web: parish.rcdow.org.uk/northwood
Off Green Lane (shopping centre); near Northwood Stn
Hillingdon Deanery (1924; cons 12 October 1954)
Administration Assistant Cheryl Myring & Siobhan Hogg
RE Co-ordinator Awaiting appointment
Safeguarding Co-ordinator Colette Quirk & Elizabeth Scudder

• Society of African Missions (SMA) White House, Watford Road, Northwood HA6 3PW
Tel: **01923 828015**
Frs Thyagu Arputham, Anthony Cussen
• Joint Support Unit, Northwood HQ, Mount Vernon Hospital, Bishops Wood Hospital, Michael Sobell House

NOTTING HILL + ST FRANCIS OF ASSISI &♿

Sunday Mass (Sat 6pm), 10, 11.30; **Holy Day Mass** 9.30, 7pm; **Weekday Mass** Mon, Tue, Thu-Sat 9.30; **Exposition** Mon, Tue, Thu, Fri 10-10.30; **Confession** Sat 10-10.30

Fr Gerard Skinner
St Francis of Assisi Church, The Presbytery, Pottery Lane W11 4NQ Tel: **020 7727 7968**
Email: nottinghill@rcdow.org.uk Web: www.stfrancisnottinghill.org.uk
North Kensington Deanery (1860)
Parish Administrator Paula Lopes McDermid **Tel: 020 7727 7968**

• Sisters of Jesus in the Temple, 28 Penzance Street W11 4QX Tel: **020 7603 3329**

OGLE STREET + ST CHARLES BORROMEO ♿

Sunday Mass (Sat 8.15pm with Neo-Catechumenate), 9, 11; **Holy Day Mass** as weekday Mass; **Weekday Mass** Tue 12.30pm, 6pm, Wed 12.30pm, Thu 12.30pm, 6pm, Fri 12.30pm, for Bank Holidays see newsletter; **Confession** Daily after Mass & on request

Fr Oscar Ardila, Fr Gary Walsh (in residence, Albanian Chaplaincy)
8 Ogle Street W1W 6HS Tel: 020 7636 2883
Email: oglestreet@rcdow.org.uk Web: oglestreetblog.wordpress.com
Off New Cavendish Street, near BT Tower

Marylebone Deanery (1862; cons 4 October 1921)
Parish Assistant Sr Pauline Forde DC
Neo-Catechumenate Communities Michael Anderson **Tel: 07955 281186**

• University Chaplaincy: see *University & Institutes of Higher Education* entry in this section
• Portland Hospital for Women & Children **Tel: 020 7580 4400**
Chaplains Fr Giles Pinnock, Fr Benedict Abuo, Fr Blaise Amadi CM, Veronica Burns
Tel 020 3312 1508
• University College Hospital, including **Elizabeth Garrett Anderson Wing**
Sunday Mass 9.45; **Holy Day Mass** 1.30pm; **Weekday Mass** Mon-Thu 1.30pm, Fri 12.15pm
Chaplains Fr Peter Harries OP, Fr Serge Stasievich, Sr Pauline Forde DC
Tel: 020 3447 3007

OLD HALL GREEN & PUCKERIDGE + ST EDMUND OF CANTERBURY & ENGLISH MARTYRS

Sunday Mass (Sat 6pm, Puckeridge); 11.30 (Old Hall Green); **Holy Day Mass** 10.30 (Puckeridge); **Weekday Mass** Wed 10.30 (Puckeridge); **Confession** Sat 5.15-5.45pm (Puckeridge)
Buntingford: **Sunday Mass** 9.15 (with term time Children's Liturgy, *2nd & 4th Sun only*) ; **Holy Day Mass** 7pm; **Weekday Mass** Tue, Thu 9.30, Fri 10.30, with **Exposition** and **Benediction** 11-11.30, Sat 9.30; **Confession** Sat 10-11

Fr Cyril Chiaha (resident at **3 Station Road, Buntingford SG9 9HT Tel: 01763 271471**),
Rev Paul O'Connor (Deacon) (clergy also serve Buntingford)
Email: oldhallgreen@rcdow.org.uk Web: parish.rcdow.org.uk/oldhallgreen

Old Hall Green + St Edmund and the English Martyrs
To rear of St Edmund's College (off A10 as signposted)
Lea Valley Deanery (1769; 1818; new church cons 2 December 1911)

Puckeridge + St Thomas of Canterbury
Off the A10, at end of Puckeridge High Street (opposite school)
Lea Valley Deanery (1926)

• St Edmund's College, Old Hall Green, Ware SG11 1DS (1793; 1853) **Tel: 01920 821504**
Priest-in-Residence Fr Peter Lyness **Tel: 01920 821504**
Lay Chaplain Paula Pierce **Tel: 01920 821334**

ORATORY + IMMACULATE HEART OF MARY ♿ ♪

Sunday Mass (Sat 6pm), 8, 10 (Sung English), 11 (Solemn Latin), 12.30pm, 4.30pm, 7pm; **Holy Day Mass** (Vigil 6.30pm), 7, 10, 12.30pm, 5.30pm, 6.30pm (Solemn Latin); **Weekday Mass** Mon-Fri 7, 12.30pm, 6pm (Latin), Sat 7, 8, 10; **Sunday Vespers** and **Benediction** 3.30pm; **Holy Day Vespers** and **Benediction** (Vigil 5.30pm); **Benediction** Tue 6.30pm; **Holy Hour** Thu 6.30pm; **Confession** (French, German, Italian, Spanish) Sat 10-12.45pm, 3-6pm, Sun after each morning Mass, 6-6.50pm, Mon-Fri 9.30-12.30pm, 3pm-6pm

Fathers of the Oratory of St Philip Neri (Oratorians) Fr Michael Lang
The Oratory SW7 2RP **Tel: 020 7808 0900**
Email: oratory@rcdow.org.uk Web: www.bromptonoratory.co.uk

Beside V&A Museum at convergence of Brompton Road and Thurloe Place; near South Kensington Stn (TfL)
Kensington & Chelsea Deanery (1854; 1884; cons 16 April 1884)
Community: Frs Julian Large (Provost), Edward van den Bergh, George Bowen, Ronald Creighton-Jobe, Charles Dilke, Patrick Doyle, John Fordham, Michael Lang, Rupert McHardy, James Tabarelli
The Little Oratory: Exercises of the Brotherhood Sun 4.30pm
Fr Martin Stamnestro (in residence)

• Congregation of Our Lady (Canonesses of St Augustine), 51 Clareville Street SW7 5AX
Tel: 020 7370 6217 / 07365 270599 Email: mgabrielrobin@outlook.com
• Brompton Hospital

OSTERLEY + ST VINCENT DE PAUL

Sunday Mass 9, 11.30, 6pm; **Holy Day Mass** 9.30, 7.30pm; **Weekday Mass** Mon 9.30, Tue 7.30pm, Wed-Sat 9.30; **Rosary** Mon, Wed-Sat after Mass, Tue 7pm before Mass; **Exposition** Sat 10-11 followed by **Benediction** at 11; **Confession** Sat 10-10.30 & on request

Fr Mark Leenane
2 Witham Road, Osterley, Isleworth TW7 4AJ Tel: 020 8560 4737
Email: osterley@rcdow.org.uk Web: parish.rcdow.org.uk/osterley
Between Eversley Crescent & Spring Grove Road
Hounslow Deanery (1934; cons 1936; 2004; cons 24 September 2005)

PADDINGTON + OUR LADY OF SORROWS A

Sunday Mass 9.30 **Holy Day Mass** as Weekday Mass (also 7pmi at Harrow Road parish); **Weekday Mass** Tue, Thu, Sat 10; **Exposition** and **Benediction** Tue, Thu, Sat 9-10; **Confession** Sat 9-10 or on request

Fr Michael Jarmulowicz (also serves Harrow Road, resident at **Presbytery, 337 Harrow Road W9 3RB** Tel: 020 7286 2170)
17 Cirencester Street W2 5SR Tel: 020 7286 2672
Email: paddington@rcdow.org.uk Web: parish.rcdow.org.uk/paddington
Off Harrow Road, near Royal Oak Stn (TfL)
North Kensington Deanery (1912; cons 1998)
Parish Administrator Mrs Mandy O'Sullivan-Whiting **Thu 10-2pm**
Maronite Rite: Sunday Mass (Sat 7pm), 11.30, 7pm; **Weekday Mass** Wed, Fri 7pm (see *Lebanese Church* entry in this section)

PALMERS GREEN + ST MONICA

Sunday Mass (Sat 6pm), 7.45, 9, 10.30, 12noon; **Holy Day Mass** 7, 9.30, 7.30pm; **Weekday Mass** 9.30 daily, preceded by **Morning Prayer** Mon-Fri 9.10 and followed by **Rosary**, Sat 9.30 preceded by **Rosary** 9.10, see weekly newsletter for other times; **Exposition** Mon-Fri 2-3pm, Sat after 9.30 Mass with **Benediction** 10.50; **Confession** Sat 10.15-10.45, 5.15-5.45pm

SECTION 3

Canon Mehall Lowry, Fr Paul Zhao SVD
The Presbytery, I Stonard Road N13 4DJ Tel: 020 8886 9568
Email: palmersgreen@rcdow.org.uk Web: www.stmonica.co.uk
Enfield Deanery (1910; 1914; cons 6 October 1985)
Parish Sister Sr Joyce Dionne, Daughters of Providence (St Brieuc) **c/o The Presbytery**
Youth Programme Co-ordinator Anna McMullan

PARSONS GREEN + HOLY CROSS ♿ ♪

Sunday Mass (Sat 5.30pm), 9.45, 11.30; **Holy Day Mass** 9.30, 7pm; **Weekday Mass** Mon, Tue, Thu, Fri 9.30; **Confession** Fri 10-10.30, Sat 4.45-5.15pm & on request

Fr Michael Daley, Fr Tibor Borovsky (in residence, Slovak and Czech Chaplain), Rev Marco Lazzaron (Deacon)
22 Cortayne Road SW6 3QA Tel: 020 7736 1068
Email: parsonsgreen@rcdow.org.uk
Web: http://www.holycrosschurchparsonsgreen.org.uk
Ashington Road off New Kings Road, opposite Munster Road; between Parsons Green & Putney Bridge Stns (TfL)
Hammersmith & Fulham Deanery (1843; 1884; 1924; cons 11 October 1928)
Parish Administrator Mrs Annie D'Souza **Catechetical Co-ordinator** Mrs Alexandra Fisher

PERIVALE + ST JOHN FISHER ♿ ♪

Sunday Mass (Sat 6.30pm), 9.30 (Family), 11.30, 6.30pm; **Holy Day Mass** (Vigil 7.30pm), 10; **Weekday Mass** Mon, Tue, Thu, Fri 10; **Exposition** Mon 10.30, Sat 5-6pm; **Confession** Sat 5.15-5.45pm & on request

Fr Peter Shekelton (Parochial Administrator)
41/42 Langdale Gardens, Perivale, Greenford UB6 8DQ Tel: 020 8997 3164
Email: perivale@rcdow.org.uk Web: parish.rcdow.org.uk/perivale
On north side of Western Avenue (A40), just past the Hoover building
Ealing Deanery (1936; 1970)
Parish Office Manager Mrs Ana Hains (Mon 9:30-2:30pm, Tue 10:30-3:30pm, Wed-Fri 9:30-2:30pm)

PIMLICO + HOLY APOSTLES A ♪

Sunday Mass (Sat 6pm), 9, 10.30 (Family), 12.30pm (Spanish) **Albanian Sunday Mass** 3 pm, *every 2 weeks*; **Holy Day Mass** (Vigil 7pm), 10, 7pm; **Weekday Mass** 9.30 (10 if a funeral); **Exposition** Wed 10-11, Sat 5-5.45pm; **Confession** Sat 5-5.30pm & by appointment

Canon Pat Browne, Fr Charles Soyombo (in residence)
47 Cumberland Street SW1V 4LY Tel: 020 7834 6965
Email: pimlico@rcdow.org.uk Web: www.holyapostlespimlico.org
Winchester Street off Lupus Street, near Pimlico Stn (TfL)
Westminster Deanery (1917; 1957; cons 10 May 1974)
Parish Sister Sr Margaret Donnelly DC
Parish Secretary Sarah Harcher **Tel: 020 7834 6965 Email: sarahharcher@rcdow.org.uk**

• Franciscan Sisters of the Heart of Jesus, 9-11 St George's Drive SW1V 4DJ
Tel: 020 7834 4020 (Convent) 020 7834 5356 (Hostel) Email: fransisuk09@gmail.com
• Sisters of Notre Dame de Namur, Bella Best House, 5B Westmoreland Terrace
SW1V 4AW Web: sndden.org
• Stella Maris, 39 Eccleston Square SW1V 1PX Tel: 020 7901 1931
Email: info@stellamarismail.org Web: www.stellamaris.org.uk
• Catholic Bishops' Conference of England and Wales, 39 Eccleston Square SW1V 1BX
Tel: 020 7630 8220 Email: secretariat@cbcew.org.uk
• Missio (APF), 23 Eccleston Square SW1V 1NU Tel: 020 7821 9755
Email: director@missio.org.uk

PINNER + ST LUKE

Sunday Mass (Sat 6pm), 9, 11; Holy Day Mass (Vigil 7.30pm), 10; Weekday Mass Mon, Tue, Thu, Fri 10; Bank Holiday Mass 12noon; Exposition after Tue 10 Mass; Confession Sat 11-11.30, 5-5.30pm

Mgr Vincent Brady
28 Love Lane, Pinner HA5 3EX Tel: 020 8866 0098
Email: pinner@rcdow.org.uk Web: parish.rcdow.org.uk/pinner
In town centre, 3 mins from Pinner Stn (TfL), off Bridge Street
Harrow Deanery (1914; 1957)
Parish Administrators Pat Williams, Noreen Linnane (Mon, Tue 9-1pm, Wed 9-12.30pm, Thu, Fri 9-1pm) Tel: 020 8866 0098 opt 2
Pastoral Assistant (Catechetics) Norah O'Hare Tel: 020 8866 0098 opt. 3
Pastoral Outreach Worker Mariola Griffiths Tel: 020 8866 0098 opt. 4

• Daughters of Charity, Farmside, 43 High Street, Pinner HA5 5PJ
Tel: 020 8866 4442 Email: pinnerdcs@gmail.com
• Diocesan Centre for Youth Ministry, 125 Waxwell Lane, Pinner HA5 3EP
Tel: 020 3757 2516 Email: youth@rcdow.org.uk Web: http://dowym.com
(see under Westminster Youth Ministry, Section 2)
• SPEC, Waxwell House, 125 Waxwell Lane, Pinner HA5 3EP
Tel: 020 3757 2500 Email: spec@rcdow.org.uk
Diocesan Retreat Centre for Young People (see under Westminster Youth Ministry, Section 2)

POLISH CHURCH 1 + OUR LADY OF CZESTOCHOWA AND ST CASIMIR A

Sunday Mass (Sat 6pm), 9, 11, 12.30pm, 3.30pm, 7pm; Holy Day Mass 10.30, 7pm
Weekday Mass Mon-Fri 10.30, 7pm, Sat 7.30; Confession 30 min before Mass

Fr Bogdan Kołodziej, Fr Leszek Buba, Fr Tomasz Mężyk
2 Devonia Road N1 8JJ Tel: 08444 874288
Email: polishchurch1@rcdow.org.uk Web: www.parafia-devonia.org.uk
Near Angel TfL Station
Islington Deanery (1905; 1930)
Parish Office Tue-Fri 5-6pm

• Polish Catholic Mission, 4 Devonia Road N1 8JJ
Tel: 020 7226 3439

Mgr Stefan Wylezek (Vicar Delegate), Canon Krzysztof Tyliszczak (Chancellor), Mgr Janusz Tworek (Financial Administrator)

POLISH CHURCH 2 + ST ANDREW BOBOLA ♿♪

Sunday Mass (Sat 6pm), 8.30, 10, 12noon, 6pm; **Holy Day Mass** 10, 12noon, 7pm; **Weekday Mass** 10, 7pm; **Confession** Mon-Fri 9.30-10, 6.30-7pm, Thu 7.30-9pm, Sat 5-6pm

Fr Marek Reczek, Canon Zygmunt Zapaśnik
1 Leysfield Road W12 9JF Tel: 020 8743 8848
Email: polishchurch2@rcdow.org.uk Web: www.bobola.church
Hammersmith & Fulham Deanery (1961)

POLISH CHURCH 3 + OUR LADY MOTHER OF THE CHURCH ♪

Sunday Mass (Sat 7pm), 8.30, 10 (Family), 11.30, 1pm, 2.30pm (*Seasonal from Sep-Jun*) 5.15pm, 7pm (Youth), 8.30pm; **Weekday Mass** 8 (Latin), 10, 3.30pm *English on 1st Fri*, 7pm

Marian Fathers (MIC) Fr Michał Kozak, Fr Wiktor Gumienny, Fr Dariusz Mazewski, Fr Klaudiusz Rokicki, Fr Piotr Szyperski
2 Windsor Road W5 5PD Tel: 020 8567 1746
Email: polishchurch3@rcdow.org.uk Web: www.parafiaealing.co.uk
Ealing Deanery (1986)

• Sisters of the Holy Name of Jesus, 57 Mount Park Road W5 2PU Tel: 020 8997 2030
Sunday Mass (Sat 5pm, Polish)
• Sisters of the Resurrection, 84 Gordon Road W5 2AR Tel: 020 8998 8954
Weekday Mass Mon-Fri 7.30
• Divine Mercy Apostolate: see *Ealing* parish entry
• Kolbe House (Nursing Home) 18 Hanger Lane W5 3HH Tel: 020 8992 4978
Sunday Mass (Sat 4.30pm)

PONDERS END + CHURCH OF MARY, MOTHER OF GOD A ♪

Sunday Mass (Sat 5pm), 8, 9.30 (Family), 11 (Sung), 12.30pm (Italian), 5pm; **Holy Day Mass** 9.30, 12.30pm, 7.30pm; **Weekday Mass** Mon, Tue, Wed, Thu, Sat 9.30, Fri 7.30pm; **Confession** Sat 10.30-11.30

Fr John B. Shewring
192 Nags Head Road, Enfield EN3 7AR
Tel: 020 8804 2149 / 07973 539907
Email: pondersend@rcdow.org.uk Web: www.marymotherofgod.church
Enfield Deanery (1912; 1921; cons 8 September 1985)
Parish Administrator Dorothy Eribankya Tel: 020 8804 2149
Catechetical Co-ordinator Steven Smyth Tel: 020 8443 4069 / 07784 186406

• Italian Catholic Centre

Fr Antonio Serra **197 Durants Road, Enfield EN3 7DE** Tel: **020 8804 2307**

POPLAR + SS MARY AND JOSEPH ♿ ☞ S

Sunday Mass (Sat 6pm), 10, Mass in Word and Sign 4.30pm *2nd Sun only, not in August;*
Holy Day Mass (Vigil 7pm), 10; **Weekday Mass** Mon, Tue 10, Wed 4pm, Thu, Fri 10 (may
vary); **Confession** Sat 5.15pm

Fr Keith Stoakes (also serves Limehouse)
Clergy House, 9 Pekin Street E14 6EZ Tel: 020 7987 4523
Email: poplar@rcdow.org.uk Web: parish.rcdow.org.uk/poplar
Church at junction of Upper North Street and Canton Street
Tower Hamlets Deanery (1816; 1856; 1954; new church cons 12 October 1960)
Parish **Administrator** Alessandro Vaglio

• Faithful Companions of Jesus, The Lodge, Hale Street E14 0BS
Tel: 020 7517 9599 Email: fcjpoplar@outlook.com Web: www.fcjsisters.org

POTTERS BAR + OUR LADY & ST VINCENT ♿ ☞

Sunday Mass (Sat 6pm), 9, 11 (with Children's Liturgy) (**Sunday Mass August** (Sat 6pm), 10);
Holy Day Mass 10, 7.30pm; **Weekday Mass** 10 as announced; **Confession** Sat 5.15–
5.45pm, Advent & Lent 10.30–11.30 (with **Exposition)**

Canon Shaun Lennard, Rev Donal Hopkins (Deacon)
243 Mutton Lane, Potters Bar EN6 2AT Tel: 01707 654359
Email: pottersbar@rcdow.org.uk Web: www.olasv.org.uk
Enfield Deanery (2006; 2006)
Catechetical **Co-ordinator** Awaiting appointment Email: parish.rcdow.org.uk/pottersbar
Parish **Safeguarding Representative** Awaiting appointment

• Potters Bar District Hospital, Elysium Potters Bar, Cuffley Manor, Cooperscroft,
Greenhill Care Home, Mayfair Lodge, Potters Grange

QUEENSWAY + OUR LADY, QUEEN OF HEAVEN ♿ ☞

Sunday Mass (Sat 5.30pm), 10, 11.30, 1pm (Ethiopian, Gheez rite); **Holy Day Mass** 9.30,
6pm; **Weekday Mass** Mon 6pm, Tue, Wed 9.30, Fri 6pm; **Holy Hour** Sat 4.15-5.15pm;
Confession Sat 4.15-5.15pm & on request

Fr Saviour Grech
4a Inverness Place W2 3JF Tel: 020 7229 8153
Email: queensway@rcdow.org.uk Web: parish.rcdow.org.uk/queensway
Queensway, opposite Bayswater Stn (TfL); close to Queensway Stn (TfL)
North Kensington Deanery (1954; 1973; cons 21 April 2002)

• Prelature of Opus Dei, 4 Orme Court W2 4RL Tel: 020 7229 7574
Mgr Nicholas Morrish, Frs Peter Bristow, Paul Hayward, James Pereiro, Gerard Sheehan,
Andrew Soane

RADLETT + ST ANTHONY OF PADUA ♫

Radlett: Sunday Mass 10; Holy Day Mass as announced; Weekday Mass Tue 10;
Confession Sun 9.30-9.50

Fr Kevin Moule, Rev Tony Barter (Deacon), Rev Anthony Curran (Deacon) (clergy also
serve London Colney and Shenley)
22 The Crosspath, Radlett WD7 8HN Tel: 01923 635541
Email: radlett@rcdow.org.uk Web: parish.rcdow.org.uk/radlett
St Albans Deanery (1905; new church 1910)
Parish Administrator Maria Crossland Tel: 01923 635541

REDBOURN (FLAMSTEAD AND MARKYATE) + ST JOHN FISHER ♿ ♫

Sunday Mass (Sat 5.30pm), 9; Holy Day Mass as announced; Weekday Mass as
announced; Confession Sat 9.45-10.15, 5.45-6.15pm

Fr Michael Mannion (also serves Wheathampstead)
1 Peppard Close, Redbourn, St Albans AL3 7EB Tel: 01582 792270
Email: redbourn@rcdow.org.uk Web: parish.rcdow.org.uk/redbourn
Dunstable Road, north of the village on the old A5
St Albans Deanery (1936; 1967; cons 22 June 2003)

RICKMANSWORTH + OUR LADY HELP OF CHRISTIANS ♿ ♫

Sunday Mass 8.30, 11, 6pm; Holy Day Mass 9.30, 7.30pm; Weekday Mass Mon-Sat 9.30;
Exposition and Confession Sun 5-5.45pm

Chorleywood: Sunday Mass 9; Holy Day Mass as announced; Weekday Mass Tue 9.30;
Confession on request & by appointment

Mill End: Sunday Mass (Sat 6pm), 10.30; Holy Day Mass as announced; Weekday Mass
Wed 9.30; Exposition and Confession Sat 5-5.45pm

Fr Andrew Gallagher, Fr Matteo Di Giuseppe (clergy also serve Chorleywood and Mill
End)
5 Park Road, Rickmansworth WD3 1HU Tel: 01923 773387
Email: rickmansworth@rcdow.org.uk Web: parish.rcdow.org.uk/rickmansworth
On main road beside roundabout at bottom of Scots Hill (east end of High Street)
Watford Deanery (1886; 1909)

ROYSTON + ST THOMAS OF CANTERBURY AND THE ENGLISH MARTYRS A ♫

Sunday Mass (Sat 6.30pm), 9, 10.30; Holy Day Mass 9.15, 7.30pm; Weekday Mass Tue
7.30pm Wed-Fri 9.15; Confession Sat 5.45pm & by appointment, with Exposition from
5.30pm

Fr Philip Knights
6 Melbourn Road, Royston SG8 7DB Tel: 01763 243117
Email: royston@rcdow.org.uk Web: www.roystoncatholicchurch.co.uk
Left side of A10 just beyond central roundabout, towards Cambridge
Stevenage Deanery (1911; 1917)

• Sisters of Providence (of the Immaculate Conception), Providence House, 4 Melbourn Road, Royston SG8 7DB Tel: 01763 250956 Email: providencemarian@yahoo.co.uk

RUISLIP + MOST SACRED HEART ♿ ♪

Sunday Mass (Sat 6pm), 9, 10.30 (Family), 12noon, 6pm; **Holy Day Mass** (Vigil 8pm), 8, 10, 8pm; **Weekday Mass** 10 and as announced; **Confession** Sat 10.30-11

Awaiting appointment, Fr Jose Netto
73 Pembroke Road, Ruislip HA4 8NN Tel: 01895 632739
Email: ruislip@rcdow.org.uk Web: parish.rcdow.org.uk/ruislip
Ruislip Manor, near traffic lights; near Ruislip Manor Stn; 1/3 mile Ruislip Stn
Hillingdon Deanery (1921; new church cons 15 June 1939)
Administrator Mrs Anne O'Connor
Catechetical Co-ordinator Mrs Jo Marsh **Tel: 01895 673983**
Parish Youth Worker Siobhan Denny

RUISLIP SOUTH + ST GREGORY THE GREAT A ♿ ♪

Sunday Mass (Sat 5.30pm), 10, 12noon, 6pm; **Holy Day Mass** 10, 7.30pm; **Weekday Mass** Mon-Wed, Fri, Sat 10; **Exposition** Sat 10.30-11.30, Mon-Wed, Fri 10.30-12.30pm; **Rosary** Mon-Wed, Fri 6pm; **Confession** Sat 10.30-11.30, 4.30-5.15pm
Live streaming from St Gregory's at **www.churchservices.tv/southruislip**

Fr Paulo Bagini
447 Victoria Road, South Ruislip HA4 0EG Tel: 020 8845 2186
Email: ruislipsouth@rcdow.org.uk Web: parish.rcdow.org.uk/ruislipsouth
Corner of Angus Drive, near South Ruislip shops/Stn
Hillingdon Deanery (1958; 1967; cons 1 November 1975)
Pastoral Assistant Sr Joanna Whooley RSHM
Parish Administrator Gillian Harrington

ST ALBANS + SS ALBAN AND STEPHEN A ♪

Sunday Mass (Sat 6pm), 8, 9 (at Mass Centre), 9.30, 11.30, 6pm; **Holy Day Mass** (Vigil 7pm) 10, 7pm; **Weekday Mass** Mon10, 7pm, Tue 10, Wed, 10, 7pm, Thu 10, *First Fri* 10, Fri 7pm, Sat10; **Exposition** Sat 10.30-11.30; **Confession** Sat 10.30-11.30;
Mass at St Albans Abbey, in the Lady Chapel Fri 12noon

Fr Michael O'Boy, Fr Andrew Bowden, Rev Brendan Day (Deacon)
14 Beaconsfield Road, St Albans AL1 3RB Tel: 01727 853585
Email: stalbans@rcdow.org.uk Web: www.albanstephen.org
Close to St Albans City Stn
St Albans Deanery (1840; 1904; cons 1977)
Mass Centre, Marshalswick (St John Fisher School)
Sunday Mass 9

• St Albans City Hospital Tel: **01727 866122** Chaplain Rev Anthony Curran (Deacon)
Tel: **01923 217994**

SECTION 3

ST ALBANS SOUTH + ST BARTHOLOMEW ♿♫

Sunday Mass (Sat 6pm), 8.30, 10.30; **Holy Day Mass** as announced; **Weekday Mass** Mon 12noon, Tue, Wed, Fri, Sat 9; **Exposition** Sat 9.30-10; **Confession** Sat 9.30-10, 5.15-5.45pm & by appointment
Mass at St Albans Abbey, in the Lady Chapel Fri 12noon

Fr Francis Antwi-Darkwah

47 Vesta Avenue, St Albans AL1 2PE Tel: 01727 850066
Email: stalbanssouth@rcdow.org.uk Web: parish.rcdow.org.uk/stalbanssouth
On Watling Street (A5183), just above the North Orbital Road/A414 roundabout
St Albans Deanery (1959; cons 9 November 1985)

• Brothers of the Sacred Heart, Watling House, 8 King Harry Lane, St Albans AL3 4AW
Tel: 01727 861969
Brs Nelson Dionne, Joseph Holthaus, Paul Vaillancourt (Superior)

ST CHARLES SQUARE (NORTH KENSINGTON) + ST PIUS X ♿♫

Sunday Mass (Sat 6pm), 9, 11; **Holy Day Mass** 8.20, 12.30pm; **Weekday Mass** Mon-Fri 8.20, preceded by **Morning Prayer** 8.05; **Confession** Sat 5.15-5.45pm

Fr Peter Wilson, Fr Brian Creak (in residence, University Chaplain, contact details below)
79 St Charles Square W10 6EB Tel: 020 8969 6844
Email: stcharlessquare@rcdow.org.uk Web: parish.rcdow.org.uk/stcharlessquare
West of Ladbroke Grove, just north of Stn (TfL) & motorway bridge
North Kensington Deanery (1937; 1955)
(Fr Brian Creak Tel: 020 8968 3373)
• Carmelite Nuns, Monastery of the Most Holy Trinity, 87 St Charles Square W10 6EA
Tel: 020 8969 8702 Email: carmelnottinghill@talktalk.net
Web: carmelitesnottinghill.org.uk Chaplain Fr Marcus Winter Tel: 020 3673 9540
Daily Mass 8.15
• Little Sisters of Jesus, 41 Bonchurch Road W10 5NN Tel: 020 8960 0440
• Princess Louise Home
• St Charles Square Centre for Health and Wellbeing (Mental Health Units)
Tel: 020 8969 2488
• St Charles Square Palliative Care, Pembridge Hospice

ST JOHN'S WOOD + OUR LADY A ♫

Sunday Mass (Sat 6pm), 9 (Sung, Children's Liturgy of the Word), 10.30 (Sung Latin, Choir), 12noon (Sung), 6pm; **Holy Day Mass** 10, 7.30pm; **Weekday Mass** Mon-Wed 10, Thu 7pm, Fri-Sat 10; **Exposition** Sat 10.30-11.15; **Confession** Sat 10.30-11, 5.15-5.45pm & by arrangement
Our Lady Queen of the World: see below

Fr Kevin Jordan, Fr Benjamin Woodley
54 Lodge Road NW8 8LA Tel: 020 7286 3214
Email: stjohnswood@rcdow.org.uk Web: www.olsjw.org.uk

Top of Lisson Grove, close to junction with St John's Wood Road (by Lords Cricket Ground)
Marylebone Deanery (1833; 1836; cons 14 May 1925)
Parish Administrator Claudia McHugh **Email:** stjohnswood@rcdow.org.uk
Parish Sister Sr Brigid Collins RSM
Safeguarding Representative Frances Uchea
Email: stjohnswoodsg@safeguardrcdow.org.uk

• Handmaids of the Sacred Heart of Jesus, 25 St Edmund's Terrace NW8 7PY
Tel: 020 7722 2756 Email: provincialsec@aol.com Web: http://aciengland.org
Chapel of Our Lady, Queen of the World: Sunday Mass 10 Exposition Wed 10-12noon
• Mercy Union Generalate, 11 Harewood Avenue NW1 6LD Tel: 020 7723 2527
9 Wimborne House, Harewood Avenue NW1 6NU Tel: 020 7723 4794
39 Alma Square NW8 9PY Tel: 020 7289 3657
91 Ashmill Street NW1 6RA
• Redemptoris Mater House of Formation, St Edward's Convent, 11 Harewood Avenue
NW1 6LD Tel: 020 7723 9364 Email: rmhf.lnd@gmail.com
Fr Lorenzo Andreini
• Hospital of St John & St Elizabeth, 60 Grove End Road NW8 9NH
Tel: 020 7806 4000 **Chaplain** Fr Hugh MacKenzie
Hospital Chapel (Church of St John of Jerusalem)
Sunday Mass 11; Weekday Mass Tue 11
• Wellington Hospital Tel: 020 7586 5959
Chaplains Fr Giles Pinnock, Fr Benedict Abuo, Fr Blaise Amadi CM, Veronica Burns
Tel 020 3312 1508

ST MARGARETS-ON-THAMES + ST MARGARET OF SCOTLAND ♿ ♂

Sunday Mass 8.30, 10.30, 6.30pm; **Holy Day Mass** 7.15, 10, 8pm; **Weekday Mass** Mon-Thu,
Sat 10; **Confession** Sat 10.30-11, Sun 10-10.20

Canon Peter Newby, Rev Joseph Estorninho (Deacon)
130 St Margarets Road, Twickenham TW1 1RL Tel: 020 8892 3902
Email: stmargaretsonthames@rcdow.org.uk Web: www.stmargaretsrcchurch.co.uk
Opposite St Margarets Stn (BR); close to Chertsey Road (A316) and Richmond Road (A305)
Upper Thames Deanery (1930; 1969)
Parish Administrator Cynthia Souza

SAWBRIDGEWORTH: *SEE BISHOP'S STORTFORD*

SHENLEY + THE GOOD SHEPHERD

Sunday Mass (Sat 5pm); **Holy Day Mass** as announced; **Weekday Mass** Wed 9.30:
Confession Sat 4.30-4.50pm

Fr Kevin Moule, Rev Tony Barter (Deacon), Rev Anthony Curran (Deacon) (clergy also
serve London Colney and Radlett, Parish Priest is resident at **22 The Crosspath, Radlett
WD7 8HN Tel: 01923 635541**)

Black Lion Hill, Shenley WD7 9DH
Email: radlett@rcdow.org.uk Web: parish.rcdow.org.uk/shenley
St Albans Deanery (1969; 1976)
Parish Administrator Maria Crossland **Tel: 01923 635541**

SHEPHERDS BUSH + THE HOLY GHOST AND ST STEPHEN A

Sunday Mass (Sat 6pm), 9.15, 11 (Family), 6pm; **Holy Day Mass** 9.30, 7pm; **Weekday Mass** Mon, Tue 9.30, Wed 7, Thu 7pm; Fri, Sat 9.30: **Exposition** Sat 10-10.45, with **Benediction**; **Confession** Sat 10.15-10.45, 5.15-5.45pm

Fr Mark Vickers
44 Ashchurch Grove W12 9BU **Tel: 020 8743 5196**
Email: shepherdsbush@rcdow.org.uk Web: www.rcshepherdsbush.org
Off Askew Road, near junction with Goldhawk Road; nearest Stn Stamford Brook (TfL)
Hammersmith & Fulham Deanery (1889; 1904; cons 24 April 1936)

• Franciscan Missionaries of Mary (Provincialate), 5 Vaughan Avenue W6 0XS
Tel: 020 8748 4077 Email: provsec@fmmuk.org Web: www.fmmii.org

SHEPPERTON + ST JOHN FISHER ♿♪

Sunday Mass (Sat 6pm), 8.30, 10.30; **Holy Day Mass** 9.30, 7pm; **Weekday Mass** Tue-Fri 9.30, Sat 10; **Rosary** Wed after Mass; **Exposition** Fri after Mass; **Confession** Sat 5.30pm

Fr Shaun Richards
15 Wood Road, Shepperton TW17 0DH **Tel: 01932 563116**
Email: shepperton@rcdow.org.uk Web: parish.rcdow.org.uk/shepperton
In Shepperton Green (sign on Shepperton - Staines road)
Upper Thames Deanery (1936; 1965)
Parish Administrator Awaiting appointment **Email: shepperton@rcdow.org.uk**
Parish Bookkeeper Traci Blundell **Email: sheppertonbookkeeper@rcdow.org.uk**

SOHO SQUARE + ST PATRICK ♿♪

Sunday Mass (Sat 6pm), 11, 5pm, 6pm (Spanish); **Holy Day Mass** 8, 12.30pm, 1.05pm, 6pm; **Weekday Mass** Mon-Fri 12.45pm; **Exposition** Mon-Fri 1.30-6pm, Sat 7-9pm; **Confession** Mon-Fri 12.15-12.40pm, Sat 5.30-6pm

Canon Alexander Sherbrooke
21a Soho Square W1D 4NR **Tel: 020 7437 2010**
Email: sohosquare@rcdow.org.uk Web: www.stpatricksoho.org
Near junction of Oxford Street and Charing Cross Road, south of Tottenham Court Road TfL Stn
Westminster Deanery (1792; 1893)
Parish Sister Sr Mary Kenefick PSMG

• Latin American Chaplaincy Fr Carlos Abajos Eguileta **Tel: 020 7820 1697**
• SOS Prayer Line **Tel: 020 7434 9211**

SOMERS TOWN + ST ALOYSIUS A ♪

Sunday Mass (Sat 6pm), 10.30, 6pm; **Holy Day Mass** 9.30, 12.30pm, 6pm; **Weekday Mass** Mon, Tue, Thu, Fri 9.30; **Confession** Sat 5pm & by appointment

Fr Jeremy Trood
20 Phoenix Road NW1 1TA Tel: 020 7387 1971
Email: somerstown@rcdow.org.uk Web: parish.rcdow.org.uk/somerstown
Off Eversholt Street, east of Euston Stn
Camden Deanery (1798; 1808; 1968; cons 24 May 1992)

• Faithful Companions of Jesus, 32 Phoenix Road NW1 1TA
Tel: 020 3435 8049 Email: fcjcommunity@fcjhouse-somerstown.co.uk
Web: www.fcjsisters.org
FCJ Spirituality Centre Email: enquiries.fcjcentre@fcjhouse-somerstown.co.uk
Web: www.fcjsisters.org/spirituality-centre-london
• Missionary Congregation of the Evangelizing Sisters of Mary, St Philomena's Convent, 70-71 Euston Square NW1 1DJ Email: nasicleme@yahoo.co.uk
• Poor Servants of the Mother of God, St Philomena's Convent, 70-71 Euston Square NW1 1DJ Email: mary.kenefick@psmgs.org.uk / frances.ennis@psmgs.org.uk
Web: www.poorservants.org
• St Pancras Hospital (Evergreen, Rochester and Oakwood Wards)
Chaplain: Awaiting appointment

SOUTHALL + ST ANSELM ♿♪

Sunday Mass (Sat 6.30pm), 8, 9.45, 11.30, 6.30pm; **Holy Day Mass** 7.30, 9.15, 12.15pm, 6.30pm; **Weekday Mass** Mon-Fri 9.15; **Exposition** Thu 10-11pm; *First Fri* Mass followed by **Exposition** 9.15, 6.30pm; **Confession** Mon-Fri 8.45-9.10, Sat 11-12noon & by appointment
Ethnic Chaplaincy Masses: Sri Lankan (Tamil) *1st Sun* 2pm; Konkani (Goan) *3rd Sat* 4pm; **Malayalam** *3rd Sun* 3pm; **Urdu** *last Sun* 3pm

Jesuits (SJ) Fr Jovito F D'Souza, Fr Edward Bermingham
Rev Stephen Khokhar (Deacon)
St Anselm's Rectory, The Green, Southall UB2 4BE Tel: 020 8574 3300
Email: southall@rcdow.org.uk Web: stanselmchurchsouthall.com
To the south of Southall Stn (BR), opposite Osterley Park Road
Ealing Deanery (1906; 1930; 1968)
Parish Evanglisation Co-ordinator Susan Cawley Email susancawley@rcdow.org.uk

• Missionaries of Charity, 41 Villiers Road, Southall UB1 3BS Tel: 020 8574 1892

SECTION 3

SPANISH PLACE + ST JAMES A ♪

Sunday Mass (Sat 6pm), 8, 10.30 (Sung Latin), 12noon, 4pm, 7pm; **Holy Day Mass** 7.15, 12.30pm, 6pm; **Weekday Mass** Mon-Fri 12.30pm, 6pm, Sat 10; **Holy Hour** Sat 4.45pm; **Confession** Mon-Fri 12-1pm; Sat 5-5.45pm

Mgr Philip Whitmore, Canon Roger Taylor (in residence), Fr Mark Elliott-Smith (in residence, Ordinariate)
22 George Street W1U 3QY Tel: 020 7935 0943
Email: spanishplace@rcdow.org.uk Web: www.sjrcc.org.uk
Bottom of Marylebone High Street; Baker Street or Bond Street TfL Stns
Marylebone Deanery (1791; 1890; cons 28 April 1949)
Parish Administrator Paul Thomson Tel: 020 3475 9097

• King Edward VII Hospital for Officers
• London Clinic
• Harley Street Clinic
Chaplains Fr Giles Pinnock, Fr Benedict Abuo, Fr Blaise Amadi CM, Veronica Burns
Tel 020 3312 1508
• Princess Grace Hospital
Chaplains as above
• University College Hospital on Westmoreland Street
Chaplains: Fr Peter Harries OP, Fr Serge Stasievich Tel: 020 3447 3007

SPITALFIELDS, E1: *SEE UNDERWOOD ROAD*

STAINES-UPON-THAMES + OUR LADY OF THE ROSARY ♿ ♪

Sunday Mass (Sat 6.30pm) 9, 11; **Holy Day Mass** 7, mid-morning as announced, 7pm; **Weekday Mass** Tue-Thu 9.15, Fri as announced; **Exposition** Tue 9.35-9.50; **Confession** Sat 5.30-6pm

Fr Philip Dyer-Perry
The Presbytery, 59 Gresham Road, Staines TW18 2BD Tel: 01784 452381
Email: staines@rcdow.org.uk Web: parish.rcdow.org.uk/staines
Near Staines Stn (BR), opposite footbridge
Upper Thames Deanery (1890; 1932)

STAMFORD HILL + ST IGNATIUS ♿ ♪

Sunday Mass (Sat 6.30pm), 8, 9.30, 11, 12.30pm (Polish), 4.30pm (Latin American), 7.30pm (Polish); **Holy Day Mass** 10, 6.30pm; **Weekday Mass** 10, Friday also 6.30pm; **Confession** after weekday Mass and by appointment

Jesuits (SJ) Fr Andrew Cameron-Mowat, Fr Piotr Kropisz, Fr John McCabe
27 High Road N15 6ND Tel: 020 8800 2121
Email: stamfordhill@rcdow.org.uk Web: parish.rcdow.org.uk/stamfordhill / www.stignatius.co.uk

Corner of High Road (A10) & St Ann's Road near Seven Sisters Stn (TfL)
Haringey Deanery (1894;1903)
Community: Frs Harold Elias, John Moffatt, Michael Smith, Br Stephen Power
Catechetical Co-ordinator Agnieszka Wiecek

- Servite Sisters, St Mary's Convent, 90 Suffolk Road N15 5RH Tel: 020 8800 2940
- Ursulines of Jesus, 149 Bethune Road N16 5DY Tel: 020 8800 4623

STANMORE + ST WILLIAM OF YORK ♿♪

Sunday Mass (Sat 5.30pm), 8, 10 (Sung); **Holy Day Mass** 9.30, 7pm; **Weekday Mass** Mon-Wed 9.30, Fri 7pm, Sat 9.30; **Confession** Sat 4.30-5.15pm

Fr Jonathan Goodall
1 Du Cros Drive, Stanmore HA7 4TJ Tel: 020 8954 1299
Email: stanmore@rcdow.org.uk Web: parish.rcdow.org.uk/stanmore
Off Marsh Lane, ¼ mile south of The Broadway
Harrow Deanery (1938; 1960)
Parish Secretary Frances Bright

- Royal National Orthopaedic Hospital, Woodland Hall Home

STANWELL + ST DAVID ♿♪

Sunday Mass (Sat 6pm), 10.30; **Holy Day Mass** 9.30, 7.30pm; **Weekday Mass** Mon, Tue 6pm, Wed 9.30, Fri 6pm; **Exposition** Fri 5.30pm; **Confession** Sat 5.15-5.45pm

The Sons of Divine Providence (FDP) Fr Sidon Sagar, Fr Carlo Mazzotta, Fr Henryk Halman (in residence) (clergy also serve Ashford and are resident at **112 Clarendon Road, Ashford TW15 2QD**)
St David's, Everest Road, Stanwell, Staines TW19 7EE Tel: 01784 255973
Email: stanwellparish@rcdow.org.uk Web: parish.rcdow.org.uk/stanwell
Upper Thames Deanery (1964; 1967)

- Ashford Hospital

STEVENAGE PARISHES A ♿♪

Bedwell, St Joseph: **Sunday Mass** (Sat 6pm), 10.30, 12noon, 6pm; **Holy Day Mass** as announced; **Weekday Mass** Wed 7pm, Thu, Fri 9.30; **Rosary** Thu, Fri after Mass; **Exposition** Wed 7.30-8.15pm; **Confession** Wed 7.30-8.30pm, Sat 5-5.45pm

Old Town, Transfiguration: **Sunday** (Sat 5pm), 9; **Holy Day Mass** 9.30; **Weekday Mass** Mon, Fri 9.30; **Confession** Sat 4.30-4.45pm

Shephall, St Hilda: **Sunday Mass** (Sat 6.30pm), 9.30 (Sung), 11 (with Children's Liturgy); **Holy Day Mass** 9.30; **Weekday Mass** Mon, Tue, Sat 9.30; **Exposition** Mon 10-11; **Confession** Sat 10, 6.15pm

Fr Michael Doherty SDS (resident at **9 Breakspear, Stevenage SG2 9SQ** Tel: 01438 352182), Fr Nigel Woollen (resident at **St Joseph's Presbytery, Bedwell Crescent, Stevenage SG1 1NJ** Tel: 01438 351243)

Administrator for the three parishes Lynne Gasston

+ St Joseph (Stevenage Bedwell)
St Joseph's Presbytery, Bedwell Crescent, Stevenage SG1 1NJ
Email: stevenagebedwell@rcdow.org.uk Web: parish.rcdow.org.uk/stevenage
Off roundabout linking Bedwell Crescent and Fairlands Way
Stevenage Deanery

+ Transfiguration of Our Lord
Grove Road, Stevenage SG1 3PX (Stevenage Old Town)
4 Basils Road, Stevenage SG1 3PX (Correspondence address)
Email: stevenageoldtown@rcdow.org.uk Web: parish.rcdow.org.uk/stevenage
Off Church Lane, east of High Street
Stevenage Deanery (1912)

• Sisters of Charity of Jesus and Mary, 3 Hitchin Road, Stevenage SG1 3BJ
Tel: 01438 354247
• Lister Hospital Tel: 01438 314333

+ St Hilda (Stevenage Shephall)
9 Breakspear, Stevenage SG2 9SQ
Email: stevenageshephall@rcdow.org.uk Web: parish.rcdow.org.uk/stevenage
Stevenage Deanery (1958; cons 1986)

STOKE NEWINGTON + OUR LADY OF GOOD COUNSEL ♿ ♪

Sunday Mass (Sat 6.30pm), 9, 11; **Holy Day Mass** 10, 7pm; **Weekday Mass** Mon-Fri 10 (followed by Marian devotions); **Zimbabwean Mass** *First Sat only* 2pm; **Holy Hour** *First Sat only* 11; **Confession** Sat 11.30-12noon, 5.30-6pm & on request

Fr Martin Tate, Fr John Rufaro Mudereri (in residence, Zimbabwean Chaplaincy)
24 Bouverie Road N16 0AJ Tel: 020 8800 5250
Email: stokenewington@rcdow.org.uk Web: parish.rcdow.org.uk/stokenewington
Hackney Deanery (1882; 1936; 1976)

• Little Sisters of the Poor, St Anne's Home, 77 Manor Road N16 5BL
Tel: 020 8826 2500 Email: ms.stanne@lsplondon.co.uk Web: www.lsplondon.co.uk
Chaplain Fr Daniel Magnier

STONEBRIDGE + THE FIVE PRECIOUS WOUNDS A ♪

Sunday Mass (Sat 6pm), 10, 12noon; **Holy Day Mass** 10, 7pm; **Weekday Mass** Mon-Wed, Fri 10; **Confession** Sat 5.15-5.45pm, Fri 10.30-11

Fr Tony Thomas, Rev Andrew Safo-Poku (Deacon)
The Presbytery, Brentfield Road NW10 8ER Tel: 020 8965 3313
Email: stonebridge@rcdow.org.uk Web: parish.rcdow.org.uk/stonebridge
Off Harrow Road (A404), 1/4 mile east of junction with North Circular Road
Brent Deanery (1926; 1957; cons 14 May 1967)

STROUD GREEN + ST PETER-IN-CHAINS ♿♪

Sunday Mass (Sat 6.30pm), 9.45 (Sung), 11.15 (Family), 7pm; **Holy Day Mass** 9, 7.30pm; **Weekday Mass** Mon-Fri 9; **Morning Prayer** 15 mins before weekday Mass; **Holy Hour** Fri 7-8pm; **Confession** Sat 6-6.20pm

Fr David Barrow

12 Womersley Road N8 9AE Tel: 020 8340 3394
Email: stroudgreen@rcdow.org.uk Web: www.stpeterinchains.com
Haringey Deanery (1894; 1896)

• Sisters of Christian Instruction (St Gildas), 36 Dickenson Road N8 9ET
Tel: 020 8340 7203 Web: sistersofstgildas.org.uk

SUDBURY + ST GEORGE ♿♪

Sunday Mass (Sat 6.15pm), 8.30, 9.45 (Family), 11.15 (Solemn), 5.30pm (Sung); **Holy Day Mass** 9.30, 8pm; **Weekday Mass** 9.30; **Exposition** with **Benediction** Sat 5.15-6pm; **Confession** Sat 5.15-6pm

Mgr Jeremy Fairhead, Fr Michael Guthrie

970 Harrow Road, Sudbury, Wembley HA0 2QE
Tel: 020 8904 2552
Email: sudbury@rcdow.org.uk Web: parish.rcdow.org.uk/sudbury
On corner of St Andrew's Avenue, east of Greenford Road / Sudbury Court Drive junction
Harrow Deanery (1924; 1926; cons 18 April 1928)
Parish Team Mgr Jeremy Fairhead, Fr Mike Guthrie, Mr Peter Kingsley (**Pastoral Assistant** and **Catechetical Co-ordinator**), Mrs Toni Miles (**Parish Secretary**)

• Northwick Park Hospital
• Wembley Hospital, Clementine Churchill Hospital

SUNBURY-ON-THAMES + ST IGNATIUS OF LOYOLA ♿♪

Sunday Mass (Sat 6pm), 9.30, 11.30; **Holy Day Mass** 9.30, 7.30pm; **Weekday Mass** Mon-Wed, Fri 9.30; **Exposition** Sat 10.30 with **Benediction** 11.15; **Confession** Sat 10.30-11.15 or on request

Fr Christian de Lisle

The Rectory, Green Street, Sunbury-on-Thames TW16 6QB Tel: 01932 783507
Email: sunburyonthames@rcdow.org.uk Web: parish.rcdow.org.uk/sunburyonthames
Main road, South Sunbury Stn (BR) / M3 interchange
Upper Thames Deanery (1862; 1869)
Parish Administrator Mrs Lavina Menezes E Fernandes Mon-Fri 10-1pm
Email: sunburyonthames@rcdow.org.uk
The Manning Room is available for hire Email: sunburyparishcentres@rcdow.org.uk

• Sunbury Nursing Home, Ashton Lodge, Beechwood Court

SECTION 3

SWISS COTTAGE + ST THOMAS MORE A

Sunday Mass 9.30, 11 (Sung), 6pm; **Holy Day Mass** 7,10, 7pm; **Weekday Mass** Mon-Fri 7,10, Sat 10; **Confession** daily, before & after Mass

Fr Stefan Hnylycia
Presbytery, Maresfield Gardens NW3 5SU Tel: 020 7435 1388
Email: swisscottage@rcdow.org.uk Web: parish.rcdow.org.uk/swisscottage
Off Fitzjohn's Avenue, near Finchley Road and Swiss Cottage TfL Stns
Camden Deanery (1938; 1968; cons 8 May 1977)

• Lakefield, Maresfield Gardens NW3 5RY Tel: 020 7794 5669
Web: www.lakefield.org.uk Catering and education centre
Pastoral Care entrusted to the Prelature of Opus Dei
• Netherhall House, Nutley Terrace NW3 5SA Tel: 020 7435 8888
Web: www.nh.netherhall.org.uk Hall of Residence for male University students
Pastoral Care entrusted to the Prelature of Opus Dei
Fr Bernard Marsh, Fr Alvaro Tintoré
• Eden Hall (Marie Curie) Hospice

TEDDINGTON (& HAMPTON WICK) + THE SACRED HEART

Sunday Mass (Sat 6.30pm), 9.30 (Family), 11.15 (Sung); **Holy Day Mass** 9.30; **Weekday Mass** Mon-Wed, Fri 9.30; **Exposition** Sat 9.30-11; **Confession** Sat 9.30-11 & by appointment

Parochial Administrator Fr Stephen Beale for Fr Reg Dunkling
262 Kingston Road, Teddington TW11 9JQ Tel: 020 8977 2986
Email: teddington@rcdow.org.uk Web: www.loguk.com/sacredheart
Upper Thames Deanery (1882; 1893; cons 14 June 1944)

• Sons of Divine Providence (FDP), 23 Lower Teddington Road, Hampton Wick KT1 4EU
Tel: 020 8977 5130 Email: info@orionecare.org Web: orionecare.org
Sunday Mass 9.30 (English), 11 (Polish); **Exposition** Sun 5-6pm; **Divine Mercy Devotion**
First Sun 2.30-3.30; **Rosary** Mon-Fri 6.30; **Weekday Mass** Mon-Fri 6pm; **Confession** by request
Community: Frs John C Perrotta, Stephen Beale
Orione Care Main Office 23 Lower Teddington Road, Hampton Wick KT1 4EU
Email: info@orionecare.org Web: orionecare.org
Colombo House, 1 Ferry Road, Teddington TW11 9NN Supported living flats for people with learning disabilities
St John's, 1 Ferry Road, Teddington TW11 9NN Tel: 020 8977 7574 Residential Care for people with learning disabilities
7 Ferry Road, Teddington TW11 9NN Young People's Support Project

TOLLINGTON PARK + ST MELLITUS

Sunday Mass (Sat 6pm), 11; **Holy Day Mass** 9.30; **Weekday Mass** Mon-Wed, Fri 9.30;
Confession Sat 10.30-11, 5-5.30pm & on request

Fr Chinedu Udo

The Presbytery, St Mellitus Church, Tollington Park N4 3AG Tel: 020 7272 3415
Email: tollingtonpark@rcdow.org.uk Web: parish.rcdow.org.uk/tollingtonpark
Off Stroud Green Road; north end of Fonthill Road, 5 mins from Finsbury Park Stn (BR/TfL)
Islington Deanery (1925; 1959)
Parish Secretary Helen Lebab Tue, Wed, Thu 10-2pm

TOTTENHAM + ST FRANCIS DE SALES ♿ ♫

Sunday Mass (Sat 7pm), 9, 11; **Holy Day Mass** 10, 7pm; **Weekday Mass** Mon-Tue 10, Wed Communion Service 10, Thu 10, Fri 7pm, Sat 10 with **Rosary** and **Exposition**; **Confession** Sat 10.30-11.15, 6-6.45pm

Fr David Lucuy Claros, Rev Juan Sola Garcia (Deacon)

729 High Road N17 8AG Tel: 020 8808 3554
Email: tottenham@rcdow.org.uk Web: parish.rcdow.org.uk/tottenham
Main road, opposite Tottenham Hotspur FC Ground
Haringey Deanery (1793; 1895)
Catechetical Co-Ordinator Marcelle Jemide Email: tottenhamcatechist@rcdow.org.uk
Parish Administrator Elisabete Veselovska (Mon-Fri 9-1pm)

TOTTENHAM (SOUTH): *SEE STAMFORD HILL*

TOTTENHAM (WEST): *SEE WEST GREEN*

TOWER HILL + THE ENGLISH MARTYRS ♿ ♫

Sunday Mass (Sat 6.30pm), 9, 11; **Holy Day Mass** 9.30, 1pm; **Weekday Mass** Tue-Fri 1pm; **Exposition** Tue-Fri 12noon-1pm, Sat 3-4pm; **Confession** before and after Mass

Oblates of Mary Immaculate (OMI) **Fr Angodage Don Joseph Alex,** Fr Raymond Warren (Superior)

30 Prescot Street E1 8BB Tel: 020 7488 4654
Email: towerhill@rcdow.org.uk Web: parish.rcdow.org.uk/towerhill
Close to junction with Mansell Street
Tower Hamlets Deanery (1865;1876)

• DeMazenod House, Spirituality Centre, 62 Chamber Street E1 8BL
Tel: 020 7702 0270 Email: demazenodhouse@oblates.co.uk

TRING + CORPUS CHRISTI ♿ ♫

Sunday Mass (Sat 5pm), 9; 10.30; **Holy Day Mass** as announced; **Weekday Mass** Mon-Wed 10, Fri 6pm; **Confession** Sat 4.15-4.45pm

Fr Sean Thornton

51 Langdon Street, Tring HP23 6BA Tel: 01442 823161
Email: tring@rcdow.org.uk Web: parish.rcdow.org.uk/tring
St Albans Deanery (1910; 1913; cons 16 February 2001)
Parish Administrator Annabelle Halliday

TWICKENHAM + ST JAMES A ♪

Sunday Mass (Sat 6pm) 10.30,12.15pm; **Holy Day Mass** 9, 7.30pm; **Weekday Mass** Mon, Tue, Thu-Sat 9, **Eucharistic Service** Wed 9; **Confession** Sat 9.45-10.45

Fr Ulick Loring

61 Pope's Grove, Twickenham TW1 4JZ Tel: 020 8892 4578
Email: twickenham@rcdow.org.uk Web: www. stjamestwickenham.org.uk
Upper Thames Deanery (1883; 1885; cons 23 July 1887)

• Religious of the Assumption, 259 Waldegrave Road, Twickenham TW1 4SY
Tel: 020 8744 1642 Email: Twickenham@assumptionreligious.org
Web: www.assumptionreligious.org
• Sisters of Mercy, 88 Pope's Grove, Twickenham TW1 4JX Tel: 020 8744 2812
• St Mary's University, Waldegrave Road, Strawberry Hill, Twickenham TW1 4SX
See entry below for *Universities and Institutes of Higher Education*

TWICKENHAM (EAST): *SEE ST MARGARETS-ON-THAMES*

UKRAINIAN CATHEDRAL: *SEE EASTERN CATHOLIC CHURCHES*

UNDERWOOD ROAD + ST ANNE ♿

Sunday Mass 10 **Holy Day Mass** as announced; **Confession** by appointment.
See entry for *Brazilian Chaplaincy* under Ethnic Chaplaincies

Missionary Community of Most Holy Providence (CMPS): Priest in Charge Fr Patrick Longo Francischini, Fr José Eduardo Viveiros Medeiros
St Anne's Church, Underwood Road E1 5AW Tel: 020 7247 7833
Email: braziliancp@rcdow.org.uk (Finances / Admin); underwood@rcdow.org.uk
(Pastoral Matters) Web: parish.rcdow.org.uk/underwoodroad
Off Vallance Road
Tower Hamlets Deanery (1850; 1855; cons 27 September 1905)
Parish and Chaplaincy Administrator Telma Melo
Pastoral Secretary Graciele Fornaciari

• **Brazilian Chaplaincy** Fr Patrick Longo Francischini (Lead Chaplain), Fr José Eduardo Viveiros Medeiros, Sr Thamires Aparecida Ciancaglio dos Reis

UNIVERSITIES AND INSTITUTES OF HIGHER EDUCATION CHAPLAINCY A

Sunday Mass 10.30 *(all year; other services term time only)*, 7.30pm; **Weekday Mass** Mon-Fri 5.30pm; **Exposition** Sun 6-7pm, Tue 6-9pm; **Confession** Sun, Mon 6-7pm.

Newman House, 111 Gower Street WC1E 6AR Tel: 020 7387 6370
Email: enquiries@universitycatholic.net Web: www.universitycatholic.net
Facebook: @newmanhouselondon

Particular Pastoral Responsibility Bishop John Sherrington

Senior Chaplain and Chaplain to LSE Fr Philip Miller
Email: frphilip@universitycatholic.net
Finance and Operations Manager Chris Castell
Email: chris@universitycatholic.net
Receptionist Team Elizabeth Elive, Anne Molloy
Email: reception@universitycatholic.net
Pastoral Associate Chris Castell
Email: chris@universitycatholic.net

Chaplains
Fr David Barrow **(University of Westminster)**
Email: davidbarrow@rcdow.org.uk (Stroud Green)
Fr Andrew Connick **(Queen Mary University of London)**
Email: a.connick@qmul.ac.uk (Wapping)
Fr Brian Creak **(Goodenough College)**
Email: bcreak@mac.com (St Charles Square)
Sr Anabel Gonzalez FMVD **(Brunel University, City University)**
Email: anabel.gonzalez@city.ac.uk
Fr Michael Holman SJ **(Imperial College)**
Email: mholmansj@jesuit.org.uk
Fr Ivano Millico **(Newman House Chaplaincy Team, Clerkenwell)**
Sr Carolyn Morrison RA **(Social Outreach Chaplain, based in Newman House)**
Email: carolyn@universitycatholic.net
Olivia Coningham-Rolls **(SOAS and Pastoral Care of Students & Staff from UCL)**
Email: o.raw@ucl.ac.uk
Fr Toby Lees OP **(King's College, London)**
Email: toby.lees@kcl.ac.uk

• Goodenough College, Mecklenburgh Square WC1 2AB

Sunday Mass 10

Fr Brian Creak (contact details above)

• St Mary's University, Waldegrave Road, Strawberry Hill, Twickenham TW1 4SX
Email: chaplaincy@stmarys.ac.uk Web: stmarys.ac.uk/chaplaincy

Sunday Mass 11 (all year); **Holy Day Mass** 1.05pm; **Weekday Mass** Mon-Fri 1.05pm
(chapel); **Confession** Mon-Fri 12.30-1pm

Chaplain Canon Peter Newby **Tel: 020 8240 4006**
Email: peter.newby@stmarys.ac.uk
Chaplaincy Administrator Grazia Hazell **Tel: 020 8240 2327**
Email: grazia.hazell@stmarys.ac.uk

SECTION 3

Choral Director Martin Foster **Tel: 020 8240 2327**
Email: martin.foster@stmarys.ac.uk

• University of Hertfordshire

Student Mass Sun 6pm at St Peter's, Hatfield South (see *Hatfield South* parish entry for other times)

Fr Innocent Odiaka MSP **(Hatfield South)** St Peter's Presbytery, Bishop's Rise, Hatfield AL10 9HN Tel: 01707 262121 Email: innocentodiaka@rcdow.org.uk

UXBRIDGE + OUR LADY OF LOURDES AND ST MICHAEL ♿ ♪

Sunday Mass (Sat 5pm) 8, 9.30, 11; **Holy Day Mass** 9.30, 7pm; **Weekday Mass** Mon 9, Tue-Wed 9.30, Fri 6pm, Sat 10; **Exposition** and **Confession** Sat 10.30-11

Fr Nicholas Schofield
Presbytery, Osborn Road, Uxbridge UB8 1UE Tel: 01895 233193
Email: uxbridge@rcdow.org.uk Web: www.catholicchurchuxbridge.org.uk
Beside Oxford Road, at junction with Harefield Road
Hillingdon Deanery (1891; 1931; cons 14 May 1936)
Pastoral Assistant Angela Atkins

• Sisters of the Sacred Hearts of Jesus and Mary, Pield Heath House, Pield Heath Road, Hillingdon UB8 3NW Tel: 01895 233092 Email: convent@pieldheathschool.org.uk
Special School Tel: 01895 258507
also Marian House Care Home, 100 Kingston Lane, Uxbridge UB8 3PW
Tel: 01895 253299
• Clare House Nursing Home

WALTHAM CROSS + OUR LADY OF THE IMMACULATE CONCEPTION AND ST JOSEPH ♿ ♪

Sunday Mass (Sat 6.30pm, 8pm Polish), 8.30, 9.45 (Polish),11.30, 6.30pm; **Holy Day Mass** 10, 8pm; **Weekday Mass** 10, Sat 11.30 (Italian); **Ukrainian Rite Liturgy** as announced; **Exposition** Fri 9.15-9.45; **Confession** Sat 10.30-11, 5.45-6.15pm

Fr John Cunningham
204 High Street, Waltham Cross EN8 7DP Tel: 01992 623156
Email: walthamcross@rcdow.org.uk Web: parish.rcdow.org.uk/walthamcross
Lea Valley Deanery (1859; 1931; cons 3 July 1971)
Parish Secretary Jacqueline Farley

WAPPING + ST PATRICK ♿ ♪

Sunday Mass (Sat 6.30pm), 10, 6.30pm; **Holy Day Mass** 10, 6.30pm; **Weekday Mass** Mon, Tue 10, Thu, Fri 6.30pm, Sat 10; **Exposition** Tue-Fri 7-8pm; **Confession** Sat, Sun 6pm

Fr Andrew Connick
The Presbytery, Dundee Street E1W 2PH Tel: 020 7481 2202
(St Patrick's Church is on Green Bank)

Email: wapping@rcdow.org.uk Web: parish.rcdow.org.uk/wapping
Off Wapping Lane; close to Wapping Stn (Overground)
Tower Hamlets Deanery (1871; 1892; cons 22 May 1902)
Parish Secretary Lucy Knights Email: lucyknights@rcdow.org.uk
Events Co-ordinator Joann Condon Email: joanncondon@rcdow.org.uk

• Jesuit Refugee Service UK, Hurtado Jesuit Centre, 2 Chandler Street E1W 2QT
Director Sarah Teather Tel: 020 7488 7310 Email: uk@jrs.net

WARE + SACRED HEART OF JESUS AND ST JOSEPH A 🎵

Sunday Mass (Sat 6.30pm), 8.30, 10.30 (Sung & Family); **Holy Day Mass** 10, 7.30pm;
Weekday Mass Mon-Thu 10; **Confession** Sat 11-11.30, 5.30-6pm *on First Sat of month*
& on request

Fr Charles Cahill, Rev Adrian Cullen (Deacon)
1 King Edward's Road, Ware SG12 7EJ Tel: 01920 462140
Email: ware@rcdow.org.uk Web: parish.rcdow.org.uk/ware
Junction of New Road (off High Street)
Lea Valley Deanery (1870; 1921; 1939)
• Carmelite Monastery, Ware Park SG12 0DT Tel: 01920 462154
Email: prioress@warecarmel.com Web: www.warecarmel.com
Chaplain Fr Anthony Baxter The Lodge, Ware Park, Ware SG12 0DS Tel: 01920 487287
Sunday Mass 11; Weekday Mass Mon-Sat 8
• Ashview, Ashwood, Camellia House, Riverside Place, Snowdrop House,
Westgate, Willowthorpe Care Homes

WARWICK STREET + OUR LADY OF THE ASSUMPTION AND ST GREGORY 🎵

Sunday Mass (Sat 6pm), 10.30 (Solemn), 5pm; **Holy Day Mass** 8, 12.45pm; **Weekday
Mass** Tue-Fri 8, Mon-Fri 12.45pm; **Exposition** Sat 5.15-5.45pm; **Confession** Mon-Fri
12.15-12.35pm & after Mass, Sat 5.15-5.45pm

in care of the Personal Ordinariate of Our Lady of Walsingham
Fr Mark Elliott Smith **(Tel: 020 7486 7026 / 07815 320761),** Mgr Keith Newton (in
residence, contact details below), Rev William Lo (Deacon)
Presbytery address: 24 Golden Square W1F 9JR
(Church & Communication address: Warwick Street W1B 5LZ Tel: 020 7734 9313)
Email: warwickstreet@rcdow.org.uk Web: parish.rcdow.org.uk/warwickstreet
Between Beak Street/Glasshouse Street; off Regent Street, close to Piccadilly Circus
Westminster Deanery (1730; 1790; cons 24 July 1928)
(Mgr Newton **Tel: 020 7440 5750**)

WATFORD + HOLY ROOD &♪

Sunday Mass (Sat 6pm), 8, 9.30, 11, 12.30pm, 2.15pm (Polish); **Holy Day Mass** as announced; **Weekday Mass** Mon, Tue 8.30, 12noon, Wed, Thu 12noon, Fri 6pm, Sat 11; **Malayalam Mass** *contact the Parish Office*; **Exposition** Tue 9-11.30, Fri 6.30-7.30pm; **Confession** Fri 6.30-7.15pm, Sat 11.30, 5pm & by appointment

Fr Gerard O'Brien, Fr Alexander Balzanella, Rev Neville Dyckhoff (Deacon)
Holy Rood Rectory, Exchange Road, Watford WD18 0PJ Tel: 01923 224085
Email: watford@rcdow.org.uk Web: parish.rcdow.org.uk/watford
Corner of Market Street and Exchange Road; office on Percy Road WD18 0QA
Watford Deanery (1883; 1890; cons 5 July 1900)
Parish Office Tel: 01923 224085

• Watford General Hospital Tel: 01923 244366

WATFORD NORTH + ST HELEN A ♪

Sunday Mass (Sat 6pm), 9, 11, 6pm; **Holy Day Mass** 10, 7pm; **Weekday Mass** Tue-Sat 10; **Exposition** Sat 9-9.50 **Confession** Sat 9-9.50

Parochial Administrator Fr Voytek Przyjalkowski, Rev Liam Lynch (Deacon)
Church of St Helen, The Harebreaks, Watford WD24 6NJ Tel: 01923 223175
Email: watfordnorth@rcdow.org.uk Web: parish.rcdow.org.uk/watfordnorth
Watford Deanery (1925; 1935)
Parish Secretary Annette Nugent Tue-Thu 9.3pm
Tel: 01923 223175

WEALDSTONE (& HARROW WEALD) + ST JOSEPH &♪

Sunday Mass (Sat 6pm), 8.15, 9.30 (Family), 11 (Sung), 12.30pm; **Holy Day Mass** 7.30, 10, 7pm; **Weekday Mass** 7.30 (not Sat), 10; *First Fri only* **Exposition** and **Confession** 6.15-6.45pm, then **Mass** 7pm; **Baptism** Sat 12noon; **Confession** Sat 10.30-11.30, 5.30-6pm

Salvatorians (SDS) Fr Thomas Malal Muchail, Fr Mario Lainez, Fr Frank Waters
St Joseph's Presbytery, 191 High Road, Harrow Weald HA3 5EE
Tel: 020 8427 1955
Email: wealdstone@rcdow.org.uk Web: www.catholicwealdstone.org
On main road, half mile north of Harrow & Wealdstone Stn (BR)
Harrow Deanery (1898; 1901; 1931)
Parish Secretary Julie Conneely **Office hours** Mon-Thu 9-2pm, Fri 9-4pm
Salvatorians (SDS) Fr Noel Keane, Fr Peter Preston
Community House, 189 High Street, Wealdstone, Harrow HA3 5DY Tel: 020 8427 2808

• Congregation of Our Lady of the Missions, 108 Spencer Road, Wealdstone, Harrow HA3 7AR Tel: 020 8861 2656 Email: provsec.uki@rndm.org.uk
Web: www.rndm.org and www.rndm-ukireland.org

WELWYN GARDEN CITY PARISHES A

St Bonaventure: **Sunday Mass** 8, 10.30; **Holy Day Mass** as announced; **Weekday Mass** Tue, Fri 9.30, Sat 10; **Confession** Sat 10.30-11

Digswell, Holy Family: **Sunday Mass** 9.30, 6pm; **Holy Day Mass** as announced; **Weekday Mass** Wed, Thu 9.30; **Confession** Thu 10-10.30

East, Our Lady Queen of Apostles: **Sunday Mass** (Sat 6pm), 11.30; **Holy Day Mass** as announced; **Weekday Mass** Mon 9.30, Tue, Fri 7 pm; **Confession** Sat 5-5.30pm

Fr Norbert Fernandes (resident at Our Lady, Queen of Apostles **Tel: 01707 323234**), Fr William Johnstone (resident at Holy Family Church **Tel: 01707 327434**)
Parish Secretary Kathryn Hubbard **Tel: 01707 322579**

+ St Bonaventure (Welwyn Garden City)
(in residence, Bishop Paul McAleenan)
81 Parkway, Welwyn Garden City AL8 6JF
Email: welwyngdncity@rcdow.org.uk Web: www.wgc-catholics.org.uk
Stevenage Deanery (1925; 1926; cons 14 September 1974)

+ Holy Family (Welwyn Garden City Digswell)
194 Knightsfield, Shoplands, Welwyn Garden City AL8 7RQ
Email: welwyngdncitydigs@rcdow.org.uk
Web: www.wgc-catholics.org.uk
Stevenage Deanery (1967; cons 13 May 2007)

+ Our Lady Queen of Apostles (Welwyn Garden City East)
141 Woodhall Lane, Welwyn Garden City AL7 3TP
Email: welwyngdncityeast@rcdow.org.uk Web: www.wgc-catholics.org.uk
Stevenage Deanery (1961; cons 18 December 1973)

• Focolare Movement (Residential Conference Centre) 69 Parkway, Welwyn Garden City AL8 6HH Tel: 01707 323620
• Queen Elizabeth II Hospital Tel: 01438 314333
• Queen Victoria Memorial Hospital, Danesbury Hospital, Isabel Hospice

WEMBLEY 1 + ST JOSEPH A

Sunday Mass (Sat 6.30pm), 9, 10.45, 12.30pm, 7.30pm; **Holy Day Mass** (Vigil 7.30pm) 9.30, 12noon; **Weekday Mass** Mon 9.30, Tue 9.30, 6.30pm, Wed 9.30, Thu 9.30, 630pm Fri 12noon, Sat 9.30; **Confession** Sat 10-10.45, **Confession** and **Exposition** Tue, Thu 7.15-8pm

Carmelites of Mary Immaculate (CMI) Fr Joseph Kaduthanam, Fr Joseph Ozhukayil Veedu Chacko, Fr Tebin Puthenpurackal
St Joseph's Presbytery, 339 High Road, Wembley HA9 6AG Tel: 020 8902 0081
Email: wembley1@rcdow.org.uk Web: parish.rcdow.org.uk/wembley
At 'The Triangle' (junction of High Road, Harrow Road & Wembley Hill Road)
Brent Deanery (1901; 1957)

SECTION 3

Parish Secretary Sr Daisylet FSM
Pastoral Assistants Sr Elizabeth Peter Panackal Purackal FSM, SrAleyamma Thottiyil Varghese FSM

• Franciscan Servants of Mary, 12 Kingsway, Wembley HA9 7QR

WEMBLEY 2 + ENGLISH MARTYRS ♿ ♒

Sunday Mass (Sat 6pm), 9, 11 (Family/with Children's Liturgy), 6pm; **Holy Day Mass** 9.30, 7pm; **Weekday Mass** Mon, Tue, Thu-Sat 9.30, preceded by **Morning Prayer** 9.15, also Wed 7pm; **Filipino Mass** *2nd Sun only* 2pm; **Exposition** Thu after Mass until 11, Sun 5-5.45pm; **Novena to Our Lady of Perpetual Help** Sat after morning Mass; **First Friday Devotion** 7-8pm; **Confession** Sat 10-10.30, 5.15-5.45pm & on request

Fr Albert Ofere
The Presbytery, Chalkhill Road, Wembley Park HA9 9EW Tel: 020 8904 2306
Email: wembley2@rcdow.org.uk Web: parish.rcdow.org.uk/wembleypark
Blackbird Hill, corner of Chalkhill Road, below Blackbird Cross
Brent Deanery (1930; 1970)

WEMBLEY 3 + ST ERCONWALD (PRESTON ROAD) ♿ ♒

Sunday Mass (Sat 5.30pm), 10 (Sung), 11.30; **Holy Day Mass** (Vigil 7pm) 9.30; **Weekday Mass** Mon-Wed, Fri 9.30; **Confession** Sat 4.30-5pm

Fr Anthony Psaila
112 Carlton Avenue East, Wembley HA9 8NB Tel: 020 8904 6031
Email: wembley3@rcdow.org.uk   Web: www.erconwald.org.uk
Off Preston Road, 400 yds east
Brent Deanery (1932; 1970)
Parish Hall Manager Elizabeth Patten Email: wembley3@rcdow.org.uk

• Sisters of La Sainte Union, 128 Elmstead Avenue, Wembley HA9 8NZ
Tel: 020 8908 3715
• Kenbrook, Birchwood Grange, Brook House

WEST DRAYTON AND YIEWSLEY + ST CATHERINE OF ALEXANDRIA ♿ ♒

Sunday Mass (Sat 7pm), 9, 11 (Sung/with Children's Liturgy), 6pm (not Easter Day, Sunday before New Year),; **Holy Day Mass** 9.30, 11, 7.30pm, (*School holidays* 9.30, 7.30pm); **Weekday Mass** Mon-Fri 9.30 as announced, Sat 10; **Confession** Sat 10.30, 6.30pm

Fr Brian Smith, Rev Nick Agule (Deacon)
20 The Green, West Drayton UB7 7PJ Tel: 01895 442777
Email: westdrayton@rcdow.org.uk Web: parish.rcdow.org.uk/westdrayton
Hillingdon Deanery (1867; 1869; cons 29 September 1893)

WEST GREEN + ST JOHN VIANNEY A

Sunday Mass (Sat 6pm), 9, 11; **Holy Day Mass** 9.15, 10 (*when school attending*), 7.30pm; **Weekday Mass** 9.15; **Confession** Sat 9.45-10.15

Fr Joe Ryan (Tel: **020 8888 9036**)
4 Vincent Road N15 3QH Tel: **020 8888 5518** (Parish Office)
Email: westgreen@rcdow.org.uk Web: stjohnvianneywestgreen.co.uk
Haringey Deanery (1927; 1959; cons 20 June 1964)
Parish Sister Sr Anabel Gonzalez Tel: **07455 544065**

• Sisters of Verbum Dei Missionary Fraternity, 4a Vincent Road N15 3QH
Tel: **020 8351 4986** Email: verbumdei.lon@gmail.com Web: uk.verbumdei.org
• Justice and Peace Commission Office, 4 Vincent Road N15 3QH
Tel: **020 8888 4222** Email: justice@rcdow.org.uk
• London Catholic Worker, Giuseppe Conlon House, 49 Mattison Road N4 1BG
Tel: **020 8348 8212** Email: londoncatholicworker@yahoo.co.uk
Web: www.londoncatholicworker.org
• Haringey Migrant Support Centre, Postal address: 386 West Green Road N15 3QL
Tel: **07544 078332** Email: info@haringeymsc.org Web: www.haringeymsc.org
New enquiries: Thu 10 Tel: **020 4566 7412**; Catch up: Thu 12-2pm Tel: **020 4566 7445**

WHEATHAMPSTEAD + ST THOMAS MORE ♿ ♪

Sunday Mass 11 (with Children's Liturgy), 5pm; **Holy Day Mass** as announced; **Weekday Mass** as announced; **Confession** as announced
Redbourn: **Sunday Mass** (Sat 5.30pm), 9; **Holy Day Mass** as announced; **Weekday Mass** as announced; **Confession** Sat 9.45-10.15, 5.45-6.15pm

Fr Michael Mannion (also serves Redbourn, resident at **1 Peppard Close, Redbourn, St Albans AL3 7EB** Tel: **01582 792270**)
7 Marford Road, Wheathampstead AL4 8AY Tel: **01582 832114**
Email: wheathampstead@rcdow.org.uk Web: parish.rcdow.org.uk/wheathampstead
St Albans Deanery (1936; 1938; 1978)

WHETSTONE + ST MARY MAGDALEN ♿ ♪

Sunday Mass (Sat 6pm, with Children's Liturgy), 9 (with Children's Liturgy), 11 (Solemn and with Children's Liturgy), 1.30pm (Polish), 4pm (Polish); **Holy Day Mass** 9.30, 5pm (Polish), 7pm; **Weekday Mass** 9.30, but Fri 12.30pm; **Exposition** Sat 4.45-5.45pm, except in August (replaced in Lent by **Stations of the Cross** at 5pm); **Confession** Sat 10-10.30, 4.45-5.45pm

Fr Gladstone Liddle
6 Athenaeum Road N20 9AE Tel: **020 8445 0838**
Email: whetstone@rcdow.org.uk Web: www.stmarymagdalens.com
Off High Road (A1000), Totteridge Lane/Oakleigh Road intersection
Barnet Deanery (1926; 1958; cons 1979)
Catechist Co-ordinator Winnie Brady Tel: **07702 094650**

WHITECHAPEL, E1: *SEE COMMERCIAL ROAD, GERMAN CHURCH AND UNDERWOOD ROAD*

WHITE CITY + OUR LADY OF FATIMA &♪ S

Sunday Mass (Sat 6pm), 9, 11, 6pm; **Holy Day Mass** 9.15, 6pm; **Weekday Mass** Mon, Tue 9.15, Wed 7.30, 12noon, Thu-Sat 9.15; **Exposition** Wed 10-12 noon, Fri 10-11, 5-6pm, Sat 10-11; **Confession** during Exposition times

Fr Richard Nesbitt, Fr Ephrem Andom (in residence, Eritrean Chaplaincy)
The Catholic Presbytery, Commonwealth Avenue, White City W12 7QR
Tel: 020 8743 8334 (Fr Ephrem Andom Tel: 020 8743 8315)
Email: whitecity@rcdow.org.uk Web: www.ourladyoffatima.org.uk
Off Bloemfontein Road, between Western Avenue / Uxbridge Road
Hammersmith & Fulham Deanery (1951; 1965; cons 17 May 1980)
Parish Administrator Collise Lynch (Mon, Wed, Fri, 10-3pm)
Parish Community Support Worker Laura Allison (Mon, Thu, Sat 10-1pm)

WHITTON + ST EDMUND OF CANTERBURY A ♪ S

Sunday Mass (Sat 6.30pm), 9.30 (Family), 11.15 (Sung), 6pm; **Holy Day Mass** 9.30, 7.30pm; **Weekday Mass** Mon-Fri 9.15, Sat 10.30; **Exposition** *First Fri* 24 hours from 10; **Confession** Sat 10-10.30

Fr Nigel Griffin
Presbytery, St Edmund's Lane, 213 Nelson Road, Whitton TW2 7BB Tel: 020 8894 9923
Email: whitton@rcdow.org.uk Web: parish.rcdow.org.uk/whitton
Right at Whitton BR Stn, left at Nelson Pub; presbytery behind the church
Upper Thames Deanery (1934; 1935; cons 29 September 1972)
Administrator Paul Hampartsoumian
Co-ordinator of Lay Ministry Louise Walton

WILLESDEN + OUR LADY OF WILLESDEN &♪

The Church is the National Shrine of Our Lady of Willesden (1930)
Sunday Mass (Sat 6pm), 9, 11 (Sung); **Holy Day Mass** (Vigil 7pm), 7, 10, 12.45pm (1962 Missal), 7.30pm (Sung); **Weekday Mass** 10, 7pm; **Exposition** Tue 10.30-6.50pm, Sat 10.30-5.50pm; **Shrine Prayers** Tue 7.30pm (*see* Catholic Societies and Organisation, Section 6, *Guild of Our Lady of Willesden*); **Confession** Tue 6.15-6.45pm, Sat 10.30-11.30, 5-5.45pm

Fr Stephen Willis, Fr Jonathan Stogdon
The Presbytery, 1 Nicoll Road NW10 9AX Tel: 020 8965 4935
Email: willesden@rcdow.org.uk Web: parish.rcdow.org.uk/willesden
At junction of Acton Lane, near Jubilee Clock, Harlesden
Brent Deanery (1886; 1931)
Shrine of Our Lady of Willesden
Catechetical Co-ordinator AnneMarie Sylvester-Charles

WILLESDEN GREEN + ST MARY MAGDALEN A 🏊

Sunday Mass (Sat 6.30pm), 9, 10.30 (Sung), 12noon (Sung), 6.30pm; **Holy Day Mass** 9.30, 6.30pm; **Weekday Mass** Mon-Sat 9.30; **Exposition** Mon-Sat 8.30-9.30, Sat 5.30-6.15pm; **Confession** Sat 10-10.30, 5.30-6.15pm

Mgr Roger Reader, Fr Allan Alvarado Gil (clergy also serve Kensal Rise, Fr Allan resident at Presbytery, 1 Wrentham Avenue NW10 3HT Tel: 020 3539 6918), Fr Ruwan Hewawasam (in residence, Sri-Lankan (Sinhalese) Chaplaincy)
Clergy House, Peter Avenue NW10 2DD Tel: 020 8451 4677
Email: willesdengreen@rcdow.org.uk Web: parish.rcdow.org.uk/willesdengreen
Harlesden Road, south side of High Road, via St Andrew's Road; not far from Willesden Green Stn (TfL)
Brent Deanery (1901; 1939; cons 1958)
Parish Administrator Kathleen Reddington
Safeguarding Claudia Tugbobo **Email:** willesdengreensg3@rcdow.org.uk

• Daughters of Wisdom (La Sagesse), 9 The Oaks, 25 Brondesbury Park NW6 7BY
Tel: 020 8830 2530
• Missionary Sisters of Christ the King (MChR) 180 Walm Lane NW2 3AX
Tel: 020 3638 4753 Email: missionary.london@gmail.com Web: www.mchr.pl
• Sisters of the Holy Family of Bordeaux, 83 St Gabriel's Road NW2 4DU
Tel: 020 8452 3844 Email: stgabriels@holyfamilybordeaux.org
Web: www.holyfamilybordeaux.org
• St Boniface Secular Institute (English Region), 44 Exeter Road NW2 4SB
Tel: 020 8438 9628 Email: hostel@institut-st-bonifatius.de
Web: www.hostel-lioba-house.de (see also *German Church* entry)
• Divine Word Missionaries (SVD), 8 Teignmouth Road NW2 4HN
Tel: 020 8452 8430 Email: svdlondon@gmail.com
Frs Albert Escoto (Praeses), Eamonn Donnelly, Krzysztof Krzyskow, John McCarthy, Martin McPake, Kevin O'Toole
• Hospitaller Order of St John of God (OH), 52 Kenneth Crescent NW2 4PN
Tel: 020 8452 8879 Email: johnoneill@sjog.org.uk Web: www.hospitaller.org.uk
Brs Malachy Brannigan (Prior), Bonaventure Gerrard, John O'Neill, Andrzej Zach
• Jesuits (SJ), Chapel of Our Lady of Mercy, 182 Walm Lane NW2 3AX
Tel: 020 8452 4304 Email: londyn@jezuici.pl / polishjesuits@rcdow.org.uk
Web: polishjesuits.co.uk
Frs Grzegorz Jankowski, Leszek Szuta, Adam Tomaszewski (Superior)
Sunday Mass (Polish) 10.30, 12noon; Mon-Sat 7.30 (English), Mon-Fri 7pm (Polish);
Exposition 30 mins before evening Mass; **Confession** 30 mins before Mass
St Francis of Assisi, Fleetwood Road NW10 1NQ
Sunday Mass (Polish) (Sat 7pm), 9, 10.30, 12noon, 7 pm; **Exposition** 30 mins before evening Mass **Confession** 30 mins before Mass
Lectio Divina: lectio.divinaOLM@gmail.com; Men of St Joseph: london.msj@gmail.com

SECTION 3

• Montfort Missionaries, 27 St Gabriel's Road NW2 4DS Tel: 020 8450 4291 / 07525 220255
Frs Nelson Cabanero, Kieran Flynn
• De Paul Trust, 247 Willesden Lane NW2 5RY Tel: 020 8830 1093
• Willesden General Hospital Tel: 020 8438 7000

WOOD GREEN + ST PAUL THE APOSTLE ♿♫

Sunday Mass (Sat 5.30pm), 8, 10 (Family), 12noon (Sung); **Holy Day Mass** 9.30, 7.30pm; **Weekday Mass** Mon-Fri 9.30, preceded by **Morning Prayer** 9.10; **Rosary** Mon, Wed-Fri after Mass; **Exposition** Sat 4.30-5.15pm; **Confession** Sat 11-12noon

Fr Perry Sykes
Presbytery & Communication Address: 22 Bradley Road N22 7SZ Tel: 020 8888 2390
(Church address: Station Road N22 7SY)
Email: woodgreen@rcdow.org.uk Web: parish.rcdow.org.uk/woodgreen
Wood Green TfL Stn (Piccadilly line), near junction with Mayes Road
Haringey Deanery (1882; 1904; 1970)

• Daughters of Divine Love, 82/84 Sylvan Avenue N22 5HY Tel: 020 8888 1898
Email: divinelovedaughters@yahoo.co.uk Web: www.ddlenglishregion.org

YEADING + ST RAPHAEL ♿♫

Sunday Mass (Sat 7pm), 9, 10.30 (Sung), 12noon; **Holy Day Mass** 9.30, 7.30pm; **Weekday Mass** Mon-Wed, Fri, Sat 9.30, with **Rosary** 9; **Exposition** *First Fri only* 7pm; **Confession** Sat 6.30pm

Fr John Welsh
St Raphael's House, Morrison Road, Yeading UB4 9JP Tel: 020 8845 1919
Email: yeading@rcdow.org.uk Web: parish.rcdow.org.uk/yeading
In Ayles Road, off Kingshill Avenue (west of Yeading Lane)
Hillingdon Deanery (1957; 1961; cons 4 May 1975)
Parish Administrator Paulina Louison

SECTION 3

CHAPLAINCIES

Information about Chaplaincies can be found at **www.rcdow.org.uk/chaplaincies**

AIRPORT CHAPELS

GATWICK AIRPORT (Diocese of Arundel & Brighton) Chapels in North and South Terminals (Diocese of Arundel & Brighton); for times of services **Tel: 01293 505540**
Web: www.gatwickairportchapel.org
HEATHROW AIRPORT St George's Chapel
See page 86 in the Parish Directory.

ARMED FORCES, PRINCIPAL CHAPLAINCIES

ARMY Fr Ian Stevenson DACG, **HQ 51 Inf Bde & HQ Army in Scotland**, Redford Cavalry Barracks, Edinburgh EH13 0PP Email: Ian.stevenson947@mod.gov.uk
ROYAL AIR FORCE Rev (Sqn Ldr) David E Skillen RAF, **Station Chaplain**, The Chaplaincy Centre, RAF Odiham, Hook RG29 1QT E-mail: David.Skillen100@mod.gov.uk
ROYAL NAVY The Very Rev David Conroy QHC VE RN **Deputy Chaplain of the Fleet**, Chaplaincy Headquarters, Tanner Building, HMS EXCELLENT, Whale Island, Portsmouth PO2 8ER E-mail: david.conroy977@mod.gov.uk

EASTERN CATHOLIC CHURCHES

Episcopal Vicar for Eastern Catholic Churches Mgr John Conneely

BELARUSIAN CATHOLIC CHURCH

Chaplain: Fr Serge Stasievich
Address: Church of St Cyril of Turau and All the Patron Saints of the Belarusian People, adjacent to Marian House, Holden Avenue N12 8HY
Tel: 020 8446 3378
Email: belarusmission@gmail.com
Web: www. belaruschurch.org.uk
Mass times: Sunday 10.30

CHALDEAN CATHOLIC CHURCH

Chaplain: Fr Andrawis Toma
Address: 38-40 Cavendish Avenue W13 0JQ
Tel: 020 8997 6370
Email: fr.andrawistoma@yahoo.com
Web: www.chaldeans.uk
Mass times: Acton West, Sunday 12.45pm

GHEEZ RITE (Eritrea)

Chaplain: Fr Ephrem Andom
Address: The Catholic Presbytery, Commonwealth Avenue W12 7QR (White City)
Tel: 020 8743 8315
Email: abbaephrem@yahoo.co.uk
Mass times: Acton East, Sunday 1pm

GHEEZ RITE (Ethiopia)

Chaplain:	Fr Ufayissa Dea Madalcho CM
Address:	1 Waller Road SE14 5LE
Tel:	07506 177622
Email:	ufiyeedm@gmail.com
Mass times:	*Queensway*, Sunday 1pm

KNANAYA

Chaplain:	Fr Mathews Valiyaputhenpura Joy
Address:	The Presbytery, Esdaile Lane Hoddesdon EN11 8DS *(Hoddesdon)*
Tel:	01992 440986
Email:	mathewsvj@rcdow.org.uk
Mass times:	*St Thomas More, Harlow CM20 1NW (Brentwood)*, 1st and 3rd Sunday 2.30pm
	St Alban, Elm Park RM12 5JX (Brentwood), 2nd and 4th Sunday 3pm

LEBANESE MARONITE CATHOLIC CHURCH

Chaplains:	Fr Antoine Achkar, Fr Aziz Azzi, Fr Youssek Eshak, Fr Fadi Kmeid
Address:	6 Dobson Close NW6 4RS
Tel:	020 7586 1801 (10.30-1.30pm)
Email:	admin@maronitechurch.org.uk
Web:	www.maronitechurch.org.uk
Mass times:	(for Lebanese) *Our Lady of Sorrows, Paddington,* Saturday 7pm; Sunday 11.30, 7pm; Wednesday, Friday 7pm
	(for Cypriots) *Holy Family Convent, 52 London Road, Enfield EN2 6EN,* Sunday 10.30

MELKITE CATHOLIC CHURCH

Chaplain:	Archimandrite Shafiq Abouzayd
Address:	46 Sunderland Avenue, Oxford OX2 8DU
Tel:	01865 514041 / 07977 495150
Email:	melkitelondon@gmail.com
Web:	www.melkite.uk
Mass times:	*St Barnabas C of E Church, Pimlico Road SW1W 8PF,* Sunday 12noon

SYRO-MALABAR CHURCH (see *Other Jurisdictions*, page 148)

Chaplain:	Fr Joseph Mukkatt **(in charge of 9 Centres in Brentwood Diocese)**
Address:	132 Shernhall Street E17 9HU
Tel:	020 8520 5877

Chaplain:	Fr Aneesh Thomas
Address:	165 Arlington Road NW1 7EX *(Camden Town)*
Tel:	07469 268402
Email:	aneeshthomas@rcdow.org.uk
Mass times:	*Feltham,* 3rd Sunday 3pm (Mass, Rosary & Catechism)
	Harefield, 2nd Sunday 5 pm (Mass, Rosary)

SECTION 3

Hayes, 2nd Sunday 2pm (Mass, Rosary & Catechism)
Hounslow, 1st Sunday 2.30 pm (Mass, Rosary & Catechism)
Stevenage Bedwell, 1st Saturday 12.30pm, 3rd Saturday 2pm (Mass, Catechism, Rosary & BVM Novena)
Watford, 2nd Saturday 9, 4th Saturday 3pm (Mass, Rosary & BVM Novena), Every Sunday 2.30-4pm (Catechism)

SYRO-MALANKARA CHURCH

Chaplain:	Fr John Alex
Address:	St John the Baptist, 349 Wanstead Park Road, Cranbrook, Ilford IG1 3TS
	St John the Baptist, Ilford (Brentwood)
Tel:	020 8554 3763

UKRAINIAN CATHOLIC CHURCH (see *Other Jurisdictions*, page 147)

Clergy:	Rt Rev Archpriest Mykola Matwijiwskyj, Fr Andriy Chornenko, Fr Taras Ditchuk (in residence), Fr Vitaly Fedun (in residence), Fr Andriy Malysh (in residence), Fr Mark Woodruff (English Liturgy Co-ordinator); Rev Ihor Dyachyk (Deacon)
Address:	Cathedral of the Holy Family, Duke Street W1K 5BQ (Correspondence etc. to 22 Binney Street W1K 5BQ)
Tel:	020 7629 1534 / 07952 180950
Email:	cathedral@ucc-gb.com
Web:	www.ucc-gb.com
Liturgies:	*Cathedral,* Sunday 8, 10,12noon, 5.15pm; *Sacred Heart Church, Horseferry Road SW1P 2EF,* 10 (English)
	Cathedral, Weekday 7, 6.15pm (Monday 6.15pm only); 2nd Saturday 4pm (English);
	Confession daily before Divine Liturgy
	Feltham, 2nd Sunday 2.30pm
	Waltham Cross, 1st & 3rd Sundays, 3pm

ETHNIC CHAPLAINCIES

Particular Pastoral Responsibility   Bishop Paul McAleenan

Co-ordinator for Ethnic Chaplaincies   Fr Philip Miller

Where a Chaplaincy is based at a parish, the name of the parish is given in italics after the address. Parish names are also in italics in the list of Mass times - please refer to the Parish Directory for the parish address.

AFRICAN CATHOLIC MISSION IN BRITAIN

Chaplain:	Rev Joseph Baffour-Awuah (Deacon)
Address:	St George's Presbytery, 132 Shernhall Street E17 9HU
Tel:	020 8521 2359 / 07786 501371
Email:	africath@clara.co.uk

ALBANIAN – KOSOVAN

Chaplain:	Fr Gary Walsh
Address:	8 Ogle Street W1W 6HS *(Ogle Street)*
Tel:	07791 054137
Email:	garywalsh2001@yahoo.com
Mass times:	*Pimlico,* 2nd and 4th Sunday 3pm
	Wood Green, 1st and 3rd Sunday 1.30pm

BRAZILIAN

Chaplains:	Fr Patrick Longo Francischini MPS (Lead), Fr José Eduardo Viveiros Medeiros MPS, Sr Thamires Aparecida Ciancaglio dos Reis MPS
Address:	St Anne's Church, Underwood Road E1 5AW *(Underwood Road)*
Tel:	020 7247 7833
Email:	braziliancp@rcdow.org.uk (Finances / Admin)
	underwoodroad@rcdow.org.uk (Pastoral Matters)
Web:	www.capelaniacblondres.uk
Mass times:	(Brazilian Masses)
	Bayswater, Saturday 4.30pm
	Brixton (Southwark), Sunday 7pm
	Crystal Palace (Southwark), Sunday 8.30
	Manor House, Sunday 5pm
	Underwood Road, Thursday 7.30pm, Saturday 7pm; Sunday 12noon
	Willesden Green, Saturday 7.45pm, Sunday 2pm

CARIBBEAN

Chaplain:	Rev Jon Dal Din (Deacon)
Address:	112 Kelmscott Road SW11 6PT
Tel:	07527 758729 / 07889 536957
Email:	jondaldin@rcdow.org.uk
President:	Lloyd Booker
Address:	17a Cambray Road SW12 0DX
Tel:	020 8675 0607

CHINESE

Chaplain:	Fr Joseph Liang
Address:	Assumption Priory, Victoria Park Square E2 9PB *(Bethnal Green)*
Tel:	020 8980 1968 / 07753 471611
Email:	josephliang1998@gmail.com
Web:	http://londonccc.wordpress.com
Mass times:	*Bethnal Green,* (Chinese) Sunday 2.15pm

CONGOLESE

Chaplain:	Fr Julien Matondo Mboko
Address:	2 Lukin Street E1 0AA *(Commercial Road)*
Tel:	020 7790 2211/ 07452 772111

Email: julienmboko@hotmail.fr / julienmboko@rcdow.org.uk
Mass times: *Highbury, (Lingala) Sunday 2pm*

CROATIAN

Chaplain: Fr Ljubomir Šimunović OFM
Address: 17 Boutflower Road SW11 1RE
Tel: 020 7223 3530
Email: hkmlondon@gmail.com
Web: www.hkmlondon.org
Mass times: *Sacred Heart Church (Cathedral Chapel of Ease), Horseferry Road SW1P 2EF, Sunday 4pm*

FILIPINO

Chaplain: Fr Francisco Cruz CM
Address: 1 Waller Road SE14 5LE
Tel: 020 7732 4119 / 07424 114644
Email: frankikocm@gmail.com
Mass times: *Feltham,* 4th Saturday 3pm
    Kilburn West, 3rd Sunday 3pm
    Lincoln's Inn Fields, 2nd Sunday 4pm
    Mill Hill, 2nd Saturday 7pm
    Philippine Embassy, 1st Friday 5.30pm
    Stonebridge, 1st Sunday 3pm
    Wembley 1, 5th Sunday 3pm

FRENCH

Chaplains: Fr Pascal Boidin sm, Fr Hubert Bonnet-Eymard sm, Fr Damien Diouf sm,
Address: Notre Dame de France, 5 Leicester Place WC2H 7BX
    (French Church)
Tel: 020 7437 9363
Mass times: See *French Church* in the Parish Directory

GERMAN

Chaplain: Fr Andreas Blum
Address: St Boniface, 47 Adler Street E1 1EE *(German Church)*
Tel: 020 7247 9529
Email: pfarrer@dkg-london.org
Mass times: See *German Church* in the Parish Directory

GHANAIAN

Chaplain: Fr Dominic Yaw Assuahene
Address: St Mary Magdalen Church, 71 Comerford Road SE4 2BA
Tel: 020 8305 8004 / 07393 613906
Email: dyassuahene@gmail.com

GOAN

Chaplain:	Fr Patrick D'Souza SFX
Address:	(Office) St Thomas of Canterbury School, Commonside East, Mitcham, CR4 1YG
Tel:	020 8665 2176
Email:	goanchaplaincy@gmail.com / goanchaplaincy@rcdow.org.uk
Address:	(Home) Ss Peter and Paul Church, 1 Cranmer Road, Mitcham CR4 4LD
Mass times:	*Cranford,* (Konkani) 4th Sunday 5pm
	Hayes, (Konkani) 1st Thursday 6pm
	Hounslow, (Konkani) 3rd Sunday 4pm
	Mitcham (Southwark), (Konkani) 2nd Sunday 3pm
	Southall, (Konkani) 3rd Saturday 4pm
	Wembley 1, (Konkani) 1st Sunday 4 pm

HUNGARIAN

Chaplain:	Fr János Csicsó
Address:	62 Little Ealing Lane W5 4EA
Tel:	020 8566 0271
Email:	hungarian.chaplaincy@btinternet.com
Web:	www.magyarkatolikusok.co.uk
Mass times:	*62 Little Ealing Lane,* 1st & 3rd Sunday 11.30

IRISH

CEO:	Eddie Gilmore
Address:	52 Camden Square NW1 9XB
Tel:	020 7482 5528
Email:	info@irishchaplaincy.org.uk
Web:	www.irishchaplaincy.org.uk
Mass times:	12noon *(First Friday only)*

ITALIAN CHURCH

Chaplains:	Fr Andrea Fulco SAC, Fr Giuseppe De Caro SAC
Address:	St Peter's Italian Church, 4 Back Hill EC1R 5EN *(Italian Church)*
Tel:	020 7837 1528
Email:	info@italianchurch.org.uk
Mass times:	See *Italian Church* in the Parish Directory

ITALIAN MISSION

Chaplain:	Fr Antonio Serra
Address:	197 Durants Road, Enfield EN3 7DE *(Ponders End)*
Tel:	020 8804 2307
Email:	mci.london@hotmail.com
Web:	www.mcilondon.org
Mass times:	*Italian Centre* Sunday 9.30, Tue, Fri 7.30pm; Adoration Fri 6.30pm

SECTION 3

Hoddesdon, Saturday 4pm
Ponders End, Sunday 12.30pm
Waltham Cross, Saturday 11.30
Confessions: 30 mins before each Mass.

KERALAN / MALAYALAM (Latin Rite)

Chaplains:	Fr Johnson Alexander, Fr Jose Netto *(resident at Ruislip)*
Address:	373 Bowes Road N11 1AA *(New Southgate)*
Tel:	07438 182888 / 07958 376955
Email:	fr.johnsonalexander@gmail.com
Mass times:	*East Ham (Brentwood),* 2nd & 4th Sunday 4pm, preceded by Catechism 3pm and Rosary 3.30pm
	Forest Gate (Brentwood), 2nd Tuesday 7pm Novena to St Anthony and Mass
	Hatfield, 3rd Saturday 6pm
	New Southgate, 2nd Sunday 3.30pm Novena to Our Lady of Perpetual Help and Mass
	Pollards Hill (Southwark), 1st Sunday 3.30pm Novena to Our Lady of Perpetual Help and Mass
	Ruislip, 1st Sunday 4pm
	Southall, 3rd Sunday 3pm, preceded by Adoration and Confession 2pm

KOREAN

Chaplain:	Fr Joong Hee Kwon
Address:	Korean Catholic Community, 104-106 Benhill Wood Road, Sutton SM1 3SR
Tel:	020 8644 1223
Email:	londoncatholic@gmail.com
Web:	www.londoncatholic.net
Mass times:	(Saturday 7pm), Sunday 11

LATIN AMERICAN

Chaplains:	Fr Carlos Abajos OAR
Address:	363 Kennington Lane SE11 5QY
Tel:	020 7820 1697
Email:	capellanialatinoamericana@gmail.com
Mass times:	*St George's Cathedral (Southwark)*, Sunday 1.3pm
	St Anthony, Forest Gate (Brentwood), Sunday 3pm
	St Anne, Vauxhall (Southwark), Sunday 1.30pm
	Stamford Hill, Sunday 4.30pm
	Soho Square, Sunday 6pm

LITHUANIAN

Chaplains:	Fr Petras Tverijonas, Fr Petras Gucevicius
Address:	21 The Oval, Hackney Road E2 9DT *(Lithuanian Church)*
Tel:	020 7739 8735

Email: parish@londonas.co.uk
Mass times: See *Lithuanian Church* in the Parish Directory

MALTESE

Chaplain: Fr Victor Camilleri OFM
Address: 47 Adler Street E1 1EE *(German Church)*
Tel: 07930 198251
Email: victorjcamilleri@gmail.com

NIGERIAN

Chaplains: Fr Peter Tochukwu Egboo, Fr Alexander Izang Atu, Fr Michael Ogunyinka
Address: 8 King Henry's Walk N1 4PB *(Kingsland)*
Tel: 07440 653821 (Fr Peter); 07432 048440 (Fr Alexander)
Email: admin@ncchapeng.org
Web: ncchapeng.org / nigeriancatholicchaplaincyenglandandwales.org
Mass times: *Dagenham (Brentwood)*, 1st Sunday 2pm
Feltham, 4th Sunday 2.30pm
Kingsland, 3rd Sunday 2pm
Mill Hill, 4th Sunday 2pm
Peckham (Southwark), 1st Sunday 2pm
Tottenham, 1st Sunday in third month of the quarter 2pm
Language Masses 2nd Sundays 2pm

POLISH

Vicar Delegate: Mgr Stefan Wylezek
Address: 2-4 Devonia Road N1 8JJ
Tel: 020 7226 3439
Email: No address supplied
Mass times: See *Polish Church 1, 2 & 3* in the Parish Directory

PORTUGUESE

Chaplain: Fr Carlos M F Gabriel
Address: Portuguese Catholic Mission, 6 Minerva Close SW9 6NZ
Tel: 020 7587 0881 / 07443 885815
Email: carlosgabriel@rcdow.org.uk / ukportuguesechaplain@gmail.com
Mass times: *Bayswater,* Sunday 9 (Confessions 10)
Camden Town, Sunday 5pm
Clapham Common (Southwark), Sunday 5pm
Cranford, 1st & 3rd Sundays12.30pm (Confessions 12noon)
Fulham1, Sunday 3pm (Confessions 2pm)
Northwood, dates as announced 7.30pm
Baptisms, weddings, house visits and individual confessions by appointment

SECTION 3

ROMANIAN
Chaplain: Fr Maricel-Irinel Mititelu
Address: 35 Cricklewood Lane NW2 1HR *(Cricklewood)*
Tel: 07721 867280
Email: romanianchaplaincy@rcdow.org.uk
Mass times: *Kingsbury Green,* Sunday 12.30pm, Tuesday 7.30pm, *First Friday only* 7.30pm
Confession 30 mins before all Masses

SLOVAK (also for CZECH)
Chaplain: Fr Tibor Borovsky (also Parish Priest of St Neots, Diocese of East Anglia)
Address: 22 Cortayne Road SW6 3QA *(Parsons Green)*
Tel: 07597 637411
Email: info@scmlondon.org / secretary@scmlondon.org
Mass times: *Our Lady of La Salette and St Joseph, 14 Melior Street SE1 3QP (Southwark)*
Sunday 1pm
Confession Sunday 12.30-12.50pm, 2.45-3.30pm
Rosary 30 mins before Mass

SPANISH
Please contact the Latin American Chaplaincy

SRI-LANKAN (SINHALESE-SPEAKING)
Chaplain: Fr Ruwan Hewawasam
Address: Clergy House, Peter Avenue NW10 2DD *(Willesden Green)*
Tel: 020 8451 4677
Email: ruwanhp@rcdow.org.uk
Mass times: *Croxley Green,* 1st Sunday 4pm
Hounslow, 2nd Sunday 4pm
Welling (Southwark), 3rd Sunday 4pm
Willesden Green, 4th Sunday 4.pm

SRI-LANKAN (TAMIL-SPEAKING)
Chaplain: Fr Elmo Arulnesan Jeyarasa
Address: 304 Garratt Lane SW18 4EH
Tel: 020 8870 6257
Email: elmojeyarasa@rcdow.org.uk
Web: www.tamil-rcchaplaincy.org.uk
Mass times: *Earlsfield (Southwark),* 4th Sunday 4.30pm
Forest Gate (Brentwood), 4th Sunday 4.30pm
Kenton, 1st Sunday 4pm
Lewisham (Southwark), 2nd Sunday 3.45pm
Southall, 1st Sunday 1.30pm
Wembley 1, 3rd Sunday 3.30pm

TRAVELLER, GYPSY AND ROMA COMMUNITIES
National
Chaplain: Rev Richard Jones (Deacon)
Email: deaconrick@walsingham.org.uk
Pastoral Co-ordinator
(Westminster): Sr Petronia Williams OSM
Address: 12 Clevelys Road E5 9JN
Tel: 020 8880 0257
Email: petroniawilliams@rcdow.org.uk / petroniaosm@yahoo.co.uk

UGANDAN
There is no Ugandan Chaplaincy, but communities meet for Mass
Mass times: Blessed Jildo Irwa & Daudi Okello Uganda Catholic Community
Kingsland, 2nd Sunday 3pm
Ugandan Croydon Catholic Community
South Norwood (Southwark), 2nd Sunday 2pm

VIETNAMESE
Chaplains: Fr John Hai Pham, Fr Tri Nguyen Van, Rev Paul Song Trong Ly (Deacon)
Address: 117 Bow Common Lane E3 4AU *(Bow Common)*
Tel: 020 7987 3477
Email: vietnamesechaplain@rcdow.org.uk / johnphamhuuhai@rcdow.org.uk
Mass times: *130 Poplar High Street E14 0AG,* Catechesis School for Vietnamese
Catholic Children Tel: 020 7536 2844
Sunday Mass 1pm (except school holidays)
Bow Common, Sunday 12noon, Monday-Wednesday 10, Thursday, Friday
8pm, Saturday 10

ZAMBIAN
Chaplain: Fr Henry Mobela
Address: 62 Eden Grove N7 8EN *(Holloway)*
Tel: 020 7607 3594 / 07495 866069
Email: kalusamobela@gmail.com / henrymobela@rcdow.org.uk
Mass times: *Clerkenwell,* 4th Saturday 3pm

ZIMBABWEAN
Chaplain: Fr John Rufaro Mudereri
Address: 24 Bouverie Road N16 0AJ *(Stoke Newington)*
Tel: 020 3802 2911 / 07943 875189 (Tue-Fri)
Email: zimbabweanchaplaincy@rcdow.org.uk
Mass times: *Stoke Newington,* 1st Saturday 2pm

SECTION 3

HM PRISON SERVICE

Particular Pastoral Responsibility Bishop Paul McAleenan, assisted by Mgr Martin Hayes

PRISON CHAPLAINCIES
National Catholic Chaplain for Prisons Awaiting appointment
CBCEW, 39 Eccleston Square SW1V 1BX
Tel: 020 7901 4857 Email: Prisons.Chaplain@cbcew.org.uk
Her Majesty's Prison and Probation Service
Roman Catholic Internal HQ Advisor Rev Paul Hargreaves (Deacon)
Tel: 07562 433656 Email: paul.hargreaves@justice.gov.uk

Co-ordinator for the Diocese Bridget Brinkley (see Feltham entry)

Bovingdon: HM Prison The Mount, Molyneaux Avenue, Hemel Hempstead HP3 0NE
Chaplains Fr Neil Scott, Rev William Lo (Deacon) **Tel: 01442 836300**
Email: neil.scott@justice.gov.uk, william.lo@justice.gov.uk
Bronzefield: HM Prison, Woodthorpe Road, Ashford TW15 3JZ
Chaplain Karen Connaughton **Tel: 01784 425690**
Email: karen.connaughton@justice.gov.uk
Feltham: HM Young Offenders Institution and Remand Centre, Bedfont Road, Feltham TW13 4ND
Chaplain Bridget Brinkley **Tel: 020 8844 5326 Email: bridget.brinkley@justice.gov.uk**
Pentonville: HM Prison, Caledonian Road N7 8TT
Chaplains Valentine Ambe, Mary Ebbasi **Tel: 020 7023 7217**
Email: valentine.ambe@justice.gov.uk, mary.ebbasi@justice.gov.uk
Wormwood Scrubs: HM Prison, PO Box 757, London W12 0AE
Chaplain Fr Chima Ibekwe **Tel: 020 8588 3200 Email: chima.ibekwe@justice.gov.uk**

HOSPITAL AND HOSPICE CHAPLAINS

Particular Pastoral Responsibility Bishop Paul McAleenan, assisted by Mgr Martin Hayes
Cardinal's Healthcare Advisors Fr Giles Pinnock and Fr Peter Harries OP
Assistant Co-ordinator of Healthcare Chaplains Rev Anthony Clark (Deacon)
For further information please see **www.rcdow.org.uk/healthcare**
In light of the Data Protection Act 1998, please indicate on entering hospital that your details may be passed to the RC Chaplain. Also state that you would like the RC Chaplain to visit you.

Hospital telephone numbers are listed after the name of the hospital, followed by the name and telephone number of the specially appointed Hospital Chaplain, where there is one, or the name in italics of the parish from which the hospital is served and the parish's telephone number.
Ashford Hospital Tel: 01784 884488 Chaplain: Frances Castledine Tel: 01784 884488

Barnet Hospital Tel: 0845 111 4000 Chaplain: Awaiting appointment
Bishops Wood Tel: 01923 835814 *Northwood* Tel: 01923 825639
Bushey BUPA Tel: 020 8950 9090 *Bushey* Tel: 020 8950 2077

Capio Nightingale Tel: 020 7535 7700 *Marylebone* Tel: 020 7723 5101

Central Middlesex Tel: **020 8965 5733** Chaplain: Fr Agustin Paunon Tel: 020 8869 2113 (Sun-Thu 9-5pm) Email: LNWH-tr.Chaplaincy@nhs.net

Charing Cross Tel: **020 3311 1056** Chaplains: Fr Giles Pinnock, Fr Benedict Abuo, Fr Blaise Amadi CM, Veronica Burns Tel: 020 3312 1508,

Chase Farm Tel: **0845 111 4000** Chaplain: Awaiting appointment

Chelsea & Westminster Tel: **020 8746 8000** Chaplain: Awaiting appointment

Clayponds Tel: **020 8560 4011** *Brentford* Tel: 020 8560 1671

Clementine Churchill Tel: **020 8872 3872** *Sudbury* Tel: 020 8904 2552

Cromwell Tel: **020 7460 2000** Chaplains: Fr Giles Pinnock, Fr Benedict Abuo, Fr Blaise Amadi CM, Veronica Burns Tel: 020 3312 1508,

Ealing Tel: **020 8967 5000** Chaplain: via Tel: 020 8967 5130 Email: LNWH-tr.Chaplaincy@nhs.net

East London & The City Mental Health NHS Trust Tel: **0845 155 5000** Chaplain: Awaiting appointment

Edenhall Marie Curie Centre Tel: **020 7794 0066** *Swiss Cottage* Tel: 020 7435 1388

Edgware Community Tel: **020 8952 2381** Chaplain: Awaiting appointment

Elizabeth Garrett Anderson Wing Chaplains: Fr Peter Harries OP, Fr Serge Stasievich Tel: 020 3447 3007

Finchley Memorial Tel: **020 8349 3121** *Finchley Church End* Tel: 020 8346 2459

Fitzroy Nuffield Tel: **020 7723 1288** *Spanish Place* Tel: 020 7935 0943

Garden House Tel: **01462 679540** *Letchworth* Tel: 01462 683504

Gordon (The) Tel: **020 8746 8733**

Great Ormond Street Tel: **020 7405 9200** Chaplains: Kate Kakande, Colette Lennon

Hammersmith, Queen Charlotte's & Chelsea Tel: **020 3313 4574** Chaplains: Fr Giles Pinnock, Fr Benedict Abuo, Fr Blaise Amadi CM, Veronica Burns Tel: 020 3312 1508

Harefield Tel: **01895 823737** *Harefield* Tel: 01895 822365

Harley Street Clinic Tel: **020 7935 7700** Chaplains: Fr Giles Pinnock, Fr Benedict Abuo, Fr Blaise Amadi CM, Veronica Burns Tel: 020 3312 1508

Harpenden BUPA Tel: **01582 763191** *Harpenden* Iel: 01582 712245

Hemel Hempstead Hospital Tel **01442 213141** Chaplains: Rev Anthony Curran (Deacon), Theresa Taylor-Brookes Tel: 01923 217994

Hendon Tel: **020 8457 4500** *Hendon* Tel: 020 8202 0560

Hertfordshire Partnership Foundation Trust Tel: **01727 804814**

Hillingdon Tel: **01895 238282** Lead Chaplain: Fr Jack Creagh Tel: 01895 279433

Homerton Tel: **020 8510 5555** *Clapton Park* Tel: 020 8525 1929

King Edward VII Tel: **020 7486 4411** *Spanish Place* Tel: 020 7935 0943

Lister (The) Tel: **020 7730 3417** *Chelsea I* Tel: 020 7589 5487

Lister Stevenage (The) Tel: **01438 314333** Chaplain: John O'Neill Tel: 01438 314333

London Clinic Tel: **020 7935 4444** *Spanish Place* Tel: 020 7935 0943

Meadow House Hospice Tel: **020 8746 8000**

Mildmay Mission Hospital Tel: **020 7613 6300** Lead Chaplain: Sr Bernie Devine SP Tel: 020 7613 6307

SECTION 3

Mile End Tel: 020 7377 7000 *Mile End* Tel: 020 8980 1845
Moorfields Eye Tel: 020 7253 3411 *Moorfields* Tel: 020 7247 8390
Mount Vernon Tel: 01923 826111 Chaplain Tel: 01438 314333

National Hospital for Neurology & Neurosurgery Chaplains: Fr Peter Harries OP, Fr Serge Stasievich Tel: 020 3447 3007
North London Hospice Tel: 020 8343 8841 *Finchley North* Tel: 020 8446 0224
North London Nuffield Tel: 020 8366 2122 *Enfield* Tel: 020 8363 2569
North Middlesex Tel: 020 8887 2000 *Edmonton* Tel: 020 8803 6631
Northwick Park Tel: 020 8864 3232 Chaplain: Fr Agustin Paunon Tel: 020 8869 2113 (Sun-Thu 9-5pm) Email: LNWH-tr.Chaplaincy@nhs.net

Peace Hospice (The) Tel: 01923 330330 *Watford* Tel: 01923 224085
Portland Hospital for Women & Children Tel: 020 7580 4400 Chaplains: Fr Giles Pinnock, Fr Benedict Abuo, Fr Blaise Amadi CM Tel: 020 3312 1508
Potters Bar Tel: 01707 653286 *Potters Bar* Tel: 01707 654359
Princess Grace Tel: 020 7486 1234 Chaplains: Fr Giles Pinnock, Fr Benedict Abuo, Fr Blaise Amadi CM Tel: 020 3312 1508

Queen Elizabeth II Tel: 01438 314333 Chaplain: John O'Neill Tel: 01438 314333
Queen Victoria Memorial Tel: 01707 365291 *Welwyn Garden City (Digswell)* Tel: 01707 327 434

Royal Brompton Tel: 020 7352 8121 Chaplain: Fr Edward van den Bergh Tel: 020 7808 0900
Royal Free Tel: 020 7794 0500 Chaplains: Fr Andrew Brookes OP, Fr Neil Fergusson OP
Royal London (Whitechapel) Tel: 020 7377 7000 Chaplains: Fr Antigon Bahati AA, Fr Crescent Iloka Tel: 020 3594 2070
Royal Marsden Tel: 020 7352 8171 Chaplain: Fr Joseph McCullough Tel: 020 8979 1890
Royal National Orthopaedic Tel: 020 8954 2300 *Stanmore* Tel: 020 8954 1299
Royal National ENT and Eastman Dental Hospitals Chaplains: Fr Peter Harries OP, Fr Serge Stasievich Tel: 020 3447 3007

St Alban's City Tel: 01727 866122 Chaplains: Rev Anthony Curran (Deacon) , Theresa Taylor-Brookes Tel: 01923 217994
St Andrew's at Harrow Bowden House Clinic Tel: 020 8966 7000 *Harrow-on-the-Hill* Tel: 020 8422 2513
St Bartholomew's Tel: 020 7377 7000 Chaplain Fr Antigon Bahati AA, Tel: 020 3465 7220
St Bernard's Tel: 020 8967 5000 Chaplain: Awaiting appointment
St Charles Square Centre for Health and Wellbeing (Mental Health Units) Tel: 020 8969 2488
St Charles Square Palliative Care, Pembridge Hospice *St Charles Square* Tel: 020 8969 6844
St John and St Elizabeth & St John's Hospice Tel: 020 7806 4000
Chaplain: Fr Hugh MacKenzie Tel: 020 7806 4040
St Joseph's Hospice Tel: 020 8525 6000 Chaplain: Awaiting appointment
St Luke's Kenton Grange Hospice Tel: 020 8382 8000 *Kenton* Tel: 020 8204 3550
St Luke's Woodside Tel: 020 8219 1800 *Muswell Hill* Tel: 020 8883 5607
St Mark's (Northwick Park) Tel: 020 8864 3232 Chaplain: Fr Augustin Paunon Tel: 020 8869 2113 (Sun-Thu 9-5pm) E-mail: LNWH-tr.Chaplaincy@nhs.net

St Mary's Tel: 020 3312 1508 Chaplains: Fr Giles Pinnock, Fr Benedict Abuo, Fr Blaise Amadi CM, Veronica Burns
St Pancras Hospital Tel: 020 7530 3500 Chaplain: Awaiting appointment
St Pancras Hospital (Evergreen, Rochester & Oakwood Wards) Chaplain: Awaiting appointment
University College (UCLH) Chaplains: Fr Peter Harries OP, Fr Serge Stasievich, Sr Pauline Forde DC Tel: 020 3447 3007
University College on Westmoreland Street Chaplains: Fr Peter Harries OP, Fr Serge Stasievich Tel: 020 3447 3007
Watford General *Watford* Tel: 01923 244366 Chaplains: Rev Anthony Curran (Deacon), Theresa Taylor-Brookes
Wellington (The) Tel: 020 7586 5959 Chaplains: Fr Giles Pinnock, Fr Benedict Abuo, Fr Blaise Amadi CM Tel: 020 3312 1508
West Middlesex Tel: 020 8321 5447 Chaplain: Sr Clementina Nasimiyu
Western Eye Tel: 020 3312 1508 Chaplains: Fr Giles Pinnock, Fr Benedict Abuo, Fr Blaise Amadi CM, Veronica Burns
Whittington Tel: 020 7272 3070 Chaplain: Fr Oliver Ugwu Tel: 020 7288 5337
Willesden Community Tel: 020 8459 1292 *Willesden Green* Tel: 020 8451 4677

SPORT

Chaplain Mgr Vladimir Felzmann **Vaughan House, 46 Francis Street SW1P 1QN**
Tel: 07810 116508 Email: vladimirfelzmann@rcdow.org.uk

UNIVERSITIES AND INSTITUTES OF HIGHER EDUCATION

See page 122 in the sParish Directory

OTHER JURISDICTIONS

BISHOPRIC OF THE FORCES

Wellington House, St Omer Barracks, Thornhill Road, Aldershot GU11 2BG
Tel: 01252 348234
Bishop of the Forces Paul Mason (2016; 2018) Email: Bishoppaulmason@gmail.com
Wellington House, St Omer Barracks, Thornhill Road, Aldershot, Hants GU11 2BG
Vicar General Fr Nicholas Gosnell Email: stmichael.stgeorge@live.co.uk
Chancellor Rev (Sqn Ldr) Neil Galloway MBE RAF **Station Chaplain (RC), HIVE, Joint Service Special Signal Unit, RAF Digby, Ashby De La Launde, Lincolnshire LN4 3LH**
Email: Neil.galloway101@mod.gov.uk
Secretary Diane Restall Email: Diane.restall654@mod.gov.uk

EPARCHY OF THE HOLY FAMILY OF LONDON

The Eparchy serves Ukrainian and Belarusian Catholics, and also Slovakian Greek Catholics
Eparchial Curia, 22 Binney Street W1K 5BQ Tel: 020 7629 1073
Email: eparchy@ucc-gb.com Web: www.ucc-gb.com

Eparch Most Rev Kenneth Nowakowski
Vicar General Rt Rev Mykola Matwijiwskyj
Chancellor Very Rev David J Senyk
See *Ukrainian Cathedral* and *Belarusian Catholic Church* under Eastern Catholic Churches in the listing above.

ORDINARIATE OF OUR LADY OF WALSINGHAM

The Ordinariate of Our Lady of Walsingham, 24 Golden Square W1F 9JR
Tel: 020 7440 5750 Email: enquiries@ordinariate.org.uk Web: www.ordinariate.org.uk
Ordinariate Clergy in the Diocese: Mgr Keith Newton (Ordinary), Frs Mark Elliott-Smith, Antony Homer (see Other Priests in the Diocese, Section 4, for contact details)
Warwick Street Parish is in the care of the Ordinariate.

PERSONAL PRELATURE OF THE HOLY CROSS AND OPUS DEI

Prelate (resident in Rome) Mgr Fernando Ocáriz
(1) 4 Orme Court W2 4RL Tel: 020 7229 7574 (Queensway)
Other centres in the diocese:
(2) Pembridge House, 29 Pembridge Square W2 4DS Tel: 020 7221 0588 (Bayswater)
(3) Dawliffe Hall, 2 Chelsea Embankment SW3 4LG Tel: 020 7351 0719 (Chelsea 1)
(4) Lakefield, 41a Maresfield Gardens NW3 5RY Tel: 020 7794 5669 (Swiss Cottage)
(5) Netherhall House, Nutley Terrace NW3 5SA Tel: 020 7435 8888 (Swiss Cottage)
(6) Ashwell House, Shepherdess Walk N1 7NA Tel: 020 7490 3296 (Hoxton)
(7) Elmore, 8 Orme Court W2 4RL Tel: 020 7243 9411 (Queensway)
Priests: Bristow, Peter (7), Hayward, Paul (1), Hnylycia, Stefan (5), Marsh, Bernard (5), Morrish, Mgr Nicholas (1), Pereiro, James (7), Sheehan, Gerard (1), Soane, Andrew (1), Tintoré, Alvaro (5)
Opus Dei Information Office, 6 Orme Court W2 4RL Tel: 020 7221 9176
Email: info.uk@opusdei.org Web: www.opusdei.org.uk

SYRO-MALABAR EPARCHY OF GREAT BRITAIN

Eparch Bishop Joseph Srampickal (2016)
Eparchial Curia, St Alphonsa Cathedral, St Ignatius Square, Preston PR1 1TT
Tel: 01722 396065 Email: smcuria@gmail.com Web: www.eparchyofgreatbritain.org

LISTED BUILDINGS
in order of Parish, Building, Address, Local Authority and Grade

Cathedral, Most Precious Blood Victoria Street SW1P 1QW City of Westminster I

Allen Hall Seminary Chapel Beaufort Street SW3 5AA Kensington & Chelsea II
Ashford, St Michael Clarendon Road TW15 2QD Spelthorne II

Bayswater, St Mary of the Angels Church and Presbytery Moorhouse Road W2 5DJ, City of Westminster II*,

Bethnal Green, Our Lady of the Assumption Victoria Park Square E2 9PB Tower Hamlets II

Bishops Stortford, St Joseph & the English Martyrs Windhill CM23 2ND East Herts II
Bow, Our Lady Refuge of Sinners and St Catherine of Siena 177 Bow Road E3 2SG Tower Hamlets II
Brentford, St John the Evangelist Boston Park Road TW8 9JF Hounslow II
Brook Green, Holy Trinity Brook Green W6 7BL Hammersmith & Fulham II*
Buntingford, St Richard of Chichester Station Road SG9 9HT East Herts II

Chelsea, St Mary Cadogan Street SW3 2QR Kensington & Chelsea II*
Chelsea, Most Holy Redeemer & St Thomas More Cheyne Row SW3 5HS Kensington & Chelsea II
Chiswick, Our Lady of Grace & St Edward High Road W4 4PU Hounslow II
Chorleywood, St John Fisher Shire Lane WD3 5NH Three Rivers II
Clerkenwell, Ss Peter & Paul Amwell Street EC1R 1UL Islington II
Commercial Road, St Mary & St Michael Lukin Street E1 0AA Tower Hamlets II
Covent Garden, Corpus Christi Maiden Lane WC2E 7NB City of Westminster II

Ealing, Abbey Church of St Benedict Charlbury Grove W5 2DY Ealing II
Ely Place, St Etheldreda Holborn Circus EC1N 6RY Camden I

Farm Street, The Immaculate Conception Farm Street W1K 3AH City of Westminster II*
French Church, Notre Dame de France Leicester Place WC2H 7BX City of Westminster II*
Fulham, St Thomas of Canterbury Rylston Road SW6 7HW Hammersmith & Fulham **Church** II*, **Presbytery** II, **War Memorial & Adjacent Tomb** II
Fulham Road, Our Lady of Dolours Fulham Road SW10 9EL Kensington & Chelsea II

Golders Green, St Edward the Confessor Finchley Road NW11 7NE Barnet II

Hammersmith, Sacred Heart School Hammersmith Road W6 7DG Hammersmith & Fulham II*
Hampstead, St Mary Holly Place NW3 6QU Camden II*
Harpenden, Our Lady of Lourdes Kirkwick Avenue, Harpenden AL5 2QH St Albans II
Harrow on the Hill, Our Lady & St Thomas of Canterbury Roxborough Park HA1 3BE Harrow II
Hatfield, Marychurch, Salisbury Square, Old Hatfield AL9 5JD Welwyn Hatfield II
Haverstock Hill, St Dominic Southampton Road NW5 4LB Camden II*
Hertford, Immaculate Conception & St Joseph St John's Street SG14 1RX East Herts II
Highgate, St Joseph Highgate Hill N19 5NE Islington II*
Holloway, Sacred Heart of Jesus Eden Grove N7 8EN Islington II
Hoxton, St Monica Hoxton Square N1 6NT Hackney II

Islington, St John the Evangelist Duncan Terrace N1 8AL Islington II
Italian Church, St Peter Clerkenwell Road EC1R 5DL Camden II*

Kensal New Town, Our Lady of the Holy Souls Bosworth Road W10 5DJ Kensington & Chelsea II
Kensington 1, Our Lady of Victories Kensington High Street W8 6AF Kensington & Chelsea II
Kensington 2, Our Lady of Mt. Carmel & St Simon Stock Kensington Church Street W8 4BB Kensington & Chelsea II
Kensington 2, Assumption Convent Kensington Square W8 5HH Kensington & Chelsea II

SECTION 3

Kentish Town, Our Lady Help of Christians Lady Margaret Road NW5 2XT Camden II

Lincoln's Inn Fields, Ss Anselm & Cecilia Kingsway WC2A 3JA Camden II

Marylebone, Our Lady of the Rosary Old Marylebone Road NW1 5QT
City of Westminster II

Mile End, Guardian Angels Mile End Road E3 4QS Tower Hamlets II

Moorfields, St Mary Eldon Street EC2M 7LS City of London II

Notting Hill, St Francis of Assisi Pottery Lane W11 4NQ Kensington & Chelsea II*

Ogle Street, St Charles Borromeo Ogle Street W1W 6HS City of Westminster II

Old Hall Green, St Edmund of Canterbury and the English Martyrs 2 Farm Lane, Old Hall
Green, Ware SG11 1DT East Herts II

Oratory, Immaculate Heart of Mary Brompton Road SW7 2RP Kensington & Chelsea II*

Pinner, St Luke Love Lane HA5 3EX Harrow II

Polish Church, Our Lady of Czestochowa Devonia Road N1 8JJ Islington II

Poplar, St Mary & St Joseph Pekin Street E14 6EZ Tower Hamlets II

Queensway, Our Lady Queen of Heaven Inverness Place W2 3JF City of Westminster II

Rickmansworth, Our Lady Help of Christians, 5 Park Road, Rickmansworth WD3 1HU
Watford II

Ruislip South, St Gregory the Great (Church and Hall) Victoria Road HA4 0EG Hillingdon II

St John's Wood, Chapel of the Hospital of St John and St Elizabeth
Grove End Road NW8 9NH City of Westminster II

St John's Wood, Our Lady Lisson Grove NW8 8LA City of Westminster II

St John's Wood, St Edward's Convent Harewood Avenue NW1 6LD City of Westminster II*

St Margarets-on-Thames, St Margaret St Margaret's Road TW1 1RL Richmond II

Shepherds Bush, The Holy Ghost and St Stephen (Church and Presbytery)
Ashchurch Grove W12 9BU Hammersmith & Fulham II

Soho Square, St Patrick Soho Square W1D 4NR City of Westminster II *

Spanish Place, St James George Street W1U 3QY City of Westminster
(Church II*, Presbytery II)

Stamford Hill, St Ignatius High Road N15 6ND Haringey II

Stanmore, St William of York Du Cros Drive HA7 4TJ Harrow II

Sudbury, St George Harrow Road HA0 2QE Brent II

Swiss Cottage, St Thomas More Maresfield Gardens NW3 5SU Camden II

Tollington Park, St Mellitus Tollington Park N4 3AG Islington II

Tower Hill, English Martyrs Prescot Street E1 8BB Tower Hamlets II

Twickenham, St Mary's University Waldegrave Road TW1 4ST Richmond I

Ukrainian Cathedral, Holy Family Duke Street W1K 5BQ City of Westminster II

Underwood Road, St Anne Underwood Road E1 5AW Tower Hamlets II*

University Chaplaincy 111 Gower Street WC1E 6AR Camden II

Wapping, St Patrick Dundee Street E1W 2PH Tower Hamlets II

Ware, Chapel of St Edmund's College Old Hall Green SG11 1DS East Herts I

Warwick Street, Our Lady of the Assumption & St Gregory Golden Square W1F 9JR
City of Westminster II*
Watford, Holy Rood Market Street WD18 0PJ Watford I
Wealdstone, St Joseph Wealdstone High Road HA3 5EE Harrow II
Wembley I, St Joseph High Road, Wembley HA9 6AG Brent II
West Drayton, St Catherine's The Green, West Drayton UB7 7PJ Hillingdon II
Willesden, Our Lady of Willesden Acton Lane NW10 9AX Brent II

CENTRAL LONDON CHURCHES

CHURCHES NEAR RAILWAY TERMINALS

CANNON STREET; FENCHURCH STREET; LONDON BRIDGE:
The English Martyrs, 26 Prescot Street E1 8BB *(Tower Hill)*
CHARING CROSS: Corpus Christi, 1 Maiden Lane WC2E 7NB *(Covent Garden)*
EUSTON; KING'S CROSS (West side); ST PANCRAS & EUROSTAR TERMINAL: St
Aloysius, Phoenix Road NW1 1TA *off Eversholt Street (Somers Town)*
KING'S CROSS (East side): The Blessed Sacrament, 165 Copenhagen Street N1 0SR
off York Way (Copenhagen Street)
LIVERPOOL STREET: St Mary Moorfields, 4-5 Eldon Street EC2M 7LS *(Moorfields)*
LONDON BRIDGE: Our Lady of La Salette & St Joseph, 14 Melior Street SE1 3QP
Tel: 020 7407 1948 *(Southwark)*
MARYLEBONE; PADDINGTON: Our Lady of the Rosary, 211 Old Marylebone Road
NW1 5QT *(Marylebone)*
VICTORIA: Westminster Cathedral, Victoria Street SW1P 1QW *(Cathedral)*
WATERLOO: St Patrick's, 26 Cornwall Road SE1 8TW Tel: 020 7928 4818 *(Southwark)*

SECTION 3

CENTRAL LOCATIONS

Services in the Churches listed will be found in the Parish Directory section, under the entry indicated here in bold and italic.

CITY (I) St Mary Moorfields, Eldon Street EC2M 7LS *north of Finsbury Circus, near Liverpool Street Stn & Moorgate TfL Stn* Tel: 020 7247 8390 *(Moorfields)*

CITY (II) The English Martyrs, 26 Prescot Street E1 8BB *off Mansell Street, near Tower of London* Tel: 020 7488 4654 *(Tower Hill)*

CITY (III) St Joseph, Lamb's Buildings EC1Y 8LE *off Bunhill Row, near Barbican Centre* Tel: 020 7628 0326 *(Bunhill Row)*

HOLBORN CIRCUS St Etheldreda, Ely Place EC1N 6RY *off Charterhouse Street, beside Holborn Circus* Tel: 020 7405 1061 *(Ely Place)*

HOLBORN KINGSWAY St Anselm and St Cecilia, Kingsway WC2A 3JA *east side just south of Holborn TfL Stn* Tel: 020 7405 0376 *(Lincoln's Inn Fields)*

LEICESTER SQUARE Notre Dame de France, Leicester Place WC2H 7BX *north side of Leicester Square* Tel: 020 7437 9363 *(French Church)*

MAYFAIR Immaculate Conception, Farm Street W1K 3AH *entrance also in Mount Street, between South Audley Street and Berkeley Square* Tel: 020 7493 7811 *(Farm Street)*

PICCADILLY CIRCUS The Assumption, Warwick Street W1R 3PA *north of Piccadilly Circus* Tel: 020 7437 1525 *(Warwick Street)*

SOHO St Patrick, Soho Square W1D 4NR *in angle between Oxford Street and Charing Cross Road; near Tottenham Court Road TfL Stn* Tel: 020 7437 2010 *(Soho Square)*

STRAND Corpus Christi, 1 Maiden Lane WC2E 7NB *off Southampton Street on north side of the Strand; near Covent Garden* Tel: 020 7836 4700 *(Covent Garden)*

VICTORIA Westminster Cathedral, Ashley Place SW1P 1LT *south side of Victoria Street, close to Victoria Stn* Tel: 020 7798 9055 *(Cathedral)*

WEST END (I) St Charles Borromeo, Ogle Street W1W 6HS *off eastern end of New Cavendish Street* Tel: 020 7636 2883 *(Ogle Street)*

WEST END (II) St James, George Street W1U 3QY *eastern end, near junction with Marylebone High Street* Tel: 020 7935 0943 *(Spanish Place)*

WEST END (III) Our Lady of the Rosary, Old Marylebone Road NW1 5QT *south side of Old Marylebone Road, by junction with Marylebone Road* Tel: 020 7723 5101 *(Marylebone)*

WEST END (IV) Tyburn Convent, 8 Hyde Park Place W2 2LJ *in Bayswater Road, close to Marble Arch* Perpetual Exposition of the Blessed Sacrament Tel: 020 7723 7262 *(Marylebone)*

PARISHES AND LONDON POSTAL DISTRICTS

Parishes are listed according to the postal address of the church or presbytery; postal district numbers following the name of a parish indicate that parts of those districts are also within the parish. Districts south of the Thames (Southwark Diocese) or east of the Lea (Brentwood) are not included.

E1	Commercial Road		N10	Muswell Hill N2
E1	German Church		N11	New Southgate N13, N14, N20, N22
E1	Tower Hill EC3		N12	Finchley (North) N3, N20
E1	Underwood Road E2		N13	Palmers Green N14, N21
E1	Wapping		N14	Cockfosters N21
E2	Bethnal Green E1		N15	Stamford Hill N16, E5
E2	Lithuanian Church		N15	West Green N8, N17, N22
E3	Bow		N16	Stoke Newington N4
E3	Bow Common E14		N17	Tottenham
E3	Mile End E1		N19	Highgate N6, N8, NW5
E5	Clapton E8, N16		N19	Archway
E5	Clapton Park E9		N20	Whetstone N12
E9	Hackney E8		N22	Wood Green N8, N11, N17
E9	Homerton E5			
E14	Limehouse		NW1	Somers Town WC1
E14	Millwall		NW1	Marylebone W1, W2
E14	Poplar		NW1	Camden Town N1, N7
			NW2	Cricklewood NW3, NW11, NW6
EC1	Bunhill Row		NW2	Dollis Hill NW10
EC1	Clerkenwell WC1, N1		NW3	Hampstead
EC1	Ely Place EC4		NW3	Swiss Cottage NW6, NW8
EC1	Italian Church		NW4	Hendon NW7, NW9
EC2	Moorfields EC1, EC3, EC4, E1		NW5	Haverstock Hill NW3, NW1
			NW5	Kentish Town NW1, N7, N19
N1	Copenhagen Street		NW6	Kilburn NW2, NW8
N1	Hoxton E2, EC2, EC1		NW6	Kilburn West
N1	Islington EC1		NW7	Mill Hill
N1	Kingsland N5, N16, E8		NW8	St John's Wood NW1, W2, W9
N1	Polish Church 1		NW9	Grahame Park
N2	Finchley (East) N3, N6, N12, NW11		NW9	Hendon (West) NW4
N3	Finchley (Church End) N12, NW11, NW7		NW9	Kingsbury Green
N4	Manor House		NW10	Kensal Rise NW6
N4	Tollington Park N7, N19		NW10	Neasden
N5	Highbury N4		NW10	Stonebridge
N7	Holloway N5, N19		NW10	Willesden
N8	Stroud Green N4, N19		NW10	Willesden Green NW2, NW6
N9	Edmonton N13, N18, N21		NW11	Golders Green NW3, N2

SW1	Westminster Cathedral		W4	Chiswick W3, W5
SW1	Pimlico		W4	Grove Park
SW3	Chelsea 1 SW1		W5	Ealing W13
SW3	Chelsea 2 SW10		W5	Polish Church 3
SW6	Fulham		W6	Brook Green W12, W14
SW6	Parsons Green		W6	Hammersmith SW6
SW6	Stephendale Road		W7	Hanwell W13
SW7	Oratory SW1, SW3, W2, W8		W8	Kensington 1 SW5, W11, W14
SW10	Fulham Road SW3, SW5, SW7		W8	Kensington 2 SW5, SW7, W11
			W9	Harrow Road
W1	Farm Street SW1		W10	Kensal New Town W9
W1	Ogle Street WC1		W10	St Charles Square
W1	Soho Square EC1, WC2		W11	Notting Hill W10
W1	Spanish Place		W12	Polish Church 2
W1	Warwick Street SW1		W12	Shepherd's Bush W3, W6
W2	Bayswater W11		W12	White City
W2	Paddington		W13	Northfields W5, W7
W2	Queensway			
W3	Acton		WC2	French Church
W3	East Acton NW10, W10, W12		WC2	Lincoln's Inn Fields EC4, WC1
W3	West Acton W5		WC2	Covent Garden SW1

DIOCESAN STATISTICS

Priests of the Diocese

Working in the Diocese	181
Chaplains / Teaching	20
Further Studies	2
Others working outside the Diocese	20
Sabbatical	6
Retired / Supply	62
Total (includes 4 Bishops)	**295**

Priests of other Dioceses

From England & Wales (includes 2 Bishops)	7
From other dioceses (includes 1 Bishop)	21
Eastern Catholic (not all resident in diocese)	18
Ethnic Chaplains (excludes Deaons and those otherwise counted, e.g. Religious)	23
Ordinariate OLW	3
Prelature of Opus Dei	9
Total working in the diocese	**81**

Priests of Religious Congregations & Societies of Apostolic Life, including Chaplains

African Missions Society 2; Assumptionists: 6; Augustinians: 8; Augustinian Recollects: 1; Benedictines (English): 8; Benedictines (Olivetan): 1; Brothers of the Sacred Heart: 1; Carmelites (Discalced): 5; Carmelites of Mary Immaculate: 3; Chemin Neuf Community: 2; Claretians: 4; Columban Fathers: 3; Comboni Missionaries 4; Consolata Fathers: 2; Divine Providence, Sons of: 5; Divine Word Missionaries: 11; Dominicans: 8; Franciscans: 2; Institute of Charity: 1; Jesuits: 29; Lebanese Maronite: 4; Marian Fathers: 6; Marist Fathers: 3; Mill Hill Missionaries: 2; Missionary Community of Most Holy Providence: 2; Missionaries of Africa: 15; Missionaries of St Paul: 4; Montfort Missionaries: 2 Oblates of Mary Immaculate: 10; Oratorians: 10; Pallottine Fathers: 5; Passionists: 4; Salvatorians: 8; Scalabrini Fathers: 1; Servites: 5; Society of Divine Vocations: 2; Spiritans 15; Stigmatines: 1; Vincentians: 6

Total for Religious	**211**

Total for Other & Religious Priests	
(includes 3 Bishops)	**292**

Permanent Deacons	**39**
Parishes	**210**

PARISH STATISTICS 2021

In the Parish Directory each parish has its deanery noted thus: *Westminster Deanery*.
The following tables are compiled from the parish returns; where no figures are given,
returns have not been received..

Mass attendance for 2021 has been counted over the last two Sundays in September and
the first two Sundays of October, following a decision of the Bishops' Conference.

Parish	Sunday Mass	Baptisms	Receptions	Marriages
Barnet Deanery				
Barnet	397	15	0	1
Burnt Oak	375	22	0	2
Cricklewood	632	45	0	8
Edgware	551	20	0	3
Finchley Church End	340	8	0	1
Finchley East	280	13	0	2
Finchley North	320	25	3	0
Golders Green	304	22	0	1
Grahame Park	240	4	0	0
Hendon	257	21	3	4
Hendon West	98	0	0	0
Mill Hill	289	41	0	3
New Barnet	263	25	2	2
Whetstone	644	37	0	7
Brent Deanery				
Dollis Hill	510	18	0	2
Kensal Rise	129	16	0	0
Kingsbury Green	505	146	0	6
Neasden	193	9	0	1
Romanian Chaplaincy	500	92	0	1
Stonebridge	259	13	0	0
Wembley 1	1299	90	0	5
Wembley 2	210	39	0	4
Wembley 3	154	8	0	0
Willesden	463	24	0	1
Willesden Green	808	61	2	6

Parish	Sunday Mass	Baptisms	Receptions	Marriages
Camden Deanery				
Camden Town	232	5	0	3
Hampstead	285	31	2	8
Haverstock Hill	566	29	2	6
Kentish Town	194	8	1	1
Kilburn	838	116	0	8
Kilburn West	65	2	0	0
Somers Town	189	21	3	1
Swiss Cottage	211	16	0	1
Ealing Deanery				
Acton	197	32	0	4
Acton East				
Acton West	203	4	0	1
Ealing	703	62	3	21
Greenford	801	99	0	8
Hanwell	593	28	0	1
Northfields	339	33	0	2
Perivale	216	20	0	2
Polish Church 3				
Southall	1363	84	1	12
Enfield Deanery				
Cockfosters	306	11	3	3
Cuffley	52	5	0	0
Edmonton	632	24	1	6
Enfield	1028	75	0	5
New Southgate	865	30	3	3
Palmers Green	780	65	1	7
Ponders End	871	41	2	1
Potters Bar	452	35	7	2
Hackney Deanery				
Clapton	235	29	0	11
Clapton Park	153	8	0	0
Hackney	392	4	0	0
Homerton	278	20	0	1
Hoxton	251	24	0	3
Kingsland	451	17	0	0
Manor House	215	34	0	0
Stoke Newington	113	9	0	0

SECTION 3

Parish	Sunday Mass	Baptisms	Receptions	Marriages
Hammersmith & Fulham Deanery				
Brook Green	646	45	0	6
Fulham 1	366	26	0	3
Fulham 2 (Stephendale Road)	127	11	0	0
Hammersmith	330	27	1	2
Parsons Green	318	23	0	0
Polish Church 2				
Shepherds Bush	427	27	2	2
White City	336	31	0	3
Haringey Deanery				
Muswell Hill	527	25	0	0
Stamford Hill	1288	81	0	3
Stroud Green	313	17	0	4
Tottenham	406	42	0	4
West Green	313	12	0	3
Wood Green	631	23	0	3
Harrow Deanery				
Harrow-on-the-Hill	421	43	1	11
Harrow North	405	11	0	6
Harrow South and Northolt	461	13	0	2
Headstone Lane	385	36	1	3
Kenton	248	14	0	3
Pinner	297	7	0	1
Stanmore	166	11	0	0
Sudbury	792	41	0	4
Wealdstone & Harrow Weald	628	46	0	6
Hillingdon Deanery				
Eastcote	200	11	0	1
Harefield	137	17	0	1
Hayes	1415	127	0	11
Heathrow Airport				
Hillingdon	404	18	0	2
Northwood	240	12	0	3
Ruislip	744	69	0	6
Ruislip South	519	31	0	1
Uxbridge	508	62	1	6
West Drayton	459	12	0	0
Yeading	508	31	10	0

Parish	Sunday Mass	Baptisms	Receptions	Marriages
Hounslow Deanery				
Brentford	213	34	0	1
Chiswick	818	20	3	5
Cranford	290	30	0	2
Feltham	1251	117	8	7
Grove Park	19	0	0	0
Heston	227	27	1	7
Hounslow	1,839	108	0	19
Isleworth	460	36	0	0
Osterley	434	27	0	4
Islington Deanery				
Archway	243	11	1	2
Bunhill Row	72	3	1	0
Clerkenwell		8	1	1
Copenhagen Street	116	4	0	0
Highbury	329	30	0	0
Highgate	350	36	0	14
Holloway	197	11	2	3
Islington	204	35	0	4
Polish Church 1	698	18	0	5
Tollington Park	116	15	0	0
Kensington and Chelsea Deanery				
Chelsea 1	328	17	6	9
Chelsea 2	325	35	0	7
Fulham Road	73	25	1	2
Kensington 1	712	36	0	5
Kensington 2	529	20	1	4
Oratory	1,544	122	22	30
Lea Valley Deanery				
Bishop's Stortford	469	39	0	7
Buntingford	105	2	0	0
Cheshunt	179	8	0	0
Hertford	140	45	0	3
Hoddesdon	368	30	2	5
Old Hall Green and Puckeridge				
Waltham Cross	610	37	1	6
Ware	41	10	0	3

Parish	Sunday Mass	Baptisms	Receptions	Marriages
Marylebone Deanery				
Farm Street	407	64	2	47
Marylebone	261	17	2	1
Ogle Street	225	5	0	1
St John's Wood	529	22	2	7
Spanish Place	774	48	7	16
University	124	1	0	0
North Kensington Deanery				
Bayswater	311	39	0	4
Harrow Road	164	9	1	0
Kensal New Town	214	16	1	0
Lebanese Church (at Paddington)	70	22	0	0
Notting Hill	378	37	0	12
Paddington	49	2	2	0
Queensway	200	2	0	0
St Charles Square	218	14	0	1
St Albans Deanery				
Berkhamsted	182	24	0	2
Borehamwood	205	43	2	3
Borehamwood North				
Harpenden	410	33	0	7
Hemel Hempstead East	302	27	0	2
Hemel Hempstead West	250	42	1	7
London Colney	105	4	1	0
Radlett	63	2	0	1
Redbourn	144	17	0	0
St Albans	687	59	3	4
St Albans South	238	16	0	3
Shenley	36	2	0	0
Tring	105	2	0	1
Wheathampstead	70	2	0	0

Parish	Sunday Mass	Baptisms	Receptions	Marriages
Stevenage Deanery				
Baldock	246	9	0	3
Hatfield	133	3	0	0
Hatfield South	292	29	0	0
Hitchin	202	39	1	4
Knebworth	167	10	1	2
Letchworth	350	27	0	4
Royston	197	20	0	0
Stevenage Bedwell	482	59	2	2
Stevenage Old Town	149	11	0	0
Stevenage Shephall	347	44	2	5
Welwyn Garden City		12	0	4
Welwyn Garden City Digswell	117	5	0	0
Welwyn Garden City East	318	45	0	3
Tower Hamlets Deanery				
Bethnal Green	117	22	1	2
Bow	226	19	0	2
Bow Common	300	77	0	1
Commercial Road	283	43	0	6
German Church	39	3	0	0
Limehouse	66	5	0	0
Lithuanian Church	205	100	0	7
Mile End	195	6	0	1
Millwall	204	7	21	1
Poplar	238	29	1	1
Tower Hill	75	11	0	1
Underwood Road	40	2	0	0
Wapping	210	15	0	5
Upper Thames Deanery				
Ashford	372	41	1	7
Hampton Hill	265	22	0	0
Hampton-on-Thames	174	10	0	0
St Margarets-on-Thames	276	14	1	1
Shepperton	165	12	0	1
Staines-upon-Thames	495	51	0	0
Stanwell	125	11	0	0
Sunbury-on-Thames	281	51	2	3
Teddington	55	1	0	0
Twickenham	289	43	5	2
Whitton	458	24	0	0

SECTION 3

Parish	Sunday Mass	Baptisms	Receptions	Marriages
Watford Deanery				
Abbots Langley	147	39	4	0
Bushey & Oxhey	150	45	0	0
Carpenders Park	301	30	0	0
Chipperfield	81	6	0	0
Chorleywood	43	0	0	0
Croxley Green	67	16	0	2
Garston	420	33	1	1
Mill End and Maple Cross	83	3	0	1
Rickmansworth	178	23	0	12
Watford	758	50	0	2
Watford North	422	43	5	3
Westminster Deanery				
Cathedral	2601	37	7	10
Covent Garden	129	6	1	4
Ely Place	100	29	0	22
French Church	529	52	0	7
Italian Church	220	83	1	11
Lincoln's Inn Fields	144	26	0	2
Moorfields	58	7	0	11
Pimlico	433	62	5	4
Soho Square	433	10	2	4
Warwick Street				
TOTAL FOR DIOCESE	**74,423**	**5,556**	**191**	**687**

Notes to the Statistics:
(1) These figures do not include those which are reported separately to Rome, e.g. those for the Eastern Catholic Churches.
(2) Baptisms, Marriages and Receptions undertaken by Ethnic Chaplaincies and recorded in parish registers are included in the above statistics.
(3) Sunday Mass attendances for the majority of the Ethnic Chaplaincies are not recorded in these figures. However, the Sunday Mass Attendance overall total for the diocese does include those who are recorded as receiving Holy Communion at home (2,048 in 2021).

JUSTICE AND PEACE CONTACTS

Here are listed the Justice and Peace contacts for each parish. If the parish is not noted below, then please contact the Parish Priest with regard to Justice and Peace matters. Please contact **justiceandpeace@rcdow.org.uk** if the details below need updating.

Cathedral John Woodhouse

Acton Patricia Waugh
Acton West Maggie Beirne

Bunhill Row Martin Pendergast
Burnt Oak Eric Moor

Cockfosters Our Common Home Group
Copenhagen Street Sr Miriam Bruder
Croxley Green Fabian Hiscock

Edmonton Lauri Clarke
Enfield Tony Sheen, Rohini Colombage

Farm Street Lisa Fraser
Feltham Monique Carayol, Miriam McEneaney
Finchley East Daniel Servini

Hampstead Santana Luis
Hanwell Angie Harris
Harpenden Graham & Liz Ryan
Harrow North Elspeth Everitt
Hatfield Angela Madden
Haverstock Hill Keiran Proffer
Hayes Gael Somerville
Headstone Lane Dominic Rodriguez
Hemel Hempstead East David Toorawa
Hemel Hempstead West Camille Fidgett
Highgate Edmund Tierney
Hitchin Ann Milner
Hounslow Mary Pierre-Harvey

Kensal Rise Oonagh O'Toole, Teresa Elkins
Kensington I Dr David Ko
Kentish Town Margaret Harvey
Kilburn West Benedict Ogbol

London Colney Rev Anthony Curran (Deacon)

New Barnet Sheila Gallagher & Fausta Valentine
Northfields Anna Maria Dupelycz

Pimlico Judyann Masters
Pinner Elizabeth Thorp

Queensway Evelyn Lopez

Ruislip Robert Nunn

St Albans Anne Rose
St Albans South Mark James
Sudbury Anne Nemeth

Tollington Park Jo Bownas
Tring Michael Demidecki

University Chaplaincy Sr Carolyn Morrison

Ware Rev Adrian Cullen (Deacon)
Wealdstone Ellen Teague
West Green Mariantha Fomenky

SECTION 3

Section 4

ARCHBISHOPS OF WESTMINSTER SINCE THE RESTORATION OF THE HIERARCHY

Cardinal Nicholas Patrick Stephen Wiseman
Born Seville, Spain, 3 August 1802; ordained Priest 11 March 1825;
ordained as Vicar Apostolic Coadjutor for the Midland District 8 June 1840;
translated to the newly-erected Diocese of Westminster 29 September 1850;
created Cardinal 30 September 1850; died 1 February 1865.

Cardinal Henry Edward Manning
Born Totteridge House, London 15 July 1808; ordained Priest 16 June 1851;
ordained as Archbishop of Westminster 8 June 1865; created Cardinal 15 March 1875; died 14
January 1892.

Cardinal Herbert Vaughan
Born Gloucester 15 April 1832; ordained Priest 28 October 1854;
ordained as Bishop of Salford 28 October 1872; translated to Westminster 8 April 1892;
created Cardinal 16 January 1893; died 19 June 1903.

Cardinal Francis Alphonsus Bourne
Born Clapham, London 23 March 1861; ordained Priest 11 June 1884;
ordained as Bishop Coadjutor of Southwark 1 May 1896; succeeded as Bishop 9 April 1897;
translated to Westminster 11 September 1903; created Cardinal 27 November 1911; died 1
January 1935.

Cardinal Arthur Hinsley
Born Selby, Yorkshire 25 August 1865; ordained Priest 23 December 1893;
ordained Bishop of the titular see of Sebastopolis in Armenia 30 November 1926;
translated to the titular see of Sardis 9 January 1930; translated to Westminster 25 March
1935; created Cardinal 13 December 1937; died 17 March 1943.

Cardinal Bernard William Griffin
Born Birmingham 21 February 1899; ordained Priest 1 November 1924;
ordained as Auxiliary Bishop of Birmingham 30 June 1938; translated to Westminster 18
December 1943; created Cardinal 18 February 1946; died 20 August 1956.

Cardinal William Godfrey
Born Liverpool 25 September 1889; ordained Priest 1916; ordained Bishop as Apostolic
Delegate 21 December 1938; translated to Liverpool 14 November 1953; translated to
Westminster 3 December 1956; created Cardinal 15 December 1958; died 22 January 1963.

Cardinal John Carmel Heenan
Born Ilford, Essex 26 January 1905; ordained Priest 6 July 1930; ordained as Bishop of Leeds 12
March 1951; translated to Liverpool 17 May 1957; translated to Westminster 2 September
1963; created Cardinal 22 February 1965; died 7 November 1975.

Cardinal George Basil Hume OSB OM
Born Newcastle-upon-Tyne 2 March 1923; ordained Priest 23 July 1950; ordained as
Archbishop of Westminster 25 March 1976; created Cardinal 24 May 1976; died 17 June 1999.

Cardinal Cormac Murphy-O'Connor
Born Reading 24 August 1932; ordained Priest 28 October 1956; ordained as Bishop of
Arundel and Brighton 21 December 1977; translated to Westminster 22 March 2000; created
Cardinal 21 February 2001; retired 3 April 2009; died 1 September 2017.

Cardinal Vincent Nichols
Born Crosby, Liverpool 8 November 1945; ordained Priest 21 December 1969; ordained as
Auxiliary Bishop of Westminster 24 January 1992; translated to Birmingham 29 March 2000;
translated to Westminster 21 May 2009; created Cardinal 22 February 2014.

SECTION 4

PRIESTS OF THE DIOCESE

Seniority by year of ordination; **r** indicates a priest who is retired.

1950

1957
r Dwyer, Peter
r Young, Henry

1960

r Scholes, Canon Bernard
r Stanley, Cedric
1961
r Fullam, Seamus
r Ward, Brian
1962
r Reynolds, Brian
r Seeldrayers, Anthony
1963
r Crewe, Hilary
r Tuck, Michael
1964
r Wilby, William
1965
Garnett, Michael
r Sharratt, Aidan
r Wahle, Francis
1966
r Egan, Patrick
r Turner, Mgr Canon Henry
1967
r Boylan, Bernard
r Brockie, Canon Michael
r Egan, Mgr Canon Thomas
1968
r Murphy, Seamus
1969
Felzmann, Mgr Vladimir

Nichols, Cardinal Vincent

1970

r Ardagh-Walter, David
r Maher, Peter
r Sharp, Peter
1971
Convery, Antony
r Foley, Patrick
Leonard, Francis
Ryan, Joseph
1972
r McGinn, Mgr Canon Paul
r O'Brien, Eamonn
1973
r Doyle, Anthony
r Munnelly, Canon Michael
r O'Connor, Timothy
r Overton, Mgr James
1974
Browne, Canon Patrick
Carroll, Patrick
Davies, Jeremy
Ponsonby Meredyth McNicholas, James
Magnier, Daniel
r Sawyer, Guy
1975
r Carroll, Edward
Connor, Christopher
Deehan, John
r Mallon, James
r Plourde, Canon Robert

Rowland, Mgr Phelim
Wiley, John
r Williamson, David
Zsidi, Gabriel
1976
Barltrop, Mgr Keith
Barnes, David
Byrne, John
Shewring, John
1977
Azzopardi, Frans
Buckley, John
Cronin, Canon Daniel
Cunningham, John
r Forde, Thomas
r Kelly, David
Law, Philip
Psaila, Anthony
1978
Baxter, Anthony
r Kirinich, Roger
r Price, Richard
Winter, Marcus
1979
Doyle, Michael
Power, Dermot

1980

Brady, Mgr Vincent
Creak, Brian
r Gullan-Steel, Stuart
Kennedy, Jim
Liddle, Gladstone
McGuckin, Terence
Ryan, Canon Paschal
1981
Doe, Anthony
Donaghy, Michael
Johnston, Michael

r McLean, Colin
O'Boyle, Mgr Seamus
Press, Francis
Scurlock, Anthony
1982
O'Neill, Dermot
r Stewart, Michael
r Whooley, John
1983
Anwyll, Mark
Duffy, James
Paris, Anthony
Phipps, Canon Terence
Stoakes, Keith
Stokes, John
Webb, Christopher
1984
Dwyer, Canon Anthony
r Gray, John
Hayes, Mgr Martin
King, Canon Gerard
McPartlan, Mgr Paul
Quinn, Gerard
Smith, Brian
r White, John
1985
Healy, Bruno
Leathem, Michael
Letellier, Robert
McAleenan, Bishop Paul
Skehan, William
Sykes, Perry
1986
r Boland, John
Cahill, Charles
r Carter, Joseph

Curry, Mgr James
Dunkling, Reginald
Hudson, Bishop
Nicholas
McLoughlin, Patrick
Mannion, Michael

1987
Davies, Canon Colin
Loring, Ulick
Sherrington, Bishop
John

1988
Carroll, Sean
Conneely, Mgr John
Fernandes, Norbert
Hannigan, Neil
r Harrington, Thomas
r Hutton, Timothy
Sherbrooke, Canon
Alexander
r Stevens, Michael

1989
Booth, Michael
Middleton, Shaun
Thornton, Sean

1990
Andom, Ephrem
Grech, Saviour
Newby, Canon Peter
Piccolomini, Charis
Seasman, Terence
Wadsworth, Mgr
Andrew

1991
Garvey, James
James, Howard
Lowry, Mehall
Morris, Allen
Przyjalkowski, Voytek
Scott, Peter-Michael

1992
r Dean, Timothy

Dermody, John
O'Doherty, Michael
O'Leary, Canon John
Salvans, Albert

1993
O'Connell, Andrew
Tastard, Terry
Wagay, Gideon
Whitmore, Mgr Philip

1994
Antwi-Darkwah,
Francis
Campbell, David
r de Lord, Richard
Harris, Peter
Lennard, Canon
Shaun
McKenna, Dominic
Welsh, John

1995
Andrew, Richard
Cullinan, Michael
Evans, David
Fairhead, Mgr Jeremy
r Graham, Donald
Lyness, Peter
MacKenzie, Hugh
McGuire, Derek
r Marriott, Canon
Richard
Reader, Mgr Roger
Reynolds, Neil
Touw Tempelmans-
Plat, Dennis F P
Woodruff, Mark

1996
r Burgess, Robin
Coker, Stephen
r Colven, Christopher
Edgar, Timothy
Hasker, Stewart
Willis, Stephen
Wilson, Canon Stuart

Woollen, Nigel

1997
Griffin, Nigel
Griffiths, Brian
Robinson, Alan
Silva, Christopher
Vipers, Christopher
Wilson, Peter

1998
Arnold, Paul
Baptiste, Philip
Gosnell, Nicholas
Lee, Clive,
Leenane, Mark
Parsons, Richard
r Rimini, Kenneth
Wang, Stephen

1999
Heslin, Matthew
Jordan, Kevin
Miller, Philip
Nguyen, Simon
Ritaccio, Antonio
r Sammarco, Anthony

2000
r Ablewhite, John
Everson, Simon
McDermott, Paul
O'Boy, Michael
Pham, John Hai
Taylor, Canon Roger
r Usher, Thomas

2001
Barrow, David
r Burton, Edward
Church, Shaun
Shekelton, Peter
Trood, Jeremy

2002
Knights, Philip
Sarsfield, Denis
Skinner, Gerard

2003
Pachuta, Robert
Schofield, Nicholas
Vickers, Mark

2004
Braz, Cristiano
Dunne, Michael
Dyer-Perry, Philip
Master, Alexander
r Pellegrini, Anthony
Ruiz-Ortiz, F Javier

2005
Daley, Michael
Mulligan, Jim
Rouco Gutierrez,
Hector
Witoń, Sławomir

2006
Conesa, Agustin
Keeley, Stewart
McKenna, John

2007
Elliott, John D A
Nesbitt, Richard

2008
Arulananthem,
Thevakingsley
Moule, Kevin
Neal, James
Reilly, David

2009
Nicol, William

2010
O'Brien, Gerard
Seaton, Stuart

2011
Bagini, Paulo
Connick, Andrew
Gallagher, Andrew
Richardson, Paul
Stokes, Graham

2012

SECTION 4

Addison, Kim
Andreini, Lorenzo
Millico, Ivano
2013
Ardila, Oscar
Pantisano, Fortunato
Pinnock, Giles
Plunkett, Martin
Tate, Martin
Walker, Mark
2014
Hyett, Derek
Jaxa-Chamiec, Andrew
O'Mahony, Brian
Richards, Shaun
2015
r Bowder, Bill
Burke, David
Chiaha, Cyril
Humphreys, Daniel
Lucuy Claros, David
2016
de Lisle, Christian
Montgomery, Tom
Ryan, Damian
Scott, John
Thomas, Tony
Udo, Chinedu
2017
Albornoz Bolivar, Julio
Bowden, Andrew J
Jarmulowicz, Michael
McMahon, Brian
Maguire, Michael
Okoro, Joseph
Quito, Carlos
Warnaby, John
2018
Allsop, Patrick
Alvarado Gil, Allan
Dunglinson, Mark

Herrero Peña, Daniel
Michael, Rajiv
Pineda, Antonio
Stogdon, Jonathan
Tabor, John
2019
Davies, Julian
Woodley, Benjamin

2020

Balzanella, Alexander
Knight, David
Soriano, Axcel
2021
Johnstone, William
Joszko, Jakub
Mangatal, Timothy
Salvagnini, Marco
2022
Cherry, David
Daley, Daniel
Di Giuseppe, Matteo
Goodall, Jonathan
Guthrie, Michael

CLERGY OF THE DIOCESE

In alphabetical order, figures following each surname indicate year of birth and of ordination to the priesthood, a place name in brackets refers to an entry in the Parish Directory section. Unless stated otherwise, all email addresses are formed: **first name+surname@rcdow.org.uk**

ARCHBISHOP

Nichols (1945; 1969) PhL, MA, MEd, STL, His Eminence Cardinal Vincent; **Archbishop's House, Ambrosden Avenue SW1P 1QJ**

AUXILIARY BISHOPS

Hudson (1959; 1986) MA, PhB, STB, STL, KC*HS, Right Rev Nicholas; **Archbishop's House, Ambrosden Avenue SW1P 1QJ** Tel: 020 7931 6061
McAleenan (1951; 1985) Right Rev Paul; **Archbishop's House, Ambrosden Avenue SW1P 1QJ** Tel: 020 7931 6062
Sherrington (1958; 1987) MA, STL, Right Rev John; **Archbishop's House, Ambrosden Avenue SW1P 1QJ** Tel: 020 7798 9060

PRIESTS

Ablewhite (1943; 2000) John; **46 Tower Court, Ely CB7 4XS** Tel: 01353 968056
Addison (1975; 2012) Kim; **The Presbytery, Rant Meadow, Hemel Hempstead HP3 8PG** Tel: 01442 210610 (Hemel Hempstead East)
Albornoz Bolivar (1981; 2017) Julio; **52 Uxbridge Road W7 3SU** Tel: 020 8567 4056 (Hanwell)
Allsop (1952; 2018) MA, Patrick; **The Presbytery, Ballance Road E9 5SS** Tel: 020 8985 1495 (Homerton)
Alvarado Gil (1982; 2018) Allan; **Clergy House, Peter Avenue NW10 2DD** Tel: 020 8451 4677 (Willesden Green, Kensal Rise)
Andom (1960; 1990) STB, STL, MTh Ephrem; **The Catholic Presbytery, Commonwealth Avenue W12 7QR** Tel: 020 8743 8315 (White City, Eritrean Chaplaincy)
Andreini (1977; 2012) Lorenzo; **11 Harewood Avenue NW1 6LD** (Superior, Redemptoris Mater House of Formation)
Andrew (1953; 1995) MA, Richard; **41 Brook Green W6 7BL** Tel: 020 7603 3832 (Brook Green)
Antwi-Darkwah (1957; 1994) STB, DIP. COUNS, Francis A; **47 Vesta Avenue, St Albans AL1 2PE** Tel: 01727 850066 (St Albans South)
Anwyll (1957; 1983) DIP. S.Comm, STL, MA, Mark; **1 Colney Hatch Lane N10 1PN** Tel: 020 8883 5607 (Muswell Hill)
Ardagh-Walter (1941; 1970) BA, David; **Flat 22, St Joseph's House, Brook Green W6 7BW** Tel: 07399 881072
Ardila (1976; 2013) Oscar; **8 Ogle Street W1W 6HS** Tel: 020 7636 2883 (Ogle Street)
Arnold (1953; 1998) MA, Paul; **St Elizabeth's Centre, South End, Much Hadham SG10 6EW** Tel: 01279 842145 (Bishop's Stortford)

SECTION 4

Arulananthem (1973; 2008) BA, STB, MA, Thevakingsley; Flat 4, 8 Morpeth Terrace SW1P 1EQ (Sabbatical)

Azzopardi (1951; 1977) Frans; Flat 3 Copper Beeches, 6 Witham Road, Isleworth TW7 4AW Tel: 020 8568 6581

Bagini (1980; 2011) Paulo; 447 Victoria Road, South Ruislip HA4 0EG Tel: 020 8845 2186 (Ruislip South)

Balzanella (1990; 2020) STL, Alexander; Holy Rood Rectory, Exchange Road, Watford WD18 0PJ Tel: 01923 224085 (Watford)

Baptiste (1971; 1998) Eugene Philip; 110 Station Road, Hampton-on-Thames TW12 2AS (Hampton-on-Thames)

Barltrop (1947; 1976) MA, STL, Mgr Keith; The Presbytery, Moorhouse Road W2 5DJ Tel: 020 7229 0487 (Bayswater)

Barnes (1944; 1976) BA, LicPsych, David; 70 Lincoln's Inn Fields WC2A 3JA Tel: 020 7405 0376 (Lincoln's Inn Fields)

Barrow (1963; 2001) BSc, MSc, STB, David; 12 Womersley Road N8 9AE Tel: 020 8340 3394 (Stroud Green)

Baxter (1944; 1978) MA, BD, MPhil, PhD, Anthony; The Lodge, Ware Park, Ware SG12 0DS Tel: 01920 487287 (Chaplain, Ware Carmel)

Boland (1947; 1986) John; Nazareth House, 162 East End Road N2 0RU (Chaplain)

Booth (1954; 1989) STL, MFT, KHS, Michael; 5970 Rancho Mission Road #248, San Diego, CA 92108, USA Tel: 619 990 1288 Email: boothmichael1954@icloud.com

Bowden (1971; 2017) BD, PgDL, STB, Andrew; 14 Beaconsfield Road, St Albans AL1 3RB (St Albans)

Bowder (1946; 2015) Bill; 19, Northfield End, Henley-on-Thames RG9 2JQ Tel: 07985 772083

Boylan (1942; 1967) Bernard; St Vincent's Nursing Home, Wiltshire Lane, Eastcote HA5 2NB (Chaplain)

Brady (1956; 1980) KGCO, Mgr Vincent G; 28 Love Lane, Pinner HA5 3EX Tel: 020 8866 0098 (Pinner)

Braz (1974; 2004) STB, Cristiano; 52 Uxbridge Road W7 3SU (Hanwell)

Brockie (1942; 1967) JCL, Canon Michael; 7 St Joseph's Cottages, 38 Cadogan Street SW3 2QU Tel: 020 7581 0868

Browne (1948; 1974) Canon Patrick; 47 Cumberland Street SW1V 4LY Tel: 020 7834 6965 (Pimlico)

Buckley (1950; 1977) John; 35 Cricklewood Lane NW2 1HR Tel: 020 8452 2475 (Cricklewood)

Burgess (1949; 1996) MA, Robin; 20 Willowmead Close W5 1PT Tel: 020 8998 4710

Burke (1975; 2015) CF, MA, STB, David; 4 Le Marchant Drive, Corunna Estate, Ludgershall, Wilts SP11 9GW (on loan to the Bishopric of the Forces)

Burton (1940; 2001) AKC, Edward; 60 Harewood Court, Wilbury Road, Hove BN3 3GL Tel: 01273 774271

Byrne (1951; 1976) John; St Lawrence's Presbytery, The Green, Feltham TW13 4AF Tel: 020 8890 2367 / 07879 058732 (Feltham)

Cahill (1955; 1986) Charles; 1 King Edward's Road, Ware SG12 7EJ
Tel: 01920 462140 (Ware)
Campbell (1955; 1994) David; c/o Archbishop's House SW1P 1QJ
Carroll (1933; 1975) Edward; 2 Delmer Court, Aycliffe Road, Borehamwood WD6 4HS
Tel: 020 8236 9565
Carroll (1947;1974) Patrick; 4 Church Close, Cuffley, Herts EN6 4LS
Tel: 01707 873308 (Cuffley)
Carroll (1956; 1988) Sean; c/o Archbishop's House SW1P 1QJ (Sabbatical)
Carter (1936; 1986) Joseph; 16 Stevenson Park, Lurgan, Craigavon, Co. Armagh BT67 9DR
Cherry (1961; 2022) David; St Lawrence's Presbytery, The Green, Feltham TW13 4AF
Tel: 020 8890 2367 / 07939 553547 (Feltham)
Chiaha (1981; 2015) BA, BPhil, MBA, BD, STB, Cyril; 3 Station Road, Buntingford SG9 9HT
Tel: 01763 271471 (Buntingford, Old Hall Green and Puckeridge)
Church (1964; 2001) STB, MA, Shaun; 16 Wellington Road, Hampton Hill TW12 1JR
(Hampton Hill)
Coker (1953; 1996) Stephen P; 3 Wissen Drive, Letchworth Garden City SG6 1FT
Tel: 07976 400954
Colven (1945; 1996) BA, Christopher G; c/o Archbishop's House SW1P 1QJ
Conesa (1973; 2006) STB Agustin; c/o Archbishop's House SW1P 1QJ (Sabbatical)
Conneely (1956; 1988) JCL, Mgr John; 70 Lincoln's Inn Fields WC2A 3JA
Tel: 020 7405 0376 (Lincoln's Inn Fields, Judicial Vicar, Episcopal Vicar for Eastern Catholic
Churches)
Connick (1982; 2011) Andrew; The Presbytery, Dundee Street E1W 2PH
Tel: 020 7481 2202 (Wapping, University Chaplaincy, Vocations Director)
Connor (1947; 1975) MA, Christopher; 165 Arlington Road NW1 7EX
Tel: 07947 561414 (Camden Town, School Chaplain)
Convery (1947; 1971) Antony; Flat 5, Francis Court, Caddington Road NW2 1RP
Creak (1940; 1980) MA, PhD, Brian; 79 St Charles Square W10 6EB
Tel: 020 8968 3373 (St Charles Square, University Chaplaincy)
Crewe (1933; 1963) Hilary; Bramley House, Half Acre, Brentford TW8 8BH
Tel: 020 8847 4550 (Chaplain)
Cronin (1952; 1977) LLM, KCHS, Canon Daniel; 72 London Road, Knebworth SG3 6HB
Tel: 01438 813303 (Knebworth)
Cullinan (1957; 1995) MA, MASt, PhD, STD, Michael; 36 Chiswick Court, Moss Lane, Pinner
HA5 3AP Tel: 020 8429 3349 (Director of Maryvale Higher Institute of Religious Sciences,
Director of BDiv Programme, and Reader in Moral Theology, Maryvale Institute,
Birmingham)
Cunningham (1952; 1977) John; 204 High Street, Waltham Cross EN8 7DP
Tel: 01992 623156 (Waltham Cross)
Curry (1960; 1986) KCHS, STB, Mgr James; The Clergy House, 16 Abingdon Road W8 6AF
Tel: 020 7937 4778 (Kensington 1)

de Lisle (1988; 2016) MA, STB, Christian; The Rectory, Green Street, Sunbury-on-Thames
TW16 6QB Tel: 01932 783507 (Sunbury-on-Thames)

de Lord (1946; 1994) STB, Richard; 18 Rannoch Court, Adelaide Road, Surbiton, Surrey KT6 4TE Tel: 020 8251 2036

Daley (1986; 2022) Daniel; 247 High Road W4 4PU Tel: 020 8994 2877 (Chiswick, Grove Park)

Daley (1959; 2005) Michael; 22 Cortayne Road SW6 3QA Tel: 020 7736 1068 (Parsons Green)

Davies (1948; 1987) Canon Colin; 4 Thirleby Road, Burnt Oak, Edgware HA8 0HQ Tel: 020 8959 1971 (Burnt Oak)

Davies (1935; 1974) Jeremy Ponsonby Meredyth ; 27 High Street, Walsingham NR22 6BY

Davies (1960; 2019) Julian; The Presbytery, Esdaile Lane, Hoddesdon EN11 8DS Tel: 01992 440986 (Hoddesdon)

Dean (1942;1992) Timothy; 7 Hutchings Lodge, High Street, Rickmansworth WD3 1EY Tel 07812 248234

Deehan (1949; 1975) MA, STB, LSS, John; 4 Lady Margaret Road NW5 2XT Tel: 020 7485 4023 (Kentish Town)

Dermody (1955; 1992) BA, John P; Priests House, Gravel Hill N3 3RJ Tel: 020 8346 2459 (Finchley Church End)

Di Giuseppe (1982; 2022) Matteo; 5 Park Road, Rickmansworth WD3 1HU Tel: 01923 773387 (Rickmansworth, Chorleywood and Mill End)

Doe (1950; 1981) BA, MA, STL, PhD, Anthony; Allen Hall, 28 Beaufort Street SW3 5AA Tel: 020 7349 5600 (Seminary)

Donaghy (1956; 1981) BD, PGCE, Michael; Cathedral Clergy House, 42 Francis Street SW1P 1QW Tel: 020 7798 9048 (Cathedral)

Doyle (1948; 1973) Anthony; Edificio Norte, Apartamento 1.5 Derecho, Calle Jorge Guillén, 17, San Pedro de Alcántara, 29670, Provincia de Málaga, Spain

Doyle (1948; 1979) Michael; Allen Hall, 28 Beaufort Street SW3 5AA Tel: 020 7349 5610 (Seminary)

Duffy (1956; 1983) James; 38 Camborne Avenue W13 9QZ Tel: 020 8567 5421 (Northfields)

Dunglinson (1959; 2018) Mark; 165 Arlington Road NW1 7EX Tel: 020 7485 2727 (Camden Town)

Dunkling (1962; 1986) Reginald; 262 Kingston Road, Teddington TW11 9JQ Tel: 020 8977 2986 (Teddington)

Dunne (1964; 2004) BA, Michael; 247 High Road W4 4PU Tel: 020 8994 2877 (Chiswick, Grove Park)

Dwyer (1952; 1984) Canon Anthony; 1 Kirkwick Avenue, Harpenden AL5 2QH Tel: 01582 712245 (Harpenden)

Dwyer (1933; 1957) BA, MA, Peter; 31 Monks Horton Way, St Albans AL1 4HA Tel: 01727 761183

Dyer-Perry (1976; 2004) STB, Philip; The Presbytery, 59 Gresham Road, Staines TW18 2BD Tel: 01784 452381 (Staines-upon-Thames)

Edgar (1956; 1996) MA, BD, AKC, Timothy; 4 Egerton Gardens NW4 4BA Tel: 020 8202 0560 (Hendon & Hendon West)

Egan (1937; 1966) MA, MSc, Patrick; **Domino's Chapel, 24 Frank Lloyd Wright Drive, PO Box 466, Ann Arbor, Michigan 48106-0466 USA** Email: fatheregan@gmail.com

Egan (1942; 1967) BEd, Mgr Canon Thomas; **Flat 2, 90 Station Road N22 7SY**
Tel: 07803 891545

Elliott (1962; 2007) John D A; **377 Mile End Road E3 4QS** Tel: 020 8980 1845
Email: jdaelliott@rcdow.org.uk (Mile End)

Evans (1959; 1995) BSc, BTh, David; **3 King Edward's Road E9 7SF**
Tel: 020 8985 2496 (Hackney)

Everson (1958; 2000) BA, Simon; **Farleigh School, Red Rice, Andover SP11 7PW**
Tel: 01264 710747 (Headmaster/Chaplain)

Fairhead (1960; 1995) MA, BTh, Mgr Jeremy; **970 Harrow Road, Sudbury, Wembley HA0 2QE** Tel: 020 8904 2552 (Sudbury)

Felzmann (1939; 1969) KCHS, DD, MSc(Eng), Mgr Vladimir; **2b Eton Avenue, Heston TW5 0HB** Tel: 07810 116508 (Catholic Chaplain for Sport)

Fernandes (1964; 1988) BD, Norbert; **141 Woodhall Lane, Welwyn Garden City AL7 3TP**
Tel: 01707 323234 (Welwyn Garden City Parishes)

Foley (1944; 1971) Patrick; **c/o Archbishop's House SW1P 1QJ**
Email: pjtwomeyfoley@gmail.com

Forde (1943, 1977) Thomas; **Garden Flat, 6 Leighton Crescent NW5 2QY**

Fullam (1932; 1961) Seamus; **c/o Archbishop's House SW1P 1QJ**

Gallagher (1981; 2011) Andrew; **5 Park Road, Rickmansworth WD3 1HU**
Tel: 01923 773387 (Rickmansworth, Chorleywood and Mill End)

Garnett (1935; 1965) MA, PhL, Michael; **Santa Apolonia 146, Apartado 319, Cajamarca, Peru**
Tel: 0051 76 363517 Email: miguelgarnett@yahoo.es (On loan, Cajamarca)

Garvey (1962; 1991) James P; **84 Pixmore Way, Letchworth Garden City SG6 3TP**
Tel: 01462 683504 (Letchworth)

Goodall (1961; 2022) BMus, Jonathan; **1 Du Cros Drive, Stanmore HA7 4TJ** (Stanmore)

Gosnell (1958; 1998) VG, SRN, BTh, MA(Ed), MA, Nicholas; **Dean, St Michael and St George, The Cathedral Church of the Bishopric of the Forces, Queens Avenue, Aldershot GU11 2BY**
Tel: 01252 315042 (Vicar General of HM Forces)

Graham (1952; 1995) STB, Donald; **Flat 4 Francis Court, Caddington Road NW2 1RP**
Tel: 020 3609 6711

Gray (1944; 1984) John; **11 St Mary's Close, Longridge, Preston. PR3 3NW**
Tel: 07739 904456

Grech (1965; 1990) MTh, MA, Saviour; **4a Inverness Place W2 3JF**
Tel: 020 7229 8153 (Queensway)

Griffin (1948; 1997) MA, BSc, Dip Th, FRSA, Nigel; **The Presbytery, St Edmund's Lane, 213 Nelson Road, Whitton TW2 7BB** Tel: 020 8894 9923 (Whitton)

Griffiths (1960; 1997) Brian; **The Presbytery, Everglade Strand NW9 5PX**
Tel: 020 8205 6830 (Grahame Park)

Gullan-Steel (1943; 1980) BD, Stuart; **Flat 13, Oakhampton House, Eeast Barton Road, Great Barton, Suffolk IP31 2RF**

SECTION 4

Guthrie (1965; 2022) Michael; **970 Harrow Road, Sudbury, Wembley HA0 2QE**
Tel: 020 8904 2552 (Sudbury, Youth Chaplain)

Hannigan (1947; 1988) Neil; **131 Glenarm Road E5 0NB** Tel: 020 8525 1929 (Clapton Park)
Harrington (1935; 1988) Thomas; **St Joseph's, Carrowmore Meadows 32, Knock, Co Mayo,**
Ireland
Harris (1951; 1994) BEd, MTh, Peter; **St Joseph's, 3 Windhill, Bishop's Stortford CM23 2ND**
Tel: 01279 654063 (Bishop's Stortford)
Hasker (1961; 1996) BA, CQSW, Stewart P; **17 Kenninghall Road E5 8BS** (Clapton)
Hayes (1956; 1984) VG, BA, BD, KCHS, Mgr Martin; **St Mary's Rectory, Draycott Terrace**
SW3 2BG Tel: 020 7931 6076 (Vicar General)
Healy (1952; 1985) Bruno J; **Tan Y Cefn, Garnfadryn, Pwllheli, Gwynedd LL53 8TG**
(Eremitical Life)
Herrero Peña (1989; 2018) Daniel; **St Peter's Church, 15 Boniface Lane, Plymouth**
PL5 3AX (On loan, diocese of Plymouth)
Heslin (1960; 1999) BA, HDipEd, STB, Matthew; **160 Long Lane, Hillingdon UB10 0EH**
Tel: 01895 234577 (Hillingdon)
Humphreys (1974; 2015) Daniel; **45 London Road, Enfield EN2 6DS** Tel: 020 8363 2569
(Enfield)
Hutton (1944; 1988) TD, FCII, Timothy; **56 Pinner Court, Pinner Road, Pinner HA5 5RN**
Tel: 020 3417 2193
Hyett (1979; 2014) BA (Hons), STB, Derek; **The Presbytery, 100a Balls Pond Road N1 4AG**
Tel: 020 7254 4378 (Kingsland)

James (1959; 1991) MA, BSc, STB, Howard; **177 Bow Road E3 2SG**
Tel: 020 8980 3961 (Bow)
Jarmulowicz (1950; 2017) BSc, MB.BS, BDiv, FRCPath, KSG Michael; **Presbytery,**
337 Harrow Road W9 3RB Tel: 020 7286 2170 (Harrow Road, Paddington)
Jaxa-Chamiec (1976; 2014) Andrew; **c/o Archbishop's House SW1P 1QJ** (Sabbatical)
Johnston (1946; 1981) MTh, MA, BD, Dip Ed, Michael; **211 Old Marylebone Road NW1 5QT**
(Marylebone)
Johnstone (1970; 2021) BA, STB, BA, MLitt, William; **194 Knightsfield, Shoplands, Welwyn**
Garden City AL8 7RQ Tel: 01707 327434 (Welwyn Garden City Parishes)
Jordan (1968; 1999) Kevin; **54 Lodge Road NW8 8LA** Tel: 020 7286 3214
(St John's Wood)
Joszko (1991; 2021) Jakub; **39 Duncan Terrace N1 8AL**
Tel: 020 7226 3277 (Islington, Copenhagen Street)

Keeley (1961; 2006) Stewart; **Presbytery, 22 Hay Lane NW9 0NG**
Tel: 020 8204 2834 (Kingsbury Green)
Kelly (1953; 1977) David; **c/o Archbishop's House SW1P 1QJ**
Kennedy (1943; 1980) Jim; **c/o Archbishop's House SW1P 1QJ** (On loan)
King (1960; 1984) Canon Gerard; **60 Highbury Park N5 2XH**
Tel: 020 7226 0257 (Highbury)

Kirinich (1953; 1978) MA, STL, Roger; **c/o Archbishop's House SW1P 1QJ**
Knight (1974; 2020) David; **4 Thirleby Road, Burnt Oak, Edgware HA8 0HQ**
Tel: 020 8959 1971 (Burnt Oak)
Knights (1960; 2002) MA, BA, PhD, Philip; **6 Melbourn Road, Royston SG8 7DB (Royston)**

Law (1950; 1977) Philip; **19 Deanscroft, Knebworth SG3 6BD Tel: 01438 816444**
Leathem (1960; 1985) Michael; **c/o Archbishop's House SW1P 1QJ**
Lee (1959; 1998) Clive; **9 Henry Road N4 2LH Tel: 020 8802 9910 (Manor House)**
Leenane (1964; 1998) BSc (Surv), BA, Mark; **2 Witham Road, Osterley, Isleworth TW7 4AJ**
Tel: 020 8560 4737 (Osterley)
Lennard (1957; 1994) Canon Shaun; **243 Mutton Lane, Potters Bar EN6 2AT**
Tel: 01707 654359 (Potters Bar)
Leonard (1936; 1971) Francis; **4 Basils Road, Stevenage SG1 3PX Tel: 01438 364165**
Letellier (1953; 1985) MA, MLitt, PhD, SSL, STD, Robert Ignatius; **7 Parker Street, Cambridge**
CB1 1JL (Further Studies)
Liddle (1948; 1980) BA, Gladstone; **6 Athenaeum Road N20 9AE**
Tel: 020 8445 0838 (Whetstone)
Loring (1946; 1987) MA, BD, BACP, Ulick; **61 Pope's Grove, Twickenham TW1 4JZ**
Tel: 020 8892 4578 (Twickenham)
Lowry (1961; 1991) Mehall; **1 Stonard Road N13 4DJ Tel: 020 8886 9568 (Palmers Green)**
Lucuy Claros (1975; 2015) David; **729 High Road N17 8AG**
Tel: 020 8808 3554 (Tottenham)
Lyness (1948; 1995) MA, Peter; **St Edmund's College, Old Hall Green, Ware SG11 1DS**
Tel: 01920 821504 (Priest-in-Residence)

MacKenzie (1962; 1995) MSc, PhL, Hugh; **Cathedral Clergy House, 42 Francis Street**
SW1P 1QW Tel: 020 7798 9055 (Cathedral, Further Studies, Hospital Chaplain)
McDermott (1970; 2000) Paul; **700 Finchley Road NW11 7NE**
Tel: 020 8455 1300 (Golders Green)
McGinn (1947; 1972) Mgr Canon Paul; **80 Pembroke Road, Ruislip HA4 8NE**
Tel: 07900 887088
McGuckin (1950; 1980) BA, STL, MA, MLitt, BD, DD, Terence; **c/o Archbishop's House**
SW1P 1QJ
McGuire (1967; 1995) Derek; **22 Roxborough Park, Harrow-on-the-Hill HA1 3BE**
Tel: 020 8422 2513 (Harrow-on-the-Hill)
McKenna (1950;1994) Dominic; **291 Shenley Road, Borehamwood WD6 1TG**
Tel: 020 8953 1294 (Borehamwood & Borehamwood North)
McKenna (1966; 2006) BA, STB, MTh, John; **82 Union Street, Barnet EN5 4HZ**
Tel: 020 8449 3338 (Barnet)
McLean (1934; 1981) Colin; **Flat 2, 165 Arlington Road NW1 7EX**
Tel: 020 7267 0214
McLoughlin (1947; 1986) BD, CertSp, MBTI, MA(Sp), Patrick; **The Presbytery, Hardie Close**
NW10 0UH Tel: 020 8451 0367 (Neasden)

McMahon (1958; 2017) MSc, BA, FdA, Brian; 186 St Johns Road, Hemel Hempstead HP1 1NR Tel: 01442 391759 (Hemel Hempstead West)

McNicholas (1944; 1974) BD, MTh, James; Sacred Heart Presbytery, London Road, Bushey WD23 1BA Tel: 020 8950 2077 (Bushey and Oxhey)

McPartlan (1955; 1984) MA, STL, DPhil, Mgr Paul; Carl J Peter Professor of Systematic Theology and Ecumenism, School of Theology and Religious Studies, The Catholic University of America, Washington DC 20064 USA Tel: 001 202 319 6515 Email: mcpartlan@cua.edu

Magnier (1949; 1974) Daniel J; St Anne's Home, 77 Manor Road N16 5BL Tel: 020 8802 0362 (Chaplain)

Maguire (1978; 2017) BSc, BD, STB, PGDip, Michael; Cathedral Clergy House, 42 Francis Street SW1P 1QW Tel: 020 7798 9098 (Cathedral)

Maher (1944; 1970) Peter; 2 Holme Close, Marston Moretaine MK43 0PT Tel: 01234 635071 / 07957 626829

Mallon (1940; 1975) James; c/o Archbishop's House SW1P 1QJ Tel: 07850 640179

Mangatal (1992; 2021) Timothy; 45 London Road, Enfield EN2 6DS Tel: 020 8363 2569 (Enfield)

Mannion (1952; 1986) Michael; 7 Marford Road, Wheathampstead AL4 8AY (Redbourn and Wheathampstead)

Marriott (1938; 1995) MA, Richard; c/o Archbishop's House SW1P 1QJ

Master (1976; 2004) Alexander; Archbishop's House, Ambrosden Avenue SW1P 1QJ Tel: 020 7798 9041 (Private Secretary to the Cardinal Archbishop)

Michael (1978; 2018) Rajiv; 41 Brook Green W6 7BL Tel: 020 7603 3832 (Brook Green)

Middleton (1962; 1989) STB, MA, Shaun; St Mary's Rectory, Draycott Terrace SW3 2BG Tel: 020 7589 5487 (Chelsea 1)

Miller (1966; 1999) MA, PhD, STL, Philip; Newman House, 111 Gower Street WC1E 6AR Tel: 020 7387 6370 (University Chaplaincy)

Millico (1972; 2012) MA, MSc, BD (Hons), STB, Ivano; 5 Amwell Street EC1R 1UL (Clerkenwell)

Montgomery (1973; 2016) BTh, Tom; 32 Hallowell Road, Northwood HA6 1DW Tel: 01923 840736 (Northwood)

Morris (1956;1991) MA, BA, BD, Allen; 243 Jockey Road, Sutton Coldfield B73 5US Tel: 0121 354 1763 (on loan, Archdiocese of Birmingham)

Moule (1954; 2008) Kevin; 22 The Crosspath, Radlett WD7 8HN Tel: 01923 635541 (Radlett and Shenley, London Colney)

Mulligan (1946; 2005) MA, BTh, James; St Paul's House, 2 Merle Avenue, Harefield UB9 6DG Tel: 01895 822365 (Harefield)

Munnelly (1949; 1973) BD, MA, Canon Michael; 4 Merry Hill Road, Bushey WD23 1DY Tel: 07932 641624

Murphy (1937; 1968) Seamus; 3 Lut Na Greine, opp. St Michael's Church, Creeslough, Co. Donegal, Ireland

Neal (1962; 2008) MA, STL, James; The Presbytery, 17 Mandeville Road, Northolt UB5 5HE Tel: 020 8864 5455 (Harrow South and Northolt)

Nesbitt (1966; 2007) Richard; **The Catholic Presbytery, Commonwealth Avenue, White City W12 7QR Tel 020 8743 8334** (White City)
Newby (1958; 1990) MA, PhL, Canon Peter; **130 St Margarets Road, Twickenham TW1 1RL** Tel: 020 8892 3902 (St Margarets-on-Thames, Chaplain, St Mary's University)
Nguyen (1958; 1999) MA, STB, Simon Thang Duc; **c/o St Anne's Home, 77 Manor Road N16 5BL** Email: Simon_hue@yahoo.co.uk (Sabbatical)
Nicol (1952; 2009) William; **c/o Archbishop's House SW1P 1QJ** (on loan, Hexham and Newcastle)

O'Boy (1968; 2000) BA, PhD, STB, MTh, STL, Michael; **14 Beaconsfield Road, St Albans AL1 3RB** (St Albans)
O'Boyle (1957; 1981) STL, Mgr Séamus; **39 Duncan Terrace N1 8AL** Tel: 020 7226 3277 (Islington, Copenhagen Street, Episcopal Vicar for Safeguarding)
O'Brien (1948; 1972) Dip RE, Eamonn; **c/o Archbishop's House SW1P 1QJ**
O'Brien (1963; 2010) Gerard; **Holy Rood Rectory, Exchange Road, Watford WD18 0PJ** Tel: 01923 224085 (Watford)
O'Connell (1963; 1993) Andrew; **c/o Archbishop's House SW1P 1QJ** (Sabbatical)
O'Connor (1949; 1973) BA, Dip Rel Ed, Timothy; **c/o Archbishop's House SW1P 1QJ**
O'Doherty (1964; 1992) Michael; **216 Dollis Hill Lane NW2 6HE** Tel: 020 8452 6158 (Dollis Hill)
O'Leary (1967; 1992) STB, PhL, PhD, Canon John; **Allen Hall, 28 Beaufort Street SW3 5AA** Tel: 020 7349 5600 (Seminary)
O'Mahony (1978; 2014) BA (Hons), BD, STB, STL, Brian; **Cathedral Clergy House, 42 Francis Street SW1P 1QW Tel: 020 7798 9098** (Cathedral)
O'Neill (1959; 1982) Dermot; **51 Nether Street N12 7NN Tel: 020 8446 0224** (Finchley North)
Okoro (1977; 2017) Joseph; **Sacred Heart Church, Park Street, Berkhamsted HP4 1HX** Tel: 01442 863845 (Berkhamsted)
Overton (1941; 1973) MA, STL, BD, Mgr James; **St Anne's Home, 77 Manor Road N16 5BL** Tel: 07930 908264
Pachuta (1977; 2003) Robert; **5 Garratt Road, Edgware HA8 9AN** Tel: 020 8952 0663 (Edgware)
Pantisano (1979; 2013) Fortunato; **Parish House, 2 Tynemouth Street SW6 2QT** Tel: 020 7736 4864 (Fulham 2 Stephendale Road)
Paris (1956; 1983) Anthony B; **The Presbytery, 4 Lord's Croft, Amesbury, Wiltshire SP4 7EP** Tel: 01980 622177 (on loan, Diocese of Clifton)
Parsons (1946; 1998) BD, MTh, MPhil, STL, DProf, AKC, Richard; **22 Boniface Walk, Harrow HA3 6PU Tel: 020 8428 3260 / 020 8864 8021** (Headstone Lane)
Pellegrini (1940; 2004) KSG, KMCO, BA, BTh, ARCO, Anthony; **16 Elm Close, North Harrow HA2 7BT** Email: asjp@btopenworld.com
Pham (1966; 2000) STB, John Hai; **117 Bow Common Lane E3 4AU** Tel: 020 7987 3477 (Bow Common, Vietnamese Chaplaincy)
Phipps (1950; 1983) MA, STL, Canon Terence; **23 St John's Street, Hertford SG14 1RX** Tel: 01992 582109 (Hertford)

SECTION 4

Piccolomini (1955; 1990) Charis; c/o Archbishop's House SW1P 1QJ
Pineda (1970; 2018) STL, STB, MA, BSc, Antonio; St Joseph's, 3 Windhill, Bishop's Stortford CM23 2ND Tel: 01279 295990 (Bishop's Stortford)
Pinnock (1967; 2013) Giles; c/o Archbishop's House SW1P 1QJ Tel: 07880 086967 Email: giles.pinnock@nhs.net (Imperial College Trust Hospitals Chaplaincy, Cardinal's Healthcare Advisor)
Plourde (1944; 1975) Canon Robert; 4 Longland Drive N20 8HA
Plunkett (1968; 2013) Martin; 32 Field End Road, Eastcote, Pinner HA5 2QT
Tel: 020 8866 6581 (Eastcote)
Power (1952; 1979) BA, BD, STL, STD, Dermot; St Anne's Home, 77 Manor Road N16 5BL
Tel: 020 3078 9346
Press (1955; 1981) Francis; St Anne's Home, 77 Manor Road N16 5BL
Price (1947; 1978) Richard; The Presbytery, Moorhouse Road W2 5DJ
Tel: 07766 871130 (Bayswater)
Przyjalkowski (1955; 1991) BD MTh, Voytek; Church of St Helen, The Harebreaks, Watford WD24 6NJ Tel: 01923 223175 (Watford North)
Psaila (1952; 1977) Anthony; 112 Carlton Avenue East, Wembley HA9 8NB
Tel: 020 8904 6031 (Wembley 3)

Quinn (1955; 1984) BA, STL, Gerard; 44 Boston Park Road, Brentford TW8 9JF
Tel: 020 8560 1671 (Brentford)
Quito (1990; 2017) Carlos; 390b Northolt Road, South Harrow HA2 8EX
Tel: 020 8864 5455 (Harrow South and Northolt)

Reader (1958; 1995) KCHS, BA, Mgr Roger; Clergy House, Peter Avenue NW10 2DD
Tel: 020 8451 4677 (Willesden Green, Kensal Rise)
Reilly (1978; 2008) MA, David; 373 Bowes Road N11 1AA
Tel: 020 8368 1638 (New Southgate, Co-ordinator of School Chaplains)
Reynolds (1938; 1962) Brian; 186a St Johns Road, Hemel Hempstead HP1 1NR
Tel: 01442 382118
Reynolds (1959; 1995) BEd Hons, Neil Francis; The Presbytery, Vale Lane W3 0DY
Tel: 020 8992 1308 (Acton West)
Richards (1962; 2014) BTh, Shaun; 15 Wood Road, Shepperton TW17 0DH
Tel: 01932 563116 (Shepperton)
Richardson (1947; 2011) Paul; 86 Fitzalan Street SE11 6QU Tel: 020 7091 4299
Rimini (1942; 1998) MISM, AIM, Kenneth; c/o Archbishop's House SW1P 1QJ
Ritaccio (1970; 1999) STB, Antonio; Allen Hall, 28 Beaufort Street SW3 5AA
Tel: 020 7349 5600 (Seminary)
Robinson (1953; 1997) KHS, MA, Alan Ian P; Corpus Christi Presbytery, Maiden Lane WC2E 7NB Tel: 020 7836 4700 (Covent Garden)
Rouco Gutierrez (1972; 2005) BA, BATS, Hector; The Presbytery, 2a Salehurst Close, Kenton HA3 0UG Tel 020 8204 3550 (Kenton)
Rowland (1949; 1975) Mgr Phelim; 4 Holly Place NW3 6QU
Tel: 020 7435 6678 (Hampstead)

Ruiz-Ortiz (1976; 2004) STB, SSL, STD, F Javier; **Allen Hall, 28 Beaufort Street SW3 5AA**
Tel: **020 7349 5600** (Seminary)
Ryan (1981; 2016) Damian; **68 Hazlewood Crescent W10 5DJ** (Kensal New Town)
Ryan (1946; 1971) Joseph; **4 Vincent Road N15 3QH Tel: 020 8888 5518** (West Green)
Ryan (1955; 1980) Canon Paschal; **7 Cheyne Row SW3 5HS**
Tel: **020 7352 0777** (Chelsea 2)

Salvagnini (1988; 2021) Marco; **The Clergy House, 16 Abingdon Road W8 6AF**
Tel: **020 7937 4778** (Kensington 1)
Salvans (1959; 1992) MTh, Albert; **c/o Archbishop's House SW1P 1QJ** (Missions)
Sammarco (1940: 1999) Anthony; **Flat 1, Croft Court, Brickwall Lane, Ruislip HA4 8JT**
Tel: **01895 638771**
Sarsfield (1962; 2002) STB, Denis; **Holy Trinity Church, London Road, Baldock SG7 6LQ**
Tel: **01462 893127** (Baldock)
Sawyer (1946; 1974) Guy; **Loreto, 47 Willow Grove, Ruislip Manor**
HA4 6DG Tel: 07944 038146
Schofield (1975; 2003) MA, STB, FSA, FRHistS, Nicholas; **The Presbytery, Osborn Road,**
Uxbridge UB8 1UE Tel: 01895 233193 (Uxbridge, Archivist Tel: **020 7938 3580**)
Scholes (1936; 1960) MA, Canon Bernard; **186b St Johns Road, Hemel Hempstead HP1 1NR**
Tel: **01442 385118**
Scott (1952; 2016) John; **Cathedral Clergy House, 42 Francis Street SW1P 1QW**
Tel: **020 7931 6041** (Cathedral)
Scott (1965; 1991) STB, Peter-Michael; **279 High Road N2 8HG Tel: 020 8883 4234**
(Finchley East)
Scurlock (1951;1981) Anthony John; **c/o Archbishop's House SW1P 1QJ**
Seasman (1990) MA, BACP, Terence; **c/o Archbishop's House SW1P 1QJ**
Seaton (1975; 2010) BA, MA, Stuart; **9 Meadow View, Harrow-on-the-Hill HA1 3DN**
Tel: **020 8422 1862** (Harrow-on-the-Hill, Catholic Chaplain, Harrow School)
Seeldrayers (1937; 1962) Anthony; **8 Burroughs Gardens NW4 4AU**
Tel: **07811 221787**
Sharp (1938; 1970) Peter; **23 The Homestead, Henry Street, Lytham, Lancs FY8 5LJ**
Tel: **01253 730803**
Sharratt (1940; 1965) BA, STL, Aidan; **St Anne's Home, 77 Manor Road N16 5BL**
Tel: **020 8809 3161**
Shekelton (1970; 2001) Peter; **42 Langdale Gardens, Perivale, Greenford UB6 8DQ**
Tel: **020 8997 3164** (Perivale)
Sherbrooke (1957; 1988) Canon Alexander; **21a Soho Square W1D 4NR**
Tel: **020 7437 2010** (Soho Square)
Shewring (1941; 1976) John; **192 Nags Head Road, Enfield EN3 7AR**
Tel: **020 8804 2149** (Ponders End)
Silva (1949; 1997) BSc, Christopher; **297 Westferry Road E14 3RS**
Tel: **020 7987 5187** (Millwall)
Skehan (1960;1985) William; **2 Lukin Street E1 0AA**
Tel: **020 7790 5911** (Commercial Road)

Skinner (1970; 2002) GRSM, LRAM, PhB, STL, Gerard; **St Francis of Assisi Church,
The Presbytery, Pottery Lane W11 4NQ** Tel: 020 7727 7968 (Notting Hill)
Smith (1958; 1984) SLitDip, Brian; **20 The Green, West Drayton UB7 7PJ**
Tel: 01895 442777 (West Drayton)
Soriano (1991; 2020) Axcel; **80 Imperial Close, Harrow HA2 7LW**
Tel: 020 8868 7531 (Harrow North)
Stanley (1935; 1960) MBE, Cedric; **1 Dunster Close, Harefield UB9 6BS**
Tel: 01895 824229
Stevens (1935; 1988) Michael; **5 Layfield Road, Newcastle-upon-Tyne NE3 5AA**
Tel: 01912 368101 Email: micste68@msn.com
Stewart (1935; 1982) Michael; **50 Bull Stag Green, Hatfield AL9 5DE**
Tel: 01707 264213
Stoakes (1958; 1983) Keith; **Clergy House, 9 Pekin Street E14 6EZ**
Tel: 020 7987 4523 (Poplar, Limehouse)
Stogdon (1988; 2018) Jonathan; **The Presbytery, 1 Nicoll Road NW10 9AX**
Tel: 020 8965 4935 (Willesden)
Stokes (1972; 2011) Graham; **80 Imperial Close, Harrow HA2 7LW**
Tel: 020 8868 7531 (Harrow North)
Stokes (1945; 1983) John; **c/o Archbishop's House SW1P 1QJ**
Sykes (1959; 1985) Perry; **22 Bradley Road N22 7SZ** Tel: 020 8888 2390 (Wood Green)

Tabor (1973; 2018) BD, John; **32 High Street, Cranford, Hounslow TW5 9RG**
Tel: 020 8759 9136 (Cranford)
Tastard (1947; 1993) MA, PhD, Terry; **38 Mulberry Court, Bedford Road N2 9DZ**
Tel: 020 3224 3039
Tate (1954; 2013) Martin; **24 Bouverie Road N16 0AJ**
Tel: 020 8800 5250 (Stoke Newington)
Taylor (1951; 2000) MA, STB, MA, Canon Roger; **22 George Street W1U 3QY**
Tel: 020 7935 0943 (Spanish Place, Vocations)
Thomas (1972; 2016) Tony; **The Presbytery, Brentfield Road NW10 8ER**
Tel: 020 8965 3313 (Stonebridge)
Thornton (1964; 1989) Sean; **51 Langdon Street, Tring HP23 6BA** Tel: 01442 823161 (Tring)
Touw Tempelmans-Plat (1949; 1995) MA, Dennis F P; **60 Rylston Road SW6 7HW**
Tel: 020 7385 4040 (Fulham 1)
Trood (1961; 2001) MA, STB, MCL, JCL, ACA Jeremy; **20 Phoenix Road NW1 1TA**
Tel: 020 7387 1971 (Somers Town, Chancellor)
Tuck (1939; 1963) Michael; **The Sanctuary, 13 The Ridings, Sunbury on Thames TW16 6NU**
Tel: 07801 790586
Turner (1941; 1966) Mgr Canon Henry; **8 Rothamsted Court, Harpenden AL5 2BZ**
Tel: 01582 965207 (Ecumenical Chaplaincy at St Albans Abbey)

Udo (1982; 2016) BD, STB, Chinedu; **The Presbytery, St Mellitus Church, Tollington Park N4
3AG** (Tollington Park)
Usher (1942; 2000) BA, Thomas; **c/o Archbishop's House SW1P 1QJ**

Vickers (1966; 2003) BA, STB, Mark; **44 Ashchurch Grove W12 9BU**
Tel: 020 8743 5196 (Shepherds Bush)
Vipers (1963; 1997) BA, Christopher J; **4/5 Eldon St EC2M 7LS Tel: 020 7247 8390**
(Bunhill Row, Moorfields, Director of Agency for Evangelisation)

Wadsworth (1961; 1990) MA, GTCL, LTCL, LRAM, Mgr Andrew; **ICEL Secretariat, 1100**
Connecticut Avenue, NW, Suite 710, Washington DC 20036-4101, USA
(Executive Director, ICEL)
Wagay (1953; 1993) BA, MA, STB, Gideon; **62 Eden Grove N7 8EN**
Tel: 020 7607 3594 (Holloway)
Wahle (1929; 1965) STL, BSc, Francis; **17 Chiltern Court, Baker Street NW1 5TD**
Tel: 020 7487 5956 Email: franciswahle@yahoo.com
Walker (1985; 2013) Mark; **85 Old Oak Common Lane W3 7DD Tel: 020 8743 5732**
(Acton East)
Wang (1966; 1998) MA, PhL, STL, PhD, Stephen; **Via di Monserrato 45, 00186 Rome, Italy**
Tel: +39 06 6868 546 (Venerable English College)
Ward (1937; 1961) Brian; **2 Evergreen Park, Tanderagee, Binion, Clonmany,**
Co. Donegal, Ireland Tel: 0035 37493 78887
Warnaby (1960; 2017) MA, BD, John; **St Joseph's Church, Oxhey Drive, South Oxhey,**
Watford WD19 7SW Tel: 020 8428 0088 (Carpenders Park and South Oxhey)
Webb (1953; 1983) Christopher; **c/o Archbishop's House SW1P 1QJ** (On loan)
Welsh (1946; 1994) John; **St Raphael's House, Morrison Road, Yeading UB4 9JP**
Tel: 020 8845 1919 (Yeading)
White (1952; 1984) John; **32 Old Brewery Close, Aylesbury HP21 7SH**
Tel: 01296 481776
Whitmore (1959; 1993) MA, DPhil, STL, Mgr Philip; **22 George Street W1U 3QY**
Tel: 020 7935 0943 (Spanish Place)
Whooley (1942; 1982) John; **24 The Crosspath, Radlett WD7 8HN**
Wilby (1939; 1964) William; **Flat 12, St Joseph's House, 42 Brook Green W6 7BW**
Wiley (1947; 1975) KJSJ, MA, BD, John; **185 Baldwins Lane, Croxley Green, Rickmansworth**
WD3 3LL Tel: 01923 231969 (Croxley Green)
Williamson (1945; 1975) STD, David; **Nazareth House, 162 East End Road N2 0RU**
Willis (1965; 1996) BA, Stephen A; **The Presbytery, 1 Nicoll Road NW10 9AX**
Tel: 020 8965 4935 (Willesden)
Wilson (1965; 1997) BA, HDipEd, Peter J; **79 St Charles Square W10 6EB**
Tel: 020 8969 6844 (St Charles Square)
Wilson (1947; 1996) MA, BSc, Canon Stuart M P; **4/5 Eldon St EC2M 7LS Tel: 020 7247**
8390 (Bunhill Row, Moorfields)
Winter (1948; 1978) Marcus; **The Lodge, 87 St Charles Square W10 6EA**
Tel: 020 3673 9540 (Notting Hill Carmel Chaplain)
Witoń (1975; 2005) STB, Sławomir; **Cathedral Clergy House, 42 Francis Street**
SW1P 1QW Tel: 020 7798 9374 (Cathedral)
Woodley (1973; 2019) BMus, ARCM, STL, Benjamin; **54 Lodge Road NW8 8LA**
Tel: 020 7286 3214 (St John's Wood)

SECTION 4

Woodruff (1959; 1995) BA, Mark; **Sainsbury Family Charitable Trusts, The Peak,**
5 Wilton Road SW1V 1AP Tel: 020 7410 0330
(English Liturgy Chaplain, Ukrainian Cathedral)
Woollen (1966; 1996) Nigel; **St Joseph's Presbytery, Bedwell Crescent, Stevenage SG1 1NJ**
Tel: 01438 351243 (Stevenage Parishes)

Young (1932; 1957) MA, Henry; **63 Heathfield Court, Heathfield Terrace W4 4LS**

Zsidi (1951; 1975) Gabriel; **c/o Archbishop's House SW1P 1QJ**

PERMANENT DEACONS

Abrahams (1960; 2017) Reginald; **160 Long Lane, Hillingdon UB10 0EH**
Tel: 01885 234577 Email: reginaldabrahams@rcdow.org.uk (Hillingdon)

Agule (1966; 2012) BSc (Acct), BA (Theol), MBA, FCA, Nick; **20 The Green, West Drayton UB7 7PJ** Tel: 01895 442777 Email: nickagule@rcdow.org.uk
(West Drayton and Yiewsley)

Barter (1956; 2017) Tony; **22 The Crosspath, Radlett WD7 8HN** Tel: 01923 635541
Email: tonybarter@rcdow.org.uk (Radlett, Shenley and London Colney)

Burke (1953; 2018) MTh, BD (Hons), PGCE, NPQH, FdA, QTS, Alex; **Ealing Abbey Parish Office, 2 Marchwood Crescent W5 2DX** Tel: 020 8862 2162
Email: alexburke@rcdow.org.uk (Ealing)

Chappell (1973; 2020) BA, MA, MSc, MPhil, MLitt, PhD, PGCE Jonathan; Permanent Diaconate, Vaughan House, 46 Francis Street SW1P 1QN
Email: jonathanchappell@rcdow.org.uk

Chelvarayan (1968; 2022) Eric Jeevaraj; **22 Roxborough Park, Harrow-on-the-Hill HA1 3BE** Email: ericchelvarayan@rcdow.org.uk (Harrow-on-the-Hill)

Clark (1945; 2008) BA, BD, LicPhil, Anthony; **700 Finchley Road NW11 7NE**
Tel: 020 8455 1300 Email:anthonyclark@rcdow.org.uk (Golders Green)

Coleman (1965; 2019) MA, LGSM, FRCO Ian; **373 Bowes Road N11 1AA**
Tel: 020 8368 1638 Email: iancoleman@rcdow.org.uk (New Southgate)

Cross (1975; 2014) FdA, BSc(Econ), MA, ACIS, Justin; **Email: justincross@rcdow.org.uk**
(diocese of East Anglia)

Cullen (1957; 2009) MBA, BSc (Hons), Adrian; **1 King Edward's Road, Ware SG12 7EJ**
Tel: 01920 462140 Email: adriancullen@rcdow.org.uk (Ware)

Curran (1971; 2012) MA, BA (Hons), PhB, Dip Coun, Anthony; **22 The Crosspath, Radlett WD7 8HN** Tel: 01923 635541 Email: anthonycurran@rcdow.org.uk (Radlett and Shenley, London Colney)

Day (1964; 2021) Brendan; **14 Beaconsfield Road, St Albans AL1 3RB**
Tel: 01727 853585 Email: brendanday@rcdow.org.uk (St Albans)

Dyckhoff (1941; 2006) OBE, FIH, FRSPH, Neville; **Holy Rood Rectory, Exchange Road, Watford WD18 0PJ** Tel: 01923 224085 Email: nevilledyckhoff@rcdow.org.uk (Watford)

Edwards (1965; 2014) FdA, BEng, PgDip, CEng, MIET, Ian; **Ealing Abbey Parish Office, 2 Marchwood Crescent, Ealing, London W5 2DX** Tel: 020 8862 2162
Email: ianedwards@rcdow.org.uk (Ealing)

Estorninho (1960; 2019) BEd, FdA, Joseph; **130 St Margarets Road, Twickenham TW1 1RL**
Tel: 020 8892 3902 Email: josephestorninho@rcdow.org.uk (St Margarets-on-Thames)

Goodall (1957; 2019) FdA, Andrew; **38 Camborne Avenue W13 9QZ** Tel: 020 8567 5421
Email: andrewgoodall@rcdow.org.uk (Northfields)

Hemming (1962; 1997) BA, MA, MPhil, PhD, Laurence; **5 Westmoreland Place SW1V 4AB**
Tel: 020 7828 2737 Email: laurencehemming@rcdow.org.uk

Hopkins (1950; 2011) FD, BA (Hons), Donal; **243 Mutton Lane, Potters Bar EN6 2AT**
Tel: 01707 654359 Email: donhopkins@rcdow.org.uk (Potters Bar)

Izundu (1952; 2018) BA, BSc (Hons), MSC, PhD, MRTPI, Kingsley; **17 Kenninghall Road E5 8BS** Tel: 020 8985 2178 Email: kingsleyizundu@rcdow.org.uk (Clapton)

Joiris de Caussin (1971; 2017) Stéphane; Email: stephanejoirisdecaussin@rcdow.org.uk (Kensington and Chelsea Deanery)

Jones (1967; 2022) Peter; **45 London Road, Enfield EN2 6DS** Email: peterjones@rcdow.org.uk (Enfield)

Khokhar (1968; 2014) FD (Telecom Engineer) Stephen; St Anselm's Rectory, The Green, Southall UB2 4BE Email: stephenkhokar@rcdow.org.uk (Southall)

Lawrence (1962; 2022) David; **700 Finchley Road NW11 7NE** Email: davidlawrence@rcdow.org.uk (Golders Green)

Leon (1968; 2022) Rolly; St Lawrence's Presbytery, The Green, Feltham TW13 4AF Tel: 020 8990 2367 Email: rollyleon@rcdow.org.uk (Feltham)

Lo (1966; 2019) HDFCT, FdA, LLB, LLM, William; Our Lady of the Assumption and St Gregory, Warwick Street W1B 5LZ Tel: 020 7734 9313 Email: williamlo@rcdow.org.uk / william.lo@justice.gov.uk (Warwick Street, HM Prison The Mount)

Lynch (1980; 2017) BSc (Hons), MA, PGdip, PGcert (Edu), QTS, Liam; Church of St Helen, The Harebreaks, Watford WD24 6NJ Tel: 01923 223175 Email: liamlynch@rcdow.org.uk (Watford North)

MacPherson (1940; 1992) MA, DMin, KHS, Duncan; **16 Ormond Drive, Hampton TW12 2TN** Tel: 020 8274 0210 Email: duncanmacpherson@rcdow.org.uk

Macken (1962; 2018) FdA, Colin; St Lawrence's, 9 The Green, Feltham TW13 4AF Tel: 020 8890 2367 Email: colinmacken@rcdow.org.uk (Feltham)

Nunn (1956; 2008) Gordon; Email: gordonnunn@rcdow.org.uk (diocese of Northampton)

O'Connor (1963; 2020) BA, PGCE, FDA, Paul; **3 Station Road, Buntingford SG9 9HT** Tel: 01763 271471 Email: pauloconnor@rcdow.org.uk (Buntingford)

O'Reilly (1970; 2019) FdA, Wayne; **60 Rylston Road SW6 7HW** Tel: 020 7385 4040 Email: waynoreilly@rcdow.org.uk (Fulham I, p/t Canary Wharf Chaplaincy)

Pereira (1963; 2007) BA (Hons) QTS, FCoT, Tito; Our Lady of Lourdes, 5 Berrymead Gardens W3 8AA Tel: 020 8992 2014 Email: titopereira@rcdow.org.uk (Acton)

Pickard (1945; 2009) Steve; Email: stevepickard@rcdow.org.uk (Retired)

Quinn (1972; 2017) FdA, Paul; Our Lady & St Michael, Crown Rise, Garston, Watford WD25 0NE Tel: 01923 673239 Email: paulquinn@rcdow.org.uk (Garston)

Safo-Poku (1955; 2020) BSc, RSPH, Andrew; The Presbytery, Brentfield Road NW10 8ER Tel: 07862 721281 Email: andrewsafopoku@rcdow.org.uk (Stonebridge)

Tsegaye (1943; 2007) BA, MSc, MCILIP, Kassa; St Thomas More, 9 Henry Road N4 2LH Tel: 020 8802 9910 Email: kassatsegaye@rcdow.org.uk (Manor House)

Wingrove (1970; 2021) Jayson; **358 Greenford Road, Greenford UB6 9AN** Tel: 020 8578 1363 Email: jaysonwingrove@rcdow.org.uk (Greenford)

Wright (1953; 2008) BSc, PhD, Simon; Email: simonwright@rcdow.org.uk (diocese of Arundel and Brighton)

Yates (1967; 2017), FdA, MA, MSC, PhD, Jeremy; **377 Mile End Road E3 4QS** Tel: 020 8980 1845 Email: jeremyyates@rcdow.org.uk (Mile End)

DEACONS IN FORMATION FOR PRIESTHOOD IN WESTMINSTER

Amari (1980; 2015) Guido
Dora (1992; 2019) Adam
Lazzaron (1987; 2022) Marco **(Parsons Green)**
Matokovic (1996; 2022) Domagoj **(Finchley East)**
Seery (1960; 2017) Ronald
Sola Garcia (1993; 2022) Juan **(Tottenham)**
Thomas (1994; 2022) Francis **(Allen Hall / Edgware)**
van der Vorst (1971; 2022) Patrick **(Beda College, Rome)**

SECTION 4

SEMINARIANS IN FORMATION FOR PRIESTHOOD IN WESTMINSTER

Allen Hall Seminary
Redemptoris Mater House of Formation
Pablo Bacho
Thomas Blackburn
Paolo Gambardella
Victor Gonzalez
Thomas Krejci
Michael Mesa
Sean Power
Robert Smialek

Extended Pastoral Placement
John Casey
Lorcán Keller

Beda College, Rome
James Boyle

Royal English College of St Alban, Valladolid
Brendan Alvares
Ashley Wells

OBITUARIES

Fr Duncan Adamson RIP

Fr Duncan died on 16 October 2022 at St Anne's Home in Stoke Newington. An Obituary will follow in the 2024 Westminster Year Book.
May he rest in peace.

Fr Desmond Baker RIP

Fr Desmond Baker – Fr Des to his former parishioners and friends – enjoyed his 12 years of retirement in his own home in St Leonards-on-Sea. He gave much appreciated assistance to local priests and became well-known to them and their parishioners. He was reliable and punctual when going to parishes for Mass and to hear confessions. Punctilious preparation of his homilies, and introductions to the scripture readings at Mass, won the appreciation of many in Arundel, Battle, Bexhill, Godalming, Hastings, Rye, St Leonards and beyond. His love of the Church and the priesthood, his devotion to the Mass and to the Blessed Sacrament were manifest, and his quiet manner and thoughtful conversation endearing. He had a love of Church history and an interest in prominent personalities, especially senior clergy, and he accrued a fund of anecdotes from his 50 years of priestly ministry which he generously shared with friends over dinner. While totally committed to the Roman Catholic Church, Fr Desmond had a love of Anglican evensong, following services broadcast on Radio 3. He made an annual pilgrimage to Canterbury on 29 December to participate in evensong in the Cathedral on the anniversary of the murder of St Thomas Becket, Archbishop of Canterbury, in 1170. It seems fitting that the venue of Fr Des' Funeral Mass is the church dedicated to St Thomas of Canterbury in St Leonards-on-Sea.

Desmond Baker was born in London on 23 June 1940. He grew up in Ealing and, with his Irish parents Victor Joseph and Anne Dorothy (formerly Keane) Baker, was a parishioner of Ealing Abbey. He was the only child of elderly parents. From a very early age he made known his desire to be a priest. Ceremonial and all things ecclesiastical were of interest to the young Desmond. His secondary education was at St Benedict's School, Ealing from 1953-58 and then, having been accepted as a student for the priesthood, he went to Campion House, Osterley – the residential house of studies run by the Jesuits to prepare men for seminary life. After two years, in September 1960, he went to Allen Hall at St Edmund's College, Ware in Hertfordshire. However, his personality made it necessary for him to discontinue formation for priesthood. The Seminary President, Mgr Butcher, wrote to Desmond's parents in July 1961, to inform them of the decision taken because of 'eccentricities of behaviour' which were not improving. It was in his best interests that he took time out, the President explained, and the door was open for him to re-apply to the Diocese after a few years. Desmond accepted the decision, recognising that there were issues that needed attention, and he communicated this in a letter to Cardinal Godfrey, Archbishop of Westminster. Desmond found employment and kept in regular contact with

Mgr Butcher by letter, telling him of his progress. He then successfully re-applied for acceptance as a student for the Diocese and he was sent to the English College in Valladolid, Spain in 1963. Desmond was by now much more at ease with himself and more out-going, having grown in confidence and with some new skills. The Rector at Valladolid was committed to assisting Desmond's development and formation, and he was successful. On 21 December 1969 Desmond was ordained to the priesthood at Ealing Abbey by Cardinal Heenan. He would not then have known that his future Bishop, Cardinal Vincent Nichols, was ordained to the priesthood on the same day, in Rome!

Fr Desmond's first appointment was to Westminster Cathedral, where he served as a Chaplain from 1970-77. He was then appointed Assistant Priest at The Immaculate Conception and St Joseph, Hertford where he remained for two years. His next appointment was to All Saints, Kenton serving as Assistant Priest for two years. He then went to St Hugh of Lincoln, Letchworth as Assistant Priest from 1981-86. He was then appointed Parish Priest at St Bede, Croxley Green where he remained one year. It was not the happiest chapter of his priesthood. Fr Desmond was not suited to the role of Parish Priest and the responsibilities and expectations that go with parish leadership. He was appointed Assistant Priest at Marychurch, Hatfield in 1987 and remained two years. In 1989 he served as a supply priest, giving assistance in various parishes in Hertfordshire before being appointed Chaplain to the Hospitaller Order of St John of God, Barvin Park in Potters Bar. It had become clear to him, and to Cardinal Hume, that his ministry should be in a rural setting and without the stress of leadership and he continued to receive professional support to help him to cope with anxiety. In 1990 he was appointed Assistant Priest at Sacred Heart, Teddington where he remained for eight years. While in the parish, he celebrated the Silver Jubilee of his Ordination with a Mass of Thanksgiving, followed by a parish party, on 26 January 1995.

In 1998 Fr Desmond moved from Teddington to London Colney, to take up his appointment as Chaplain at All Saints, the diocesan Pastoral Centre. He showed a keen interest in the work of SPEC, the Centre for Youth Ministry and remained at London Colney until 2002. He then went to live in the presbytery at Borehamwood North, available for permanent supply ministry. After a year he moved to Gunnersbury as priest in residence and available for supply ministry. The need for a temporary resident priest took him to Buntingford, from September 2003 to March 2005. He was then appointed to Mill End and Maple Cross parish as Parochial Administrator, where he served until his retirement in 2009 and his move to the house formerly owned by his parents in St Leonards-on-Sea.

Fr Desmond's happiest years were spent in Letchworth, as Assistant Priest. He wrote that in these years he felt particularly happy and fulfilled. He also experienced much happiness living with privacy and independence in retirement and being of service to local priests and parishioners. He regularly participated at deanery meetings, contributing thoughtfully to discussions. He was able to keep in touch with friends and to enjoy meals with them, talking about the lives of members of the families and the lives of 20th and 21st century political figures. In June 2021 he returned to Letchworth for the belated celebration of his 80th birthday – Covid restrictions prevented a celebration in 2020. On 17 January 2020 – before the Covid lockdown announced in March – Fr Desmond celebrated the Golden

Jubilee of his Ordination, hosted by the parish of Bexhill-on-Sea where he was well known from regular supply ministry. Bishop Richard Moth and Bishop Paul McAleenan were among those who participated at the Mass of Thanksgiving. On the actual date of his Golden Jubilee, 21 December 2019, Fr Desmon wrote to Cardinal Vincent to thank him for the letter of congratulations that he received, and commented: '…to be able to look back on 50 years of faithful ministry in the priesthood is indeed a great joy and I warmly reciprocate your good wishes and extend to you my own congratulations on attaining your own Golden Jubilee. It has been a great privilege to serve as a priest in the Metropolitan See of Westminster'. Fr Desmond died peacefully at the age of 81 in hospital on 20 December 2021, just a day short of the 52nd anniversary of his Ordination.
May he rest in peace.

Fr Antony Brunning RIP

It is sometimes said: 'You die how you live'. Fr Tony Brunning had a smile on his face throughout the period he was receiving end of life care at Nazareth House in Hammersmith. Before that, and over the years, he always had a benign smile that radiated joy and peace, his inner self being portrayed by his physiognomy. Yet there was also a characteristic nervousness that he brought with him from his childhood. He laughed at himself and at events when anxious in ways that did not cause anxiety in others, but which seemed to disarm and put people at ease. He also had the child-like qualities of openness, interest and awe when encountering other people and various situations. Essentially shy and humble, Fr Tony was a compassionate man and a priest who was accepting of other people in their variety and their needs. He was a channel of God's love and mercy, an effective minister of the Church who loved others unconditionally.

Born in Mile End Hospital on 5 May 1940 to Thomas Charles and Lena Marie Agnes (formerly Payne) Brunning, Antony was baptised in the church of the Holy Ghost and St Stephen, Shepherds Bush within a month of his birth. When he was just three months old, his father was killed in a bombing raid on the RAF station at Biggin Hill where he was based. The young Antony or Tony, as he was known, was educated initially at the Convent of the Sacred Heart, Hammersmith and then at St Benedict's School, attached to Ealing Abbey and its community of Benedictine monks. On 30 March 1952 he was confirmed at Ealing Abbey, taking the name Joseph. From an early age he felt the call to priesthood. As a boy he was devout, serious and hardworking, and regularly served weekday and Sunday Mass in Shepherds Bush, with his mother and one sister, Josephine, also being practising Catholics. He was accepted as a student for the priesthood and at the age of 18 he went to Allen Hall, then at St Edmund's College, Ware. Seminary reports describe Tony as being conscientious and dedicated to the life and work of the seminary, while also being rather nervous and young in his manner. He excelled in Latin throughout his time at the seminary (1958-64) and was then ordained to the priesthood in Westminster Cathedral by Archbishop (later Cardinal) John Heenan on 23 May 1964.

Fr Tony Brunning's first appointment was to the parish of All Saints, Kenton where he served as Assistant Priest from 1964-72. His letter of appointment, dated 30 June 1964 and sent to him by the Vicar General, required him to take up his appointment within a

SECTION 4

week of its receipt! During these years he was Chaplain to St Gregory's Secondary School in Kenton. His next appointment was to St Anselm's, Southall, where he served as Assistant Priest from 1972-78 when he was appointed Parish Administrator. While in that parish he ministered as part-time Chaplain at HMP Wormwood Scrubs, from 1977-87. Fr Tony worked well with lay people, religious sisters and other clergy as a good team leader who enabled the gifts of others in the service of the parish. His next appointment was to the parish of St Gabriel's, South Harrow and St Bernard's, Northolt, where he served as Parish Priest, based in Northolt, from 1987-97. In 1992 he set about redeveloping the church at South Harrow, supported by the diocese after an analysis of the needs and the way forward. He appealed to the parishioners for financial support, praising them for generously reducing the parish debt from £160,000 to £15,000 in just six years. People responded to his simplicity of life and dedication to his parishioners' pastoral, sacramental and spiritual needs and shared his vision for St Gabriel's.

In 1997 Fr Tony took up his appointment as full-time Hospital Chaplain at St Mary's, Paddington, living in the presbytery at Harrow Road until 2003, when he moved to live in the Marylebone presbytery. He remained in this appointment until 2008 when, at the age of 68, he was appointed to Westminster Cathedral to join the College of Chaplains. In 2014 he retired, leaving Cathedral Clergy House to live independently at the Almshouses, operated by the St Joseph's Society in Brook Green, soon after celebrating the Golden Jubilee of his ordination to the priesthood. In June 2020 it was necessary for him to move to Nazareth House in Finchley, with some health issues needing attention, a few months after the death of his beloved sister, Josephine. Following discharge from the Whittington Hospital in November 2021, Fr Tony went to Nazareth House in Hammersmith for nursing care. He was always appreciative of the care and support given by the Sisters and staff, and by the diocese.

A keen supporter of Brentford Football Club, he rejoiced in its promotion to the Premier League last season. He also took delight in family gatherings and celebrations over the years, for he was very much the 'family chaplain'. He enjoyed board games, walking holidays and real ale. He died peacefully on 25 April, slipping away gently and knowing that he would be going to the Lord, who called him to priestly ministry in his childhood and sustained him over 57 years of priestly life and ministry. His funeral date is the anniversary of his ordination when his mortal remains rest before the altar and he is supported by the loving prayers of so many, just as he was when he was ordained. 'Death does not sever the bonds of love', as Fr Tony said in the homily at his Golden Jubilee Mass in May 2014.

May he rest in peace.

Fr Dominic Byrne RIP

Fr Dominic Byrne, Parish Priest of St Theodore of Canterbury, Hampton-on-Thames died at the age of 66 at Kingston Hospital just four days after being admitted for emergency treatment. It was known to him and to those close to him that he had health issues that would shorten his life. But he lived life to the full and brought much joy to the lives of many. His untimely death on 6 December shocked and saddened many, and since his death stories of his life continue to be shared among those who knew and loved him. Dom, as he was known to his family and close friends, was born in Birmingham on 28 February 1955. His parents, Arthur and Bernadette, had four other children, born after their brother. When Dominic was two years old the family moved to Beckbury in Shropshire and after another couple of years to Wellington in the same county where they settled. The young Dominic went to the local Catholic primary school and then to the local boys' grammar school from 1965-71. He was academically bright, with a particular interest and ability in languages. At school he learned to play the piano and developed this talent to become an accomplished pianist, whilst he also enjoyed drama. It was not surprising that his faith, abilities and interests prompted application to the seminary for A-level education and vocational discernment at Ushaw College near Durham. However, in 1973, having been there for two years, he left to pursue studies in Law at Queen's College, Oxford, where he developed his interests in student politics, amateur dramatics and social life. The degree he was awarded could have been stronger, but his broader education was strengthened by his extra-curricular endeavours, including involvement with the Catholic Chaplaincy. After graduation Dominic studied for Civil Service exams and in 1977 began work with the then-Foreign Office Department for Overseas Development. He served for eight years in London and overseas, rising to the rank of Principal with his own Section. His work involved countries including Bangladesh, Ghana, Zambia, southern Africa and Malawi. While living in Malawi he encountered an elderly Dutch missionary priest and conversations with him, and a retreat with the Carmelites, reignited a sense of vocation to the priesthood. He applied to the Diocese of Westminster and was sent to the Venerable English College, Rome in September 1985, where he was awarded a Licence in Moral Theology, STL.

Dominic was ordained to the Priesthood on 19 July 1991 in Wellington by Bishop John Crowley, who was then an auxiliary Bishop of Westminster. Fr Dominic's first appointment as a priest was to Enfield, where he served from 1991-93. He then spent a short time at Westminster Cathedral before taking up an appointment as Assistant Priest at Osterley where he became Parochial Administrator. This was followed by a few months as Assistant Priest in Kenton before he went to study Canon Law in Leuven, Belgium in 1995 where he remained for five and a half years. In 2001 he returned to the Cathedral briefly, before taking up his appointment as Parish Priest at Shepperton where he served from 2001-07. During this time he lectured at Heythrop College, London University and gave assistance to the Marriage Tribunal as a Defender of the Marriage Bond, also helping to process applications from priests overseas requesting temporary supply ministry in the Diocese. His next appointment was to Hendon, where he served as Parish Priest from September 2007 until he took up his appointment as Parish Priest at Hampton-on-Thames after a few months sabbatical with the Redemptorists in Tucson, Arizona. Fr Dominic was Parish Priest at St Theodore's, Hampton-on-Thames from January 2019 until his death. During this time ministry became restricted due to the coronavirus, but parishioners were understanding and rallied to give all the support that was possible, aware that Fr Dominic had evident health issues. He maintained the practice of telephoning his mother every day at 6pm.

SECTION 4

As a priest in parish ministry Fr Dominic could be, and usually was, exceedingly kind, caring and compassionate. But he did not suffer fools gladly. On occasion he could react badly to some people or situations and then regret any harshness of word or deed. He paid careful attention to the preparation of his Sunday homilies, and was interested in what his fellow priests might be intending to say in theirs. He wanted his parishioners to have an adult faith, nurtured not only by his homilies but also by their own reading, study and reflection. As a teacher, he used the knowledge gained from his study for a JCL and then a JCD to educate and inspire his Canon Law students at Heythrop. He was proud of his four-horned biretta with its green pom-pom, but not too proud to laugh at it! He helped his students to understand that Canon Law is directed towards the pastoral care of people, with compassion and honesty, and for their salvation. His extensive knowledge and his willingness to share it, coupled with anecdotes from parish life, made him a valued and much-loved lecturer and a respected and convivial member of the Canon Law Society.

Throughout his life Fr Dominic maintained and developed interests from his early years, including theatre, ballet, classical music, opera, musicals, languages, politics, genealogy and astronomy and, perhaps above all, food and cooking. His tastes were truly universal for both food and drinks. His family and friends enjoyed the lavish hospitality with accomplished cuisine. An exceptionally generous and kind host, Fr Dominic quickly put his guests at ease, especially when his sharp wit and acute mimicry were part of the event. Many will recall enjoying an apéritif with their host, who would move between the drinks trolley, the cooker and his piano to play whatever piece of music he was currently practicing and would agree that his minestrone soup was like no other! His collection of cookery books seemed to outnumber his library of theological and Canon Law tomes. He rarely seemed to use the same recipe twice. Meals with Fr Dominic were always occasions of both serious and frivolous conversation, merriment and laughter, especially when he was prevented from taking himself too seriously. He was as attentive to the needs of his exotic cats as he was to his guests. After supper a visit to the garden to observe the rings of Saturn through the state-of-the-art telescope was not uncommon, or being shown recent additions to his collection of silver objects in the display cabinet. His sense of adventure and desire for that which was new was not confined to the kitchen – his range of interests and lively mind were admired by all who knew him.

At times Fr Dominic seemed to need the approval of others – he could have times of self-doubt and could be easily wounded. This was a result of his deep sensitivity. But we cannot doubt the approval he will receive from the God whom he knew, loved and served as a priest, ministering love and compassion to God's people in their variety and frailty.

May he rest in peace.

Canon Philip Cross RIP

Born in North London on 9 March 1936 and baptised in infancy at Our Lady of Muswell, Muswell Hill, Philip Hugh Cross wanted to be a priest from the age of 18 years. He was devout, good-natured and good-humoured. His parents, William and Ethel, had become

Catholics and passed the faith on to Philip and to their daughter Joan. At the time of Philip's application to the diocese for acceptance as a student for the priesthood, when in his late 20s, the local Parish Priest at Our Lady and St Michael, Garston described Philip's late father as a 'saint', and his late mother as 'a most remarkable woman', and Philip as 'a most loyal son of the Church'. The Parish Priest had known Philip since seven years of age, and commended him to the diocese: 'Take him', he wrote.

The young Philip was educated at Loreto College, St Albans from the age of five to seven, then at St Columba's College in St Albans for a year before going to Hardenwick Preparatory School for boys in Harpenden until 1951. This was followed by a year at Pitmans College in Finchley. At the age of 30, he left the family business and went to Campion House, Osterley in preparation for seminary formation. There he was described as the best in his year at Latin, and as one of the outstanding students. After two years he 'graduated' and went to Allen Hall Seminary in Ware. Because of his age it might have been expected that his formation for priesthood would continue at the Beda in Rome, but it was thought prudent that he remain in England because of a possible recurrence of jaundice – he had a serious bout while at Campion House and this had delayed his move. He then had health issues while at Allen Hall, including several attacks of hepatitis, interrupting his studies and prolonging his time at the seminary.

He was ordained to the priesthood at St Bartholomew's, St Albans South by Bishop Christopher Butler OSB, Auxiliary Bishop of Westminster, on 25 May 1974, when 38 years of age. Fr Philip brought to his priestly ministry maturity and experience of life 'in the world'. His first appointment was to the parish of Our Lady of Victories, Kensington where he served as Assistant Priest from 1974-79. He was then appointed Assistant Priest at Our Lady and St Michael's, Garston (where he and his family used to live) until 1984 when he took up appointment as Parish Priest at All Saints, Kenton where he remained for 16 years. On 25 May 1999 he marked the Silver Jubilee of his Ordination with Mass celebrated by Bishop Vincent Nichols, then Bishop in North London, followed by a parish party. He included on his prayer card: 'In thanksgiving to God and to everyone who shares in the Bread of Life'. He lamented the departure of the Sisters of Jesus and Mary from Kenton in 1995, writing to the Vicar General: 'We shall miss them immensely and will be hard pressed to replace them. We shall endeavour to mobilise the laity in the pastoral and catechetical areas that the Sisters covered so well – and in the prayer life.' He did not shy away from the demands of ministry. During his time in Kenton he was very involved with the expanding Northwick Park Hospital, with St Gregory's Catholic College and St Luke's Hospice, serving on the Board of Management with fellow Christians and members of other faiths before, and following completion of this much appreciated local facility.

St Bede's, Croxley Green was Fr Philip's next parish, serving as Parish Priest from 2000 until his retirement at the end of September 2012. While at St Bede's, Fr Philip was appointed Canon of the Metropolitan Cathedral Chapter, joining the diocesan College of Consultors. He also oversaw the creation of a substantial extension of the parish hall to meet the needs of the growing parish community. By the autumn of 2009, Canon Philip recognized that early retirement would suit him – he had become tired and, in his own words: 'increasingly worn out by parish life'. He asked to retire when 74 rather than the usual 75 years of age. He expressed the hope that he would live with, and care for his

SECTION 4

beloved sister Joan who had Alzheimer's. He also made known his plan to be buried in the grave of Joan's late husband, Primo Signorini, in North Watford Cemetery. Joan died on Christmas Day 2017. He spent the last years of his life at St Anne's Home, Stoke Newington. He was much loved by the Little Sisters of the Poor, staff and residents. In 2017 he wrote: 'I can look back over 40 years of constant happiness in the priesthood and it's not finished yet'. On 3 May 2022 Canon Philip was called from St Anne's Home to Heaven by the Lord, on the Feast of St Philip and St James.

Throughout his years of priestly ministry Canon Philip recognized and encouraged the contribution of other priests, Religious Sisters and parishioners in the life and work of the Church. He had a natural warmth and was a promoter of priestly fraternity while never being 'clerical'. He accompanied some of the former Anglican clergy whose faith journey led them to the Catholic Church, and for many, priesthood. He enjoyed his model railway, an expansive Hornby train set in a large room of the presbytery at Croxley Green, complete with village shops and even sheep. He was thoughtful, kind and wise and loved to relax in the company of family and friends. He had an easy, gentle manner and a good sense of fun. A good listener, he was non-judgmental and affirming of people and, above all, loved being a priest. In an interview with seminarians in 2015 he counselled: 'whatever you do, you must do it with love. That's what enables you to do it. And pray for the gift of perseverance, that once you have placed your hand on the plough you may not give up but may keep on to the end.'

May he rest in peace.

Fr Kevin Eastell RIP

Fr John Kevin Eastell BA, STh, MEd, PhD had a love of learning. An accomplished writer of papers and articles on education, theology, ecumenism and significant people of the 15th century including John Fisher, Thomas More, Thomas Cranmer and John Stokesley, his legacy lives on not only by his contribution to history and scholarship but also through his ministry as an Anglican and in the Catholic Church, and as a devoted husband of Ann and father of Dominic.

Born in Yorkshire on 11 May 1942, the young Kevin was educated locally in Cleckheaton in West Yorkshire. At the age of 16 he began studies as a Junior at Kelham near Newark, Nottinghamshire , a college founded for the education of Anglicans preparing for ministry and run by the Society of the Sacred Mission. He then spent a year with the Manchester Industrial Mission from 1960-61. Studies at Kelham continued for a further two years before Kevin went to Wells Theological College in 1963 for three years. He was ordained as a priest on 24 December 1967 to be Assistant Curate at St Peter's, Horbury in Wakefield until 1969, when he went to St Bartholomew's, Armley in Leeds where he served as Assistant Curate until 1972. Kevin and Ann were married on 31 January 1970 and their son, Dominic, was born in December of that year. He was appointed Vicar of St Margaret's, Toxteth in Liverpool where he served from 1972-76. During this time he was a member of the Liverpool Diocesan Education Committee. St Peter's in Formby, Liverpool was his next appointment, where he served as Vicar from 1976-82. The Eastells then moved to Manchester, where Kevin served as Vicar at St Paul's in Royton from 1982-88. In

Manchester he was Secretary of the Manchester Diocesan Adult Education Committee, Chair of West Pennine Housing Association and a member of the Manchester Diocesan Ministerial Education Committee. His journey in ministry, and south, brought him to London, where he served as Diocesan Director for Professional Ministry from 1988-96. From 1992-96 Kevin was a Tutor with the Open University Course EH26 Adult Education, and in 1994 he was an Examiner in the Open University Faculty of Education.

Kevin and Ann were received and confirmed in the Catholic Church on 1 November 1996. This took place in Angers, France at the Cathedral dedicated to St Maurice. Now living in Angers, Kevin undertook studies at the local Catholic University. As a Catholic, he wrote of his appreciation for the Church: 'The hospitality of the Catholic Church has been most impressive and in faith terms it has been a wonderful experience to rediscover peace of mind and soul. That experience can never be denied and becoming Catholics has been confirmed as the right decision for both my wife and myself … I have never regarded ordination as a right to be claimed and ultimately all an individual can do is to offer one's life for the glory of God'. Kevin's desire was for his ministry in the Church of England to be fulfilled as a Catholic priest. Recommendations for his acceptance for ordination were made by many, including the late Fr Michael Hopley OSB of Ealing Abbey, who stated that Kevin 'is a man of integrity, is conscientious and has a great concern for others. I fully support his application for admission to the priesthood and have no hesitation in commending him'. Others commented on Kevin's long-standing Catholic faith, his intelligence, communication skills, spirituality, pastoral care for people and his good sense of humour. Kevin was ordained as a Catholic priest on 9 November 2002 at Our Most Holy Redeemer and St Thomas More, Chelsea by Bishop James O'Brien, Auxiliary Bishop of Westminster.

Fr Kevin returned to France and continued his involvement with the Catholic University as a Professor and Director of the distinguished Moreanum Centre. In 2003 he established an English-speaking Church community in Anjou in the Diocese of Angers with the blessing of Bishop Jean-Louis Bruguès. Fr Kevin wanted to provide ministry to English-speaking Catholics and he wanted others to share his appreciation for St Thomas More. He was pleased when given a visiting professorial chair at the University of Polonia in Poland to give lectures on St Thomas More and the English Renaissance and Reformation, and was instrumental in establishing a distance learning Diploma in Thomas More Studies. He was also involved with arrangements for an international Thomas More academic conference in Argentina. From January to April 2004 he went on a weekly visit to Paris to lecture to students from the University of Minnesota on St Thomas More and the European Renaissance. Then in May he travelled to Kalamazoo, near Chicago, to give a paper at a Medieval Conference on St Thomas More's 'Letter to Bugenhagen' and the principles of Church unity. In July of that same year he was involved with the arrangements for and delivery of a conference to celebrate Hungary joining the European Union. For Fr Kevin the excitement was enhanced because St Thomas More set his 'Dialogue of Comfort' in the besieged city of Buda.

In November 2011 he was in London for the launch of Cardinal Vincent Nichols' 237-page book St John Fisher, Bishop and Theologian in Reformation and Controversy. St John Fisher was executed at Tower Hill in June 1535, a few weeks before the execution of St

Thomas More. Both men gave their lives for the Catholic faith, having stood up to King Henry VIII, and both were canonised in 1935. Fr Kevin assisted the Cardinal with the task of publishing the MA thesis written while the latter was a postgraduate student at the University of Manchester in the early 1970s and wrote the Afterword, giving a brief survey of significant research and scholarship on the Reformation in England since the Cardinal's thesis was written.

Fr Kevin kept himself busy with both his pastoral and academic apostolate, sharing his love of the Lord and his love for St Thomas More with energy and enthusiasm. In May 2017, he retired but continued to support the mission of the Chaplaincy based at the Church of Notre Dame de la Chapelle in Doué La Fontaine in Anjou. The patrons of the Chaplaincy, Our Lady and St Thomas More, continued to inspire and motivate him. In recent months his deteriorating health required treatment and care in hospital, where he celebrated his 80th birthday on 11 May, dying peacefully there on 30 May. His funeral took place locally on 14 June.

St Thomas More's influence lives on. The impressive bronze statue by Leslie Cubitt Bevis on Cheyne Walk, around the corner from the church where Fr Kevin was ordained, describes St Thomas More as Scholar, Statesman and Saint. Fr Kevin was certainly a scholar and a man of letters and learning, and we pray that he will enjoy the fullness of life with the God whom he knew, loved and served in the company of the saints.

May he rest in peace.

Fr David Irwin RIP

St Thomas More is quoted on the prayer card produced to mark the Reception of David Irwin into Full Communion with the Catholic Church on 31 May 1994: 'Thank you, dear Jesus, for all you have given me, for all you have taken away from me, for all you have left me'. In February 1994 Canon David wrote to his parishioners in the parish of St Andrew and St Francis of Assisi, Willesden Green: 'the General Synod of the Church of England has taken the final steps and the ordination of women to the priesthood is now legal … I cannot accept this as God's will for his church … the only possible and honourable thing is to withdraw'. Canon David resigned, as did many other clergy who believed that the Church of England had left them and the Church of England did not have the authority to ordain women to the priesthood. This decision was not easy for him. His letter went on: 'after almost 18 years of ministry here, this is not a step I have taken lightly. I have been tremendously happy and fulfilled here. It would be tempting to carry on as though nothing had happened, but that would be impossible and indeed culpable for it would be going against truth'. He completed his ministry in the Church of England by celebrating the Easter liturgies with his parishioners, soon after his 50th birthday. His conscience led him to be reconciled with the Catholic Church and to offer himself for ordination as a Catholic priest. He received encouragement from Cardinal Hume and those who worked closely with him, including the now Cardinal Vincent Nichols, then Bishop in North London.

David John Irwin was born in Portsmouth on 1 March – St David's Day – 1944. His sister, Ann, recalls that from the age of four, when David was asked what he wanted to be when he grew up, he replied he 'wanted to be in the Church'. His secondary education was at Worthing High School for Boys from 1955-62. He then spent a year working with the Sheffield Industrial Mission. From 1963-66 he studied Theology at King's College London, and then went to study at Warminster Theological College. In May 1967 David was ordained as a deacon and in June 1968 as a priest by Bishop Mervyn Stockwood at Southwark Cathedral. He served as Curate in Sydenham from 1967-70, then as Curate in Ealing from 1970-76. He then ministered in Willesden, Gladstone Park and, from 1983, as Vicar of St Andrew and St Francis of Assisi, Willesden Green and Gladstone Park. His energy and enthusiasm transformed the parish. Approachable and friendly, he built up the community and used his musical abilities as a singer and organist to ensure the dignified celebration of the liturgy. However, when things occasionally went wrong, he could find it hard to conceal his displeasure. During his time in Willesden Green he ministered as a hospital chaplain and as chair of governors of the parish school and as a member of the deanery synod standing committee. He went as a commissary to two Ghanian dioceses, Kumasi and Cape Coast, 1986-94 and was appointed Honorary Canon of these Anglican dioceses. He worked collaboratively with other clergy in the parish and with parishioners. He came to the Catholic Church as a popular and effective pastor.

David was ordained as a Deacon of the Catholic Church on 18 July 1995 and in the same year, on 4 December, as a Priest – his fourth ordination! He was appointed Assistant Priest at Our Lady's, St John's Wood where he had served as the lay Pastoral Assistant, then Deacon, from 1995-99. His next appointment was the Sacred Heart of Jesus parish, Holloway Road as Parish Priest, from 1999-2003. In 1998 he was given additional responsibilities as Spiritual Director to the Union of Catholic Mothers in the Diocese. Having moved on from Holloway Road and, after 12 months' sabbatical leave, Fr David was appointed Parish Priest at St Peter-in-Chains, Stroud Green from 2004 until 2010 when he went to live in the Rectory at St James, Spanish Place. In 2010 Fr David was appointed Co-ordinator for the Ethnic Chaplaincies then, in 2014, Episcopal Vicar, as this work included engagement with the Archdiocese of Southwark and the Diocese of Brentwood. He was deeply committed to the work of the chaplaincies and to the welfare of the Chaplains, showing them fatherly concern. In 2014 he was appointed Conventual Chaplain *Ad Honorem* to the British Association of the Sovereign Military Order of Malta, having served as a Magistral Chaplain since 2005. Fr David had been involved previously as a spiritual director with the OM's Lourdes pilgrimages since 1999. Other OM pilgrimages took him to Lebanon, Walsingham and Holywell.

Fr David moved from Spanish Place in 2019 at the usual retirement age of 75. He had been very happy there, but was beginning to find the 42-step climb to his rooms challenging! He went to live in the bungalow in Findon Village, Worthing rented from the Church of England Pensions Board since 1994 on his departure from the C of E. He was relieved to know that the Diocese of Westminster's Sick and Retired Priest Fund would meet the cost of the monthly rent, council tax and water rates. Fr David continued involvement with the Order of Malta as Principal Chaplain, but stood down as the Senior Chaplain for the Lourdes Pilgrimage, and also as Spiritual Director for the UCM after 20 years in this role. In his retirement he provided greatly appreciated supply ministry in local parishes, including Arundel and West Grinstead. In 2020 he stood down as Co-ordinator of the Ethnic Chaplaincies, because travelling to and from London had become more challenging due to health issues and the restrictions caused by the coronavirus pandemic. In his letter to the Ethnic Chaplains, dated 7 December 2020, he wrote: 'I have come to realise that since retiring and moving back to West Sussex it is difficult to get to London as frequently as is necessary to do this job properly. I would like to thank all of you for your kindness to me over the 10 years in the job. It has been a great joy to be able to share a little in the vibrant life of your communities and I hope I may have been of some help in your work. For my part I have found this to have been one of the most rewarding of the tasks I have undertaken'.

Those who serve as Ethnic Chaplains, other priest-colleagues, friends and parishioners in many parishes in the Church of England and in the Diocese of Westminster have cause to be grateful to Fr David for his dedication to priestly life and ministry – one of service that was affirming and enabling of others as disciples of the Lord. He was kindly and cheerful, infectiously so, and his easy-going and affable manner, warm smile and evident sense of fun put people at ease, including the sick and the poor. He gave of himself generously and his positive attitude made people feel good about themselves and their role in the life and work of the Church.

In December 2020 Fr David celebrated his silver jubilee of ordination as a Catholic Priest with Mass, followed by a convivial lunch with friends in a local pub. He found his true home in the Catholic Church. A 'priests' priest' who retained some Anglican preferences, he won the affection of all, because of his commitment to the Lord and the Church and his desire to serve all entrusted to his care.

May he rest in peace.

Fr Kevin McDevitt RIP

Kevin McDevitt was born in Faughanvale, Co. Derry on 8 September 1943. He had six brothers and two sisters, born to his parents Rose and James McDevitt. His secondary school education was with the Christian Brothers in Enniscorthy, Co. Wexford from 1955-59. He then went to college at St Mary's, Dundalk in Co. Louth until 1962, before entering the Marist Novitiate in Dublin from 1962-63. An older brother, Vincent, had already joined the Holy Ghost Fathers. From 1964-65 Kevin studied philosophy at University College Dublin and then theology at the Marist House of Studies, Mount St Mary's, Milltown in Dublin. He was ordained to the priesthood on 20 December 1969 at Clonliffe College by John Charles McQuade, Archbishop of Dublin.

Fr Kevin SM was appointed school chaplain in Dundrum, Dublin where he also taught Religious Education, from 1970-74. He was then appointed to serve the parish of St Joseph, Blantyre, Glasgow where he gained much pastoral experience while supporting the life and work of the parish. His next appointment was to London, as a member of the Irish Chaplaincy in Britain, based at St Mellitus parish, Tollington Park from 1976-82. He saw himself as a missionary priest, ministering where the Lord had sent him. During Lent 1982 he transferred to the parish of Our Lady of Lourdes, Acton where he served as Assistant Priest, having completed his work with the Irish Chaplaincy. He had considered applying for incardination in Dublin and also San Antonio, Texas where he spent four months in 1982. But he found happiness in the diocese of Westminster and sought incardination, having ministered here for 10 years. With the blessing of his Marist superiors, he applied and was accepted. 'Naturally, we regret his departure, and I'm sure Kevin will prove to be a very good and zealous priest, wrote the Provincial Superior in support of the request. On 6 February 1987 he was formally incardinated as a priest of the diocese of Westminster in a simple ceremony at Archbishop's House, followed by afternoon tea hosted by Cardinal Basil Hume OSB.

In 1987 Fr Kevin was appointed Assistant Priest at Sacred Heart parish, Berkhamsted with special responsibility for the Hemel Hempstead West area of Gadebridge and Warners End. His ministry included chaplaincy to John F Kennedy Secondary School in Hemel. He described schools as a particular type of parish and saw the need for neighbouring schools to work together for the good of the students. In a letter to Cardinal Hume, in November 1988, he wrote: 'You rightly mentioned that no Catholic school can act in isolation, as we are part of each other'. The following year he was appointed Priest in Charge at Hemel Hempstead West and then, in 1991, he was appointed Parish Priest of Hatfield. In 1997 he moved from Hatfield to take up his appointment as Parish Priest of the Church of the Transfiguration, Kensal Rise until 2003. During this time he was asked to take a seminarian on pastoral placement. He was expecting a deacon, and said to the seminarian: 'You're not a deacon, what good is that? I thought you were a deacon but you're a student, a student – a kind of non-person!' The student was not a golfer, and put down by Fr Kevin as 'one of those modern priests who go to the theatre and restaurants'. But he and the student developed a good and lasting rapport. In 2004 Fr Kevin was appointed Parish Priest of St Gabriel's, Archway. He was kept busy with parish work, and in local hospitals and schools. He developed a particular apostolate to the homeless and excluded, to those with mental health issues and addictions. In February 2010 he wrote to the Archbishop, Vincent Nichols, explaining his need to stand down from the Pontifical Mission Societies, Missio, and his work with the Holy Childhood – children helping children – and the APF Red Boxes. He had been involved with this work for 20 years. Having celebrated his 40th anniversary of ordination, and aged 67, it was time to hand on this work to a younger priest. He enjoyed the celebrations marking his anniversary, when parishioners at Archway organized a surprise Mass and party, and was much pleased by the appearance of his five brothers and two sisters who arrived just minutes before the start of Mass. Ten years later, his Golden Jubilee of Ordination was celebrated in Blackwater, Enniscorthy, Co. Wexford in January 2020 with the local community and friends who travelled from London.

Fr Kevin left Archway and returned to Ireland in the autumn of 2014 to retire. He went to live in the Curate's house in Blackwater. There he received support from the Secular Clergy Common Fund and the Westminster Sick and Retired Priests Fund and appreciated the welcome he received from Bishop Denis Brennan and local clergy. He helped out in the local parish, celebrating Mass, hearing confessions and assisting with pastoral ministry. In a letter to Cardinal Vincent in December 2015, he wrote that he was grateful to have the opportunity of more time for prayer and reflection, and to visit family and friends – and to enjoy golf! He wrote about missing the golfing fraternity that was an important part of his life while in Westminster. Playing golf with priests of the diocese of

Ferns brought much joy, as did the annual competition with Westminster diocese. Throughout his life he followed the Gaelic games of hurling and football, rejoicing in the successes of Donegal and other northern teams.

He was popular in the parishes where he served and formed many lasting friendships, embracing life and people, and not slow in expressing his opinions. At times he could be argumentative, displaying some rough edges, but not far beneath the surface was a kind and generous heart. He cared for and about people who were poor, vulnerable and disadvantaged. In 2020 on a visit to London Fr Kevin was given a warm reception at the St Gabriel's Community Centre in Archway. Among the guests were people who had been homeless and helped by him to find accommodation, and members of the Chinese Catholic community who were given a place to meet by him when he was Parish Priest. Throughout his ministry he was committed to the work of education and supported staff and students of the schools in his various parishes. In children he saw hope for the future. Towards the end of 2020 he had become unwell and needed surgery and treatment. After some respite, his health deteriorated. The last few months of his life were spent in Kilbeggan, in a house he had built adjacent to the home of his sister, and his health declined rapidly. He died peacefully on Sunday 20 March 2022 in the Midland Regional Hospital in Tullamore, Co. Offaly. A few days earlier Cardinal Vincent phoned and spoke with Fr Kevin, who was by then very frail. The call gave him encouragement as he bore his suffering while preparing himself for God's call. In a message to the congregation at the Funeral Mass on 22 March the Cardinal's words were read by Fr Sean Carroll: '…I extend to Fr Kevin's family and friends my condolences and the assurance of my prayers for the repose of his soul, that he may rest in peace and rise in glory. I express to them, and to all who are here in Kilbeggan, my appreciation for his priestly ministry in the diocese of Westminster and elsewhere. We give thanks to God for calling Fr Kevin to serve the Church as a priest, and we give thanks to Fr Kevin for 52 years of priestly ministry, celebrating the Sacraments of the Church and bringing to those in his care the compassion and mercy of God. May he receive the reward of his labours and be embraced in the loving arms of Jesus whom he knew, loved and served'.

May he rest in peace.

Fr Séamus McGeoghan RIP

Séamus McGeoghan was born seven weeks early on 31 March 1945, to Alice and Joseph, in his grandmother's house in Omagh, Co Tyrone. He was the eldest of 11 siblings. The McGeoghan family moved to Hanwell in West London in 1949. The young Séamus attended the parish primary school from the age of five, and at 11 years of age he went to Gunnersbury Grammar School for boys, from 1956-63. He was good in the classroom, less so on the sports field. He felt the call to priesthood from an early age and told his parents about his sense of vocation. He was persuaded by his father to work as a trainee accountant and this he did for a year, working with a firm in Acton. In 1964 he went to study for the priesthood at Allen Hall, St Edmund's College, Ware, having passed eight O Levels and three A Levels. He excelled at studies and earned the nickname 'Doctor'. After two years he continued his formation for the priesthood at the Venerable English College in Rome. Although he arrived in the world early, seminary records show that he was not an early riser in the morning! This characteristic endured over the years, annoying to some and endearing to others.

Séamus was ordained to the priesthood at the church of Our Lady and St Joseph, Hanwell on 5 October 1969 by Cardinal John Heenan, then Archbishop of Westminster. How could he have known then that his classmate from the English College, Cardinal Vincent Nichols, ordained later in the same year, would be presiding and preaching at his Funeral Mass ? Fr Séamus' First Mass was in the same church the following day and later in the month was his celebration of the first of many family weddings. His first appointment was to Our Lady of the Rosary, Marylebone, where he served as Assistant Priest from 1970-74. He was then appointed to St Joseph's, Wembley where he remained until 1980. He served as Parish Priest at St Mary Magdalene, Willesden Green from 1980-84. He then went to St Paul's, Wood Green and remained there for seven years. He had a short placement at Carpenders Park in 1991 before being appointed to Northwood for a few months. He then went to Hackney, briefly, before being appointed Parish Priest at East Acton where he served from 1992-2000. His final appointment was to St Thomas of Canterbury and the English Martyrs, Royston where he served as Parish Priest from 2000 for 16 years until his retirement.

Fr Séamus was always committed to education, seeing it as the route to opportunity and choices. He wanted to share with others what he had received – knowledge and skills from a good education – and he did so generously. As a seminarian he helped others who were struggling with studies. On visits to Cambridge, further up the A10, he introduced friends from Allen Hall to bookshops and favourite restaurants. He also benefited from the love that was received and given in a large and close family. He was a loving priest who shared his faith, knowledge and experience freely.

He retired from full time ministry in 2016. As his health declined, his need for care increased. At St Vincent's Nursing Home in Eastcote he was well cared for, and comfortable. He formed deep friendships among staff and residents and welcomed many former parishioners who visited him. Since March 2020 the visits were restricted due to the coronavirus pandemic. A few months earlier, in October 2019, Fr Séamus celebrated the Golden Jubilee of his ordination to the priesthood, and did do in the company of family and friends. Ten years before that he celebrated the 40th anniversary of ordination in Royston. Those who were there recall a large but gentle man preaching with conviction, powerfully.

Many friends remember his small red Robin Reliant 3-wheel car and exhilarating journeys on fast roads. He enjoyed travelling to Ireland to see family and friends, including former parishioners who had returned to live there. Intelligent, cheerful and self-deprecating, he enjoyed company and was himself good company. He was accepting of people with their strengths and weaknesses and an avid reader and collector of books on a wide range of subjects. He excelled at billiards and snooker, unrestricted by his portly frame, also mastering IT and technology. From an early age he supported Queens Park Rangers and went to see them play in White City. For all his intelligence he loved to watch the soaps on television, Corrie and Eastenders in particular. Despite health issues for many years, he did not succumb to self-pity but remained cheerful and positive, helped by his innate sense of humour and joie de vivre. He appreciated the kindness of others, and he was unfailingly kind himself, and humble. Fr Séamus died peacefully at the age of 76 at St Vincent's Care Home in Eastcote on 10 February 2022.

May he rest in peace.

Fr David Wilson RIP

Fr David Wilson had one sibling, Corinne, his older sister to whom he was very close and who died in 2010. But he had become part of the large family of L'Arche, with whom he lived in France from 1987 until his death on 1 July 2022. He was born to Gilbert and Lucille in London on 16 August 1938. David's French-Canadian mother was a practising Catholic, whilst his father – a senior professor of archaeology at Imperial College, London – was not a Catholic (until many years later), but was supportive of the Catholic ethos of the family home in Knightsbridge. Part of David's early childhood was spent with his mother in Montreal during World War II. When back in England, St Mary's, Cadogan Street was the church where David attended Mass daily, when he became aware of a vocation to the priesthood. His application to the diocese, in 1964 at the age of 25, was supported by the Parish Priest, Bishop David Cashman. At this time David was a recent postgraduate of London University, where he studied for a Diploma in Education. Before that he studied at St Edmund Hall, Oxford, from 1959-62 and was awarded his Bachelor of Arts in Geography. He had also done National Service in the Army from 1957-59. His school education was at Ampleforth from 1952-56, preceded by five years at St Martin's Preparatory School, North Yorkshire. In September 1964 David began his formation as a student for the priesthood at Allen Hall, Ware in Hertfordshire. His parents were keen to contribute to the cost of his accommodation and studies, then £300 p.a., and a cheque for the full amount was sent for the first year of studies – David was expected to persevere! David was assigned to Ss Sebastian and Pancras, Kingsbury Green as a Deacon in 1969. He won the appreciation of the Parish Priest and parishioners for being hard-working and a man of prayer. His approach to catechetics was innovative and effective as he shared his faith with, and taught, children at non-Catholic schools on Saturday mornings. He worked with the choir, teaching new hymns as he helped the parish become more liturgically up-to-date in the post-Vatican II era. When his time in the parish has come to completion, the Parish Priest wrote about David's contribution to the life of the parish to the Rector of Allen Hall Seminary: 'His impact on the parish was tremendous and everybody was sorry when he had to go ... a tireless worker from menial work (polishing floors!) to top class organization. He was a most spiritual man and had time for everybody. I can thoroughly recommend him as a most suitable candidate for Ordination'. On 29 June 1970 David was ordained to the priesthood in the chapel at St Edmund's College by Bishop Victor Guazzelli (Auxiliary Bishop of Westminster from May 1970 until he retired in December 1996).

The Annunciation, Burnt Oak was Fr David's first appointment as a newly ordained priest. He served in the parish from 1970-72, when he went to Lille, France to study for a Licence in Theology with the aim of returning to teach in the seminary. In response to Cardinal Heenan's invitation to undertake further studies, he wrote: 'I believe that for theology to be truly living it must not lose sight of the pastoral situation'. In 1974 he was appointed 'Chaplain to the Handicapped in the Diocese', based at St Vincent's in Carlisle Place SW1. Working with two Religious Sisters, he created original programmes for catechetics and care for people with disabilities and their families, setting up the centre at St Joseph's in Hendon.

In 1987 Fr David returned to France to work with L'Arche, founded in 1964 as a worldwide federation of people with and without learning disabilities, now in over 30 countries, working together for a world where all belong. He spent the rest of his priesthood among people with special needs and differently gifted, and with people devoted to the care of people that some others found difficult to understand or accept. He, and others, demonstrated the kind of love that embraced people unconditionally, sacrificing his options in favour of those whose options were restricted not through choice but circumstances. Alongside ministry at L'Arche, he served the local parish and forged links with local clergy and parishioners of the diocese of Arras. Every five years his contract for continuing ministry in France was renewed at his request, with the support of L'Arche and the Bishop of Arras. Meanwhile he maintained regular contact with the diocese of Westminster, sending regular letters and information bulletins to successive Archbishops of Westminster. In 2016 he retired from active ministry and chose to remain in France with L'Arche in Ambleteuse. The following year his health began to decline and his need for care increased. He was transferred to a care home close to where he had been living to receive 24-hour care. In a letter to Cardinal Vincent in April 2017, the Regional Leader at L'Arche wrote: 'It is a mystery to see how, after all these years of ministry at L'Arche, Fr David has become and will become closer still to the reality lived by our members with disabilities'. He continued to have many visitors, and he was regularly taken out for trips.

In August 2018 Fr David celebrated his 80th birthday and in June 2020 he celebrated the Golden Jubilee of his Ordination to the Priesthood. Writing to congratulate him, Cardinal Vincent let Fr David know: 'I join many people who will be thanking God for all the gifts that He gives. Among those gifts, one of the most precious is a vocation to the Priesthood … When we find this vocation and follow it generously our lives are marked by a profound sense of peace and happiness'. Peace and happiness were gifts that Fr David shared with those with whom he so generously shared his life.

He also had a great love of theatre and came to appreciate opera on discovering that some could be humorous. Despite all the years spent in France, he remained 'very, very English … His simplicity in his relations, his sense of humour and sometimes even his eccentricity were noticed and appreciated', as was noted in the notice of his death on 1 July. He was a familiar figure rollerblading on the embankment at Ambleteuse and on the ice skating rink. He eschewed clericalism associated with self-interest, privilege and entitlement. On a visit to Rome he had to make a clerical collar by cutting a plastic bottle to be suitably attired to meet the Pope. Over the years he remained faithful to his twice-daily routine of time for quiet prayer and bible study. His homilies were brief – they did not have to be long because the way he lived spoke volumes. Over the years he travelled widely, visiting L'Arche communities and leading retreats and delivering training to staff and volunteers. Wherever he went, and with everyone he met, he shared his commitment to the value of every person as he worked to promote the dignity of all. His very presence, and his ubiquitous smile, were visible signs of his love for all.

In recent years Fr David's own needs enabled members and friends of L'Arche to embrace him with the care and compassion he had so readily extended to others. When increased frailty necessitated his transfer to the retirement home, he continued to influence the lives of others by his faith, his gentleness and his trust in the Lord. He received the Sacrament of the Sick on 27 June and four days later passed peacefully into the loving embrace of the Lord whom he knew, loved and served. On the day of his death the L'Arche community expressed sadness, writing of Fr David: 'We are at the same time sad and grateful for everything he has brought to everyone and to the whole community including the parish, the village and around the world. His kindness, his humility, his unconditional love for everyone … we give thanks that we have known and loved him'. Fr David's Funeral Mass and burial took place on 4 July in Ambleteuse, Pas de Calais in northern France.

May he rest in peace.

DIOCESAN CLERGY ANNIVERSARIES

JANUARY

1	Cardinal Francis Bourne (1935)
	Fr Brendan Soane (2000)
2	Fr Cyril Wilson (1988)
3	Fr Donald Campbell (1985)
	Fr Denis Cantwell (1995)
4	Fr Bernard Canham (1990)
	Fr William Brown (2001)
6	Fr Thomas Anderson (1974)
	Fr Thomas McNamara (1976)
	Mgr Graham Leonard (2010)
	Mgr Ralph Brown (2014)
7	Fr John T Carberry (1988)
8	Fr John Kearsey (2004)
	Mgr Anthony Stark (2020)
10	Mgr Ernest T Bassett (1990)
	Fr William Kahle (1993)
	Fr Patrick Nolan (2014)
11	Fr Mark Coningsby (2014)
12	Fr Arthur P Mintern (1993)
14	Cardinal Henry Manning (1892)
	Fr Peter Lyons (1998)
15	Canon James Hathway (1976)
	Fr Anthony Busuttil (2013)
	Mgr Mark Langham (2021)
16	Fr Edward Hinsley (1976)
	Canon Frederick Smyth (2007)
	Fr Seamus Noctor (2019)
	Mgr John Klyberg (2020)
17	Fr Edward Dering Leicester (1977)
	Fr George O'Connor (1989)
18	Fr Gerry Ennis (2000)
	Fr Robin Whitney (2012)
19	Fr Oldrich Trnka (2003)
20	Mgr George Leonard (1993)
	Fr Thomas Gardner (1995)
	Fr Stephen Bartlett (2012)
21	Preb Ronald Pilkington (1975)
22	Cardinal William Godfrey (1963)
23	Fr Derek Jennings (1995)
	Fr Bernard McCumiskey (2021)
24	Fr Adrian Walker (2019)
25	Fr Bernard Fisher (1990)
26	Bishop Patrick Casey (1999)
29	Fr Frederick Vincent (1973)

30	Fr Joseph Fehrenbach (1985)
	Fr Patrick Howard (2000)
	Fr Philip Dayer (2005)
31	Fr Kidane Lebasi (2021)

FEBRUARY

1	Mgr Edward Dunderdale (2001)
2	Fr Charles Lowe (1978)
	Bishop Philip Harvey (2003)
	Fr James McCormick (2009)
3	Fr Hugh Bishop (1984)
6	Fr Patrick McEvoy (1974)
	Canon William Ward (1993)
	Canon Daniel Kay (2003)
	Fr Kenneth McCabe (2013)
7	Fr George Haines (2000)
	Fr Michael John Groarke (2008)
9	Canon George Groves (1997)
10	Fr Seamus McGeoghan (2022)
11	Fr Alan Body (1988)
12	Fr Joseph Francis (1984)
	Canon Edward Armitage (1987)
	Mgr Canon Francis Bartlett (1992)
13	Mgr Canon Maurice Kelleher (1994)
15	Cardinal Nicholas Wiseman (1865)
	Fr Richard Wakeling (1988)
	Fr Leo Straub (2000)
	Mgr Canon Adrian Arrowsmith (2014)
16	Mgr Bernard Chapman (1999)
	Fr John Kirwin (2003)
	Canon Patrick Davies (2010)
19	Fr Ronald Aylward (2010)
20	Fr Joseph Scholles (1983)
21	Fr Michael Hollings (1997)
	Canon Peter Bourne (2001)
	Fr Cathal McGonagle (2010)
22	Deacon James Richards (2014)
23	Canon John O'Callaghan (1981)
24	Mgr Canon Arthur Rivers (1978)
25	Fr Charles McMenemy (1976)
	Fr Archibald Bardney (1985)
	Fr Andrew Clancy (1986)
26	Fr Brian Heaney (2013)
27	Fr Nicholas Lambert (1976)

SECTION 4

Canon Michael Richards (1997)
Canon Charles McGowan (2006)
Canon Peter Moore (2006)

28 Fr Joseph Gilligan (1990)
Fr John Taylor (2005)

29 Fr Frank Rochla (1992)
Fr John McCoy (2012)

MARCH

6 Mgr Frederick Row (1974)
Mgr Canon Clement Parsons (1980)
Fr Geoffrey Webb (2014)
Fr Timothy McCarthy (2018)

7 Fr Henry Dodd (1992)
Fr Harold Riley (2003)

8 Fr Thomas Nobbs (1977)

9 Fr Paul Lenihan (1992)

14 Canon Jeremiah Galvin (1973)
Fr Reginald Watt (1975)
Fr Vincent Crewe (2021)

15 Fr Walter Donovan (1981)

17 Cardinal Arthur Hinsley (1943)
Fr Michael Buckley (1993)
Fr Lionel Keane (1997)
Fr Charles Connor (2005)
Canon Digby Samuels (2018)

18 Fr John Nelson-Turner (2015)

20 Canon Desmond Swan (1995)
Fr Edward Bushey (1996)
Fr Nicholas Kavanagh (2018)
Fr Gerard Burke (2019)
Fr Kevin McDevitt (2022)

21 Fr James de Felice (1978)

22 Fr Edward Higgs (1988)

23 Fr Peter Day (2006)

24 Fr John Gill (1985)
Fr Pat Heekin (2006)

25 Mgr Richard Kenefeck (1982)

27 Fr Cormac Rigby (2007)
Fr James Brand (2013)

30 Fr William Hutchinson (1984)

APRIL

1 Canon Edward Matthews (2020)

3 Fr Francis Kenney (1987)
Fr Charles Austin Garvey (2020)

4 Fr Peter Dunn (1974)
Fr Robert Holmes-Walker (2010)

5 Fr David Evans (1989)

6 Mgr Canon Frederick Miles (2020)

7 Fr John Keep (2002)
Fr John O'Halloran (2020)
Fr John Helm (2020)

9 Fr Ronald Cox (1994)
Fr Thomas Hookham (1998)
Fr James Wooloughan (2003)
Fr Gerard Meaney (2010)

10 Mgr Canon John M T Barton (1977)
Fr Brian Laycock (2004)

11 Fr John Bebb (1975)
Bishop James O'Brien (2007)
Mgr John Coghlan (2020)

12 Fr John Mills (1975)
Fr Anton Cowan (2016)

13 Fr Albert Davey (1987)

14 Fr Michael Hendry (1994)

15 Fr John Seabrook (2020)

16 Fr Clement Tigar (1976)
Mgr Canon Lancelot Long (1978)
Fr Bernard McGuinness (1978)

19 Fr Joseph McEntee (1978)
Canon Harold Winstone (1987)
Fr Anthony Conlon (2020)

20 Fr Patrick Smyth (1978)

21 Canon Reginald Fuller (2011)

22 Fr Herbert Crees (1974)
Fr Robert Tollemach (1998)
Fr John Robson (2000)

23 Canon Frank Martin (2002)

24 Canon Clement Rochford (1978)
Fr Derek McClughen (1991)

25 Canon Francis Hegarty (2004)
Fr Antony Brunning (2022)

27 Fr Stanley Harrison (1973)
Mgr John F McDonald (1992)

28 Canon John Longstaff (1986)

29	Fr Michael Moriarty (1996)

MAY

2	Fr John Farrelly (1990)
	Fr John Coughlan (1997)
	Fr Francis Finnegan (1999)
	Fr Edward Bilsborrow (2007)
3	Canon Philip Cross (2022)
4	Fr Raymond Tomalin (1996)
5	Canon Herbert Welchman (1982)
	Fr Denys Lucas (1995)
6	Fr John Hathway (1995)
	Fr Anthony Potter (2003)
7	Fr Alastair Russell (1997)
9	Fr Bernard Lagrue (1995)
10	Fr Patrick Keegan (1992)
	Mgr Canon Oliver Kelly (1995)
	Canon Denis Britt-Compton (2002)
	Fr Charles Mercer (2005)
	Fr Frederick de L'Orme (2016)
11	Fr Thomas Kean (1981)
13	Mgr Stephen Shaw (1998)
14	Fr Peter Boshell (1993)
15	Fr William O'Brien (2004)
	Fr Patrick Sammon (2018)
20	Fr Stanislaus Savage (1975)
	Fr Michael Markey (2014)
22	Fr Ronald Richardson (1999)
	Fr Charles MacMahon (2003)
23	Fr Bernard Bussy (1992)
	Fr Hugh McAleese (1994)
	Fr Matthew Burrows (2010)
24	Fr Denis Ward (1978)
	Fr Philip Rogers (1995)
	Fr Michael Garvey (2002)
	Fr Denis Nottingham (2002)
25	Mgr Denis McGuinness (1993)
	Fr John Oldland (1995)
26	Canon Patrick J Murphy (1974)
	Fr John Murray (1995)
30	Fr Albert Purdie (1976)
	Fr Kevin Eastell (2022)
31	Canon Reginald Crook (1990)

	Fr John Luke (2003)
	Fr Kevin Greene (2004)

JUNE

1	Fr Philip Carpenter (1992)
	Bishop Victor Guazzelli (2004)
	Fr Denis Patrick Watters (2019)
2	Fr Stephen Finnegan (1993)
	Fr Damien McManus (1997)
4	Fr Joseph Rees (2007)
	Fr William McConalogue (2009)
8	Fr Harold Hamill (2016)
9	Mgr David Norris (2010)
10	Fr John Harrington (2007)
11	Fr Vincent McCarthy (1974)
	Fr Francis Davis (2003)
13	Canon Alfonso de Zulueta (1980)
14	Fr George Lee (1987)
	Canon Vincent Berry (2020)
16	Fr Michael Pinot de Moira (2013)
17	Cardinal Basil Hume OSB (1999)
18	Fr Michael Connor (2007)
19	Cardinal Herbert Vaughan (1903)
20	Fr Thomas Kiernan (2013)
21	Fr J Brian Campbell (1983)
22	Fr Anthony Turbett (2000)
26	Fr John Moran (1988)
	Mgr Canon Roderick More O'Ferrall (1991)
	Canon Christopher Tuckwell (2020)
27	Fr Raleigh Addington (1980)
28	Canon Denis Crowley (1980)
29	Fr Richard Fitzgibbon (2006)
30	Fr Christopher Bedford (2008)

JULY

1	Mgr Anthony Howe (2011)
	Fr David Wilson (2022)
3	Fr William M Brown (1989)
	Fr George Ennis (2007)
4	Fr Joseph Anthony Carr (1999)
6	Fr Terence Wardle (2010)

SECTION 4

7	Canon Alfred Cuming (1978)
	Fr Frank Morrall (1995)
	Fr John Power (2002)
8	Fr Joseph Gardner (1992)
9	Fr Christopher Pemberton (1983)
	Fr John Norton (1989)
10	Fr Peter Harris (1976)
	Fr Thomas Kelly (1983)
12	Fr Daniel Higgins (1996)
14	Mgr Canon Joseph Williams (1991)
15	Fr Christopher McKenna (2003)
16	Fr Michael Giffney (1987)
	Canon John McKenzie (1988)
17	Fr Horatio Hosford (2014)
	Fr Frederick Jackson (2020)
19	Canon Peter Gilburt (2017)
21	Canon Philip Moore (1976)
	Fr Anthony O'Sullivan (1997)
	Fr Norman Kersey (1999)
	Canon Herbert Veal (2005)
22	Fr Tom Allan (2007)
26	Fr George Fonseca (1998)
	Fr David Roderick (2005)
27	Fr Graham Feint (2000)
28	Fr Ralph Gardner (1976)
	Fr Patrick Whyte (1988)
	Deacon Sydney Adams (2005)
30	Fr Calum MacLean (1982)
	Fr Vincent Commerford (1997)
31	Fr Albert Vaughan (1995)

AUGUST

1	Fr Richard Johnson (1992)
	Fr Ignatius Tonna (1993)
2	Fr Thomas Stack (1984)
	Fr Michael Archer (2014)
	Fr Thomas Quinn (2019)
3	Mgr Canon John Mostyn (1981)
4	Fr Christopher Gawecki (2019)
5	Fr William Lynagh (1977)
	Fr Alan Fudge (2011)
6	Fr Anthony Sacré (2015)
9	Fr John Greene (1980)

11	Fr Laurence Allan (1981)
	Fr Guy Martin Heal (2009)
12	Fr Roderick Cuming (1981)
	Fr Wilfrid Soggee (1990)
	Fr John Milne (2001)
	Fr Joseph Finnegan (2002)
	Fr John D'Arcy Dutton (2013)
14	Fr Philip Dwerryhouse (1986)
15	Fr John Adam (1979)
	Fr Bernard Mortimore (1980)
16	Canon Denis O'Sullivan (1983)
	Fr Peter Latham (2005)
17	Mgr Walter Drumm (2015)
19	Canon George Davey (1986)
	Fr Leslie Cole (1997)
	Fr Michael Durand (2018)
20	Cardinal Bernard Griffin (1956)
	Fr Joseph McVeigh (1977)
	Fr Desmond Mullin (1988)
21	Fr Percival Fielden (1990)
	Fr Edward Houghton (2009)
23	Fr Daniel Horan (2020)
24	Fr Patrick Cassidy (2007)
25	Mgr Canon Herbert Haines (2004)
	Fr Raymond Legge (2015)
	Fr Sean McWeeny (2016)
26	Fr Peter Keenan (1984)
27	Mgr John Coonan (1979)
	Fr Norman Wrigley (2015)
29	Fr Edward Fowler (1973)
	Fr Michael Lynam (1984)
	Fr Colin Whatling (2021)
31	Fr William Rees (1984)
	Canon Maurice O'Leary (1997)

SEPTEMBER

1	Cardinal Cormac Murphy-O'Connor (2017)
2	Fr Gerard Strain (1980)
3	Deacon Timothy Marsh (2013)
6	Canon Michael Roberts (2004)
	Fr Stephen Delany (2021)
7	Canon John F Marriott (1977)

10	Fr Thomas Burke (2018)
11	Fr William Erby (1974)
	Mgr Canon Cuthbert Collingwood (1980)
	Fr James Whitehead (1983)
12	Fr Leslie Wood (1984)
14	Fr William Ruhman (1978)
	Fr Leonard Collingwood (1985)
15	Fr Brian Connaughton (1979)
	Fr Robert Gates (2014)
16	Canon Nicholas Kelly (1988)
	Fr Patrick David O'Driscoll (2016)
17	Fr Frederick Thomas (1986)
	Fr John Pakenham (1987)
18	Canon John L Wright (1978)
19	Fr Alan Ashton (2014)
	Fr Patrick Lyons (2015)
20	Fr Des O'Neill (2008)
	Fr Austin Hart (2013)
21	Fr George Ingram (1992)
23	Fr Godfrey Wilson (1998)
24	Mgr Peter Anglim (2016)
26	Fr James Loughnane (1993)
	Fr Bernard Lang (2005)
	Fr Lance Joseph Boward (2011)
	Mgr Augustine Hoey (2017)
27	Deacon Robert Levett (2021)
28	Fr Robert Newbery (1981)
	Fr Gerard Barry (1998)
30	Fr Michael O'Dwyer (1977)
	Fr Joseph Murray (1989)
	Fr John B Elliott (2017)

OCTOBER

1	Fr Barry Ffrench (2019)
2	Canon Des Sheehan (2004)
5	Fr John Fleming (1974)
	Fr Walter Meyjes (1987)
6	Fr Denis Murphy (1999)
	Fr George Dangerfield (2018)
7	Fr Thomas Daniel (1984)
	Canon Peter Phillips (2014)
8	Fr Thomas Allan (1982)

10	Fr Norman Fergusson (1986)
	Fr Arthur Moraes (2008)
12	Fr James Finn (1977)
	Canon John P Murphy (1989)
13	Fr Norman Brown (2017)
14	Fr John Woods (2002)
	Fr Barry Carpenter (2012)
16	Mgr Canon Terence Keenan (1984)
	Fr Duncan Adamson (2022)
18	Fr John Eveleigh Woodruff (1976)
	Fr John Murphy (2005)
19	Fr John Farrell (1983)
21	Fr Richard Berry (1989)
22	Fr David Cullen (1974)
	Fr Herbert Keldany (1988)
	Fr Ben Morgan (2005)
23	Fr Joe Gibbons (2002)
	Fr Dermot McGrath (2012)
24	Fr John Halvey (1990)
	Fr Ken Dain (2010)
25	Fr Andrew Moore (1994)
	Fr John Kearney (2007)
	Fr John Miller (2020)
26	Fr John Clayton (1992)
	Fr George Talbot (2004)
	Fr David Irwin (2021)
27	Fr Colin Kilby (1985)
29	Fr Joseph Eldridge (1993)
30	Canon William Gordon (1976)
31	Fr William Dempsey (2008)

NOVEMBER

1	Fr Horace Tennant (2000)
2	Mgr Canon George Tomlinson (1985)
	Fr Terence Brady (1989)
5	Fr Eric Chadwick (1993)
6	Fr Peter Geraerts (1980)
7	Cardinal John Carmel Heenan (1975)
	Canon Charles Carr (1985)
	Fr Raymond Geraerts (1995)
8	Fr Jeremiah Ryan (2001)
	Fr Peter Stevens (2019)
9	Fr George Barringer (1978)

	Fr James Ethrington (1981)			Fr John Donlan (2006)
10	Fr Richard M Sutherland (1974)		18	Canon Bernard George (1980)
	Fr John Spencer (1980)		19	Canon John Shaw (1981)
11	Fr Gerald Freely (2013)			Fr Edward Gwilliams (1981)
12	Fr James R Coughlan (1974)			Fr Edward Scanlan (1992)
	Fr Peter Johnson (2000)			Fr William Campling (1996)
14	Fr Maurice Ryan (1983)			Canon John McDonald (2016)
	Canon Louis Marteau (2002)			Fr Bernard Crowe (2019)
16	Fr Ian Dommerson (1996)		20	Fr Desmond Baker (2021)
17	Fr Samuel Steer (1996)		21	Fr Clive Godwin (1974)
20	Canon Louis Thomas (2017)		22	Fr David Palmer (2020)
22	Mgr Reginald Butcher (1976)		23	Fr Ian Dickie (2012)
	Fr Christopher Fullerton (1980)		24	Fr Manoel Gomes (1989)
24	Canon Edmund Hadfield (1982)		25	Deacon Ron Saunders (2007)
25	Fr Joseph Doyle (1978)			Canon Charles Acton (2016)
	Canon Joseph Geraerts (1979)		26	Fr Alan O'Connor (1992)
	Fr John Galvin (2010)			Fr Bernard Lavin (1999)
	Canon John Formby (2015)		27	Fr Andrew Morley (1993)
26	Fr James Woodward (1976)		28	Mgr Canon Joseph Collings (1978)
	Fr William Wood (1986)			Fr Gerard Mulvaney (1996)
	Fr Anthony John Cooke (2007)			Fr James A Duffy (2020)
27	Fr Joseph Scally (1995)		29	Fr Robert Bradley (1976)
	Fr Peter O'Reilly (2005)		30	Canon Alexander Stewart (1976)
29	Fr Christopher Hamilton-Gray (2012)		31	Fr Wilfrid Trotman (1976)
	Fr Brian Nash (2014)			Fr Stephen Rigby (1978)
30	Canon Arthur Welland (1978)			Fr George Swanton (1979)
				Fr Dennis Skelly (1996)
				Fr Michael Ware (1998)

DECEMBER

3	Fr Harold Purney (1983)
4	Fr Peter Allen (1978)
	Mgr Wilfrid Purney (1987)
	Fr Benedict Westbrook (1989)
6	Fr John Harper-Hill (1998)
	Mgr Alexander Groves (1998)
	Fr Dominic Byrne (2021)
11	Fr Dalton Haughey (1991)
12	Fr Laurence Kingseller (1975)
13	Fr Jeremiah Daly (1974)
14	Deacon Michael Bykar (2008)
15	Fr Francis Donovan (1983)
	Fr Robert Joseph Barry (2018)
16	Mgr George Tancred (2002)

OTHER PRIESTS IN THE DIOCESE

The entry in brackets following each surname indicates the diocese, order, congregation or society to which the priest belongs. A place name in brackets refers to a parish entry where further details may be found.

a.a.	Assumptionist		OAR	Augustinian Recollect
CCN	Chemin Neuf Community		OCarm	Carmelite
CM	Vincentian		ODC	Carmelite (Discalced)
CMF	Claretian Missionary		OFM	Franciscan (Friar Minor)
CMI	Carmelite of Mary Immaculate		OFMCap	Capuchin Friar
CMPS	Missionary Community of Most Holy Providence		OMI	Oblate of Mary Immaculate
			OP	Dominican
CP	Passionist		OSA	Augustinian
CS	Scalabrini Father		OSB	Benedictine
CSS	Stigmatine		OSM	Servite
CSSp	Spiritan		SAC	Pallottine
CSSR	Redemptorist		SC	Brothers of the Sacred Heart
FDP	Sons of Divine Providence		SCJ	Sacred Heart Father
FMVD	Verbum Dei Missionary Fraternity		SDS	Salvatorian
IC	Rosminian (Institute of Charity)		SDV	Society of Divine Vocations
IMC	Consolata Father		SJ	Jesuit
LMO	Lebanese Maronite Order		SM	Marist
MAfr	Missionary of Africa (White Father)		SMA	Society of African Missions
MHM	Mill Hill Missionary		SMM	Montfort Missionary
Mccl	Comboni Missionary		SSC	Columban Father
MIC	Marian Father		SSP	Society of St Paul
MSFS	Fransalian		SVD	Divine Word Missionary
MSP	Missionary Society of St Paul			

RETIRED BISHOPS

Campbell (OSA, Bishop Emeritus of Lancaster) Michael; **55 Fulham Palace Road W6 8AU** (Hammersmith)

Crowley (Bishop Emeritus of Middlesborough) John; **Flat 2, Francis Court, Caddington Road NW2 1RP Tel: 020 8452 6200** (Cricklewoood)

BISHOP

Nowakowski (Eparch of the Eparchy of the Holy Family in London) Kenneth; **22 Binney Street W1K 5BQ** (Ukrainian Cathedral)

PRIESTS

Abuo (Ogoja) Benedict; **41 Brook Green W6 7BL Email: benedict.abuo@nhs.net** (Brook Green, Imperial College Trust Hospitals Chaplaincy)

Achkar (LMO) Antoine; **6 Dobson Close NW6 4RS Tel: 020 7586 1801** (Lebanese Maronite Church)

Adayi (CSSp) Daniel; **94 Bath Road, Hounslow TW3 3EH Tel: 020 8570 1693**
(Hounslow)
Addison (OSM) Paul; **264 Fulham Road SW10 9EL (Fulham Road)**
Adusei-Poku (CSSp) Patrick; **5 Berrymead Gardens W3 8AA Tel: 020 8992 2014 (Acton)**
Akoeso (OSB) Bernard M; **c/o Archbishop's House SW1P 1QJ**
Alex (OMI) Angodage Don Joseph; **30 Prescot Street E1 8BB (Tower Hill)**
Alexander (Keralan Chaplaincy) Johnson; **373 Bowes Road N11 1AA**
Tel 07438 182888 (New Southgate)
Anderson (MAfr) Donald; **64 Little Ealing Lane W5 4XF (Brentford)**
Angga Indraswara (SJ) Heinrich; **Copleston House, 221 Goldhurst Terrace NW6 3EP**
(Kilburn)
Antwi-Boasiako (CSSp) Paul; **Our Lady and St Michael Catholic Church, Crown Rise,**
Garston WD25 0NE Tel: 01923 673239 (Garston)
Anywanwu (CM) Akobundu; **2 Flower Lane NW7 2JB Tel: 020 8959 1021 (Mill Hill)**
Anzioli (MCCJ) Angelo; **16 Dawson Place W2 4TJ (Bayswater)**
Armstrong (CM) Raymond; **2 Flower Lane NW7 2JB Tel: 020 8959 1021 (Mill Hill)**
Arputham (SMA) Thyagu; **White House, Watford Road, Northwood HA6 3PW**
(Northwood)
Ashu (CM) John; **2 Flower Lane NW7 2JB Tel: 020 8959 1021 (Mill Hill)**
Atu (Nigerian Chaplaincy) Alexander Izany; **8 King Henry's Walk N1 4PB**
Tel: 07432 048440 (Kingsland)
Atunaya (CSSp) David; **15 St John's Villas N19 3EE Tel: 020 7272 8195 (Archway)**
Azzi (LMO) Aziz; **6 Dobson Close NW6 4RS Tel: 020 7586 1801 (Lebanese Maronite**
Church)

Baczewski (SJ) Adam; **182 Walm Lane NW2 3AX Tel: 020 8452 4304**
(Willesden Green)
Bahati (a.a.) Antigon Claude; **Assumption Priory, Victoria Park Square E2 9PB**
(Bethnal Green, Barts Health NHS Trust)
Bailham (OP) Joseph; **St Dominic's Priory, Southampton Road NW5 4LB**
(Haverstock Hill)
Baka (CSSp) Benedict; **Our Lady and St Michael Catholic Church, Crown Rise, Garston**
WD25 0NE Tel: 01923 673239 (Garston, School Chaplain)
Banayag (OSA) Tomas; **55 Fulham Palace Road W6 8AU (Hammersmith)**
Banseh (MAfr) Matthew; **15 Corfton Road W5 2HP (Ealing)**
Barnes (SJ) Michael; **Copleston House, 221 Goldhurst Terrace NW6 3EP (Kilburn)**
Beale (FDP) Stephen; **23 Lower Teddington Road, Hampton Wick KT1 4EU (Teddington)**
Bermingham (SJ) Edward; **St Anselm's Rectory, The Green, Southall UB2 4BE (Southall)**
Bevan (OSB) Alexander; **Ealing Abbey, Charlbury Grove W5 2DY (Ealing)**
Birchall (SJ) David; **114 Mount Street W1K 3AH (Farm Street)**
Blake (OCD) Mathew; **41 Kensington Church Street W8 4BB (Kensington 2)**
Blum (Cologne) Andreas; **47 Adler Street E1 1EE (German Church)**
Boidin (SM) Pascal; **5 Leicester Place WC2H 7BX (French Church)**

Bolivar (OSA) Arthur; 55 Fulham Palace Road W6 8AU (Hammersmith)
Bonelli (IMC) Carlo; 3 Salisbury Avenue N3 3AJ (Finchley Church End)
Bonnet-Eymard (SM) Hubert; 5 Leicester Place WC2H 7BX (French Church)
Borovsky (Slovak Chaplaincy, and also for Czech) Tibor; 22 Cortayne Road SW6 3QA
(Parsons Green)
Bossy (SJ) Michael; 114 Mount Street W1K 3AH (Farm Street)
Bowen (Oratorian) George; The Oratory, Brompton Road SW7 2RP (Oratory)
Braum (Fréjus–Toulon) Barry; 8 Hyde Park Place W2 2LJ (Tyburn Convent Chaplain)
Bristow (Opus Dei) MA, STD, Peter; 8 Orme Court W2 4RL (Queensway)
Brunet (CCN) Christophe; 29 Bramley Road N14 4HE (Cockfosters)
Buba Leszek; 2 Devonia Road N1 8JJ Tel: 020 7226 9944 (Polish 1)
Burns (OSB) BA, STB, Peter; Ealing Abbey, Charlbury Grove W5 2DY (Ealing)

Cabanero (SMM) Nelson; 27 St Gabriel's Road NW2 4DS (Willesden Green)
Calcutt (MAfr) Richard; 64 Little Ealing Lane W5 4XF (Brentford)
Cameron-Mowat (SJ) Andrew; 27 High Road N15 6ND (Stamford Hill)
Camilleri (OFM, Maltese Chaplaincy) Victor; 47 Adler Street E1 1EE Tel: 07930 198251
Email: victorjcamilleri@gmail.com (German Church)
Chantry (MHM) Anthony; 23 Eccleston Square SW1V 1NU (Pimlico)
Chimire (SJ) Inos; Copleston House, 221 Goldhurst Terrace NW6 3EP (Kilburn)
Choi (OSA) Jacob; 19 Hoxton Square N1 6NT (Hoxton)
Chornenko Andriy; 22 Binney Street W1K 5BQ Tel: 020 7629 1073
(Ukrainian Cathedral)
Ciebien Krzysztof; 2 Devonia Road N1 8JJ Tel: 020 7704 7662 (Polish 1)
Clifford (OSA) Barry; 55 Fulham Palace Road W6 8AU (Hammersmith)
Creighton-Jobe (Oratorian) Ronald; The Oratory, Brompton Road SW7 2RP (Oratory)
Csicsó (Pecs) János; 62 Little Ealing Lane W5 4EA (Brentford)
Cullen (MAfr) David; 64 Little Ealing Lane W5 4XF (Brentford)
Cummins (MAfr) Joseph; 64 Little Ealing Lane W5 4XF (Brentford)
Cummins (MAfr) Thomas; 64 Little Ealing Lane W5 4XF (Brentford)
Curci (MCCJ) Carmine; 16 Dawson Place W2 4TJ (Bayswater)
Curran (CM) Eugene; 2 Flower Lane NW7 2JB (Mill Hill)
Cussen (SMA) Anthony; White House, Watford Road, Northwood HA6 3PW
(Northwood)

D'Souza (SJ) Jovito F; St Anselm's Rectory, The Green, Southall UB2 4BE (Southall)
Daly (SAC) Thomas; 358 Greenford Road, Greenford UB6 9AN (Greenford)
De Caro (SAC) Giuseppe; 4 Back Hill, Clerkenwell Road EC1R 5EN (Italian Church)
De Marchi (MCCJ) Benito; 16 Dawson Place W2 4TJ (Bayswater)
Devereux (OMI) Thomas; New Priory, Quex Road NW6 4PS (Kilburn)
Diame (CSSp) Jean Pascal; 63 Somerset Road, New Barnet EN5 1RF (New Barnet, School
Chaplain)
Dilke (Oratorian) Charles; The Oratory, Brompton Road SW7 2RP (Oratory)
Dillon (OMI) Paschal; 237 Goldhurst Terrace NW6 3EP (Kilburn)

Dionne (SC) Nelson; 8 King Harry Lane, St Albans AL3 4AW (St Albans South)
Diouf (SM) Damien; 5 Leicester Place WC2H 7BX (French Church)
Ditchuk Taras; 22 Binney Street W1K 5BQ Tel: 020 7629 1073 (Ukrainian Cathedral)
Doherty (SDS) Michael; 9 Breakspear, Stevenage SG2 9SQ
Tel: 01438 352182 (Stevenage Parishes)
Doherty (CP) Tiernan; St Joseph's Retreat, Highgate Hill N19 5NE (Highgate)
Donnelly (SVD) Eamonn; 8 Teignmouth Road NW2 4HN (Willesden Green
Doyle (Oratorian) Patrick; The Oratory SW7 2RP (Oratory)
Dukiya (CSSp) Jerome; 373 Bowes Road N11 1AA Tel: 020 8368 1638 (New Southgate)
Dunn (OP) Michael; St Dominic's Priory, Southampton Road NW5 4LB (Haverstock Hill)

Edgar (OP) Leo; St Dominic's Priory, Southampton Road NW5 4LB (Haverstock Hill)
Egboo (Nigerian Chaplaincy) Peter Tochukwu; 8 King Henry's Walk N1 4PB
Tel: 07440 653821 (Kingsland)
Egenonu (CSSp) Erasmus; 247 High Road W4 4PU Tel: 020 8994 2877
(Chiswick, Grove Park)
Ekuma (OCD) Taddeus; 41 Kensington Church Street W8 4BB (Kensington 2)
Elias (SJ) Harold; St Ignatius Church, 27 High Road N15 6ND (Stamford Hill)
Elliott-Smith (Ordinariate) MA, DipRAM, GRSM, LRAM, Mark; 22 George Street W1U 3QY
Tel: 020 7486 7026 / 07815 320761 Email: markelliottsmith@rcdow.org.uk
(Warwick Street)
Enehizena (CSSp) Moses; 15 St John's Villas N19 3EE (Archway)
Enuh (CM) Chinedu; 2 Flower Lane NW7 2JB (Mill Hill)
Eshak (LMO) Youssef; 6 Dobson Close NW6 4RS Tel: 020 7586 1801 (Lebanese
Maronite Church)
Escoto (SVD) Albert; 8 Teignmouth Road NW2 4HN (Willesden Green)
Ezenwosu (MSP) Walter; 115 Hertford Road N9 7EN (Edmonton)

Fedun Vitaly; 22 Binney Street W1K 5BQ Tel: 020 7629 1073 (Ukrainian Cathedral)
Fernandes (Goa and Daman); 60 Rylston Road SW6 7HW Tel: 020 7385 4040 (Fulham 1)
Fitzharris (SVD) Kieran; 8 Teignmouth Road NW2 4HN (Willesden Green)
Flynn (SMM) Kieran; 27 St Gabriel's Road NW2 4DS (Willesden Green)
Fordham (Oratorian) John; The Oratory, Brompton Road SW7 2RP (Oratory)
Frances (OAR) Jose; 18 Cheniston Gardens W8 6TQ (Kensington 1)
Fulco (SAC) Andrea; 4 Back Hill, Clerkenwell Road EC1R 5EN (Italian Church)

Gałuszka Marek; Priest's House, Gravel Hill N3 3RJ Tel: 07523 545493
(Finchley Church End)
Ganeri (OP) Martin St Dominic's Priory, Southampton Road NW5 4LB (Haverstock Hill)
Gerrard (MAfr) John; 15 Corfton Road W5 2HP (Ealing)
Gorham (OSB) STB, Timothy; Ealing Abbey, Charlbury Grove W5 2DY (Ealing)
Gowkielewicz (MIC) Andrzej; 1 Courtfield Gardens W13 0EY (Ealing)
Gucevicius (Vilnius) Petras; 21 The Oval, Hackney Road E2 9DT Tel: 020 7739 8735
(Lithuanian Church)

Gumienny (MIC) Wiktor; 2 Windsor Road W5 5PD Tel: 020 8567 1746 (Polish 3)

Halman (FDP) Henryk; 112 Clarendon Road, Ashford TW15 2QD (Ashford, Stanwell)
Harries (OP) BSc, BD, Peter; St Dominic's Priory, Southampton Road NW5 4LB
Email: peter.harries2@nhs.net (Haverstock Hill)
Hassan (OSA) Gabriel; 19 Hoxton Square N1 6NT (Hoxton)
Hayward (Opus Dei) LLB, JCD, Paul; 4 Orme Court W2 4RL (Queensway)
Heap (MAfr) Michael; 15 Corfton Road W5 2HP (Ealing)
Hemer (MHM) John; 28 Beaufort Street SW3 5AA Tel: 020 7349 5618 (Seminary)
Hewawasam (Sri-Lankan (Sinhalese) Chaplaincy) Ruwan; Clergy House, Peter Avenue
NW10 2DD Tel: 020 8451 4677 (Willesden Green)
Hewitt Stephen; c/o Archbishop's House SW1P 1QJ
Hnylycia (Opus Dei) BSc, PGCE, Stefan; The Presbytery, Maresfield Gardens NW3 5SU
(Swiss Cottage)
Holman (SJ) Michael; Copleston House, 221 Goldhurst Terrace NW6 3EP (Kilburn)
Homer (Ordinariate, School Chaplain) Antony; Email: antonyhomer@rcdow.org.uk
Howard (SJ) Damian; 114 Mount Street W1K 3AH (Farm Street)

Ifeanyi (CSSp) Fidelis; Our Lady and St Michael Catholic Church, Crown Rise, Garston
WD25 0NE Tel: 01923 673239 (Garston, School Chaplain)
Isah (Abeokuta, Nigeria) Daniel; Presbytery, 337 Harrow Road W9 3RB Tel: 020 7286
2170 (Harrow Road, Paddington)
Isek (MSP) Agbor; St Peter's Presbytery, Bishop's Rise, Hatfield, Herts AL10 9HN
(Hatfield Marychurch and Hatfield South)

Januszkiewicz Canon Jerzy; c/o Polish Catholic Mission in England and Wales
Jenish (CP) Edwin; St Joseph's Retreat, Highgate Hill N19 5NE (Highgate)
Johnson (Focolare Movement) Francis Thomas; 138 Parkway, Welwyn Garden City
AL8 6HP Tel: 01707 339242 (Welwyn Garden City)

Kaduthanam (CMI) Joseph; St Joseph's Presbytery, 339 High Road, Wembley HA9 6AG
(Wembley 1)
Kasereka (a.a.) Justin; Assumption Priory, Victoria Park Square E2 9PB (Bethnal Green)
Katthula (CMF) Joseph; Botwell House, Botwell Lane, Hayes UB3 2AB (Hayes)
Keane (SDS) Noel; Salvatorian Community House, 189 High Street, Wealdstone, Harrow
HA3 5DY (Wealdstone)
Kelly (MAfr) Peter; 64 Little Ealing Lane W5 4XF (Brentford)
King (SJ) Nicholas; 114 Mount Street W1K 3AH (Farm Street)
Kmeid (LMO) Fadi; 6 Dobson Close NW6 4RS Tel: 020 7586 1801 (Lebanese Maronite
Church)
Kołodziej Bogdan; 2 Devonia Road N1 8JJ Tel: 020 7226 9944 (Polish 1)
Koloth (CP) George; St Joseph's Retreat, Highgate Hill N19 5NE (Highgate)
Kozak (MIC) Michał; 2 Windsor Road W5 5PD Tel: 020 8567 1746 (Polish 3))

SECTION 4

Kropisz (SJ) Piotr **St Ignatius Church, 27 High Road N15 6ND (Stamford Hill)**
Krzyskow (SVD) Krzysztof; **8 Teignmouth Road NW2 4HN (Willesden Green)**
Kukla MgrTadeusz; **1 Kensington Gate W8 5NA Tel: 020 7589 6664 / 07976 728716**
Email: tadeuszkukla@yahoo.co.uk
Kurumeh (CSSp) Jude; **5 Berrymead Gardens W3 8AA Tel: 020 8992 2014 (Acton)**

Lainez (SDS) Mario; **191 High Road, Harrow Weald HA3 5EE (Wealdstone)**
Lang (Oratorian) Michael; **The Oratory, Brompton Road SW7 2RP (Oratory)**
Large (Oratorian) Julian; **The Oratory, Brompton Road SW7 2RP (Oratory)**
Leggett (MAfr) Raymond; **15 Corfton Road W5 2HP (Ealing)**
Lew (OP) Lawrence; **St Dominic's Priory, Southampton Road NW5 4LB (Haverstock Hill)**
Liang (Jianxi, Chinese Chaplaincy) Joseph; **Assumption Priory, Victoria Park Square E2 9PB Tel: 07753 471611 (Bethnal Green)**
Lobo Ratu (SVD) Nicodemus; **112 Twickenham Road, Isleworth TW7 6DL (Isleworth)**
Loewenstein (OP) Rudolf; **St Dominic's Priory, Southampton Road NW5 4LB (Haverstock Hill)**
Longo Francischini (MPS) Patrick; **St Anne's Church, Underwood Road E1 5AW (Underwood Road)**

McCabe (SJ) John; **St Ignatius Church, 27 High Road N15 6ND (Stamford Hill)**
McCambridge (OSB) Ambrose; **Ealing Abbey, Charlbury Grove W5 2DY (Ealing)**
McCarthy (SVD) John; **8 Teignmouth Road NW2 4HN (Willesden Green)**
McFadden (OMI) John; **New Priory, Quex Road NW6 4PS (Kilburn, University Chaplaincy)**
McFlynn (Irish Chaplaincy) Gerry; **52 Camden Square NW1 9XB Tel: 020 7482 5528 (Kentish Town)**
McGowan (OCD) John; **41 Kensington Church Street W8 4BB (Kensington 2)**
McHardy (Oratorian) Rupert; **The Oratory, Brompton Road SW7 2RP (Oratory)**
McLoughlin (SAC) Joseph; **358 Greenford Road, Greenford UB6 9AN (Greenford)**
McMillan (SJ) Keith; **Copleston House, 221 Goldhurst Terrace NW6 3EP (Kilburn)**
McPake (SVD) Martin; **8 Teignmouth Road NW2 4HN (Willesden Green)**
Maher (OMI) Brian; **New Priory, Quex Road NW6 4PS (Kilburn)**
Malal Muchail (SDS) Thomas; **191 High Road, Harrow Weald HA3 5EE (Wealdstone)**
Malysh Andriy; **22 Binney Street W1K 5BQ Tel: 020 7629 1073 (Ukrainian Cathedral)**
Markey (SSC) Gerard; **12 Blakesley Avenue W5 2DW (Ealing)**
Marsh (Opus Dei) DIC, STD, Bernard; **Netherhall House, Nutley Terrace NW3 5SA (Swiss Cottage)**
Marsh (OSA) Robert; **15 Dorville Crescent W6 0HH (Hammersmith)**
Matwijiwskyj Rt Rev Mykola; **22 Binney Street W1K 5BQ Tel: 020 7629 1073 (Ukrainian Cathedral)**
Mazewski (MIC) Dariusz; **1 Courtfield Gardens W13 0EY Tel: 07427 748605 (Ealing)**
Mazzotta (FDP) Carlo; **112 Clarendon Road, Ashford TW15 2QD (Ashford, Stanwell)**
Mboko (Congolese Chaplaincy) Julien Matondo; **2 Lukin Street E1 0AA (Commercial Road)**
Mbu'i (SVD) Vincent; **Cathedral Clergy House, 42 Francis Street SW1P 1QW (Cathedral)**

Medeiros (MPS) José Eduardo Viveiros; St Anne's Church, Underwood Road E1 5AW (Underwood Road)

Mężyk Tomasz; 2 Devonia Road N1 8JJ (Polish 1)

Michałek Maciej; c/o Holy Family Convent, 52 London Road, Enfield EN2 6EN
Email: jeszuam@interia.pl (Enfield)

Mignolli (CSS) Natalino; 2 Leigh Gardens NW10 5HP (Kensal Rise)

Mititelu (Iasi, Romanian Chaplaincy) Maricel-Irinel; The Presbytery, 22 Hay Lane NW9 0NG
Tel: 07721 867280 (Kingsbury Green)

Mobela Henry; 62 Eden Grove N7 8EN Tel: 07495 866069 (Holloway)

Moffatt (SJ) John; St Ignatius Church, 27 High Road N15 6ND (Stamford Hill)

Moneke (CSSp) Damian-Mary; 94 Bath Road, Hounslow TW3 3EH Tel: 020 8570 1693 (Hounslow, Heathrow Airport)

Morrish (Opus Dei) MA, STD, Mgr Nicholas; 4 Orme Court W2 4RL (Queensway)

Morrone (SDV) Luigi; 15 The Green, Heston Road, Heston TW5 0RL (Heston)

Mudereri (Zimbabwean Chaplaincy) John Rufaro; 24 Bouverie Road N16 0AJ (Stoke Newington)

Murray (OMI) Terence; New Priory, Quex Road NW6 4PS (Kilburn)

Mutimutema (SJ) Clarence; Copleston House, 221 Goldhurst Terrace NW6 3EP (Kilburn)

Mway-Zeng (SDS) Richard; The Presbytery, 96 The Crescent, Abbots Langley, Watford WD5 0DS (Abbots Langley, Chipperfield)

Narcher (SVD) Clement; 112 Twickenham Road, Isleworth TW7 6DL (Isleworth)

Netto (Quilon) Jose; 73 Pembroke Road, Ruislip HA4 8NN Tel: 01895 632739 (Ruislip)

Newman (CMF) Chris; Botwell House, Botwell Lane, Hayes UB3 2AB (Hayes)

Newton (Ordinariate) Mgr Keith; 24 Golden Square W1F 9JR
Tel: 020 7440 5750 (Warwick Street)

Ngolele (SJ) Christophere; Copleston House, 221 Goldhurst Terrace NW6 3EP (Kilburn)

Nicholson (SJ) Paul; 114 Mount Street W1K 3AH (Farm Street)

Nnatuanya (CSSp) Vincent; 45 London Road, Enfield EN2 6DS Tel: 020 8363 2569 (Enfield)

Nolan (MAfr) Francis; 64 Little Ealing Lane W5 4XF (Brentford)

Nopparat Ruankool (SJ) Charles; Copleston House, 221 Goldhurst Terrace NW6 3EP (Kilburn)

Nowotnik (Birmingham) Jan; 39 Eccleston Square SW1V 1BX (CBCEW)

Nunn (OSB) MMus, Alban; Ealing Abbey, Charlbury Grove W5 2DY (Ealing)

Nyamali (OCD) Theophilus; 41 Kensington Church Street W8 4BB (Kensington 2)

Nyarko Clement; 17 Churchfield Path, off Church Lane, Cheshunt EN8 9EG (Cheshunt)

O'Brien (OSM) Chris; 264 Fulham Road SW10 9EL (Fulham Road)

O'Brien (a.a.) Tom; 16 Nightingale Road, Hitchin SG5 1QS (Hitchin)

O'Byrne (CMF) John; Botwell House, Botwell Lane, Hayes UB3 2AB (Hayes)

O'Dell (a.a.) Andrew; 16 Nightingale Road, Hitchin SG5 1QS (Hitchin)

O'Donovan (SAC) Liam; 358 Greenford Road, Greenford UB6 9AN (Greenford)

O'Malley (SSC) Daniel; 12 Blakesley Avenue W5 2DW (Ealing)

SECTION 4

O'Reilly (OMI) Lorcan; 14 Quex Road NW6 4PL (Kilburn)
O'Reilly (SJ) Paul; Copleston House, 221 Goldhurst Terrace NW6 3EP (Kilburn)
O'Shea (Brentwood) Canon Brian; 15 Sheridan Place, Roxborough Park,
Harrow-on-the Hill HA1 3BQ Tel: 07809 591516 (Harrow)
O'Toole (SVD) Kevin; Nazareth House, 162 East End Road N2 0RU (Finchley East)
Odiaka (MSP) Innocent; St Peter's Presbytery, Bishop's Rise, Hatfield, Herts AL10 9HN
(Hatfield Marychurch and Hatfield South)
Ofere (Warri) Albert; The Presbytery, Chalkhill Road, Wembley Park HA9 9EW
Tel: 020 8904 2306 (Wembley 2)
Oguagwu (MSP) Noel; 115 Hertford Road N9 7EN (Edmonton)
Ogunyinka (Ijebu-Ode, Nigeria) Michael; 8 King Henry's Walk N1 4PB
Tel: 07440 653821 (Nigerian Chaplaincy, Kingsland)
Ozhukayil Veedu Chacko (CMI) Joseph; St Joseph's Presbytery, 339 High Road, Wembley
HA9 6AG (Wembley 1)

Panato (MCCJ) Pasquino; 16 Dawson Place W2 4TJ (Bayswater)
Paunon Agustin (Filipino/Hospital Chaplaincy, based at London North West Healthcare NHS
Trust HA1 3UJ); Room 235, Block 4, Hodgson Court, Nightingale Avenue, Harrow HA1
3GH Tel: 020 8869 2112 Mobile: 07880 558225 (Harrow-on-the-Hill)
Pember (CSSp) David; 63 Somerset Road, New Barnet EN5 1RF (New Barnet)
Pereiro (Opus Dei) PhD, STD, James; 8 Orme Court W2 4RL (Queensway)
Pérez Jiménez (SJ) Luis Orlando; Copleston House, 221 Goldhurst Terrace NW6 3EP
(Kilburn)
Perrotta (FDP) John; 23 Lower Teddington Road, Hampton Wick KT1 4EU (Teddington)
Phelan (OMI) Michael; New Priory, Quex Road NW6 4PS (Kilburn)
Podador (SDV) Ritche; 15 The Green, Heston Road, Heston TW5 0RL (Heston)
Preston (SDS) Peter; Salvatorian Community House, 189 High Street, Wealdstone, Harrow
HA3 5DY (Wealdstone)
Puthenpurackal (CMI) Tebin; 339 High Road, Wembley HA9 6AG (Wembley 1)

Quan (CSSp) Ignatius; 15 St John's Villas N19 3EE Tel: 020 7272 8195 (Archway)

Rajewski Bartosz; 167 West Hendon Broadway NW9 7EB Tel: 07449 801752
Email: chaplaincy@pcmew.org.uk Web: www.dalondon.org.uk (Hendon West)
Reczek, Marek; 1 Leysfield Road W12 9JF Tel: 07973 923026 (Polish 2)
Riezu (OAR) Robert; 18 Cheniston Gardens W8 6TQ (Kensington 1)
Robinson (SJ) Dominic; 114 Mount Street W1K 3AH (Farm Street)
Rockey (CP) Thomas; St Joseph's Retreat, Highgate Hill N19 5NE (Highgate)
Rokicki (MIC) Klaudiusz; 2 Windsor Road W5 5PD Tel: 020 8567 1746 (Polish 3)
Rout (OFM) Paul; 2a Eton Avenue, Heston TW5 0HB (Heston)
Ruankool (SJ) Charles Nopparat; Copleston House, 221 Goldhurst Terrace NW6 3EP
(Kilburn)
Ryall (OSM) Patrick; 264 Fulham Road SW10 9EL (Fulham Road)
Ryan (SSC) Thomas; 12 Blakesley Avenue W5 2DW (Ealing)

Sagar (FDP) Sidon 112 Clarendon Road, Ashford TW15 2QD (Ashford, Stanwell)

Salter (Eparchy of the Holy Family) John A T; 1 St James Close, Bishop Street N1 8PH
Tel: 020 7359 0250 (Islington)

Satur (OSM) Allan; 264 Fulham Road SW10 9EL (Fulham Road)

Sawadogo (MAfr) Augustin; 15 Corfton Road W5 2HP (Ealing)

Seenan (MAfr) Hugh; 64 Little Ealing Lane W5 4XF (Brentford) and
15 Corfton Road W5 2HP (Ealing)

Serra (Italian Mission) Antonio; 197 Durants Road, Enfield EN3 7DE
Tel: 020 8804 2307 (Ponders End)

Sheehan (Opus Dei) MA, STD, Gerard; 4 Orme Court, London W2 4RL Tel: 020 7229 7574
(Queensway)

Shipperlee (OSB) BD, BA, Abbot Martin; Ealing Abbey, Charlbury Grove W5 2DY (Ealing)

Shorter (MAfr) Aylward; 64 Little Ealing Lane W5 4XF (Brentford)

Skeats (OP) Thomas; St Dominic's Priory, Southampton Road NW5 4LB (Haverstock Hill)

Smith (SJ) Michael; St Ignatius Church, 27 High Road N15 6ND (Stamford Hill)

Smith (MAfr) Peter; 64 Little Ealing Lane W5 4XF (Brentford)

Smyth (CMF) Paul; Botwell House, Botwell Lane, Hayes UB3 2AB (Hayes)

Soane (Opus Dei) BSc, STD, Andrew; 4 Orme Court W2 4RL (Queensway)

Soyombo Charles; 47 Cumberland Street SW1V 4LY (Pimlico)

Ssuuna (OSM) Fulgensio; 264 Fulham Road SW10 9EL (Fulham Road)

Stamnestro Martin; The Oratory, Brompton Road SW7 2RP (Oratory)

Stapleford (OSB) BA, Thomas; Ealing Abbey, Charlbury Grove W5 2DY (Ealing)

Starkey (MAfr) Denis; 64 Little Ealing Lane W5 4XF (Brentford)

Stasievich (Belarusian) Serge; Marian House, Holden Avenue N12 8HY (Finchley North)

Strange Mgr Roderick; St Mary's University, Waldegrave Road, Twickenham TW1 4SX
Tel: 020 8240 8288   Email: roderick.strange@stmarys.ac.uk (Twickenham)

Sulik (SJ) Ladislav; 114 Mount Street W1K 3AH (Farm Street)

Sullivan (CCN) Pascal; 29 Bramley Road N14 4HE (Cockfosters)

Susairaj (OMI) Johnson; New Priory, Quex Road NW6 4PS (Kilburn)

Szuta (SJ) Leszek; 182 Walm Lane NW2 3AX Tel: 020 8452 4304 (Willesden Green)

Szyperski (MIC) Piotr; 2 Windsor Road W5 5PD Tel: 020 8567 1746 (Polish 3)

Tabarelli (Oratorian) James; The Oratory, Brompton Road SW7 2RP (Oratory)

Tatsidjodoung (a.a.) Adams; 16 Nightingale Road, Hitchin SG5 1QS (Hitchin)

Taylor (OSB) Abbot Dominic; Ealing Abbey, Charlbury Grove W5 2DY (Ealing)

Thomas Aneesh (Syro-Malabar Chaplaincy); 165 Arlington Road NW1 7EX
(Camden Town)

Thomas (Nottingham) Canon Christopher; 39 Eccleston Square SW1V 1BX (CBCEW)

Thomas (IC) Tom; 14 Ely Place EC1N 6RY (Ely Place)

Tintoré (Opus Dei) Alvaro; Netherhall House, Nutley Terrace NW3 5SA
(Swiss Cottage)

Toma Andrawis (Chaldean Chaplaincy); 38 - 40 Cavendish Avenue W13 0JQ

Tomas (IMC) Luis; 3 Salisbury Avenue N3 3AJ (Finchley Church End)

Tomaszewski (SJ) Adam; 182 Walm Lane NW2 3AX Tel: 020 8452 4304
(Willesden Green)
Tran (a.a.) Joseph Quoc Cuong; Assumption Priory, Victoria Park Square E2 9PB
(Bethnal Green)
Travers (CM) Noel; 2 Flower Lane NW7 2JB (Mill Hill)
Tverijonas MA, Petras; 21 The Oval, Hackney Road E2 9DT (Lithuanian Church)
Tworek Mgr Janusz; 2 Devonia Road N1 8JJ Tel: 07970 150712 (Polish 1)
Tyliszczak Canon Krzysztof; 2 Devonia Road N1 8JJ Tel: 07710 198765 (Polish 1)

Ugoagwu (MSP) Noel; 115 Hertford Road N9 7EN (Edmonton)
Ugwu (CSSp) Oliver; 15 St John's Villas N19 3EE Tel: 020 7272 8195
(Archway, Hospital Chaplaincy)

Valiyaputhenpura Joy (Knanaya Chaplaincy) Mathews; The Presbytery, Esdaile Lane,
Hoddesdon EN11 8DS Tel: 01992 440986 (Hoddesdon)
van den Bergh (Oratorian) Edward; The Oratory, Brompton Road SW7 2RP (Oratory)
Van (Vinh, Vietnam) Tri Nguyen; 117 Bow Common Lane E3 4AU Tel: 020 7987 3477
(Bow Common, Vietnamese Chaplaincy)
Vico (CS) Alberto; Villa Scalabrini, Green Street, Shenley WD7 9BB
Tel: 020 8207 5713 (Borehamwood North)

Wallbank (MAfr), Christopher; 64 Little Ealing Lane W5 4XF (Brentford)
Walsh (Albanian Chaplaincy) Gary; 8 Ogle Street W1W 6HS
Tel: 020 7636 2883 (Ogle Street)
Warren (OMI) Raymond; 30 Prescot Street E1 8BB (Tower Hill)
Waters (SDS) Francis; St Joseph's Presbytery, 191 High Road, Harrow Weald HA3 5EE
(Wealdstone)
Wildsmith (MAfr) Edward; 64 Little Ealing Lane W5 4XF (Brentford)
Woo (MAfr) Edward; 64 Little Ealing Lane W5 4XF (Brentford)
Wylezek Mgr Stefan; 2 Devonia Road N1 8JJ Tel: 020 7226 3439 (Polish 1)

Xavier (OCD) Tijo; 41 Kensington Church Street W8 4BB (Kensington 2)

Yacub (SJ) Chester; Copleston House, 221 Goldhurst Terrace NW6 3EP (Kilburn)

Zabbey (OSA) Anthony; 19 Hoxton Square N1 6NT (Hoxton)
Zapaśnik Canon Zygmunt; 1 Leysfield Road W12 9JF (Polish 2)
Zeng (SDS) Dieudonne; The Presbytery, 96 The Crescent, Abbots Langley, Watford
WD5 0DS (Abbots Langley, Chipperfield)
Zhao (SVD) Paul; 1 Stonard Road N13 4DJ (Palmers Green)

RELIGIOUS CONGREGATIONS AND SOCIETIES OF APOSTOLIC LIFE (MEN)

A place name in italics refers to a parish entry, where further details may be found.

African Missions, Society of (SMA)
White House, Watford Road, Northwood
HA6 3PW *(Northwood)*
Arputham, Thyagu **(Superior)**
Cussen, Anthony

Assumptionists (a.a.)
(1) Assumptionist Priory, Victoria Park Square
E2 9PB *(Bethnal Green)*
(2) 16 Nightingale Road, Hitchin SG5 1QS
(Hitchin)
Bahati, Antigon Claude (1)
Kasereka, Justin (1)
O'Brien, Tom (2)
O'Dell, Andrew (2)
Tatsidjodoung, Adams (2)
Tran, Joseph Quoc Cuong (1)

Augustinians (OSA)
(1) 55 Fulham Palace Road W6 8AU
(Hammersmith)
(2) 19 Hoxton Square N1 6NT *(Hoxton)*
(3) 15 Dorville Crescent W6 OHH
(Hammersmith)
Banayag, Tomas (1) **(Parish Priest)**
Bolivar, Arthur (10
Campbell, Bishop Michael (1)
Choi, Jacob (2)
Clifford, Barry (1) **(Prior)**
Hassan, Gabriel (2) **(Parish Priest)**
Marsh, Robert (3) **(Provincial)**
Zabbey, Anthony (2) **(Prior)**
Brothers:
McLaren, Michael (1)
Tan, David (1)

Augustinian Recollects (OAR)
18 Cheniston Gardens W8 6TQ
(Kensington 1)
Riezu, Robert **(Prior)**

Benedictines (OSB - English Congregation)
Charlbury Grove W5 2DY *(Ealing)*
Bevan, Alexander
Burns, Peter
Gorham, Timothy
McCambridge, Ambrose **(Parish Priest)**
Nunn, Alban
Shipperlee, Martin
Stapleford, Thomas
Taylor, Dominic **(Abbot)**

Carmelites, Discalced (OCD)
41 Kensington Church Street W8 4BB
(Kensington 2)
Blake, Mathew
Ekuma, Taddeus **(Prior & Parish Priest)**
McGowan, John
Nyamali, Theophilus
Xavier, Tijo

Carmelites of Mary Immaculate (CMI)
St Joseph's Presbytery 339 High Road,
Wembley HA9 6AG *(Wembley 1)*
Kaduthanam, Joseph
Ozhukayil Veedu Chacko, Joseph
Puthenpurackal, Tebin

Charity, Institute of (IC - Rosminians)
14 Ely Place EC1N 6RY *(Ely Place)*
Thomas, Tom

SECTION 4

Chemin Neuf Community (CCN)
29 Bramley Road N14 4HE
(Cockfosters)
Brunet, Christophe **(Parish Priest)**
Sullivan, Pascal
Deacon:
Wood, Ted

Claretian Missionaries (CMF - Missionaries,
Sons of the Immaculate Heart of Mary)
**Botwell House, Botwell Lane, Hayes UB3
2AB** *(Hayes)*
Katthula, Joseph
Newman, Chris
O'Byrne, John
Smyth, Paul **(Superior)**

Columban Fathers (SSC)
12 Blakesley Avenue W5 2DW *(Ealing)*
Markey, Gerard
O'Malley, Daniel **(Superior)**
Ryan, Thomas

Comboni Missionaries (MCCI - Verona
Fathers)
Comboni House, 16 Dawson Place W2 4TJ
(Bayswater)
Anzioli, Angelo **(Superior)**
Curci, Carmine
De Marchi, Benito
Panato, Pasquino

Consolata Fathers (IMC)
3 Salisbury Avenue N3 3AJ
(Finchley Church End)
Bonelli, Carlo
Tomas, Luis **(Superior)**

Divine Providence, Sons of (FDP)
**(1) 23 Lower Teddington Road, Hampton
Wick KT1 4EU** *(Teddington)*
**(2) 112 Clarendon Road, Ashford
TW15 2QD** *(Ashford)*
Beale, Stephen (1)

Halman, Henryk (2)
Mazzotta, Carlo (2)
Perrotta, John C (1) **(Superior)**
Sagar, Sidon (2)

Divine Word Missionaries (SVD)
(1) 8 Teignmouth Road NW2 4HN
(Willesden Green)
**(2) 112 Twickenham Road, Isleworth TW7
6DL** *(Isleworth)*
(3) 42 Francis Street SW1P 1QW
(Cathedral)
(4) 1 Stonard Road N13 4DJ *(Palmers
Green)*
Donnelly, Eamonn (1)
Escoto, Albert (1) **(Praeses)**
Fitzharris, Kieran (1)
Krzyskow, Krzysztof (1)
Lobo Ratu, Nicodemus (2)
McCarthy, John (1)
McPake, Martin (1)
Mbu'i, Vincent (3)
Narcher, Clement (2)
O'Toole, Kevin *(Nazareth House, Finchley)*
Zhao, Paul (4)

Dominicans (OP - The Order of Preachers)
**St Dominic's Priory, Southampton Road
NW5 4LB (***Haverstock Hill)*
Dunn, Michael
Edgar, Leo
Ganeri, Martin **(Provincial)**
Harries, Peter
Keenan, Oliver
Lew, Lawrence **(Parish Priest)**
Loewenstein, Rudolf
Skeats, Thomas

Franciscans (OFM)
Camilleri, Victor *(German Church)*
Rout, Paul *(Heston)*

Hospitaller Order of St John of God (OH)
52 Kenneth Crescent NW2 4PN
(Willesden Green)
Brothers:
Brannigan, Malachy **(Prior)**
Gerrard, Bonaventure
O'Neil, John
Zach, Andrzej

Jesuits (SJ - Society of Jesus)
**(1) Provincial Curia, 114 Mount Street
W1K 3AH** *(Farm Street)*
**(2) Farm Street Church, 114 Mount Street
W1K 3AH** *(Farm Street)*
**(3) St Ignatius Church, 27 High Road
N15 6ND** *(Stamford Hill)*
**(4) Polish Jesuits, 182 Walm Lane
NW2 3AX** *(Willesden Green)*
**(5) Copleston House, 221 Goldhurst
Terrace NW6 3EP** *(Kilburn)*
**(6) St Anselm's Rectory, The Green, Southall
UB2 4BE** *(Southall)*
Angga Indraswara, Heinrich (5)
Baczewski, Adam (4)
Barnes, Michael (5)
Bermingham, Edward (6)
Birchall, David (2)
Bossy, Michael (2)
Cameron-Mowat, Andrew (3)
Chimire, Inos (5)
D'Souza, Jovito F (6)
Elias, Harold (3)
Holman, Michael (5)
Howard, Damian (1,2) **(Provincial)**
King, Nicholas (2)
Kropisz, Piotr (3)
McCabe, John (3)
McMillan, Keith (5)
Moffatt, John (3)
Mutimutema, Clarence (5)
Ngolele, Christopere
Nicholson, Paul (2)

O'Reilly, Paul (5)
Pérez Jiménez, Luis Orlando (5)
Robinson, Dominic (2)
Ruankool, Charles Nopparat (5)
Smith, Michael (3)
Sulik, Ladislav (2)
Szuta, Leszek (4)
Tomaszewski, Adam (4)
Yacub, Chester (5)
Brother:
Power, Stephen (3)

Lebanese Maronite Order (LMO)
6 Dobson Close NW6 4RS
(Lebanese Church)
Achkar, Antoine
Azzi, Aziz
Eshak, Youssef
Kmeid, Fadi

Malta, Order of (SMOM)
13 Deodar Road SW15 2NP

Marian Fathers (MIC)
(1) 2 Windsor Road W5 5PD *(Polish Church 3)*
(2) 1 Courtfield Gardens W13 0EY *(Ealing)*
Gowkielewicz, Andrzej (2)
Gumienny, Wiktor (1)
Kozak, Michał (1) **(Parish Priest)**
Mazewski, Dariusz (1,2) **(Provincial
Delegate)**
Rokicki, Klaudiusz (1)
Szyperski, Piotr (1)

Marist Fathers (SM)
5 Leicester Place WC2H 7BX
(French Church)
Boidin, Pascal **(Parish Priest)**
Bonnet-Eymard, Hubert **(Superior)**
Diouf, Damien

Mill Hill Missionaries
Chantry, Anthony *(Missio)*
Hemer, John *(Allen Hall Seminary)*

SECTION 4

Missionary Community of Most Holy Providence (MPS)
St Anne's Church, Undwerwood Road E1 5AW *(Underwood Road)*
Longo Francischini, Patrick **(Priest in Charge)**
Medeiros, José Eduardo Viveiros

Missionaries of Africa (MAfr - White Fathers)
(1)15 Corfton Road W5 2HP *(Ealing)*
(2) 64 Little Ealing Lane W5 4XF *(Brentford)*
Anderson, Donald (2)
Banseh, Matthew (1)
Calcutt, Richard (2)
Cullen, David (2)
Cummins, Joseph (2)
Cummins, Thomas (2)
Heap, Michael (1)
Nolan, Francis (2)
Seenan, Hugh (1, 2) **(Superior** and **Provincial)**
Shorter, Aylward (2)
Smith, Peter (2)
Starkey, Denis (2)
Wallbank, Christopher (2) **(Superior)**
Wildsmith, Edward (2)
Woo, Edward (2)
Brothers:
Murphy, Nicholas (1)
O'Reilly, Patrick (2)

Missionary Society of St Paul (MSP)
(1) 115 Hertford Road N9 7EN
(Edmonton)
(2) St Peter's Presbytery, Bishop's Rise, Hatfield AL10 9HN *(Hatfield Marychurch & Hatfield South)*
Ezenwosu, Walter (1)
Isek, Agbor (2)
Odiaka, Innocent (2)
Ugoagwu, Noel (1)

Montfort Missionaries (SMM)
27 St Gabriel's Road NW2 4DS
(Willesden Green)
Cabanero, Nelson
Flynn, Kieran

Oblates of Mary Immaculate (OMI)
(1) New Priory, Quex Road NW6 4PS
(Kilburn)
(2) 237 Goldhurst Terrace NW6 3EP
(Kilburn)
(3) 1 Stafford Road NW6 5RS *(Kilburn West)*
(4) 30 Prescot Street E1 8BB *(Tower Hill)*
(5) Denis Hurley House, 14 Quex Road NW6 4PL *(Kilburn)*
Alex, Angodage Don Joseph (4) **(Parish Priest)**
Devereux, Thomas (1)
Dillon, Paschal (2)
McFadden, John (3)
Maher, Brian (1)
Murray, Terence (1) **(Parish Priest)**
O'Reilly, Lorcan (5)
Phelan, Michael (1)
Susairaj, Johnson (1)
Warren, Raymond (4)

Oratorians
The Oratory, Brompton Road SW7 2RP
(Oratory)
van den Bergh, Edward
Bowen, George
Creighton-Jobe, Ronald
Dilke, Charles
Doyle, Patrick
Fordham, John
Lang, Michael **(Parish Priest)**
Large, Julian **(Provost)**
McHardy, Rupert
Tabarelli, James

Pallottine Fathers (SAC)
(1) 358 Greenford Road, Greenford UB6 9AN *(Greenford)*
(2) 4 Back Hill EC1R 5EN *(St Peter's Italian Church)*
Daly, Thomas (1)
De Caro, Giuseppe (2)
Fulco, Andrea (2)
McLoughlin, Joseph (1)
O'Donovan, Liam (1)

Passionists (CP)
St Joseph's Retreat, Highgate Hill, N19 5NE *(Highgate)*
Doherty, Tiernan **(Rector)**
Jenish, Edwin
Koloth, George **(Parish Priest)**
Rockey, Thomas

Sacred Heart, Brothers of the (SC)
8 King Harry Lane, St Albans AL3 4AW *(St Albans South)*
Brothers:
Dionne, Nelson
Holthaus, Joseph
Vaillancourt, Paul **(Superior)**

Salvatorians (SDS - Society of the Divine Saviour)
(1) 96 The Crescent, Abbots Langley WD5 0DS *(Abbots Langley, Chipperfield)*
(2) Salvatorian Community House, 189 High Street, Wealdstone, Harrow HA3 5DY and **The Presbytery, 191 High Street, Wealdstone HA3 5EE** *(Wealdstone)*
(3) 9 Breakspear, Stevenage SG2 9SQ *(Stevenage Shephall)*
Doherty, Michael (3) **(Superior)**
Keane, Noel (2)
Lainez, Mario (2)
Malal Muchail, Thomas (2)
Mway-Zeng, Richard (1) **(Provincial)**
Preston, Peter (2)
Waters, Frank (2)

Zeng, Dieudonne (1)

Scalabrini Fathers (CS)
Green Street, Shenley WD7 9BB *(Borehamwood North)*
Vico, Alberto

Servites (OSM - Friar Servants of Mary)
264 Fulham Road SW10 9EL *(Fulham Road)*
Addison, Paul
O'Brien, Chris
Ryall, Patrick
Satur, Allan **(Parish Priest)**
Ssuuna, Fulgensio
Brother:
Gethins, Patrick

Society of Divine Vocations (SDV)
15 The Green, Heston Road, Heston TW5 0RL *(Heston)*
Podador, Ritche
Morrone, Luigi

Spiritans (CSSp - Congregation of the Holy Spirit)
(1) 63 Somerset Road, New Barnet EN5 1RF *(New Barnet)*
(2) 15 St John's Villas N19 3EE *(Archway)*
(3) 94 Bath Road, Hounslow TW3 3EH *(Hounslow)*
(4) Our Lady and St Michael Catholic Church, Crown Rise, Garston WD25 0NE *(Garston)*
(5) Heathrow Airport, Hounslow TW6 1BP
(6) 45 London Road, Enfield EN2 6DS *(Enfield)*
(7) 247 High Road W4 4PU *(Chiswick, Grove Park)*
(8) 5 Berrymead Gardens W3 8AA *(Acton)*
(9) 373 Bowes Road N11 AA *(New Southgate)*
Adayi, Daniel (3)
Adusei-Poku, Patrick (8)

SECTION 4

Antwi-Boasiako, Paul (4)
Atunaya, David (2)
Baka, Benedict (4)
Diame, Jean Pascal (1)
Dukiya, Jerome (9)
Enehizena, Moses (2)
Ifeanyi, Fidelis (4)
Kurumeh, Jude (8)
Moneke, Damian-Mary (3, 5)
Nnatuanya, Vincent (6)
Onyema Egenonu, Erasmus (7)
Pember, David (1)
Quan, Ignatius (2)

Stigmatine Fathers (CSS)
2 Leigh Gardens NW10 5HP *(Kensal Rise)*
Mignolli, Natalino

Vincentians (CM - Congregation of the Mission)
2 Flower Lane NW7 2JB *(Mill Hill)*
Anywanwu, Akobundu
Armstrong, Raymond
Ashu, John
Curran, Eugene **(Superior)**
Enuh, Chinedu
Travers, Noel

RELIGIOUS CONGREGATIONS AND SOCIETIES OF APOSTOLIC LIFE (WOMEN)

Place-names refer to a parish entry, where further details may be found.

Adoratrices, Handmaids of the Blessed Sacrament and of Charity (AASC): Kensington 2

Adorers of the Sacred Heart (OSB) - Tyburn Nuns: Marylebone

Carmelites (ODC): St Charles Square, Ware

Columban Sisters (MSSC): Bow

Comboni Missionary Sisters (CMS): Chiswick

Congregation of Our Lady (Canonesses of St Augustine) (CSA): Oratory

Congregation of Our Lady of the Missions (RNDM): New Southgate, Wealdstone

Congregation of La Sainte Union des Sacrés Coeurs (LSU): Bethnal Green, Holloway, Kentish Town, Wembley 3

Congregation of the Sisters of Nazareth (CSN): Brook Green, Finchley East

Daughters of Charity of St Vincent de Paul (DC): Cathedral, Mill Hill, Pinner

Daughters of Divine Love (DDL): Borehamwood North, Wood Green

Daughters of Mary, Mother of Mercy DMMM): Edgware

Daughters of Providence (St Brieuc) : Palmers Green

Daughters of St Paul (FSP): Kensington 1

Dominican Sisters (Congr. of Newcastle, Natal) (OP): Bushey, Cricklewood, Edgware, Harpenden

Faithful Companions of Jesus (FCJ): Isleworth, Poplar, Somers Town

Franciscan Servants of Mary (FSM): Wembley 1

Franciscan Sisters of the Heart of Jesus (FCJ): Pimlico

Franciscan Missionaries of Mary (FMM): Shepherds Bush

Franciscan Sisters of Mill Hill (OSF): Mill Hill

Franciscan Sisters of Our Lady of Victories: Cathedral

Handmaids of the Holy Child Jesus (HHCJ): Edmonton

Handmaids of the Sacred Heart of Jesus (ACI): St John's Wood

Institute of the Blessed Virgin Mary (Loreto Sisters) (IBVM): Acton West

Institute of Our Lady of Mercy: Highbury

Little Company of Mary (LCM): Ealing, Gunnersbury

Little Sisters of Jesus: Hoxton, St Charles Square

Little Sisters of the Poor (LSP): Stoke Newington

Marist Sisters (SM): Archway

Medical Mission Sisters (Society of Catholic Medical Missionaries - SCMM): Acton, Hanwell, Northfields

Missionary Community of Divine Providence (MPS): Underwood Road

Missionaries of Charity (MC): Kensal New Town, Southall

Missionary Congregation of the Evangelizing Sisters of Mary (MCESM): Somers Town

Missionary Sisters of Christ the King (MChR): Willesden Green

SECTION 4

Missionary Sisters of the Immaculate (PIME): Chiswick

Missionary Sisters of Our Lady of Africa (White Sisters) (MSOLA): Ealing

Missionary Sisters of the Society of Mary (SMSM): French Church

Pallottine Missionary Sisters (SAC): Clerkenwell

Poor Clares (OSC): Barnet

Poor Handmaids of Jesus Christ (PHJC): Hendon

Poor Servants of the Mother of God (PSMG): Brentford, Hampton-on-Thames, Somers Town

Religious of the Assumption (RA): Bayswater, Kensington 2, Twickenham

Religious of Mary Immaculate (RMI): Kensington 2

Religious of the Sacred Heart of Mary (RSHM): Northfields

Religious Sisters of Charity (RSC): Acton, Hackney

School Sisters of Notre Dame (SSND): Copenhagen Street

Servants of Mary (OSM): Clapton, Stamford Hill

Sisters of Charity of Jesus and Mary (SCJM): Letchworth, Stevenage

Sisters of Charity of St Jeanne Antide (S de C); Sisters of St Martha: Ealing

Sisters of Charity of St Paul (Selly Park) (SP): Hackney

Sisters of Christian Instruction (St Gildas) (SCI): Barnet, Stroud Green

Sisters of the Cross and Passion (CP) Fulham Road, Islington

Sisters of the Holy Family of Bordeaux (HFB): Kilburn, Willesden Green

Sisters of the Holy Family of Nazareth (CSFN): Enfield

Sisters of the Holy Name of Jesus: Polish Church 3

Sisters Hospitallers of the Sacred Heart (HSC): Fulham Road

Sisters of the Infant Jesus (IJS): Acton East

Sisters of Jesus and Mary (rjm): Kensal Rise

Sisters of Jesus in the Temple (SJT): Notting Hill

Sisters of Mercy (RSM): Clapton Park, Cricklewood, Feltham, Hillingdon, Kensal New Town, St John's Wood, Twickenham

Sisters of Notre Dame de Namur (SND): Pimlico

Sisters of Our Lady of the Missions: Wealdstone

Sisters of Our Lady of Sion (NDS): Bayswater

Sisters of Providence (of the Immaculate Conception): Royston

Sisters of the Resurrection (CR): Ealing, Polish 3

Sisters of the Sacred Heart of Jesus (St Jacut) (SSCJ): Finchley East

Sisters of the Sacred Hearts of Jesus and Mary (Chigwell): Uxbridge

Sisters of St Dorothy (SSD): Hampstead

Sisters of St Joseph of Peace (CSJ): Cricklewood, Hanwell

Sisters of St Louis (SSL): New Southgate

Sisters of St Marcellina (IM) : Hampstead

Sisters of Saint Mary of Namur (SSMN): Harrow-on-the-Hill

Sisters of St Paul de Chartres (SPC): Highbury

Society of the Holy Child Jesus (SHCJ): Brook Green

Society of Marie Auxiliatrice: Muswell Hill

Society of the Sacred Heart (RSCJ): Brook Green

Ursulines of Jesus (UJ): Stamford Hill

Verbum Dei Missionary Fraternity (FMVD):
West Green

Wisdom (La Sagesse) Daughters of (DW):
Archbishop's House, Willesden Green

Pope's Worldwide Prayer Network
UNITED KINGDOM
(formerly the Apostleship of Prayer)

- Praying with the Pope each day and with the whole Church
- Offering ourselves each day to the heart of Jesus in apostolic readiness
- A simple prayer pathway that anyone can join

Together we make each day different.

National Office
Jesuit Community, St Ignatius, 27 High Road Stamford Hill, N15 6ND
prayernetwork@jesuit.org.uk   07432 591117
www.popesglobalprayer.net

SECTION 4

Conference of Religious in England and Wales (COREW) - 'Providing Strength through Unity'
The Conference supports the leaders of the religious communities of England and Wales. COR aims to help men and women Religious face the challenges and needs of 21st century society. The aim is to focus on agreed initiatives and provide religious leaders with the support and educational resources that enable them to serve their individual communities better. Over the past 60 years the Conference has identified key needs for its members who themselves have worked tirelessly serving our communities to improve the lives of parishioners through their educational, healthcare and prayer roles, social justice and pastoral work.
Contacts
Nalini Nathan **General Secretary**
Tel: 020 3255 1085 Email: generalsecretary@corew.org
Bernadette Kehoe **Communications & Development Lead**
Tel: 07719 311667 Email: communications@corew.org
Christine Considine **Administrative Co-ordinator**
Email: admin@corew.org
70-71 Euston Square NW1 1DJ
Web: www.corew.org Twitter: @OfReligious Instagram: religiouslifeleaders

Consecrated Women
See *Conscecrated Women* under Catholic Societies and Organisations, Section 6

The Grail A grant-making body, supporting activities consonant with the aims of the former Grail Secular Institute. See *Grail, The* under Catholic Societies and Organisations, Section 6

The Leaven A Carmelite way of life for single or widowed Catholic women
See *Carmelite Secular Institute* under Catholic Societies and Organisations, Section 6

St Boniface Secular Institute (English Region) 44 Exeter Road NW2 4SB
Tel: 020 8438 9628 Email: hostel@institut-st-bonifatius.de
Web: www.hostel-lioba-house.de
See *German Church* and *Willesden Green* parish entries

Servants of the Word (SW) An ecumenical congregation based in Acton at **31a Lynton Road W3 9HL Tel: 020 8993 8113**

Servite Secular Institute (SSI) A life of service through vows of chastity, poverty and obedience in union with others of like mind, remaining in their own circumstances. Women of prayer living in the world as Servants of Mary.
Email: vocations@ssi.org.uk Web: www.ssi.org.uk

Section 5

CATHOLIC SCHOOLS

All schools are listed under the local authority area in which they are situated, and, for primary schools, the name of the parish is also indicated. In the case of secondary schools and colleges the name of the deanery is only given where that is different from the local authority area in which the school or college is situated. The Parish Priest normally acts as Chaplain for primary schools. In secondary schools and colleges, the name of the Chaplain is given.

Unless stated otherwise, all schools are voluntary aided and co-educational, and all primary schools are junior and infant. (A) indicates that the school is an Academy. (+N) indicates that the school has a nursery. (RO) indicates that the school is in the trusteeship of a Religious Order. (R) indicates that it is recognised as Catholic by the Cardinal Archbishop; all other schools are in the trusteeship of the Diocese. All schools with websites are to be found listed at **www.rcdow.org.uk.**

Statistics

Primary (Aided & Academy)	150
Primary (Independent)	9
Secondary (Aided & Academy)	38
Secondary (Independent)	3
All-age (Aided & Academy)	1
All-age (Non-maintained Special)	2
All-age (Independent)	2
VI Form Colleges	2
Total	**207**

CITY OF WESTMINSTER   (213)

PRIMARY SCHOOLS

Our Lady of Dolours: (+N) (3381) 19 Cirencester Street W2 5SR
Tel: 020 7641 4326 Email: admin@ourladydolours.co.uk
Head Mrs Sarah Alley (Paddington)

St Edward: (+N) (3432) Lisson Grove NW1 6LH
Tel: 020 7723 5911 Email: office@stedwardsprimary.co.uk
Executive Head Mr Martin Tissot Head of School Mrs Anne Thomas (St John's Wood) (RO)

St Joseph, Maida Vale: (+N) (3473) Lanark Road W9 1DF
Tel: 020 7286 3518 Email: office@stjosephsschool.org.uk
Head Dr Ninette Fernandes Viana (St John's Wood)

St Mary of the Angels: (+N) (3532) Shrewsbury Road W2 5PR
Tel: 020 7792 1883 Email: office@stmaryangels.co.uk
Head Mrs Mary Wilson (Bayswater)

S c h o o l s

St Vincent, Marylebone: (+N) (3610) St Vincent Street W1U 4DF
Tel: 020 3146 0743 Email: office@stvincentsprimary.org.uk
Head Miss Marina Coleman (Spanish Place)

St Vincent de Paul: (+N) (3611) Morpeth Terrace SW1P 1EP
Tel: 020 3351 5990 Email: office@svpschool.co.uk
Head Mr Nathaniel Scott Cree (Cathedral)

Independent
St Christina (6225) (Girls) 25 St Edmund's Terrace NW8 7PY
Tel: 020 7722 8784 Email: office@saintchristinas.org.uk
Head Mr Alistair Gloag (St John's Wood) (RO)

Westminster Cathedral Choir School: (6197) (Boys) Ambrosden Avenue SW1P 1QH
Tel: 020 7798 9081 Email: office@choirschool.com
Head Mr Neil McLaughlan (Cathedral)

SECONDARY SCHOOL
St George: (A) (4809) Lanark Road W9 1RB
Tel: 020 7328 0904 Email: office@stgeorgesrc.org
Executive Head - Trust CEO Mr Martin Tissott Acting Deputy Trust CEO Mr James Martin
Head of School Mr Cathal Gregory (Marylebone Deanery)
Chaplains Fr John McFadden and Jo Ronayne

LONDON BOROUGH OF BARNET (302)
PRIMARY SCHOOLS
The Annunciation: (Infants +N) (3500) Thirleby Road, Edgware HA8 0HQ
Tel: 020 8959 2325 Email: office@annunciationinf.barnetmail.net
Executive Head Mrs Carol Minihan (Burnt Oak)

The Annunciation: (Junior) (3514) The Meads, Edgware HA8 9HQ
Tel: 020 8906 0723 Email: office@annunciationjnr.barnetmail.net
Executive Head Mrs Carol Minihan (Burnt Oak)

Blessed Dominic: (+N) (3511) Great Strand NW9 5PE
Tel: 020 8205 3790 Email: office@blesseddominic.barnetmail.net
Head Mrs Geraldine Pears (Grahame Park)

Our Lady of Lourdes Catholic Primary, Finchley: (+N) (3501) Bow Lane N12 0JP
Tel: 020 8346 1681 Email: office@olol.barnetmail.net
Head Miss Barbara Costa (Finchley East)

Sacred Heart, Whetstone: (3510) 2 Oakleigh Park South N20 9JU
Tel: 020 8445 3854 Email: office@sacredheart.barnetmail.net
Head Mrs Geraldine Porter (Whetstone)

St Agnes, Cricklewood: (+N) (3502) **Thorverton Road NW2 IRG**
Tel: **020 8452 4565** Email: office@stagnes.barnetmail.net
Head Mrs Susan O'Reilly (Cricklewood)

St Catherine, Barnet: (+N) (3504) **Vale Drive, Barnet EN5 2ED**
Tel: **020 8440 4946** Email: office@stcatherines.barnetmail.net
Head Miss Maureen Kelly (Barnet)

St Joseph, Hendon: (3509) **Watford Way NW4 4TY**
Tel: **020 8202 5229** Email: office@stjosephs.barnet.sch.uk
Executive Head Dr James Lane (Hendon)

St Theresa: (3507) **East End Road N3 2TD**
Tel: **020 8346 8826** Email: office@sttheresas.barnetmail.net
Executive Head Miss Barbara Costa (Finchley Church End)

St Vincent, Mill Hill: (3506) **The Ridgeway NW7 IEJ**
Tel: **020 8959 3417** Email: office@stvincents.barnet.sch.uk
Head Miss Marie Tuohy (Mill Hill)

Independent
St Anthony School for Girls: (6008) (Girls) **Ivy House, 94-96 North End Road NW11 7SX**
Tel: **020 3869 3070** Email: info@stanthonysgirls.co.uk
Head Mr Donal Brennan (Golders Green)

SECONDARY SCHOOLS
Bishop Douglass Catholic High: (A) (5408) **Hamilton Road N2 0SQ**
Tel: **020 8444 5211/3** Email: schooladmin@bishopdouglass.barnet.sch.uk
Executive Head Mr Martin Tissot **Head of School** Mrs Michelle Henderson
Chaplain Fr Kevin Ryan SX

Finchley Catholic High: (5405) (Boys) **Woodside Lane N12 8TA**
Tel: **020 8445 0105** Email: info@finchleycatholic.org.uk
Head Mrs Niamh Arnull **Chaplain** Martina Locatelli

St James Catholic High: (5407) **Great Strand NW9 5PE**
Tel: **020 8358 2800** Email: admin@st-james.barnet.sch.uk
Head Mrs Carolyn Laws **Chaplain** Mariella Signorini

St Michael Catholic Grammar: (5404) (Girls) **Nether Street N12 7NJ**
Tel: **020 8446 2256** Email: office@st-michaels.barnet.sch.uk
Head Mr Michael Stimpson **Chaplain** Fr Jean Diame CSSp (RO)

SECTION 5

LONDON BOROUGH OF BRENT   (304)

PRIMARY SCHOOLS

The Convent of Jesus & Mary: (Infants +N) (3507) **21 Park Avenue NW2 5AN**
Tel: **020 8459 5890** Email: admin@conventinf.brent.sch.uk
Executive Head Miss Elsa Fonseca (Willesden Green)

Our Lady of Grace, Dollis Hill: (A) (Infants +N) (3510) **Dollis Hill Avenue NW2 6EU**
Tel: **020 8450 6757** Email: admin@ologinfants.brent.sch.uk
Head Mrs Philomena Bourne (Dollis Hill)

Our Lady of Grace, Dollis Hill: (A) (Junior) (3500) **Dollis Hill Lane NW2 6HS**
Tel: **020 8450 6002** Email: admin@ologjuniors.brent.sch.uk
Head Mr Stephen McGrath (Dollis Hill)

Our Lady of Lourdes, Willesden: (+N) (3508) **Wesley Road NW10 8PP**
Tel: **020 8961 5037** Email: admin@lourdes.brent.sch.uk
Interim Head Mrs Marie Halpin (Stonebridge)

Federation of St Joseph Infant and Junior Schools, Wembley:
St Joseph's Infant, Wembley: (Infants +N) (3509) **Waverley Avenue, Wembley HA9 6TA**
Tel: **020 8903 6032** Email: admin@sjinf.brent.sch.uk
Executive Head Mrs Amanda Whelan (Wembley 1)

St Joseph' Catholic Junior, Wembley: (Junior) (3501) **Chatsworth Avenue, Wembley HA9 6BE**
Tel: **020 8902 3438** Email: admin@sjinf.brent.sch.uk
Executive Head Mrs Amanda Whelan **Associate Head** Mr Mark Betts (Wembley 1)

St Joseph, Willesden: (+N) (5203) **Goodson Road NW10 9LS**
Tel: **020 8965 5651** Email: admin@stjo.brent.sch.uk
Head Miss Dawn Titus (Willesden)

St Margaret Clitherow, Neasden: (A) (+N) (3511) **Quainton Street NW10 0BG**
Tel: **020 8450 3631** Email: admin@clitherow.brent.sch.uk
Head Ms Ilira Heath (Wembley 2)

St Mary, Kilburn: (+N) (3602) **Canterbury Road NW6 5ST**
Tel: **020 7624 3830** Email: admin@marycps.brent.sch.uk
Head Mrs Bridget Pratley (Kilburn)

St Mary Magdalen: (Junior) (3505**) Linacre Road NW2 5BB**
Tel: **020 8459 3159** Email: admin@marymag.brent.sch.uk
Executive Head Miss Elsa Fonseca (Willesden Green)

St Robert Southwell: (+N) (3506) **Slough Lane NW9 8YD**
Tel: **020 8204 6148** Email: admin@robsouth.brent.sch.uk
Head Miss Honor Beck (Kingsbury Green)

SECONDARY SCHOOLS
Newman Catholic College: (5407) (Boys) **Harlesden Road NW10 3RN**
Tel: **020 8965 3947** Email: office@ncc.brent.sch.uk
Acting Head Mr Andy Dunne **Chaplain** John Roche

St Claudine's Catholic School for Girls (A) (5404) (Girls) **Crownhill Road NW10 4EP**
Tel: **020 8965 2986** Email: office@cjmlc.co.uk
Head Mrs Louise McGowan **Chaplain** Ann-Marie Sylvestercha

St Gregory Catholic Science College: (A) (5406) **Donnington Road, Harrow HA3 0NB**
Tel: **020 8907 8828** Email: schooloffice@stgregorys.harrow.sch.uk
Head Mr Andrew Prindiville **Chaplain** Julian Carlsson

LONDON BOROUGH OF CAMDEN   (202)
PRIMARY SCHOOLS
Our Lady, Camden: (+N) (3655) **Pratt Street NW1 0DP**
Tel: **020 7485 7997** Email: admin@ourladys.camden.sch.uk
Executive Head Mrs Juliette Jackson **Associate Head** Ms Moya Richardson (Camden Town)

Rosary: (+N) (3391) **238 Haverstock Hill NW3 2AE**
Tel: **020 7794 6292** Email: admin@rosary.camden.sch.uk
Head Miss Sophie Kennedy (Haverstock Hill)

St Dominic, Camden: (+N) (3429) **Southampton Road NW5 4JS**
Tel: **020 7485 5918** Email: admin@stdominics.camden.sch.uk
Head Ms Jennifer O'Prey (Haverstock Hill)

St Eugene de Mazenod: (3649) **Mazenod Avenue, Quex Road NW6 4LS**
Tel: **020 7624 4837** Email: admin@steugene.camden.sch.uk
Executive Head Mrs Juliette Jackson (Kilburn)

St Joseph, Macklin Street: (+N) (3482) **Macklin Street, Drury Lane WC2B 5NA**
Tel: **020 7242 7712** Email: admin@stjosephs.camden.sch.uk
Executive Head Mrs Juliette Jackson (Lincoln's Inn Fields)

St Patrick, Kentish Town: (+N) (3560) **Holmes Road NW5 3AH**
Tel: **020 7267 1200** Email: admin@stpatricks.camden.sch.uk
Executive Head Ms Jennifer O'Prey (Kentish Town)

Independent
St Anthony's Preparatory: (6181) (Boys) **90 Fitzjohn's Avenue NW3 6AA**
Tel: **020 7431 1066** Email: shoffice@stanthonysprep.co.uk
Head Mr Richard Berlie (Hampstead) **Chaplain** Mgr Phelim Rowland (R)

SECTION 5

St Mary's, Hampstead: (6084) (Girls) **47 Fitzjohn's Avenue NW3 6PG**
Tel: 020 7435 1868 Email: office@stmh.co.uk
Head Mrs Harriet Connor-Earl (Swiss Cottage) (R)

SECONDARY SCHOOLS

La Sainte Union: (5041) (Girls) **Highgate Road NW5 1RP**
Tel: 020 7428 4600 Email: general@lsu.camden.sch.uk
Head Mrs Sophie Fegan **Chaplain** Shirley Taylor (RO)

Maria Fidelis Catholic School FCJ: (4652 **1-39 Drummond Crescent NW1 1LY**
Tel: 020 7387 3856 Email: office@mariafidelis.camden.sch.uk
Head Ms Helen Gill **Chaplain** Sr Ellen McCarthy FCJ (RO)

LONDON BOROUGH OF EALING (307)

PRIMARY SCHOOLS

Holy Family School: (2000) **Vale Lane W3 0DY**
Tel: 020 8992 3980 Email: admin@holyfamily.ealing.sch.uk
Head Mr Thomas Doherty (Acton West)

Mount Carmel: (+N) (3500) **Little Ealing Lane W5 4EA**
Tel: 020 8567 4646 Email: info@mountcarmel.ealing.sch.uk
Head Mrs Clare Walsh (Brentford)

Our Lady of the Visitation: (3503) **Greenford Road, Greenford UB6 9AN**
Tel: 020 8575 5344 Email: admin@olovrc.com
Head Miss Kathleen Coll (Greenford)

St Anselm, Southall: (3505) **Church Avenue, Southall UB2 4BH**
Tel: 020 8574 3906 Email: office@st-anselms.ealing.sch.uk
Acting Head Rev Tito Pereira (Deacon) (Southall)

St Gregory, Ealing: (+N) (3506) **Woodfield Road W5 1SL**
Tel: 020 8997 7550 Email: admin@st-gregorys.ealing.sch.uk
Head Awaiting appointment (Ealing)

St John Fisher, Perivale: (+N) (3504) **Sarsfield Road, Perivale UB6 7AF**
Tel: 020 8799 0970 Email: admin@st-johnfisher.ealing.sch.uk
Acting Head Miss Rebecca Sullivan (Perivale)

St Joseph, Hanwell: (+N) (3507) **York Avenue W7 3HU**
Tel: 020 8567 6293 Email: admin@st-josephs.ealing.sch.uk
Head Mr Julian Rakowski (Hanwell)

St Raphael: (3508) **Hartfield Avenue, Northolt UB5 6NL**
Tel: 020 8841 0848 Email: admin@st-raphaels.ealing.sch.uk
Head Miss Tracey Brosnan (Yeading)

St Vincent, Ealing: (3509) 1 Pierrepoint Road W3 9JR
Tel: 020 8992 6625 Email: admin@stvps.co.uk
Head Mrs Monica McCarthy (Acton)

Independent
St Benedict Junior: (6606) 5 Montpelier Avenue W5 2XP
Tel: 020 8862 2054 Email: juniorschool@stbenedicts.org.uk
Head Mr Robert Simmons **Chaplain** Dom Andrew Hughes OSB (R)

SECONDARY SCHOOL
The Cardinal Wiseman School: (4603) Greenford Road, Greenford UB6 9AW
Tel: 020 8575 8222 Email: info@wiseman.ealing.sch.uk
Head Mr Daniel Coyle **Chaplain** Mary Boland

Independent
St Benedict Senior: (6006) 54 Eaton Rise W5 2ES
Tel: 020 8862 2254 Email: seniorschool@stbenedicts.org.uk
Head Mr Andrew Johnson **Chaplain** Dom Alexander Bevan OSB (RO)

PRIMARY & SECONDARY SCHOOL
Independent
St Augustine Priory School: (6005) (Girls) Hillcrest Road W5 2JL
Tel: 020 8997 2022 Email: office@sapriory.com
Head Mrs Sarah Raffray (R)

LONDON BOROUGH OF ENFIELD (308)

PRIMARY SCHOOLS
Our Lady of Lourdes: (3504) The Limes Avenue N11 1RD
Tel: 020 8361 0767 Email: office@ololschool.enfield.sch.uk
Head Mrs Gillian Hood (New Southgate)

St Edmund, Enfield: (3501) Hertford Road N9 7HJ
Tel: 020 8807 2664 Email: office@st-edmunds.enfield.sch.uk
Head Awaiting appointment (Edmonton)

St George, Enfield: (3502) Gordon Road, Enfield EN2 0QA
Tel: 020 8363 3729 Email: office@st-georges.enfield.sch.uk
Head Mr Paul O'Rourke (Enfield)

St Mary, Enfield: (+N) (5403) Durants Road, Enfield EN3 7DE
Tel: 020 8804 2396 Email: office@st-marys.enfield.sch.uk
Head Miss Maeve Creed (Ponders End)

St Monica, Enfield: (3503) Cannon Hill, Cannon Road N14 7HE
Tel: 020 8886 4647 Email: office@st-monicas.enfield.sch.uk
Head Mrs Kate Baptiste (Palmers Green)

SECTION 5

Schools

SECONDARY SCHOOLS

St Anne Catholic High for Girls: (4706) (Girls) Oakthorpe Road N13 5TY
Tel: 020 8886 2165 Email: admin@st-annes.enfield.sch.uk
Head Mrs Emma Loveland **Chaplain** Salvatore La Barbera

St Ignatius College: (3500) (Boys) Turkey Street, Enfield EN1 4NP
Tel: 01992 717835 / 760520 Email: enquiries@st-ignatius.enfield.sch.uk
Head Mrs Mary O'Keefe **Chaplain** John Dawson (RO)

LONDON BOROUGH BOROUGH OF HACKNEY (204)

PRIMARY SCHOOLS

Our Lady and St Joseph: (+N) (3371) Buckingham Road N1 4DG
Tel: 020 7254 7353 Email: admin@olsj.hackney.sch.uk
Head Mrs Aoife O'Grady (Kingsland)

St Dominic, Hackney: (+N) (2900) Ballance Road E9 5SR
Tel: 020 8985 0995 Email: admin@stdominics.hackney.sch.uk
Head Mrs Deirdre Finan (Homerton)

St Monica, Hackney: (+N) (3553) 43 Hoxton Square N1 6QN
Tel: 020 7739 5824 Email: office@st-monicas.hackney.sch.uk
Head Mrs Amanda Ruthven (Hoxton)

St Scholastica (+N) (3659) Kenninghall Road E5 8BS
Tel: 020 8985 3466 Email: officeadmin@st-scholasticas.hackney.sch.uk
Head Mrs Sandra Brierley (Clapton)

SECONDARY SCHOOLS

Cardinal Pole: (4714) 205 Morning Lane E9 6LG
Tel: 020 8985 5150 Email: enquiries@cardinalpole.co.uk
Head Mr Adam Hall **Chaplain** James Ryan

Our Lady's Catholic High School: (4641) (Girls) 6-16 Amhurst Park N16 5AF
Tel: 020 8800 2158 Email: officeadmin@olchs.co.uk
Head Mr Andy English **Chaplain** Sr Dominico Savio (RO)

LONDON BOROUGH OF HAMMERSMITH & FULHAM (205)

PRIMARY SCHOOLS

The Good Shepherd: (+N) (3602) Gayford Road W12 9BY
Tel: 020 8743 5060 Email: admin@goodshepherdrc.lbhf.sch.uk
Head Mrs Imogen Lavelle (Shepherds Bush)

Holy Cross, Fulham: (+N) (3354) Basuto Road SW6 4BL
Tel: 020 7736 1447 Email: admin@holycross.lbhf.sch.uk
Executive Head Mrs Kathleen Williams **Associate Head** Mrs Catherine MacGonigal
(Parsons Green)

Larmenier & Sacred Heart: (+N) (3649) **41a Brook Green W6 8DH**
Tel: **020 8748 9444** Email: admin@larshrc.lbhf.sch.uk
Head Miss Jennifer McGinty (Brook Green)

St Augustine: (3378) **Disbrowe Road W6 8QE**
Tel: **020 7385 4333** Email: admin@staugustinesrc.lbhf.sch.uk
Head Mr Martin Kincaid (Hammersmith)

St John XXIII: (+N) (3645) **1 India Way W12 7QT**
Tel: **020 8743 9428** Email: admin@stjohnxxiii.lbhf.sch.uk
Head Mrs Karen Cunningham (White City)

St Mary: (+N) (3529) **Masbro Road W14 0LT**
Tel: **020 7603 7717** Email: admin@stmarysrc.lbhf.sch.uk
Head Ms Robina Maher (Brook Green)

St Thomas of Canterbury: (3648) **Estcourt Road SW6 7HB**
Tel: **020 7385 8165** Email: admin@stthomasrc.lbhf.sch.uk
Executive Head Mrs Karen Wyatt **Head of School** Miss Jo Breslin (Fulham 1)

SECONDARY SCHOOLS
The London Oratory: (A) (5400) (Boys) **Seagrave Road SW6 1RX**
Tel: **020 7385 0102** Email: admin@los.ac
Head Mr Daniel Wright **Chaplain** Fr George Bowen (RO)

Sacred Heart High: (A) (3394) (Girls) **212 Hammersmith Road W6 7DG**
Tel: **020 8748 7600** Email: info@sacredh.lbhf.sch.uk
Head Mrs Sharon O'Donovan **Chaplain** Vicky Lorenzato (RO)

LONDON BOROUGH OF HARINGEY (309)
PRIMARY SCHOOLS
Our Lady of Muswell: (+N) (3500) **Pages Lane N10 1PS**
Tel: **020 8444 6894** Email: office@ourladymuswell.haringey.sch.uk
Head Mrs Angela McNicholas (Muswell Hill)

Federation of St Francis de Sales Infant and Junior Schools, Haringey:
St Francis de Sales: (Infants+N) (3507) **Brereton Road N17 8DA**
Tel: **020 8808 2923** Email: admin@sfds.haringey.sch.uk
Head Dr James Lane (Tottenham)

St Francis de Sales: (Junior) (3501) **Brereton Road N17 8DA**
Tel: **020 8808 2923** Email: admin.junior@sfds.haringey.sch.uk
Head Dr James Lane (Tottenham)

St Gildas: (Junior) (3509) **1 Oakington Way N8 9EP**
Tel: **020 8348 1902** Email: admin@st-gildas.haringey.sch.uk
Executive Head Mrs Angela McNicholas (Stroud Green)

SECTION 5

St Ignatius: (+N) (3502) **St Ann's Road N15 6ND**
Tel: **020 8800 2771** Email: head@st-igs.haringey.sch.uk
Head Mr Con Bonner (Stamford Hill)

St John Vianney: (+N) (3510) **Stanley Road N15 3HD**
Tel: **020 8889 8421** Email: admin@st-johnvianney.haringey.sch.uk
Head Mr Stephen McNicholas (West Green)

St Martin de Porres: (+N) (3508) **Blake Road N11 2AF**
Tel: **020 8361 1445** Email: admin@st-martinporres.haringey.sch.uk
Head Mrs Louise Fleming (Wood Green)

Federation of St Mary Priory Infant and Junior Schools:
St Mary Priory: (Infants +N) (3505) **Hermitage Road N15 5RE**
Tel: **020 8800 9305** Email: admin@stmarysrcpriory.haringey.sch.uk
Head Mrs Jane Ronan (Stamford Hill) (RO)

St Mary Priory: (Junior) (3503) **Hermitage Road N15 5RE**
Tel: **020 8800 9305** Email: admin@stmarysrcpriory.haringey.sch.uk
Head Mrs Jane Ronan (Stamford Hill) (RO)

St Paul: (3504) **Bradley Road N22 4SZ**
Tel: **020 8888 7081** Email: admin@st-pauls.haringey.sch.uk
Executive Head Mrs Louise Fleming **Head of School** Mr Peter O'Shaughnessy (Wood Green)

St Peter-in-Chains: (Infants) (3506) **3 Elm Grove N8 9AJ**
Tel: **020 8340 6789** Email: admin@st-peter-in-chains-rc.haringey.sch.uk
Executive Head Mrs Angela McNicholas (Stroud Green)

SECONDARY SCHOOL
St Thomas More: (A) (4703) **Glendale Avenue N22 5HN**
Tel: **020 8888 7122** Email: admin@stthomasmoreschool.org.uk
Executive Head Mr Martin Tissot **Head of School** Mr Alex Rosen

LONDON BOROUGH OF HARROW (310)
PRIMARY SCHOOLS
St Anselm, Harrow: (3501) **Roxborough Park, Harrow HA1 3BE**
Tel: **020 8422 1600** Email: office@st-anselms.harrow.sch.uk
Head Mrs Maria O'Connell (Harrow-on-the-Hill)

St Bernadette, Harrow: (A) (3500) **Clifton Road, Kenton, Harrow HA3 9NS**
Tel: **020 8204 8902** Email: office@stbernadette.harrow.sch.uk
Head Mr David O'Farrell (Kenton)

St George, Harrow: (A) (3508) **Sudbury Hill, Harrow HA1 3SB**
Tel: **020 8422 1272** Email: office@stgeorges.harrow.sch.uk
Head Mrs Deirdre Monaghan (Sudbury)

St John Fisher: (A) (3505) **Melrose Road, Pinner HA5 5RA**
Tel: **020 8868 2961** Email: office@st-johnfisher.harrow.sch.uk
Head Ms Nina Pignatiella (Harrow North)

St Joseph, Harrow: (A) (3507) **Dobbin Close, Belmont, Harrow HA3 7LP**
Tel: **020 8863 8531** Email: office@stjosephs.harrow.sch.uk
Head Mr Christopher Briggs (Wealdstone)

St Teresa, Harrow: (+N) (3504) **Long Elmes, Harrow Weald HA3 6LE**
Tel: **020 8428 8640** Email: schooloffice@st-teresas.harrow.sch.uk
Head Mrs Laura Thornton (Headstone Lane)

SECONDARY SCHOOLS

Sacred Heart Language College: (A) (4700) (Girls) **186 High Street, Wealdstone HA3 7AY**
Tel: **020 8863 9922** Email: enquiries@tshlc.harrow.sch.uk
Head Miss Geraldine Higgins **Chaplain** Marie Wright

Salvatorian College: (A) (5400) (Boys) **High Road, Harrow Weald HA3 5DY**
Tel: **020 8863 2706** Email: admin@salvatorian.harrow.sch.uk
Executive Head Mr Martin Tissot (RO)

SIXTH FORM COLLEGE

St Dominic: (8600) **Mount Park Avenue, Harrow-on-the-Hill HA1 3HX**
Tel: **020 8422 8084** Email: stdoms@stdoms.ac.uk
Principal Mr Andrew Parkin **Chaplain** Awaiting appointment

LONDON BOROUGH OF HILLINGDON   (312)

PRIMARY SCHOOLS

Botwell House: (+N) (3401) **Botwell Lane, Hayes UB3 2AB**
Tel: **020 8573 2229** Email: botwell@ibotwell.co.uk
Head Mr Kevin Oakley (Hayes)

Sacred Heart, Ruislip: (+N) (3405) **Herlwyn Avenue, Ruislip HA4 6EZ**
Tel: **01895 633240** Email: office@shpsruislip.org
Head Ms Theresa McManus (Ruislip)

St Bernadette, Hillingdon: (+N) (3402) **160 Long Lane, Hillingdon UB10 0EH**
Tel: **01895 232298** Email: office@stbernadetteschool.co.uk
Head Mrs Colette Acres (Hillingdon)

St Catherine, West Drayton: (+N) (3403) **Money Lane, West Drayton UB7 7NX**
Tel: **01895 442839** Email: office@stcatherine.co.uk
Head Miss Elizabeth Doonan (West Drayton)

St Mary, Uxbridge: (+N) (3404) **Rockingham Close, Uxbridge UB8 2UA**
Tel: **01895 232814** Email: office@stmarysuxbridge.org.uk
Head Miss Ann Shevlin (Uxbridge)

SECTION 5

St Swithun Wells: (+N) (3400) Hunters Hill, South Ruislip HA4 9HS
Tel: 01895 808194 Email: admin@ssw.school
Head Mrs Kristy Davis (Ruislip South)

SECONDARY SCHOOL
The Douay Martyrs: (A) (5408) Edinburgh Drive, Ickenham, Uxbridge UB10 8QY
Tel: 01895 679400 Email: office@douaymartyrs.co.uk
Head Ms Fiona McCloskey **Chaplain** Luisa Foley

NON-MAINTAINED SPECIAL SCHOOL
Pield Heath House: (7006) Pield Heath Road, Hillingdon UB8 3NW
Tel: 01895 258507 Email: admin@pieldheathschool.org.uk
Head Sr Julie Rose **Chaplain** Eryl D'Souza (RO)

LONDON BOROUGH OF HOUNSLOW   (313)

PRIMARY SCHOOLS
Our Lady & St John: (+N) (3502) Boston Park Road, Brentford TW8 9JF
Tel: 020 8560 7477 Email: admin@stjohnrc.hounslow.sch.uk
Head Mrs Susan Cunningham (Brentford)

The Rosary: (3941) 10 The Green, Heston TW5 0RL
Tel: 020 8570 4942 Email: office@rosary.hounslow.sch.uk
Executive Head Mrs Karen Cunningham **Head of School** Miss Fiona Bass (Heston)

St Lawrence: (+N) (3503) Victoria Road, Feltham TW13 4AF
Tel: 020 8890 3878 Email: office@st-lawrence.hounslow.sch.uk
Head Mr Leo Duggan (Feltham)

St Mary, Chiswick: (+N) (3505) Duke Road W4 2DF
Tel: 020 8994 5606 Email: office@stmarys.hounslow.sch.uk
Head Miss Joan Harte (Chiswick)

St Mary, Isleworth: (+N) (3504) South Street, Isleworth TW7 7EE
Tel: 020 8560 7166 Email: office@smi.hounslow.sch.uk
Head Mr Farley Marsh (Isleworth)

St Michael's and St Martin's: (+N) (3507) Belgrave Road, Hounslow TW4 7AG
Tel: 020 8572 9658 Email: office@stmichaelrc.hounslow.sch.uk
Head Mrs Nicola Duggan (Hounslow)

SECONDARY SCHOOLS
Gumley House: (A) (5400) (Girls) St John's Road, Isleworth TW7 6XF
Tel: 020 8568 8692 Email: general@gumleyhouse.com
Head Mr Stephen Byrne **Chaplain** Celia Hannigan (RO)

Gunnersbury: (5401) (Boys) **The Ride, Boston Manor Road, Brentford TW8 9LB**
Tel: **020 8568 7281** Email: office@gunnersbury.hounslow.sch.uk
Head Mr Kevin Burke

St Mark: (A) (4800) **106 Bath Road, Hounslow TW3 3EJ**
Tel: **020 8577 3600** Email: staffroom@st-marks.hounslow.sch.uk
Head Mrs Andrea Waugh-Lucas **Chaplain** Ivan Cižmárik

LONDON BOROUGH OF ISLINGTON (206)

PRIMARY SCHOOLS

Blessed Sacrament: (+N) (3643) **Boadicea Street N1 0UF**
Tel: **020 7278 2187** Email: admin@blessedsacrament.islington.sch.uk
Head Ms Alexandra Fernandez-Madden(Copenhagen Street)

Christ the King: (+N) (3633) **55 Tollington Park N4 3QW**
Tel: **020 7272 5987** Email: admin@ctks.co.uk
Executive Head Mr John Lane (Tollington Park)

Sacred Heart, Islington: (3384) **68 George's Road N7 8JN**
Tel: **020 7607 3407** Email: admin@sacredheart.islington.sch.uk
Head Mr John Lane (Holloway)

St Joan of Arc, Highbury: (+N) (3631) **Northolme Road N5 2UX**
Tel: **020 7226 3920** Email: office@st-joanofarc.islington.sch.uk
Head Miss Clare Campbell (Highbury)

St John the Evangelist: (+N) (3456) **Duncan Street N1 8BL**
Tel: **020 7226 1314** Email: office@stjohnevangelist.islington.sch.uk
Head Miss Stephanie Day (Islington)

St Joseph: (+N) (3483) **Highgate Hill N19 5NE**
Tel: **020 7272 1270** Email: office@st-josephs.islington.sch.uk
Head Miss Clare McFlynn (Highgate) (RO)

St Peter and St Paul, Islington: (+N) (3575) **Compton Street EC1V 0EU**
Tel: **020 7253 0839** Email: parentsupport@stpetersandstpauls.islington.sch.uk
Head Miss Tracey Peters (Clerkenwell)

SECONDARY SCHOOL

St Aloysius: (4651) (Boys) **Hornsey Lane N6 5LY**
Tel: **020 7561 7800** Email: enquiries@sta.islington.sch.uk
Head Mrs Paula Whyte **Chaplain** Fr David Pember CSSp

SECTION 5

ROYAL BOROUGH OF KENSINGTON AND CHELSEA   (207)

PRIMARY SCHOOLS

Oratory: (3379) Bury Walk, Cale Street SW3 6QH
Tel: 020 7589 5900 Email: info@oratory.rbkc.sch.uk
Head Mrs Jane Griffiths (Oratory) (RO)

Our Lady of Victories: (+N) (5200) Clareville Street SW7 5AQ
Tel: 020 7373 4491 Email: info@olov.rbkc.sch.uk
Head Mr Christopher McPhilemy (Kensington 1)

St Charles: (+N) (5201) 83 St Charles Square W10 6EB
Tel: 020 8969 5566 Email: info@st-charles.rbkc.sch.uk
Head Miss Ann Slavin (St Charles Square)

St Francis of Assisi: (+N) (3437) Treadgold Street W11 4BJ
Tel: 020 7727 8523 Email: info@franassisi.rbkc.sch.uk
Executive Head Mrs Kathleen Williams (Notting Hill)

St Joseph, Chelsea: (+N) (3477) Cadogan Street SW3 2QT
Tel: 020 7589 2438 Email: info@stjosephs.rbkc.sch.uk
Executive Head Mrs Karen Wyatt (Chelsea 1)

St Mary, East Row: (+N) (3542) East Row W10 5AW
Tel: 020 8969 0321 Email: info@st-marys.rbkc.sch.uk
Executive Head Miss Ann Slavin (Kensal New Town)

The Servite: (+N) (3613) 252 Fulham Road SW10 9NA
Tel: 020 7352 2588 Email: office@serviteprimaryschool.co.uk
Head Mrs Kathleen Williams (Fulham Road) (RO)

Independent

St Philip's Preparatory School: (6104) (Boys) 6 Wetherby Place SW7 4NE
Tel: 020 7373 3944 Email: office@stpschool.co.uk
Head Mr Alexander Wulffen-Thomas (Kensington 2) (RO)

SECONDARY SCHOOLS

The Cardinal Vaughan Memorial School: (A) (5402) (Boys) 89 Addison Road W14 8BZ
Tel: 020 7603 8478 Email: office@cvms.co.uk
Head Mr Paul Stubbings Chaplain Mgr Roger Reader

All Saints Catholic College: (4801) St Charles Square W10 6EL
Tel: 020 8969 7111 Email: info@allsaintscc.org.uk
Head Mr Andrew O'Neill Chaplain Bonny Sunny (North Kensington Deanery)

St Thomas More Language College, Chelsea: (4861) Cadogan Street SW3 2QS
Tel: 020 7589 9734 Email: info@stm.rbkc.sch.uk
Head Dr Trevor Papworth Chaplain Fr Anthony Homer

Independent
More House School: (6202) (Girls) **22 Pont Street SW1X 0AA**
Tel: **020 7235 2855** Email: office@morehouse.org.uk
Head Ms Faith Hegarty (RO)

SIXTH FORM COLLEGE
St Charles Catholic Sixth Form College: (8600) **74 St Charles Square W10 6EY**
Tel: **020 8968 7755** Email: enquiries@stcharles.ac.uk
Principal Mr Martin Twist **Chaplain** James Holland (North Kensington Deanery)

LONDON BOROUGH OF RICHMOND (318)

PRIMARY SCHOOLS
The Sacred Heart, Teddington: (3320) **St Mark's Road, Teddington TW11 9DO**
Tel: **020 8977 6591** Email: info@sacredheart.richmond.sch.uk
Head Ms Brenda Green (Teddington)

St Edmund, Whitton: (3315) **St Edmund's Lane, Nelson Road, Whitton TW2 7BB**
Tel: **020 8894 7898** Email: office@st-edmunds.richmond.sch.uk
Head Mrs Carmel Moreland (Whitton)

St James, Twickenham: (+N) (3316) **260 Stanley Road, Twickenham TW2 5NP**
Tel: **020 8898 4670** Email: info@st-james.richmond.sch.uk
Head Mr Ciaran Beatty (Twickenham)

PRIMARY AND SECONDARY SCHOOL
St Richard Reynolds Catholic College Federation:
St Richard Reynolds (Primary): (2000) **Clifden Road, Twickenham TW1 4LT**
Tel: **020 8325 4630** Email: primary@srrcc.org.uk
Head Mr Richard Burke (Twickenham)

St Richard Reynolds Catholic College: (4000) **Clifden Road, Twickenham TW1 4LT**
Tel: **020 8325 4630** Email: office@srrcc.org.uk
Head Mr Richard Burke **Chaplain** Rebecca Walker (Upper Thames Deanery)

Independent
St Catherine Catholic School: (6008) (Girls) **Cross Deep, Twickenham TW1 4QJ**
Tel: **020 8891 2898** Email: admissions@stcatherineschool.co.uk
Head Mrs Johneen McPherson **Chaplain** Mary Ryan (RO) (Upper Thames Deanery)

LONDON BOROUGH OF TOWER HAMLETS (211)

PRIMARY SCHOOLS
English Martyrs: (+N) (3619) **St Mark Street E1 8DJ**
Tel: **020 7709 0182** Email: admin@englishmartyrs.towerhamlets.sch.uk
Head Ms Bronagh Nugent (Tower Hill)

SECTION 5

Our Lady and St Joseph: (+N) (3667) Wade's Place E14 0DE
Tel: 020 3764 8860 Email: office@olsj.co.uk
Head Mr Patrick Devereux (Poplar)

St Agnes, Bow: (+N) (3397) Rainhill Way E3 3ES
Tel: 020 8980 3076 Email: info@st-agnes.towerhamlets.sch.uk
Head Ms Brid McDaid (Bow)

St Anne's and Guardian Angels, Whitechapel: (+N) (100950) Underwood Road E1 5AW
Tel: 020 7247 6327 Email: office@stannesgaprimary.com
Head Mrs Sheila Mouna (Underwood Road)

St Edmund, Millwall: (+N) (3431) 299 West Ferry Road E14 3RS
Tel: 020 7987 2546 Email: admin@st-edmunds.towerhamlets.sch.uk
Head Awaiting appointment (Millwall)

St Elizabeth: (+N) (2003) Bonner Road E2 9JY
Tel: 020 8980 3964 Email: school@st-elizabeth.uk
Head Miss Angelina John (Bethnal Green)

St Mary and St Michael: (+N) (2002) Sutton Street E1 0BD
Tel: 020 7790 4986 Email: admin@sm-sm.co.uk
Head Mrs Rachel Mahon (Commercial Road)

SECONDARY SCHOOLS
Bishop Challoner Catholic Federation of Schools:
Bishop Challoner: (4726) (Girls) 352 Commercial Road E1 0LB
Tel: 020 7791 9500 Email: info@bishop.towerhamlets.sch.uk
Acting Executive Headteacher Mr J P Morrison
Head of Girls School Ms Chantelle Easmon-Johnson Chaplain Awaiting appointment

Bishop Challoner: (4298) (Boys) 352 Commercial Road E1 0LB
Tel: 020 7791 9500 Email: info@bishop.towerhamlets.sch.uk
Acting Executive Headteacher Mr J P Morrison
Head of Boys School Mr Bryan Young Chaplain Awaiting appointment

COUNTY OF HERTFORDSHIRE (919)
PRIMARY SCHOOL (ENFIELD DEANERY)
Pope Paul: (3975) Baker Street, Potters Bar EN6 2ES
Tel: 01707 659755 Email: admin@popepaul.herts.sch.uk
Head Mrs Elizabeth Heymoz (Potters Bar)

PRIMARY SCHOOLS (LEA VALLEY DEANERY)
Sacred Heart, Ware: (3424) Broadmeads, Ware SG12 9HY
Tel: 01920 461678 Email: admin@sacredheart312.herts.sch.uk
Head Mrs Michelle Fusi (Ware)

St Augustine, Hoddesdon: (+N) (3345) Riversmead, Hoddesdon EN11 8DP
Tel: 01992 463549 Email: admin@staugustines.herts.sch.uk
Head Mrs Gillian Napier (Hoddesdon)

St Cross: (3408) Upper Marsh Lane, Hoddesdon EN11 8BN
Tel: 01992 467309 Email: admin@stcross.herts.sch.uk
Head Miss Joanne Walsh (Hoddesdon)

St Joseph, Bishop's Stortford: (+N) (3318) Great Hadham Road, Bishop's Stortford
CM23 2NL Tel: 01279 652576 Email: admin@stjosephs207.herts.sch.uk
Head Mr Peter Coldwell (Bishop's Stortford)

St Joseph, Hertford: (+N) (3341) North Road, Hertford SG14 2BY
Tel: 01992 583148 Email: admin@stjosephs255.herts.sch.uk
Executive Head Mrs Michelle Fusi **Head of School** Mr Martin Maloney (Hertford)

St Joseph, Waltham Cross: (+N) (3327) Royal Avenue, Waltham Cross EN8 7EN
Tel: 01992 629503 Email: admin@stjosephs351.herts.sch.uk
Head Mrs Barbara O'Connor (Waltham Cross)

St Paul, Cheshunt: (+N) (3423) Park Lane, Cheshunt EN7 6LR
Tel: 01992 635060 Email: admin@stpauls373.herts.sch.uk
Head Mrs Katie Wooton-Greer (Cheshunt)

St Thomas of Canterbury: (3367) High Street, Puckeridge, near Ware SG11 1RZ
Tel: 01920 821450 Email: admin@stcanterbury.herts.sch.uk
Head Mrs Michelle Keating (Old Hall Green and Puckeridge)

PRIMARY SCHOOLS (ST ALBANS DEANERY)
St Adrian: (+N) (3389) Watling View, St Albans AL1 2PB
Tel: 01727 852687 Email: admin@stadrians.herts.sch.uk
Head Miss Aideen Porter (St Albans South)

St Alban & St Stephen: (3421) Cecil Road, St Albans AL1 5EG
Tel: 01727 866668 Email: admin@ssas.herts.sch.uk
Head Ms Clare Moore (St Albans)

St Albert the Great: (3391) Acorn Road, Rant Meadow, Hemel Hempstead HP3 8DW
Tel: 01442 264835 Email: admin@albertthegreat.herts.sch.uk
Head Mrs Kathryn Little (Hemel Hempstead East)

St Bernadette, London Colney: (+N) (3416) Walsingham Way, London Colney AL2 1NL
Tel: 01727 822489 Email: admin@stbernadette.herts.sch.uk
Head Mrs Sandra Lavelle-Murphy (London Colney)

SECTION 5

St Cuthbert Mayne: (Junior) (3386) Clover Way, Gadebridge, Hemel Hempstead HP1 3EA
Tel: 01442 253347 Email: admin@cuthbertmayne.herts.sch.uk
Head Awaiting appointment (Hemel Hempstead West)

St Dominic, Harpenden: (+N) (3401) Southdown Road, Harpenden AL5 1PF
Tel: 01582 760047 Email: admin@stdominic.herts.sch.uk
Head Miss Clare O'Sullivan (Harpenden)

St John Fisher, St Alban's: (3403) Hazelmere Road, Marshalswick, St Albans AL4 9RW
Tel: 01727 861077 Email: admin@sjfisher.herts.sch.uk
Head Miss Patricia O'Donnell (St Albans)

St Rose: (Infants +N) (3409) Green End Road, Boxmoor, Hemel Hempstead HP1 1QW
Tel: 01442 398855 Email: admin@stroses.herts.sch.uk
Head Mrs Ella Ryan (Hemel Hempstead West)

St Teresa, Borehamwood: (+N) (3384) Brook Road, Borehamwood WD6 5HL
Tel: 020 8953 3753 Email: admin@stteresas.herts.sch.uk
Acting Head Mrs Jacquie Tucker (Borehamwood)

St Thomas More, Berkhamsted: (+N) (3402) Greenway, Berkhamsted HP4 3LF
Tel: 01442 385060 Email: admin@stmore.herts.sch.uk
Executive Head Mrs Kathryn Little (Berkhamsted)

Independent

St Columba's College: (6136) (Boys) Preparatory School, 8 King Harry Lane,
St Albans AL3 4AW
Tel: 01727 862616 Email: collegeadmin@stcolumbascollege.org
Interim Head Mr David Shannon-Little (St Albans South) (RO)

PRIMARY SCHOOLS (STEVENAGE DEANERY)

Holy Family, Welwyn Garden City (+N) (3404) Crookhams, Welwyn Garden City AL7 1PG
Tel: 01707 375518 Email: admin@holyfamily.herts.sch.uk
Head Mrs Kate Linnane (Welwyn Garden City Digswell)

Our Lady, Hitchin: (A) (3399) Old Hale Way, Hitchin SG5 1XT
Tel: 01462 622555 Email: admin@ourladys.herts.sch.uk
Head Awaiting appointment (Hitchin)

Our Lady, Welwyn Garden City: (+N) (3382) Woodhall Lane, Welwyn Garden City
AL7 3TF
Tel: 01707 324408 Email: admin@ourladys527.herts.sch.uk
Head Mr Richard Curry (Welwyn Garden City East)

St John, Baldock: (A) (+N) (3413) Providence Way, Baldock SG7 6TT
Tel: 01462 892478 Email: admin@stjohns4.herts.sch.uk
Head Mr Tom Timson (Baldock)

St Margaret Clitherow, Stevenage: (3397) Monkswood Lane SG2 8RH
Tel: 01438 352863 Email: admin@clitherow.herts.sch.uk
Head Miss Carmela Puccio (Stevenage Shephall)

St Mary, Royston: (A) (+N) (5200) Melbourn Road, Royston SG8 7DB
Tel: 01763 246021 Email: admin@st-marys-royston.herts.sch.uk
Head Mrs Julia Pearce (Royston)

St Philip Howard (3388) Woods Avenue, Hatfield AL10 8NN
Tel: 01707 263969 Email: admin@sphoward.herts.sch.uk
Head Mrs Mairead Ann Waugh (Hatfield)

St Thomas More, Letchworth: (A) (3400) Highfield, Letchworth Garden City SG6 3QB
Tel: 01462 620670 Email: admin@strcjmi.herts.sch.uk
Head Mrs Jane Perry (Letchworth)

St Vincent de Paul, Stevenage: (+N) (3977) Bedwell Crescent, Stevenage SG1 1NJ
Tel: 01438 729555 Email: admin@stvincent.herts.sch.uk
Head Mr Jonathan White (Stevenage Bedwell)

PRIMARY SCHOOLS (WATFORD DEANERY)

Divine Saviour: (A) (+N) (3410) Broomfield Rise, Abbots Langley WD5 0HW
Tel: 01923 265607 Email: admin@divinesaviour.herts.sch.uk
Head Mrs Helen Wilson (Abbots Langley)

The Holy Rood: (A) (+N) (3985) Greenbank Road, Watford WD17 4FS
Tel: 01923 223785 Email: admin@holyrood.herts.sch.uk
Head Mrs Emma Brand (Watford)

Sacred Heart, Bushey: (3415) Merryhill Road, Bushey WD23 1SU
Tel: 01923 01923 901179 Email: admin@sacredheart682.herts.sch.uk
Executive Head Mrs Linda Payne (Bushey and Oxhey)

St Anthony: (+N) (3428) Croxley View, Watford WD18 6BW
Tel: 01923 226987 Email: admin@stanthonys.herts.sch.uk
Head Mrs Elaine Harrold (Watford)

St Catherine of Siena: (A) (5211) Horseshoe Lane, Garston, Watford WD25 7HP
Tel: 01923 676022 Email: admin@st-catherine.herts.sch.uk
Head Ms Nicola Kane (Garston)

St John, Rickmansworth: (A) (3398) Berry Lane, Mill End, Rickmansworth WD3 7HG
Tel: 01923 774004 Email: admin@stjohns705.herts.sch.uk
Executive Head Mrs Patricia O'Donnell (Mill End)

SECTION 5

St Joseph, South Oxhey: (+N) (3383) Ainsdale Road, South Oxhey, Watford WD19 7DW
Tel: 020 8428 5371 Email: admin@stjosephs775.herts.sch.uk
Head Mrs Linda Payne (Carpenders Park)

SECONDARY SCHOOLS (HERTFORDSHIRE)

John F Kennedy: (4619) Hollybush Lane, Hemel Hempstead HP1 2PH
Tel: 01442 266150 Email: admin@jfk.herts.sch.uk
Head Mr Paul Neves Chaplain Calum Moore (St Albans Deanery)

John Henry Newman: (A) (5413) Hitchin Road, Stevenage SG1 4AE
Tel: 01438 314643 Email: admin@jhn.herts.sch.uk
Head Mr Clive Mathew Chaplain Fr Philip Law (Stevenage Deanery)

Loreto: (A) (4620) (Girls) Hatfield Road, St Albans AL1 3RQ
Tel: 01727 856206 Email: admin@loreto.herts.sch.uk
Head Mrs Maire Lynch Chaplain Shane McCarthy (RO) (St Albans Deanery)

Nicholas Breakspear: (A) (5412) Colney Heath Lane, St Albans AL4 0TT
Tel: 01727 860079 Email: admin@nbs.herts.sch.uk
Head Mr Declan Linnane Chaplain Fr Fidelis Ifeanyi CSSp (St Albans Deanery)

St Joan of Arc: (A) (5418) High Street, Rickmansworth WD3 1HG
Tel: 01923 773881 Email: admin@joa.herts.sch.uk
Head Mrs Bernadette O'Hanlon Chaplain Rev Liam Lynch (Deacon)
(Watford Deanery)

St Mary, Bishop's Stortford: (5422) Windhill, Bishop's Stortford CM23 2NQ
Tel: 01279 654901 Email: info@stmarys.net
Head Mr Andrew Celano Chaplain Daniel D'Cruz (Lea Valley Deanery)

St Michael: (A) (5417) High Elms Lane, Garston, Watford WD25 0SS
Tel: 01923 673760 Email: admin@stmichaelscatholichighschool.co.uk
Head Mr Edward Conway Chaplain Fr Benedict Baka CSSp (Watford Deanery)

Independent

St Columba College: (6025) (Boys) King Harry Lane, St Albans AL3 4AW
Tel: 01727 855185 Email: collegeadmin@stcolumbascollege.org
Interim Head Mr David Shannon-Little Chaplain Br Nelson Dionne SC (RO)
(St Albans Deanery)

NON-MAINTAINED SPECIAL SCHOOL
St Elizabeth Centre: (7006) South End, Much Hadham SG10 6EW
Tel: 01279 843451 Email: schooloffice@stelizabeths.org.uk
Director of Education and Skills Development Mr Alec Clark
Head of School Mrs Samantha Steinke-Sanderson Principal Mrs Teresa Glynn
(RO) (Lea Valley Deanery)

PRIMARY AND SECONDARY SCHOOL
Independent
St Edmund's College and Prep: (6115) Old Hall Green, Ware SG11 1DS
Tel: 01920 821504 Email: enquiries@stedmundscollege.org
Head Mr Matthew Mostyn
Priest-in-Residence Fr Peter Lyness Lay Chaplain Paula Peirce (Lea Valley Deanery)

COUNTY OF SURREY   (936)

PRIMARY SCHOOLS
Our Lady of the Rosary: (3461) Park Avenue, Staines-upon-Thames TW18 2EF
Tel: 01784 453539 Email: info@ourlady.surrey.sch.uk
Head Miss Patricia McNicholas (Staines-upon-Thames)

St Ignatius, Sunbury: (3459) Green Street, Sunbury-on-Thames TW16 6QG
Tel: 01932 785396 Email: admin@st-ignatius.surrey.sch.uk
Head Mrs Charlotte Hendy (Sunbury)

St Michael, Ashford: (3915) Feltham Hill Road, Ashford TW15 2DG
Tel: 01784 253333 Email: info@st-michaels.surrey.sch.uk
Head Mr John Anthony Lane (Ashford)

SECONDARY SCHOOL
St Paul College: (5411) Manor Lane, Sunbury-on-Thames TW16 6JE
Tel: 01932 783811 Email: info@st-pauls.surrey.sch.uk
Head Mr James McNulty Chaplain Carlise Jones (Upper Thames Deanery)

Section 6

CATHOLIC SOCIETIES AND ORGANISATIONS

Inclusion in this section does not necessarily imply a recommendation of the group nor an endorsement of views expressed by it.

AID TO THE CHURCH IN NEED

ACN is a Pontifical Foundation directly under the Holy See. As a Catholic charity, it supports the faithful wherever they are persecuted, oppressed or in need, through prayer, information and action. Founded in 1947 by Fr Werenfried van Straaten, whom Pope St John Paul II named 'an outstanding Apostle of Charity', the organisation is now at work in around 140 countries. Undertaking thousands of projects every year, the charity provides emergency support for people experiencing persecution, transport for clergy and catechists, funding for media and evangelisation projects, grants for church building, Mass stipends, subsistence support for priests and religious and training for seminarians.

ACN UK is a registered charity in England and Wales [1097984] and Scotland [SC040748].
National Director Dr Caroline Hull **Head of Community Outreach for England, Scotland and Wales** Lorraine McMahon **Aid to the Church in Need UK, 12-14 Benhill Avenue, Sutton SM1 4DA Tel: 020 8662 8668 Email: acn@acnuk.org**

ANSCOMBE BIOETHICS CENTRE

A national Catholic Research Centre, established by the Catholic Bishops of England and Wales in 1977. It seeks to promote understanding of Catholic teaching on healthcare and biotechnology issues through research and educational outreach. The Centre engages in scholarly dialogue with academics and practitioners of different traditions, and contributes to public policy debates and consultations. In addition to academic conferences and seminars, it also runs educational programmes for, and gives advice to, healthcare professionals, biomedical scientists, students and the wider Catholic community.
Director Prof David Albert Jones **The Anscombe Bioethics Centre, 82-83 St. Aldate's, Oxford OX1 1RA Tel: 07734 964620 Email: admin@bioethics.org.uk Web: www.bioethics.org.uk**

ARCHCONFRATERNITY OF ST STEPHEN

The Archconfraternity of St Stephen exists to promote and encourage high standards of altar serving. Servers can be enrolled into the Guild with permission of their Parish Priest once they have been serving for at least six months and made their First Communion. Please contact the Hon Secretary or Diocesan Director for details on how a parish can be affiliated to the Guild.
National Director Fr Dennis F P Touw Tempelmans-Plat (Fulham I) **Diocesan Director** Fr Keith Stoakes (Poplar / Limehouse) **Hon President** Paul Briers KCHS
Hon Secretary Marc Besford **Email: secretary@guildofststephen.org**

ASSOCIATION FOR LATIN LITURGY

(Under the patronage of the Bishops' Conference of England & Wales)
Latin liturgy and Gregorian chant for the Church of today.

We promote the use of Latin in the *Novus Ordo* and the Church's inheritance of Gregorian Chant, working especially to enable the faithful to participate fully in the Latin liturgy in its contemporary form. We arrange meetings with sung Masses, Vespers and Benediction in Latin, talks, chant days, publish our journal *Latin Liturgy*, engage in liturgical studies, liaise with the hierarchy, and produce liturgical booklets for congregations. Our latest publication, the Introits of the *Graduale Parvum*, provides simple but authentic settings for all Sundays of the year in Latin and English, suitable for small choirs and for congregations. Work on settings of the other chants of the Propers is well advanced. The *Graduale Parvum* is now distributed by the C T S.

Contact Membership Secretary **173 Davidson Road, Croydon CR0 6DP**
General enquiries Email: enquiries@latin-liturgy.org Web: www.latin-liturgy.org /
www.facebook.com/latinliturgy

ASSOCIATION FOR THE PROPAGATION OF THE FAITH (APF)

Part of the Missio network, the Association for the Propagation of the Faith (APF) builds much needed infrastructure in predominantly impoverished, remote areas – from chapels and schools, to orphanages, clinics and dispensaries. Requested by the local community, our support transforms lives and creates a hub from which the young Church can flourish and grow, spreading the Good News of the Gospel, ministering to the faithful and delivering essential services in health and education through the Red Mission boxes and the World Mission Sunday annual collection.

Diocesan Director Fr Carlos Quito **Email: carlosquito@rcdow.org.uk**
Mill Hill Appealer for the Diocese Fr John Hemer MHM
Tel: 020 7349 5609 Email: johnhemer@gmail.com
National Office for Missio 23 Eccleston Square SW1V 1NU (Reg. Charity No. 1056651)
Tel: 020 7821 9755 Email: apf@missio.org.uk Web: www.missio.org.uk

ASSOCIATION OF MARY HELP OF CHRISTIANS

To promote personal devotion to, and public honour of Our Lady under the title 'Help of Christians'. A prayer meeting is held on the fourth Saturday of each month at 3.30pm at **9 Henry Road N4 2LH Contacts** Rev Kassa Tsegaye (Deacon) **120 Seaford Road N15 5DT**, Fr Hugh Preston SDB **Tel: 07806 803683**

ASSUMPTION SISTERS AND YOUNG ADULTS MINISTRY

The Religious of the Assumption, founded by St Marie Eugenie, are committed to the Christian education of young people. We accompany university students and young professionals from 18-30s and offer a programme of Catholic retreats, pilgrimages, events and monthly masses with socials to enable them to meet regularly in a friendly, spiritual environment.

Address: Maria Assumpta Chapel **21 Kensington Square W8 5HH**
Email: youth@assumptionvolunteers.org Web: www.assumptionreligious.org
Facebook: Religious of the Assumption UK Instagram: assumptionuk

ASSUMPTION VOLUNTEERS

Catholic Gap Year and short term volunteer opportunities: overseas in India, the Philippines, Rwanda, Lithuania, Belgium, Italy, Latin-America or in the UK in Newcastle-upon-Tyne and Middlesbrough. Volunteer in educational and social projects connected with the Assumption Sisters worldwide. There are 10 subsidised placements each year; share your skills and your life with young people in poor communities around the world and let them teach you a new way of living.

Contact Anne Marie Salgo **Volunteer Co-ordinator, 20 Kensington Square W8 5HH**
Email: vc@assumptionvolunteers.org.uk Web: www.assumptionvolunteers.org.uk
Facebook: Assumption Volunteers

BANNEUX ND. INTERNATIONAL UNION OF PRAYER

Promulgates the message given by Our Lady at Banneux under the title 'Virgin of the Poor' by showing films and leading retreats and pilgrimages.
Secretary Lisa Pirie **1 Lines Road, Stevenage SG1 3DJ** Tel: 07500 288384
Email: banneuxndgb@gmail.com

BEGINNING EXPERIENCE

A Catholic ministry for men and women who find themselves single again following divorce, separation or the death of a partner. It offers a weekend programme which seeks to encourage participants to close the door gently on the past and to approach life with more confidence and hope in the future.
Contact Freda Bacon **Tel: 01322 838415,** or Maura Heaney **Tel: 07795 498445**
Email: besouthofengland@gmail.com Web: www.beginningexperience.org.

CAFOD (CATHOLIC AGENCY FOR OVERSEAS DEVELOPMENT)

CAFOD (Charity number 09387398) is the official overseas development and relief agency of the Catholic Church in England and Wales. In over 30 countries we reach people in poverty with practical help. Through our global Church network, one of the largest in the world, we have the potential to reach everyone in greatest need, save lives and relieve suffering.
In emergencies we provide immediate relief. Our long-term re-building programmes focus on clean water, sanitation, sustainable livelihoods and peace-building. Our Campaign work challenges the structures and behaviours that drive poverty, injustice and harm the natural world. We campaign for global justice, so that every woman, man and child can live a full and dignified life.
Support can be offered through donations, prayer, volunteering and campaigning.
CAFOD's Lent Family Fast Day is on Friday 3 March 2023 and Harvest Fast Day is on Friday 6 October 2023 and donation envelopes will be available in churches in the weeks preceding.
Contact Tony Sheen **CAFOD Westminster Volunteer Centre, 29 Bramley Road N14 4HE**
Tel: 020 8449 6970 Email: westminster@cafod.org.uk Web: cafod.org.uk

CARITAS CHRISTI

International secular institute for women living a celibate life. For the single or widowed.
Web: www.ccinfo.org

SECTION 6

CARITAS SOCIAL ACTION NETWORK

CSAN is the official agency of the Catholic Bishops' Conference of England and Wales for domestic social action. We support and facilitate our network of over 50 Catholic dioceses and independent charities. Our members provide help for families and children, the elderly, homeless people, refugees, the disabled, and prisoners. The national team strives to develop the network, advance the education, training, practice and formation of those active in Catholic social action, and offer a coherent Catholic voice on social justice in the public arena. CSAN is a member of *Caritas Internationalis* within the *Caritas Europa* group.

Chairman of Trustees Rt Rev Terence Drainey **Vice-Chairman** Sr Lynda Dearlove
CEO Raymond Friel **Romero House, 55 Westminster Bridge Road SE1 7JB**
Tel: 020 7870 2210 Email: admin@csan.org.uk Web: www.csan.org.uk

CARMELITES OF THE DISCALCED CARMELITE SECULAR ORDER

Carmelite Seculars, together with the friars and nuns, are sons and daughters of the Order of Our Lady of Mount Carmel and St Teresa of Jesus. They share the same charism. It is one family with the same spiritual possessions, the same call to holiness and the same apostolic mission. There are four groups that meet regularly within the Westminster diocese.

Contact Mark Courtney **Tel: 020 8288 0536** Email: mark.courtney@oxon.org
Web: www.secularcarmel.org.uk

CARMELITE SECULAR INSTITUTE (THE LEAVEN)

The Leaven, the Secular Institute of Our Lady of Mount Carmel, is a secular institute for single women and widows founded in 1949. There are currently members in England, Scotland, Italy and Australia. The individual apostolate of members is rooted in a life of prayer drawing on the rich spiritual heritage of the Carmelites and each member lives her everyday life wherever she finds herself: alone, with family or friends. Our members work in various jobs including nursing, teaching, in factories and cleaning. The commitment to service and contemplation is shown in the vows they take of poverty, celibacy and obedience.

Contact Angela Kneale **8 Fulwell Court, St Leger Drive, Great Linford, Milton Keynes MK14 5HB** Email: theleavensi@gmail.com

CARMELITE THIRD ORDER (ANCIENT OBSERVANCE)

Carmel-in-London offers laity and diocesan clergy the opportunity to deepen their following of Christ within one of the Church's most ancient spirituality traditions, combining contemplative reflection with prophetic service and action for justice. Drawing inspiration from the prophet Elijah, the Blessed Virgin Mary and the Saints of Carmel, we form praying communities in the heart of the Church at the service of all God's people, through formal Carmelite Third Order gatherings and more diverse Carmelite Spirituality Groups. A Carmelite Third Order Group of the Ancient Observance (O.Carm) meets regularly in Westminster Diocese, alongside the monthly Carmel-in-the-City Spirituality Group. **Contact** Sylvia Lucas
Email: sylvia_lucas@btinternet.com Web: www.carmelinthecity.org.uk

CATENIAN ASSOCIATION

International Association of Catholic men, with over 250 local groups in the UK including 20+ in Westminster diocese. Catenians support each other, their families and friends, their clergy and parishes, vocations, young people, and many charities each year. We share our faith as friends and meet monthly to renew friendships, share a meal, organise events, and unload the daily stresses and strains of modern living.

Contact Declan O'Farrell (Director) **Tel: 07866 523092 Email:** declanofarrell@hotmail.com

CATHOLIC ARCHIVES SOCIETY

The Catholic Archives Society promotes and advises on listing, management and preservation of records of dioceses, religious foundations and institutions of the Catholic Church. It is a voluntary organisation founded in 1979 to promote the care of the archives of the Roman Catholic Church in the United Kingdom and Republic of Ireland, so enabling them:
• To be used for the efficient administration of the diocese, parish, religious foundation or lay society they concern.
• To be available for research and cultural uses

Contact: catholicarchivesociety@gmail.com **Web:** www.catholicarchivesociety.org
Twitter: @CatholicArcSoc

CATHOLIC ASSOCIATION FOR RACIAL JUSTICE

The Catholic Association for Racial Justice is an independent charity, and a membership organisation. CARJ works with people of diverse backgrounds, in Church and society, to create a more just, more equal, more co-operative community. We do this through education, advocacy and facilitating mutual support among:
· schools, families and young people in marginalised communities
· Gypsies, Roma and Traveller communities
· those working in poor urban communities
· those suffering discrimination based on race, caste, religion and social class.
Wherever possible, CARJ works in formal or informal partnership with members, friends and fellow citizens who share our basic values.

Chair Mrs Yogi Sutton **Catholic Association for Racial Justice, 9 Henry Road N4 2LH**
Tel: 020 8802 8080 Email: info@carj.org.uk **Web:** www.carj.org.uk

CATHOLIC ASSOCIATION OF PERFORMING ARTS

Members are encouraged to use their talents to help others, work with like-minded performers, enjoy social and networking opportunities, explore their spiritual side and encourage the performance and publication of Catholic plays and scripts.
Chaplain Fr Alan Robinson **Secretary** Kenneth Michaels
Email: kennethmichaels@hotmail.com **Web:** www.caapa.org.uk

SECTION 6

CATHOLIC CHARISMATIC RENEWAL

Details about Catholic Charismatic Renewal, including contacts for International, National, Diocesan and local groups, prayer groups and communities, and how to subscribe to our quarterly e-newsletter are through **Email: ccrcentre.goodnews@gmail.com**, or visit **Web: www.ccr.org.uk**

CATHOLIC CONCERN FOR ANIMALS

(Registered Charity 231022) CCA is the principal animal welfare organisation within the Catholic Church worldwide and we exist to promote and care for the well-being and protection of all of God's creation and work within the spirit of *Laudato Si'*, the Encyclical on the Environment by Pope Francis.
Contact Chris Fegan **Tel: 07817 730472 Email: chrisfegancca@gmail.com**
Web: www.catholic-animals.com

CATHOLIC EDUCATION SERVICE

CES is the education agency of the Bishops' Conference. Founded by the Vicars-Apostolic in 1847, its principal aim remains to represent the collective view of the bishops to central government and other national agencies in the field of education. It also supports the work of diocesan education services and religious orders who are trustees of schools. In the Catholic sector across England and Wales there are 2,204 schools and colleges educating over 853,000 students. There are also 4 Catholic universities and 8 other Catholic higher education institutions. **Chair** The Rt Rev Marcus Stock, Bishop of Leeds **Director** Paul Barber
39 Eccleston Square SW1V 1BX Tel: 020 7901 1900
Email: general@catholiceducation.org.uk Web: www.catholiceducation.org.uk

CATHOLIC EVANGELISATION SERVICES

Produce Catholic teaching resources on DVD to equip parishes, schools and colleges. A wide range of CaFE (Catholic Faith Exploration) resources are available for sacramental preparation, parish renewal, chaplaincy groups and to support the RE curriculum in secondary schools.
Director David Payne **PO Box 333, St Albans AL2 1EL Tel: 0845 050 9428**
Email: resources@faithcafe.org Web: www.faithcafe.org www.youthcafe.org

CATHOLIC EVIDENCE GUILD

For the training and provision of public speakers on the Catholic Faith.
Enquiries Mr Phil Gough **Email: catholic.reconquista@outlook.com**
YouTube: Catholic Reconquista

CATHOLIC FAMILY HISTORY SOCIETY

The Society exists to help and encourage those who have Catholic ancestry in England, Wales and Scotland to research their family history. Details of membership, publications and resources are obtainable through the website or by email.
Email: cfhsrecords@gmail.com Web: http://catholicfhs.online

CATHOLIC GRANDPARENTS ASSOCIATION

The Catholic Grandparents Association is a global organisation of the faithful. An integral part of the Catholic Grandparents Association is setting up branches at the parish level. These act as prayer and support groups for grandparents. Grandparents have a unique vocation that must be fostered and cherished in the spirit of St Joachim and St Anne, the grandparents of Jesus and parents of Mary. **PO Box 90, Walsingham, Norfolk NR21 1AQ Tel: 01328 560333**

CATHOLICS IN FUNDRAISING

A network to share best practice amongst Catholics working in fundraising for charities. Meets twice a year in London for a topical presentation, discussion and networking. There is also a LinkedIn group 'Catholics in Fundraising, UK'
Contact John Green **Email: jgreen@jesuit.org.uk**

CATHOLIC MEDICAL ASSOCIATION

For Catholic members of the medical and healthcare professions
39 Eccleston Square SW1V 1BX Tel: 020 7901 4895 Fax: 020 7901 4819
Chairman of Westminster Branch Rev Dr Michael Jarmulowicz **337 Harrow Road W9 3RB**
Tel: 020 7286 2170 Email: secretary@catholicmedicalassociation.org.uk
Web: www. catholicmedicalassociation.org.uk

CATHOLIC MISSIONARY UNION OF ENGLAND AND WALES

The national forum and information centre of the missionary societies and congregations - lay and religious - working in mission and human development projects overseas. It promotes mission, coordinates the annual parish mission appeals by the member societies and is a consultative body to the Bishops' Conference.
Secretary Richard Owens **CMU Secretariat, Office 4, 106 Lord Street, Southport PR8 1LF**
Email: secretariat@cmu.org.uk Web: www.cmu.org.uk

CATHOLIC PEOPLE'S WEEKS

Established in 1945, CPW runs educational, residential events which provide the opportunity for people to combine study of their faith with thoughtful joyous liturgy, time to reflect and relax, community experience and a holiday for young and old. New programme each January.
Email: chaircpw@gmail.com Web: www.catholicpeoplesweeks.org

CATHOLIC POLICE GUILD

Founded in 1914 by Mgr Howlett for Catholic members of policing in London. Since 1974 a national organisation for those in policing and broader law enforcement. **Chairman of London Metropolitan & City Region** Alex Blatchford **Tel: 07788 988588**
Email: alex.blatchford@catholicpoliceguild.co.uk Web: www.catholicpoliceguild.co.uk

SECTION 6

CATHOLIC RECORD SOCIETY

Founded in 1904 to make available material for study of the Catholic history of England and Wales since the Reformation, publishing transcripts of diaries; letters and biographies; legal, court and official papers; and records of old Catholic missions, seminaries, colleges and convents. Since then its purview has broadened considerably; it hosts an annual conference and its peer-reviewed academic journal, *British Catholic History*, is published twice a year by Cambridge University Press.

Contact Hon Secretary Dr Scholastica Jacob   **Email: secretary@crs.org.uk**
Web: www.crs.org.uk

CATHOLIC TRUTH SOCIETY

We believe in helping people to discover, nurture and share their faith, by providing honest and compelling answers to life's deepest questions. Everything we do is authentic, accessible, and authoritative. You can rely on us to tackle the important issues of life and faith, to make the complicated easy to understand, and that the works we publish are in line with the teachings of the Catholic Church.

Chair Rt Rev Paul Hendricks MA PhL VG, Auxiliary Bishop in Southwark Archdiocese
General Secretary Pierpaolo Finaldi **Publishing Office 42-46 Harleyford Road SE11 5AY**
Tel: 020 7640 0042 Fax: 020 7640 0046 Email: orders@CTSbooks.org
Web: www.CTSbooks.org

CATHOLIC UNION OF GREAT BRITAIN AND C.U. CHARITABLE TRUST

The Catholic Union of Great Britain (CUGB) was founded in 1870 and is the voice of the Catholic laity working to educate the Government, Parliament and wider society to ensure that our Catholic values and interests are presented to key decision makers who determine legislation and social policy. The funding of CUGB is by annual or life individual membership subscription or donation. **President** Rt. Hon. Sir Edward Leigh MP **Director** Nigel Parker
The Catholic Union of Great Britain (CUGB), St Maximilian Kolbe House, 63 Jeddo Road W12 9EE Tel: 020 8749 1321 Email: info@catholicunion.org.uk Web: catholicunion.org.uk
The Catholic Union Charitable Trust (CUCT) was launched in 2015. Its principal aim is to advance Catholic moral, social and spiritual teaching by means of conferences, lectures, training and seminars. The funding of the CUCT is by donations which are eligible for gift aid.
Chairman James Bogle **Secretary** Tom Martin
The Catholic Union Charitable Trust (CUCT), St Maximilian Kolbe House, 63 Jeddo Road W12 9EE Tel: 020 8749 1321 Email: info@cuct.org Web: cuct.org

CATHOLIC VOICES

An Apologetics project that has spread to 22 countries. Set up to train spokespersons for radio and TV interviews, it now also offers speakers to parishes, chaplaincies, and schools. It holds topical briefings when the Church is in the news, runs a blog (www.cvcomment.org) and has led to publications, including 'How to Defend the Faith Without Raising Your Voice'. It offers bespoke media trainings for dioceses and Catholic organisations in the UK and abroad. Independent of the Bishops' Conference, it is supported as part of their 'Confidently Catholic' agenda, encouraging lay people 'to know and live their faith with courage and give witness to it with confidence'.

Lead Co-ordinator Brenden Thompson **Email:** info@catholicvoices.org.uk
Web: www.catholicvoices.org.uk **Twitter:** @CatholicVoices.

CATHOLIC WOMEN'S LEAGUE

The Catholic Women's League was founded in 1906. It is a Catholic agency uniting Catholic women in a bond of friendship and encouraging them to use their talents in the service of the Church and the community, reaching out to every area of concern.

Contact Veronica Comparini, President Westminster Branch **Tel: 01442 258684**
Email: veedotcomp@gmail.com, Jean Clarke, National Secretary **Email:** natsec@cwlhq.org.uk
Web: catholicwomensleaguecio.org.uk

CHRISTIAN LIFE COMMUNITY

Small groups of Christians who meet regularly to help each other deepen their life of prayer. CLC's special characteristic is the spirituality of St Ignatius, helping members to integrate prayer with action in their daily lives.

National Chaplain Br Alan Harrison SJ **Diocesan Representative** Jackie Gill **(Administrator)** 114 Mount Street W1K 3AH **Email:** president@clcew.org.uk

COMMUNITY OF SANT'EGIDIO

The Community of Sant'Egidio is a 'Church Public Lay Association' which began in Rome in 1968. The different communities, spread across 73 countries, share the same spirituality and principles which characterise the way of Sant'Egidio: Prayer, Communicating the Gospel, Solidarity with the Poor, Ecumenism, and Dialogue. The Community regularly gathers for common prayer, as a pathway to becoming familiar with Jesus' words, presenting to the Lord the needs of poor people, our own needs and the needs of the whole world.

Sant'Egidio, in London as elsewhere, lives in service to the poor in friendship and familiarity, considering them as brothers and sisters, especially the homeless and the elderly. Feel free to contact us for details regarding our services throughout the year and at Christmastime.

Email: info@santegidio.org.uk **Web:** www.santegidio.org.uk **Facebook:** @santegidiolondon
Twitter: @santegidiouk **Instagram:** @santegidiouk

COMMUNITY OF THE RISEN LORD

The mission of the Community of the Risen Lord (CRL) UK is to bring life-transforming renewal both to parishes and dioceses, with outreach and pastoral activities based on the teaching of the Catholic Church. Meetings are held at St. Joseph's Pastoral Centre, Hendon, from 3.30-5.30 pm on 2nd and 4th Sundays.

Contact: Sonia Tissera **(UK Co-ordinator),** Niru Fernando **and** Eric Jeevaraj **(Co-Group Team)** 70 Roxeth Green Avenue, South Harrow HA2 8AG **Tel:** 07957 117928
Email: ericc2210@gmail.com **Web:** www.crlmain.org

SECTION 6

CONSECRATED WOMEN

Vatican II restored the Order of Virgins, which dates from the early Church. Canon 604 speaks of this form of consecrated life, mentioned in the Catechism (paras 922-4). We are consecrated publicly by the Bishop to live an independent life within the local church community. Each woman is autonomous, and her pattern of life is planned by herself and approved by the Bishop. She is responsible for her own finances. Other women are consecrated as widows; our vow is for life. Those who wish meet annually for a week at Hyning monastery. This kind of religious life combines freedom with commitment.
Contact: Gosia Brykczynska OCV **148 Carlyle Road W5 4BJ Tel: 020 8560 0120**
Email: gosia.brykczynska@protonmail.com

CONSTANTINIAN ORDER OF ST GEORGE

Internationally recognised ancient and charitable Catholic Order of Knighthood under the custodianship of the Royal House of Bourbon Two Sicilies.
Grand Master HRH The Duke of Castro **Prior** HE Vincent Cardinal Nichols, Archbishop of Westminster **Sub-Prior** Most Rev George Stack, Archbishop Emeritus of Cardiff; **Chief Chaplain for Ireland** Most Rev Dr Raymond Field, Auxiliary to the Archbishop of Dublin;
Delegate for Britain and Ireland Awaiting appointment;
Vice-Delegates HE Mr John Bruton **(Ireland)**, The Rt Hon Lord Murphy of Torfaen **(Great Britain)**, The Hon Sir Peter Caruana **(Gibraltar)**
Contact Sacred Military Constantinian Order of St George
12 Queen's Gate Gardens SW7 5LY Tel: 020 7594 0275
Email: chancery@constantinian.org.uk Web: www.constantinian.org.uk

DEPARTMENT FOR EVANGELISATION AND DISCIPLESHIP

Mission Directorate
Director Fr Jan Nowotnik **Mission Adviser** Elliot Vanstone **Administrator and Committees Secretary** Kinga Kosterska
The Directorate carries out the work as dictated by the Bishops in assisting the local Church to achieve the priorities indicated below, communicating the Bishops' vision and working with Diocesan evangelisation personnel, leaders of New Movements, CYMFed and Catholic resource providers who support evangelisation and catechesis in a parish context.
Tel: 020 7901 4882 Email: kinga.kosterska@cbcew.org.uk Web: www.cbcew.org.uk
• The Department for Evangelisation and Discipleship helps the local Church to make the joy of the Gospel a reality in England and Wales. It does this by promoting the work of mission in line with the themes presented in *Evangelii Gaudium*, The Directory for Catechesis and The Pastoral Conversion of the Parish Community in the Service of the Mission of the Church.
Chair Archbishop Mark O'Toole (Archbishop of Cardiff and Bishop of Menevia)
Secretary Fr Jan Nowotnik
• National Office for Vocation
The National Office for Vocation (NOV), is part of the Department, working to help people hear God's Call. This is done by:
• Building a culture of vocation within the Church of England & Wales

• Working with youth and youth organisations to nurture young people into leadership and responsibility in the Church

• Working with the Department for Evangelisation and other ecclesial bodies to help people grow in their baptismal calling as disciples of Jesus Christ.

Director Sr Elaine Penrice **Discipleship Promoter** James Ryan

Email: enquiries@ukvocation.org **Web** www.ukvocation.org

• The Department of Dialogue and Unity is in dialogue with many faith communities. For Christian unity it works with Churches Together in England, English and Welsh Anglican Roman Catholic Community and with Churches Together in Britain and Ireland. It has separate dialogues with Methodists, the United Reformed Church, the Eastern Orthodox Church, the Oriental Orthodox Church, the Jews and the Muslims.

The Department assists diocesan co-ordinators with dialogue with Christian denominations and other faith communities by providing ongoing formation.

Chair Archbishop Bernard Longley (Archbishop of Birmingham)

Secretary Fr Jan Nowotnik (National Ecumenical Officer for England and Wales)

EMMANUEL COMMUNITY

A Public Association of the Faithful, recognised by the Holy See, for lay people, priests, deacons and consecrated men and women. **Web:** www.emmanuel.info

ENGLISH CATHOLIC HISTORY ASSOCIATION

To promote interest and encourage research into English and Welsh Catholic history. Helps preserve relevant documents. Arranges regular meetings/visits. Members' quarterly newsletter.

Secretary Mrs Angela Hodges **45 High Street, Stoke sub Hamdon, Somerset TA14 6PR**

Tel: 01935 823928 Email: secretary@echa.org.uk Web: www.echa.org.uk

FOCOLARE MOVEMENT

An international, ecclesial movement which began in 1943 in Trent, Northern Italy, when Chiara Lubich and the small group of people around her experienced God's personal love and the transformative power of putting the words of the Gospel into practice. The Focolare Movement's principal aim is to help bring about the fulfilment of Jesus' prayer: 'That all may be one'. In this country Focolare has a national conference centre in Welwyn Garden City and local groups in various locations.

Focolare Centre for Unity, 69 Parkway, Welwyn Garden City AL8 6JG

Tel: 01707 323620 Email: cfu@focolare.org.uk Web: www.focolare.org/gb

FRIENDS OF THE HOLY FATHER

To pray for the Holy Father's intentions, study and promote his teaching. Supports a fund assisting in defraying expenses of his Apostolic Ministry. **Chair** John Langan

Secretary Mary Maxwell **23a Vincent House, Vincent Square SW1P 2NB**

Email: fhfenquiries@gmail.com Web: www.thefriendsoftheholyfather.org

FRIENDS OF THE HOLY LAND

Friends of the Holy Land, an ecumenical and non-political charity, fosters resilience and hope among Christians in the Holy Land. Our efforts flow from Christians through Christians to Christians. We seek to raise awareness of the daily challenges faced by Christians living in the Holy Land, supporting them with prayers and fund-raising, and encouraging Christians to visit the Holy Land and meet local Christian communities. We provide funding to meet emergency needs for the most vulnerable, and support sustainable projects mainly in education, employment, health and housing, which ultimately make a difference to individual Christians and their families. Cardinal Nichols is the Founding Patron.

Contact Office Manager **Friends of the Holy Land, Farmer Ward Road, Kenilworth CV8 2DH Tel: 01926 512980 Email: office@friendsoftheholyland.org.uk Web: www.friendsoftheholyland.org.uk Facebook@friendsoftheholyland Twitter@Social_FHL**

FRIENDS OF THE ORDINARIATE OF OUR LADY OF WALSINGHAM

The aim of the Friends (Charity No. 1142667) is to raise money from across the Catholic community to support the work and mission of the Ordinariate. In particular we assist with the training and support of priests and invest in churches owned or used by the Ordinariate..

Contact Nicolas Ollivant **c/o 24 Golden Square W1F 9JR** Email: ollivant@gmail.com Web: http://friendsoftheordinariate.org.uk/

FRIENDS OF THE *VENERABILE* (THE ENGLISH COLLEGE IN ROME)

Founded in 1985, the Friends (Charity no. 1075141) support students of the College, who will be our future priests with prayers, encouragement and financial help. Over £385,000 has been given to the College since 1985 for various projects. In 2018 the Friends started an additional Pilgrimage Fund (Restricted) to assist the College when pilgrimages are arranged.

Contact Mike Lang **Tel: 01364 644811** Email: mikelang537@btinternet.com Web: www.friendsofenglishcollegerome.org.uk

GOOD COUNSEL NETWORK

A Catholic, pro-life pregnancy centre in central London providing friendship and practical help and ongoing support of all kinds to assist pregnant women to choose life for their children. We have Daily Mass and Adoration in our Centre. We provide speakers and run a monthly day of prayer and fasting for the end of abortion. We provide post-abortion counselling, too. We welcome volunteers who wish to help us in our work.

Director Clare McCullough **The Good Counsel Network, PO Box 46679 NW9 8ZT Tel: 020 7723 1740** Email: info@goodcounselnetwork.com Web: www.goodcounselnetwork.com Blog: mariastopsabortion.blogspot.com

GRAIL, THE

The Grail has always worked to share its Christian inspiration and values with the world by encouraging awareness of God's presence in the individual, communities and creation, in the belief that to help one person to grow is to help to build the world. Today this work is being continued through the making of small grants to other charities or groups whose work

embodies these values. For full details of eligibility and application forms **contact**
Email: president@grailsociety.org.uk Web: www.grailsociety.org.uk

GUILD OF OUR LADY OF RANSOM

Supporting evangelisation in England and Wales. Principal means: Encouraging prayer,
evangelisation, and innovation in our Church. Offering financial support to charities promoting
the Catholic faith in England and Wales, and parishes through each of our dioceses.
Contact Master Mgr John Armitage **Project Manager** Nazar Alsamarai
79a Barking Road E16 4HB Email: info@guild-ransom.co.uk Web: www.guild-ransom.co.uk

GUILD OF OUR LADY OF WILLESDEN

The Guild is open to all and meets every Tuesday at **Our Lady of Willesden, Nicoll Road
NW10 9AX** after the 7pm Mass. Its purpose is to pray for the intentions and protection of
London through the intercession of Our Lady of Willesden.
Guild Master Fr Stephen Willis

GUILD OF ST AGATHA

Catholic Association of Bellringers. **Guild Office, 1 Albert Road, Bournemouth BH1 1BZ**
Diocesan Representative Canon Shaun Lennard **243 Mutton Lane, Potters Bar EN6 2AT**
Tel: 01707 654359

HOLY SEPULCHRE, EQUESTRIAN ORDER OF THE

To strengthen in its members the Christian life, in fidelity to the Pope and the teachings of the
Church, observing the principles of charity for assistance to the Holy Land; to aid the
charitable, cultural and social works and institutions of the Church in the Holy Land, particularly
those of and in the Latin Patriarchate of Jerusalem, with which the Order maintains ties; to
support the propagation of the Faith there, involving in this work Catholics scattered
throughout the world, united in charity by the symbol of the Order; and also all brother
Christians; and to sustain the rights of the Catholic Church in the Holy Land.
Contact Howard Field **Email: westminstersecretary@eohsj.org.uk** Web: https://eohsj.org.uk

HOUSING JUSTICE

Through national membership we offer advice and training on delivering services to people
who are homeless or in housing need; facilitate and co-ordinate frontline services, including a
London-wide winter shelters forum; and campaign for better legislation. We support the
development of services nationwide and champion alternative solutions, notably housing co-
operatives and community land trusts. Members are available to speak to groups or after
Masses about homelessness and housing. We also co-ordinate the annual Homeless Sunday in
October.
Chief Executive Kathy Mohan **The Foundry, Unit 2.11, 17 Oval Way SE11 5RR**
Tel: 020 3752 5635 Email: info@housingjustice.org.uk Web: www.housingjustice.org.uk

SECTION 6

IMPACT

Young people making a difference (13-17 year-olds) trains young people to become leaders in life using the 'See, Judge, Act' method. See '**Young Christian Workers**' for more details.

JOHN PAUL II FOUNDATION FOR SPORT (JP2F4S)

Launched by Pope Benedict XVI during his visit to Britain, to honour the memory of St John Paul II and his vision for sport, this charity enables the setting up of clubs in parishes and schools, supports clubs in need of advice and guidance and produces educational materials for schools and parishes. Catholic in inspiration, working with all and for all, its purpose is summed up in its strapline: 'Educating young people through sport'.
Contact Mgr Vladimir Felzmann CEO **John Paul II Foundation for Sport, Vaughan House, 46 Francis Street SW1P 1QN Email: vladimirfelzmann@rcdow.org.uk**

KNIGHTS OF ST COLUMBA

Fraternal order of Catholic men supporting the mission of the Church and the spiritual, intellectual and material welfare of its members and their families.
**Head Office, 75 Hillington Road South, Glasgow G52 2AE Tel: 0141 883 5700
Email: headoffice@ksc.org.uk**
Provincial Grand Knights: Province 11 Dale Stuart **Province 29** Jim Pugh
Province 30 Anthony Berkeley

LATIN MASS SOCIETY

Founded in 1965, LMS is an association of Catholic faithful and a registered charity with around 2,000 members, predominantly lay, drawn from every age, group and walk of life. It is dedicated to the use and wider provision of the Traditional Latin Mass (the *Missale Romanum 1962*) and other Sacraments. Working with its network of local representatives, the Society organises pilgrimages, retreats, days of recollection, training conferences for priests and servers, conferences for the general public, research and campaigning. It is a supporter of the Gregorian Chant Network (**www.gregorianchantnetwork.org**). Details of its sodality for altar servers, the Society of St Tarcisius (**www. lms.org.uk/society-st-tarcisius**), and family and youth affiliates can be obtained from the London office. It also publishes a quarterly magazine, *Mass of Ages*. Its online shop offers books and DVDs on the Traditional Mass and devotions.
Contact National Office **9 Mallow Street EC1Y 8RQ**
Tel: 020 7404 7284 Email: info@lms.org.uk Web: lms.org.uk

LAY DOMINICANS

Lay members of the Order of Preachers called to the four pillars of prayer, study, community, and preaching within the lay state. Members may be married or single and make a lifelong commitment to the Order. Lay Dominicans preach the Gospel for the salvation of souls, after the example of St Dominic, through varied apostolates and professions. The London fraternity meets on the second Sunday of each month at the shrine of Our Lady of the Rosary and St Dominic, Southampton Road NW5 4LB.
President Catherine Wallis-Hughes **Tel: 07807 348223**
Email: catherinewallishughes@gmail.com

LAY MISSION AND VOLUNTEER NETWORK

An informal group of Catholic missionary and volunteer organisations which offer faith-based volunteering overseas. Co-ordinators meet to share ideas and resources and each summer run a residential week-long pre-departure training course for volunteers. This training course is also open to those going to volunteer abroad with religious orders who may not have access to training.

Each organisation has its own charism and sending practice (opportunities, countries, length of service, age range). If you'd like to volunteer with one of us contact details for each website can be found on **Facebook page LMVN**

LIFE ASCENDING MOVEMENT (FORMERLY THE ASCENT)

For Christians in middle and later life helping them grow spiritually and to take up their responsibilities as members of the Church through friendship, spirituality and mission, with parish-based regular meetings.

National President Colin Blagdon **19 Lymington Road, Stevenage SG1 2PE**
Tel: 01438 216247 Web: www.lifeascending.org.uk

LONDON CATHOLIC WORKER

LCW is part of the international Catholic Worker movement founded in 1933 by Dorothy Day and Peter Maurin. CW communities are houses of hospitality for the poor as well as places to perform the works of mercy and organise resistance to the works of war, injustice and violence. The movement practises hospitality, active non-violence, gentle personalism and voluntary poverty. Each community is independent, with no HQ. We need full-time live-in community members and volunteers, as well as part-time volunteers and donations in cash or in kind. **Contact** London Catholic Worker **49 Mattison Road N4 1BG Tel: 020 8348 8212** Email: londoncatholicworker@yahoo.co.uk Web: www.londoncatholicworker.org

LONDON JESUIT CENTRE

The Centre runs courses and events specializing in theology, spirituality, and social and environmental justice issues, from beginner to MA level. Its aim is to be of service to the Church in London and beyond by proclaiming the gospel through adult formation. The LJC offers retreat days and retreats in daily life (with some online), and spiritual direction for lay people and clergy. It is also home to the Heythrop Library (established 1614), one of the largest collections of theology and philosophy in Europe. The Library is open to researchers, academics, students and those with a serious interest in theology, philosophy and related disciplines. **Contact:** ljc@jesuit.org.uk Web: www.londonjesuitcentre.org

MALTA, ORDER OF (BRITISH ASSOCIATION)

A British charity and a religious order of the Church, supporting in the UK, inter alia, The Orders of St John Care Trust, soup kitchens in London, Oxford, Cambridge, Colchester and St Andrews and pilgrimages for the sick to Lourdes and Walsingham.
British Association Sovereign Military Order of Malta, Craigmyle House, 13 Deodar Road SW15 2NP Tel: 020 7286 1414 Email: basmom@btconnect.com.

SECTION 6

MARIST WAY

The Marist Way is the lay branch of the Marist Congregation, bringing together people who wish to participate in the life and mission of the Church in the `Spirit of Mary', a way envisaged by Jean-Claude Colin, founder of the Marists, who are Priests, Sisters, Brothers and Laity.

Marists endeavour to think, feel, judge and act as Mary did, at Nazareth and at Pentecost All Marists believe that Mary maintains a special interest in bringing the women and men of our time into contact with her Son, Jesus. They feel called to share in this concern of Mary's and to become part of her family to work on her behalf. The term `the work of Mary' describes this essentially missionary spirit.

Contact Mrs Pat O'Connor **12 Harrow Road, Linthorpe, Middlesbrough TS5 5PD**
Tel: 01642 814486 Email: patriciaoconnor44@gmail.com Facebook: Marist Way England

MARRIAGE CARE

We provide marriage preparation and relationship counselling to thousands of couples each year through a network of centres and professionally accredited volunteers. Visit our website to book a place on a marriage preparation course for those marrying in the Catholic Church or for a counselling appointment. If you are interested in helping us support couples in your community, we would love to hear from you; please visit the website also.

Registered office (Charity number 218159): Marriage Care, Huntingdon House, 278 Huntingdon Street, Nottingham NG1 3LY Tel: 0800 389 3801
Email: info@marriagecare.org.uk Web: www.marriagecare.org.uk

MARRIAGE ENCOUNTER

Provides weekends for couples and those who are engaged, in association with priests and religious, to enrich their lives through improving communication.

Web: http://wwme.org.uk/

MING-AI (LONDON) INSTITUTE

An education institute promoting links between our diocese and the Church in Hong Kong and China. It provides an MA degree programme in Chinese Cultural Heritage Management (validated by Middlesex University) and a wide range of leisure, Chinese cookery, language and calligraphy classes. Ming-Ai specialises on British Chinese Culture Heritage projects, and has an outreach project to demonstrate Chinese culinary skills to the schools' food & technology classes.

Chairman Professor Jonathan Liu **Dean** Ms Chungwen Li
Ming-Ai (London) Institute, 1 Cline Road N11 2LX
Tel: 020 8361 7161 Email: enquiry@ming-ai.org.uk Web: www.ming-ai.org.uk / www.britishchineseheritagecentre.org.uk

MISSIO

The Pope's official charity for overseas mission, with 120 offices worldwide under the co-ordination of the Pontifical Mission Societies in Rome. We are the Holy Father's chosen instrument for sharing the Gospel and building the Church throughout the world.

Together, the Missio offices globally support 1,069 dioceses in 157 countries. It is the only Catholic charity which supports the 40% of the Universal Church that is too new, young or poor to support itself. We aim to follow Christ's example by helping everyone in need, regardless of background or belief.

Missio comprises four branches which work together: the Association for the Propagation of the Faith (APF), the Society of St Peter the Apostle (SPA), Mission Together (MT), and the Pontifical Missionary Union (PMU).

National Director Fr Anthony Chantry MHM

National Office for Missio 23 Eccleston Square SW1V 1NU (Reg. Charity No. 1056651)
Tel: 020 7821 9755 Email: info@missio.org.uk Web: www.missio.org.uk
Diocesan Director Fr Carlos Quito **Email:** carlosquito@rcdow.org.uk

MISSION TOGETHER (HOLY CHILDHOOD)

Part of the Missio network, Mission Together (MT) provides such things as healthcare and education for the world's poorest children, regardless of background or belief. It supports vulnerable children via educational, medical and welfare projects through schools, orphanages, health centres, children's homes and nutrition programmes. The food, education, medications, shelter, and formation that MT provides fulfil both the children's spiritual and practical needs.

National Office for Missio 23 Eccleston Square SW1V 1NU (Reg. Charity No. 1056651)
Tel: 020 7821 9755 Email: missiontogether@missio.org.uk Web: www.missio.org.uk
Diocesan Director Fr Philip Baptiste **Email:** philipbaptiste@rcdow.org.uk

NATIONAL BOARD OF CATHOLIC WOMEN

A consultative body to the Bishops' Conference of England & Wales with consultative status within the United Nations, with representatives from 32 Catholic organisations and the dioceses. A forum in which women are enabled to share their views and concerns and make recommendations at all levels.

Tel: 07724 685780 Email: nbcwpres@gmail.com Web: nbcw.co.uk

NATIONAL COUNCIL FOR LAY ASSOCIATIONS (ENGLAND AND WALES)

A consultative body to the Bishops' Conference, consisting of lay apostolic national organisations, liaison representatives, advisors & executive. **Adviser** Bishop Tom Williams
President Val Ward **Tel:** 07711 121415 **Email:** valward19@yahoo.co.uk
Secretary Debbie Cottam **Tel:** 07778 266059 **Email:** deborahcottam@outlook.com

NEOCATECHUMENAL WAY

The Neocatechumenal Way is an itinerary of Catholic formation lived in small communities within the parish. It helps people different in age, social background, mentality and culture, to rediscover and to live the immense riches of their baptism. They meet on a regular basis to celebrate the Liturgy of the Word and the Eucharist, going through various stages similar to those of the 'catechumenate' of the Early Church. The Neocatechumenal Way is governed by a Statute approved by the Holy See. **Email:** ncway.gb@gmail.com
Web: www.camminoneocatecumenale.it

SECTION 6

NEWMAN ASSOCIATION

National association of Catholic laity and clergy, with local circles in London and Hertfordshire
Web: http://www.newman.org.uk/

OUR LADY'S CATECHISTS

See entry for the *Catholic Women's League*

PAX CHRISTI

Pax Christi is a gospel-based international movement for peace, open to all. We strive to help the Church and wider community to proclaim and make peace through its work for reconciliation and the promotion of a culture of peace and non-violence. We offer a wide range of materials for education, reflection and campaigning for peace. Pax Christi also produces material for parishes each year to encourage support for Peace Sunday (the Pope's World Peace Message), celebrated on the 2nd Sunday in Ordinary Time.
National President Archbishop Malcolm McMahon OP **CEO** Awaiting appointment
St Joseph's, Watford Way NW4 4TY Tel: 020 8203 4884 Email: info@paxchristi.org.uk
Web: www.paxchristi.org.uk

PONTIFICAL MISSIONARY UNION (PMU)

Part of the Missio network, the Pontifical Mission Union (PMU) is responsible for encouraging all the faithful to have passion for mission and evangelisation. As Catholics we are encouraged to share the love of God through our words and actions with our global family.
National Office for Missio 23 Eccleston Square SW1V 1NU (Reg. Charity No. 1056651)
Tel: 020 7821 9755 Email: info@missio.org.uk Web: www.missio.org.uk
Diocesan Director Fr Carlos Quito **Email: carlosquito@rcdow.org.uk**

POPE'S WORLDWIDE PRAYER NETWORK

The Network (formerly the Apostleship of Prayer) is co-ordinated by the National Co-ordinator, Fr Eddy Bermingham SJ. Its renewal was mandated by Pope Benedict, then by Pope Francis. The 175 year-old ministry is active in almost 100 countries, inviting the faithful to pray the Monthly Intentions of the Holy Father. It offers the Daily Prayer Pathway, expanding the traditional Morning Offering, whilst the new 'Way of the Heart' renews the much-loved devotion to the Sacred Heart. All parishes are invited and encouraged to pray with the Pope.
Email: eberminghamsj@jesuit.org.uk Web: https://www.praywiththepope.net
Twitter: @PraywiththePope

PRAY AS YOU GO

Pray As You Go is a daily prayer session produced by the Jesuits in Britain, designed to be with you wherever you are, to help you pray whenever you find time. Pray As You Go also provides audio retreats and extra Ignatian resources. Available as an app for iOS and Android, as a podcast, or online at **www.pray-as-you-go.org**

PRISON ADVICE & CARE TRUST (FORMERLY THE BOURNE TRUST)

Pact is the national Catholic charity working to support prisoners, people with convictions and their families. We work in courts, prisons and in the community to support people to make a fresh start, and to minimise the harm that can be caused by imprisonment to people who have committed offences, on families and on communities. If you or someone you know needs support, call free, confidential helpline **0808 808 3444**, email **helpline@prisonadvice.org.uk** or fill in the webform at **prisonadvice.org.uk/forms/contact-our-helpline**. If interested in the criminal justice system, please get in touch for information about volunteer opportunities.
**29 Peckham Road SE5 8UA Tel: 020 7735 9535 Email: ParishAction@prisonadvice. org.uk
Web: www.prisonadvice.org.uk**

PROJECT 2030

Our group enables Catholics in their 40s to get together at a social and spiritual level. Events include Masses, retreats, walks, meals, museum visits, pilgrimages, holidays, and other opportunities to meet up together.
**National Office: St John's, 266 Wellington Road North, Heaton Chapel SK4 2QR
Contact** Rev Hugh Hanley SCJ **Email: project2030@btinternet.com
Web: www.fortysomethings.net**

RETROUVAILLE

A lifeline for troubled marriages, helping heal and renew marriages in distress. For couples who are finding it difficult to communicate; who argue about everything or live in silence; who feel alone, lonely and distant; who may think separation and divorce are their only options.
**Tel: 07887 296983 / 07973 380443 Email: retrouvailleukinfo@gmail.com
Web: www.retrouvaille.org.uk**

ST BARNABAS SOCIETY (SUCCESSOR TO THE CONVERTS' AID SOCIETY)

For the assistance of needy former clergy and religious received into the Catholic Church.
Secretary Fr Paul Martin **Windsor House, Heritage Gate, East Point Business Park, Sandy Lane West, Oxford OX4 6L** Tel: 01865 513377 **Email: directorstbarnabas@gmail.com
Web: www.stbarnabassociety.org.uk**

ST FRANCIS LEPROSY GUILD

The Guild was founded in 1895 to help those suffering from leprosy. It supports leprosy hospitals, treatment centres, rehabilitation centres and residential care for people suffering from or affected by leprosy in 12 countries, as well as projects to eradicate leprosy one community at a time. **Chair of Trustees** Michael Forbes Smith **CEO** Clare McIntosh
**73 St Charles Square W10 6EJ Email: enquiries@stfrancisleprosy.org
Web: www.stfrancisleprosy.org**

SECTION 6

ST FRANCIS OF ASSISI CATHOLIC RAMBLERS CLUB

Organises Sunday walks in London and the Home Counties throughout the year. Rambles on additional days and further afield are occasionally provided, plus other social activities.
Contact Membership Secretary stfrancisramblers@gmail.com for an information pack or for further details go to **www.stfrancisramblers.ukwalkers.com**

ST JOSEPH'S SOCIETY (FORMERLY THE AGED POOR SOCIETY)

This charity provides almshouse accommodation for elderly / retired Roman Catholics who are of limited means and able to live independently.
Contact: St Joseph's Society **42 Brook Green W6 7BW**
Tel: 020 7603 9817 Email: stjosephssociety@yahoo.co.uk

ST VINCENT DE PAUL SOCIETY

The St Vincent de Paul Society (SVP) is an international Christian society, Catholic in character and origin. The Society's mission is to bear witness to Christ's love and to put his teaching into practice. With mutual support, friendship and encouragement, members seek to reach out and extend their commitment through person-to-person care for those disadvantaged, neglected or in need. They seek to identify the causes of need, provide items of furniture, clothing and food where appropriate and offer the hand of friendship. In these ways members aim to develop their own spiritual lives, strengthening their own faith and deepening their love of God and their neighbour.
Contact St Vincent de Paul Society **Romero House, 55 Westminster Bridge Road SE1 7JB**
Tel: 020 7703 3030 Email: info@svp.org.uk **Web:** www.svp.org.uk

ST VINCENT'S FAMILY PROJECT

TheProject provides support to young families in South Westminster. We believe that early help to families will reduce or prevent the many potential crises families and children can face through school and adolescence. At present, there are several aspects to our project, giving priority to those most in need:
Family Space, a service for young families which aims to support the whole family through Drop Ins, Creche, one to one support opportunities, support groups, parenting and healthy living courses.
Creative Art Therapies for children between the ages of 4 and 13 years. We accept referrals from local schools, children's services, and other agencies working with children.
Our six Vincentian Values are being respectful, inspired, travellers together, professional, holistic, and compassionate.
St Vincent's Family Project, Methodist Central Hall, Storey's Gate
SW1H 9NH Tel: 020 7654 5351 Email: info@svfp.org.uk **Web:** www.svfp.org.uk

SECULAR CLERGY COMMON FUND

Chief Administrator Awaiting appointment **Secretary** Angela Rowe **Tel: 07537 185800**
Email: secretary@secularclergy.org.uk **Westminister Administrator** Mgr Phelim Rowland

SECULAR CLERGY NEW COMMON FUND

Chief Administrator Mgr Canon Nicholas Rothon **Tel: 020 8852 5420**
Diocesan Representative Fr Graham Stokes **Tel: 020 8868 7531**

SECULAR FRANCISCAN ORDER (OFS)

The members of the Secular Franciscan Order, founded by St Francis of Assisi, number more than 500 in the UK. They make a lifetime Profession to join the Order, but remain in their secular state living in the world. Their rule and life is dedicated to observing the Gospel of Christ in the secular world by going from Gospel to life and life to Gospel. They support each other in their endeavours by gathering regularly in local fraternities, and in the spirit of the beatitudes they seek to share the love of God with all people and all of creation.
Contact: Email: info@ofsgb.org Web: www.ofsgb.org

SION CENTRE FOR DIALOGUE & ENCOUNTER

A centre for study and growth in mutual understanding between Christians and Jews, as well as other faiths and cultures. As a place to listen, learn, reflect and respect we offer a regular programme of courses and lectures, as well as times for reflection and prayer. Our specialist library has staff available to assist with research. Outside groups also use our facilities for their own seminars, training and meetings. The Centre is run by the Sisters of Our Lady of Sion.
34 Chepstow Villas W11 2QZ Tel: 020 7313 8286
Email: sioncentrefordialogue@gmail.com Web: https://sioncentre.org/

SOCIETY OF CATHOLIC ARTISTS

Aims to encourage high standards in Church art, to assist prospective patrons in the selection of suitable artists and craftsmen and to provide fellowship to those who have the arts and Catholicism in common.
Email: maryjeandonaghey5@gmail.com Web: www.catholicartists.co.uk

SOCIETY OF OUR LADY OF LOURDES

The Society promotes devotion to Our Lady of Lourdes by enabling and encouraging pilgrims to visit Lourdes, minimising barriers of costs and disability, and by organising services and talks in her honour during our pilgrimage in May and through its *Pilgrims Way* magazine and social media.
c/o Church of the Immaculate Heart of Mary, Botwell Lane, Hayes UB3 2AB
Tel: 020 8848 9833 Web: www.soll-lourdes.com www.facebook.com/groups/soll.lourdes/

SOCIETY OF ST AUGUSTINE OF CANTERBURY

The Society (founded in 1922) exists for the promotion and advancement of the Roman Catholic religion in England and Wales, principally through assistance in the maintenance of Archbishop's House, Westminster.
Secretary Richard Collyer-Hamlin **77 Gibbon Road, Kingston upon Thames, Surrey KT2 6AE**
Tel: 07970 401731 Email: richardcollyerhamlin@hotmail.com
Web: www.staugustineofcanterbury.org.uk

SECTION 6

SOCIETY OF ST GREGORY

The national Catholic society promoting understanding, active participation and good practice in the celebration of the liturgy. It organises summer schools, lectures and study for all who are engaged in liturgy and music. The journal *Music and Liturgy* (available by subscription) contains articles, news, reviews and a practical liturgy planner.

Contact Society Secretary **7 Nore Farm Avenue, Emsworth, Hampshire PO10 7NA**
Web: www.ssg.org.uk

SOCIETY OF ST JOHN CHRYSOSTOM

Founded in 1926 to encourage greater knowledge, understanding and appreciation of the tradition of the Eastern Churches, to promote Catholic-Orthodox unity and to support the Eastern Catholic Churches. Publishes *Chrysostom* three times a year.

Email: johnchrysostom@btinternet.com **Web:** www.orientalelumen.org.uk
President Cardinal Vincent Nichols, Archbishop of Westminster
Chair Fr Mark Woodruff **Tel: 07710 024505 Email: as above**
Membership & General Enquiries Mrs Ola Stayne **22 Esher Avenue, Walton on Thames KT12 2TA Email: miss_ola0127@yahoo.pl**

SOCIETY OF ST PETER THE APOSTLE (SPA)

Part of the Missio network, the Society of St Peter the Apostle trains the Church leaders of tomorrow, bringing the love of Christ to vulnerable communities, and passing on the gift of faith to future generations in over 157 countries around the world. Every year Missio's SPA supports the training of 30,000 future priests and 11,000 religious sisters in the mission dioceses. Only SPA, as the Pope's own charity, has this unique role throughout the world.

Diocesan Director for Missio Fr Carlos Quito **Email: carlosquito@rcdow.org.uk**
National Office for Missio 23 Eccleston Square SW1V 1NU (Reg. Charity No. 1056651)
Tel: 020 7821 9755 Email: spa@missio.org.uk Web: www.missio.org.uk

STELLA MARIS (APOSTLESHIP OF THE SEA)

Stella Maris is the official maritime agency of the Catholic Church in Great Britain. It is a registered charity (number 1069833) reliant on the annual Sea Sunday appeal and donations to sustain its ministry. 90% of world trade is carried by ship. Seafarers and fishers often work in dangerous conditions suffering loneliness, deprivation and exploitation. It deploys chaplains and ship visitors who welcome merchant seafarers / fishers to our shores and provide for their pastoral / practical needs – regardless of creed or nationality. Catholic seafarers / fishers also have the opportunity to receive the sacraments. Stella Maris provides chaplains on board cruise ships, works to maintain seafarers' centres inside ports, and collaborates with industry bodies to speak up for seafarers' / fishers' rights. It relies on a network of valued contacts and volunteers to sustain its development.

CEO / European Regional Co-ordinator Martin Foley **Stella Maris (AoS), 39 Eccleston Square W1V 1BX Tel: 020 7901 1931**
Email: info@stellamarismail.org Web: www.stellamaris.org.uk

TEAMS (EQUIPES NOTRE-DAME)

International movement for married couples of all ages whose purpose is to help couples live fully the Sacrament of Marriage. Groups of 4-6 couples, with a chaplain or spiritual advisor, meet monthly in each others' homes to support, pray and discuss Scripture. There are over 13,500 such Teams around the world.
Email: info@teamsgb.org.uk Web: www.teamsgb.org.uk

THE VINCENTIAN VOLUNTEERS LIMITED

A challenging and fulfilling Gap Year in the UK for 18-35 year olds of any nationality, living in small communities serving people who are vulnerable, in the spirit of St Vincent de Paul.
Contact Marion Osuide **St Matthew's Presbytery, Worsley Road, Eccles, Manchester M30 8BL** Tel: 07708 314996 Email: marion@vincentianvolunteers.org.uk
Web: www.vincentianvolunteers.org.uk

THINKING FAITH

The online journal of the Jesuits in Britain. Articles to help you think about your faith and think, through your faith, about the world. Visit **www.thinkingfaith.org** to see the latest content, search the archive and subscribe to regular email alerts.
114 Mount Street W1K 3AH Tel: 020 7499 0285 Email: editor@thinkingfaith.org

UNION OF CATHOLIC MOTHERS

National organisation for the preservation of the family and sanctification of the home.
Diocesan President Mrs Iona De Souza **47 Redfern Avenue, Whitton TW4 5NA**
Tel: 020 8894 2366 Email: ionadesouza@aol.com
Spiritual Director Fr Michael Johnston **Email: michaeljohnston@rcdow.org.uk**

YOUNG CHRISTIAN WORKERS & IMPACT

A movement of apostolic formation, for young people between 13 and 30. Through a programme of enquiry in small groups in parishes and schools, YCW educates and trains young people for their mission of Christian service in everyday life. It enables them to become apostles to other young people and prepares them for the responsibilities of adult Christian life. YCW also produces educative enquiry discussion material and arranges numerous training events, including residential weekends.
Contact YCW HQ **St Anthony's Presbytery, Eleventh Street, Trafford Park, Manchester M17 1JF** Tel: 0161 872 6017 Email: info@ycwimpact.com
Web: www.ycwimpact.com

YOUTH 2000

Seeks to raise up a new generation of saints to evangelise the nations by inviting young people (aged 16-35) to encounter Jesus Christ, at the heart of the Catholic Church. Led by young people for young people, Y2K hosts weekend Prayer Festivals, where young adults are introduced to the essentials of the Catholic faith: Mass, Eucharistic Adoration, Confession, Scripture and Devotion to Our Lady. These festivals provide opportunities to build friendships,

experience God's love and receive the grace of conversion. Youth 2000 also runs a Mission Team, where young people across the country are invited to join the mission and play their unique role in the vision of building a civilization of love. **Charity No. 1000371**
Contact Youth 2000 **Pilgrim Bureau, Friday Market Place, Walsingham NR22 6EG**
Email: info@youth2000.org Web: http://youth2000.org

WALSINGHAM ASSOCIATION

The Association exists to spread devotion to Our Lady of Walsingham and encourage pilgrimage to her Shrine. Founded in 1933, the Association has branches throughout the country, which new members are invited to join, or become one of its many individual members. It is open to all who seek to deepen their devotion to Our Lady, joining in daily prayer with members nationwide and supporting prayerfully the growth and development of the Shrine.
Contact Walsingham Association **Pilgrim Bureau, Friday Market Place, Walsingham, Norfolk NR22 6EG Tel: 01328 800953 Email: enquiries@walsinghamassociation.org.uk**
Web: www.walsinghamassociation.org.uk/

WORLD APOSTOLATE OF FATIMA (ENGLAND AND WALES)

A Public Association of the Faithful (Charity Number 1198986) erected to promote Our Lady's call to live the Gospel more profoundly through prayer, penance, offering up daily duties in a spirit of sacrifice, daily recitation of the Rosary and the Five First Saturdays Communion of Reparation to the Immaculate Heart of Mary.
To host the National Pilgrim Statue and the Relics of Ss Francisco and Jacinta Marto, **contact** stamfordnicky@yahoo.co.uk or **info@worldfatima-engalndwales.org.uk**. For further information on WAF (England & Wales) **web: https://worldfatima-englandwales.org.uk/**
Diocesan Representative Nestor Baniqued **Tel: 07799 226269**
Diocesan Spiritual Director Fr Richard Nesbitt **Email: whitecity@rcdow.org.uk**
National President Jerry Rivera **42 Blenheim Gardens, Kingston upon Thames KT2 7BW**
Email: national.president@worldfatima-englandwales.org.uk

WORLD COMMUNITY FOR CHRISTIAN MEDITATION

Promotes the prayer of Christian meditation as taught by John Main, monk of Ealing Abbey, simple practical wisdom that brings the truths of faith alive in our own experience.
Lido Centre, 63 Mattock Lane W13 9LA Tel: 020 8280 2283
Email: uk@wccm.org Web: www.wccm.org / www.wccm.uk

OTHER USEFUL ADDRESSES

Catholic Communications Network
39 Eccleston Square SW1V 1BX Tel: 020 7901 4800 Email: ccn@cbcew.org.uk

Catholic Safeguarding Standards Agency
39 Eccleston Square SW1V 1BX Tel: 020 7901 1920
Email: admin@catholicsafeguarding.org.uk Web: https://www.catholicsafeguarding.org.uk/

Catholic Spirituality Network (CSN, formerly CNRS, NRM)
A national network of individuals and groups including prayer guides, spiritual companions, chaplains, Retreat Centre teams, pastoral workers and clergy. We are the Catholic member group of the Ecumenical Retreat Association. We produce two newsletters a year and organize an annual conference, open to all, and day events around the country.
Catholic Spirituality Network (CSN), c/o St George's Cathedral, Westminster Bridge Road SE1 7HY Tel: 07756 864754
Email: catholicspiritualitynetwork@gmail.com Web: www.csn.retreats.org.uk

Churches Together in England
27 Tavistock Square WC1H 9HH Tel: 020 7529 8131

Independent Catholic News - the UK's daily on-line Catholic news service
Tel: 020 7267 3616 Web: www.indcatholicnews.com

Jesuit Refugee Service [JRS-UK]
Hurtado Jesuit Centre, 2 Chandler Street E1W 2QT Tel: 020 7488 7310
Fax: 020 7488 7329 Email: uk@jrs.net

Mary's Meals
Sets up school feeding programmes in some of the world's poorest communities where poverty and hunger prevent children from gaining an education. Currently 2.27 million children are fed one good nutritious meal every school day in countries such as Malawi, Liberia, Haiti, India, South Sudan, Lebanon and Syria.
13 Hippodrome Place W11 4SF Tel: 0800 698 1212
Email: London.admin@marysmeals.org Web: www.marysmeals.org.uk

The Retreat Association
PO Box 1130, Princes Risborough, Bucks HP22 9RP
Tel: 01494 569056 Email: info@retreats.org.uk Web: www.retreats.org.uk

Society for the Protection of Unborn Children (SPUC)
Our principal aims and objectives are:
· To affirm, defend and promote the existence and value of human life from the moment of conception until natural death;
· To defend and protect human life generally and in particular, whether born or unborn;
· To defend, assist and promote the life and welfare of mothers during pregnancy and of their children from the time of conception up to, during and after birth.
SPUC pursues these aims through engaging in political lobbying and campaigns, educating young people and the public, publishing academic research, fighting legal battles, and through other forms pro-life work.
SPUC, Unit B, 3 Whitacre Mews, Stannary Street SE11 4AB
Tel: 020 7091 7091 Email: information@spuc.org.uk

women@thewell
Provides services for the most vulnerable women caught in multiple cycles of abuse, we aim to support women whose lives are entangled in the sex trade to exit. Providing a broad range of

services which are women centred and trauma responsive. They include advice, advocacy, outreach, therapeutic services and specialist exiting support to women. In addition we provide a range of training and consultancy services to other agencies nationally and internationally that support women at risk.

54/55 Birkenhead Street WC1H 8BB Tel: 020 7520 1710 Email: info@watw.org.uk or for training needs: training@watw.org.uk Web: www.watw.org.uk

Section 7

THE CYCLE OF PRAYER

The liturgical year has been divided into six periods. We are asked to use the intentions during the current period, both corporately and in personal prayer, as well as on specific Days of Prayer. Parish Priests are asked to make the Cycle known by displaying and distributing copies in their churches, and to issue a reminder when a new period of the Cycle begins. When a Day of Special Prayer occurs on a Sunday, it is sufficient to announce the Day at the beginning of Mass and to include a suitable petition in the Universal Prayer. An introductory leaflet and leaflets for the seasons as well as model intercessions are available on the Bishops' Conference Liturgy Office website: **www.liturgyoffice.org.uk** .

ADVENT/CHRISTMAS 2022

Intentions: Migrants and Refugees; Expectant Mothers.

Migrants' Day	Saturday 3 December	St Francis Xavier
Expectant Mothers	especially on 18 December	4th Sunday of Advent

ORDINARY TIME: TO SPRING 2023

Intentions: Peace on Earth; Openness to the Word of God; Christian Unity; The Sick and Those who Care for Them; Victims of Trafficking and Those who Work to Combat it; Racial Justice; The Unemployed.

Peace Day	Sunday 15 January	2nd Sunday in O.T.
Octave of Prayer for Christian Unity		18 – 25 January
Sunday of the Word of God	Sunday 22 January	3rd Sunday in O.T.
Racial Justice Day	Sunday 5 February	3 Sundays before Lent 1
Day for Victims of Trafficking	Wednesday 8 February	St Josephine Bakhita
World Day for the Sick	Saturday 11 February	Our Lady of Lourdes
Europe	Tuesday 14 February	Ss Cyril and Methodius
Day for the Unemployed	Sunday 19 February	Sunday before Lent 1

LENT 2023

Intentions: Candidates for the Sacraments (especially on the Sundays of Lent); Women; The Needy and Hungry of the World; Penitents and Wanderers.

World Day of Prayer	Friday 3 March	1st Friday in March
Lent Fast Day	Friday 3 March	Friday, 1st Week of Lent

EASTER 2023

Intentions: New Members of the Church; Vocations; The Right Use of the Media; The Church; Human Work.

Europe	Saturday 29 April	St Catherine of Siena
World Day of Prayer for Vocations	Sunday 30 April	4th Sunday of Easter
Human Work	Monday 1 May	St Joseph the Worker
Day of Prayer for Victims and Survivors of Sexual Abuse	Tuesday 9 May	Tuesday, 5th Week of Easter
World Communications Day	Sunday 21 May	7th Sunday of Easter
The Church	Sunday 28 May	Pentecost

ORDINARY TIME: SUMMER 2023 (until September)

Intentions: A Deeper Understanding between Christians and Jews; Those who Suffer Persecution, Oppression and Denial of Human Rights; Europe; Human Life; Seafarers.

Day for Life	Sunday 18 June	3rd Sunday in June
Those who suffer persecution	Thursday 22 June	Ss John Fisher and
		Thomas More
Sea Sunday	Sunday 9 July	2nd Sunday in July
Europe	Tuesday 11 July	St Benedict
Europe	Sunday 23 July	St Bridget of Sweden
Europe	Wednesday 9 August	St Teresa Benedicta
		of the Cross

ORDINARY TIME: AUTUMN 2023 (September to OLJC, King of the Universe)

Intentions: Students and Teachers; The Spread of the Gospel; The Harvest; The Fruits of Human Work, and the Reverent Use of Creation; Justice and Peace in the World; All Victims of War; Young People; Prisoners and their Families.

The Care of Creation	Friday 1 September	1 September
Education Day	Sunday 10 September	2nd Sunday in September
Evangelii Gaudium Day	Sunday 17 September	3rd Sunday in September
The Harvest	Sunday 24 September	Sunday 22–28 September,
	or whenever harvest festivals are held	
Harvest Fast Day	Friday 6 October	1st Friday in October
Prisons Week	8 -14 October	2nd Week in October
World Mission Day	Sunday 22 October	penultimate Sunday in
		October
Remembrance Day	Sunday 12 November	2nd Sunday in November
World Day of the Poor	Sunday 19 November	33rd Sunday in O.T.
Youth Day	Sunday 26 November	Christ the King

ADVENT/CHRISTMAS 2023

Intentions: Migrants and Refugees; Expectant Mothers.

Migrants' Day	Sunday 3 December	St Francis Xavier
Expectant Mothers	especially on 24 December	4th Sunday of Advent

Dated Days of Prayer are also repeated against the relevant date; the symbol § indicates a reference to the Cycle of Prayer.

THE HOLY FATHER'S PRAYER INTENTIONS 2022/23

DECEMBER 2022
For voluntary not-for-profit organisations: We pray that volunteers and not-for-profit organisations committed to human development may find people dedicated to the common good and ceaselessly seek out new paths to international co-operation.

JANUARY 2023
For educators: We pray that educators may be credible witnesses, teaching fraternity rather than competition and helping the youngest and most vulnerable above all.

FEBRUARY 2023
For parishes: We pray that parishes, placing communion at the centre, may increasingly become communities of faith, fraternity and welcome towards those most in need.

MARCH 2023
For victims of abuse: We pray for those who have suffered harm from members of the Church; may they find within the Church herself a concrete response to their pain and suffering.

APRIL 2023
For a culture of peace and non-violence: We pray for the spread of peace and non-violence, by decreasing the use of weapons by states and citizens.

MAY 2023
For Church movements and groups: We pray that Church movements and groups may rediscover their mission of evangelization each day, placing their own charisms at the service of needs in the world.

JUNE 2023
For the abolition of torture: We pray that the international community may commit in a concrete way to ensuring the abolition of torture and guarantee support to victims and their families.

JULY 2023
For a Eucharistic life: We pray that Catholics may place the celebration of the Eucharist at the heart of their lives, transforming human relationships in a very deep way and opening to the encounter with God and all their brothers and sisters.

AUGUST 2023
For World Youth Day: We pray the World Youth Day in Lisbon will help young people to live and witness the Gospel in their own lives.

SEPTEMBER 2023
For people living on the margins: We pray for those persons living on the margins of society, in inhumane life conditions; may they not be overlooked by institutions and never considered of lesser importance.

OCTOBER 2023
For the Synod: We pray for the Church, that she may adopt listening and dialogue as a lifestyle at every level, and allow herself to be guided by the Holy Spirit towards the peripheries of the world.

NOVEMBER 2023
For the Pope: We pray for the Holy Father; as he fulfills his mission, may he continue to accompany the flock entrusted to him, with the help of the Holy Spirit.

DECEMBER 2023
For persons with disabilities: We pray that people living with disabilities may be at the centre of attention in society, and that institutions may offer inclusive programmes which value their active participation.

SPECIAL COLLECTIONS 2023

Collection	Announce	Collect	Send to
Racial Justice *	29 Jan	5 Feb	CaTEW via Finance, Vaughan House
Cardinal's Lenten Appeal ****	19 Feb	During Lent	Finance, Vaughan House
CAFOD Family Fast Day * (Friday 3 Mar)	26 Feb	5 Mar	CAFOD, Romero House, 55 Westminster Bridge Road SE1 7JB
Holy Places ** (Good Friday)	2 Apr	7 Apr	Finance, Vaughan House
Priest Training Fund ****	23 Apr	30 Apr	Finance, Vaughan House
Catholic Communications Network **	14 May	21 May	CaTEW via Finance, Vaughan House
Day for Life ***	11 Jun	18 Jun	CaTEW Finance Department, CBCEW, 39 Eccleston Square SW1V 1BX
Peter's Pence **	25 Jun	2 Jul	Finance, Vaughan House
Stella Maris ***	2 Jul	9 Jul	Stella Maris, 39 Eccleston Square SW1V 1BX
Catholic Education Service *	3 Sep	10 Sep	Finance, Vaughan House
Evangelii Gaudium Appeal ***	10 Sep	17 Sep	CaTEW via Finance, Vaughan House
CAFOD Harvest Fast Day * (Friday 6 Oct)	1 Oct	8 Oct	CAFOD, Romero House, 55 Westminster Bridge Road SE1 7JB
World Mission Sunday **	15 Oct	22 Oct	Missio, 23 Eccleston Square SW1V 1NU
Sick & Retired Priests ****	30 Oct	6 Nov	Finance, Vaughan House
Missionary Orders Annual Appeal *		Any time	The Order concerned

* Optional
** Mandatory, Holy See
*** Mandatory, CBCEW
****Mandatory, Diocesan

LITURGICAL INFORMATION

Universal Calendar

Announcements from the Congregation for Divine Worship:

(1) The Optional Memorial of St Gregory of Narek, Abbot & Doctor, is celebrated on 27 February.

(2) The Optional Memorial of St John of Avila, Priest & Doctor, is celebrated on 10 May.

(3) The Optional Memorial of St Paul VI, Pope, is celebrated on 29 May.

(4) The Memorial of the Blessed Virgin Mary, Mother of the Church, is celebrated on the Monday after Pentecost.

(5) St Irenaeus (28 June) is now described as Bishop, Doctor & Martyr.

(6) St Mary Magdalene, hitherto celebrated as a Memorial on 22 July, is now kept as a Feast. Texts for Mass and the Office remain as hitherto, except for the Proper Preface, now approved in English translation.

(7) The Memorial of St Martha on 29 July is celebrated as the Memorial of Ss Martha, Mary and Lazarus.

(8) The Optional Memorial of St Hildegard of Bingen, Virgin & Doctor, is celebrated on 17 September.

(9) The Optional Memorial of St Faustina Kowalska, Virgin, is celebrated on 5 October.

(10) The Optional Memorial of St John XXIII, Pope, is celebrated on 11 October.

(11) The Optional Memorial of St John Paul II, Pope, is celebrated on 22 October.

(12) The Optional Memorial of the Blessed Virgin Mary of Loreto is celebrated on 10 December.

Further information may be found on the Bishops' Conference Liturgy Office website: **www.liturgyoffice.org.uk** . For Ss Gregory of Narek, Hildegard of Bingen and John of Avila further information is here:

https://www.vatican.va/roman_curia/congregations/ccdds/documents/adnexus-decreto-dottori.pdf

Variations from the Universal Calendar

Where no indication of rank is given, the celebration is an Optional Memorial.

(1) National

Proper prayers are found in the Proper of Saints in the Roman Missal; readings may be taken from the appropriate Common in the Lectionary, where Proper readings are not provided.

12 January	St Aelred of Rievaulx	
19 January	St Wulstan, Bishop	
14 February	**Ss Cyril, Monk and Methodius, Bishop, Patrons of Europe**	Feast
1 March	**St David, Bishop, Patron of Wales**	Feast
17 March	**St Patrick, Bishop, Patron of Ireland**	Feast
21 April	St Anselm, Bishop & Doctor	
23 April	**St George, Martyr, Patron of England**	Solemnity
24 April	St Adalbert, Bishop & Martyr	
	St Fidelis of Sigmaringen, Priest & Martyr	

29 April	**St Catherine of Siena, Virgin & Doctor, Patron of Europe**	Feast
4 May	**The English Martyrs**	Feast
19 May	St Dunstan, Bishop	
25 May	St Bede the Venerable, Priest & Doctor	Memorial
27 May	**St Augustine of Canterbury**	Feast
5 June	St Boniface, Bishop & Martyr	Memorial
9 June	St Columba, Abbot	
16 June	St Richard of Chichester, Bishop	
20 June	St Alban, Protomartyr	
22 June	**Ss John Fisher, Bishop, and Thomas More, Martyrs**	Feast
23 June	St Etheldreda (Audrey), Abbess	
1 July	St Oliver Plunket, Bishop & Martyr	
11 July	**St Benedict, Abbot, Patron of Europe**	Feast
23 July	**St Bridget of Sweden, Religious, Patron of Europe**	Feast
9 August	**St Teresa Benedicta of the Cross (Edith Stein), Virgin & Martyr, Patron of Europe**	Feast
26 August	Blessed Dominic (Barberi) of the Mother of God, Priest	
30 August	Ss Margaret Clitherow, Anne Line and Margaret Ward, Martyrs	
31 August	St Aidan, Bishop, and the Saints of Lindisfarne	
3 September	**St Gregory the Great, Pope & Doctor**	Feast
4 September	St Cuthbert, Bishop	
19 September	St Theodore of Canterbury, Bishop	
24 September	Our Lady of Walsingham	Memorial
9 October	**St John Henry Newman**	Feast
10 October	St Paulinus of York, Bishop, (or St Denis, Bishop, and his Companions, Martyrs, or St John Leonardi, Priest - transferred from 9 October)	
12 October	St Wilfrid, Bishop	
13 October	St Edward the Confessor	
26 October	Ss Chad and Cedd, Bishops	
3 November	St Winifride, Virgin	
7 November	St Willibrord, Bishop	
16 November	St Edmund of Abingdon, Bishop	
	St Margaret of Scotland	
17 November	St Hilda, Abbess	
	St Hugh of Lincoln, Bishop	
	St Elizabeth of Hungary, Religious	
30 November	**St Andrew, Apostle, Patron of Scotland**	Feast
29 December	**St Thomas Becket, Bishop & Martyr, Patron of the Parish Clergy**	Feast

Thursday after Pentecost

Our Lord Jesus Christ, the Eternal High Priest   Feast

full texts at https://www.liturgyoffice.org.uk/Calendar/Sanctoral/OLJC-full.pdf

(2) Diocesan

Proper prayers are found in the Diocesan Proper (either in booklet form or available online) or National Proper in the Missal; readings are taken from the appropriate Lectionary Common.

3 February	Ss Laurence, Dunstan, Theodore, Archbishops of Canterbury	Memorial
19 April	St Alphege, Bishop	Memorial
24 April	Ss Erkenwald and Mellitus, Bishops	Memorial
20 June	St Alban, Protomartyr	Memorial
27 June	St John Southworth, Priest & Martyr	Memorial
	(Solemnity in the Cathedral)	
1 July	**Dedication of the Cathedral**	Feast
	(Solemnity in the Cathedral)	
13 October	**St Edward the Confessor**	Feast
	(Solemnity in the City of Westminster)	
29 October	Blessed Martyrs of Douai College	Memorial
16 November	St Edmund of Abingdon, Bishop	Memorial

(3) Local

Each church celebrates as a Solemnity its Feast of Title, and, if it is consecrated, the Anniversary of Dedication. Falling on a Sunday of Ordinary Time or Sunday in the octave of Christmas they replace the liturgy of that Sunday. On Sundays of Advent, Lent or Easter or on another Solemnity they are transferred to the following day. These celebrations may also, for pastoral reasons, be transferred to an ordinary Sunday or other suitable day.

If the Anniversary of Dedication is unknown, it may be transferred to the Sunday before All Saints. If the church is dedicated to a title of Our Lady not found in the Calendar, the titular feast is kept on the Solemnity of the Assumption; if dedicated to a title of Our Lord Jesus Christ not found in the Calendar, the titular feast is kept on the Feast of the Transfiguration.

(4) Holy Days of Obligation for England and Wales in 2023

Epiphany of the Lord	Friday 6 January
Ascension of the Lord	Thursday 18 May
Corpus Christi	Sunday 11 June
Ss Peter and Paul	Thursday 29 June
Assumption BVM	Tuesday 15 August
All Saints	Wednesday 1 November
Christmas	Monday 25 December

(5) Calendar for the 1962 Missal

The Calendar for the *Missale Romanum 1962* is available in booklet form and online from the Latin Mass Society (see section 6).

(6) Additional Days of Prayer

(1) The World Day of Prayer for the Care of Creation is kept on 1 September. Liturgical resources are available at **www.liturgyoffice.org.uk/Calendar/Cycle/AutumnCP.shtml#Harvest**

(2) The Day of Prayer for Victims and Survivors of Abuse is kept on Tuesday of the 5th Week of Easter. The Pontifical Commission has produced resources on its website: **http://www.protectionofminors.va/content/tuteladeiminori/en.html** .

Choice of Mass to be celebrated
(1) Mass *ad libitum* in Ordinary Time
Where a Mass is to be celebrated *ad libitum*, the priest may choose:

from the Mass formula of the preceding Sunday or any one of the Sundays in Ordinary Time, even with some of the prayers taken from any another Sunday in Ordinary Time or from the prayers for Various Needs and Occasions; or

from the Mass of a Saint noted in the calendar as an optional memorial, or of a saint noted in the Martyrology for that day; or

from any Mass for the dead, although the formulas of the daily Mass for the dead may only be used if the Mass is actually said for the dead; or

a Mass for Various Needs; or

a Votive Mass.

(2) Occasions when Mass texts of the day may be replaced

	V1	V2	V3	D1	D2	D3
1. Solemnities of precept						
2. Sundays in the seasons of Advent, Lent and Easter	✗	✗	✗	✗	✗	✗
3. Holy Thursday, Easter Triduum						
4. Solemnities not of precept, All Souls						
5. Ash Wednesday, weekdays of Holy Week	✗	✗	✗	✓	✗	✗
6. Days in the octave of Easter						
7. Sundays of Christmas and Sundays in Ordinary Time	✓	✗	✗	✓	✗	✗
8. Feasts						
9. Weekdays in the season of Advent from 17 to 24 December						
10. Days in the octave of Christmas	✓	✗	✗	✓	✓	✗
11. Weekdays in the season of Lent						
12. Obligatory memorials						
13. Weekdays in the season of Advent to 16 December						
14. Weekdays in the season of Christmas from 2 January	✓	✓	✗	✓	✓	✗
15. Weekdays in the season of Easter						
16. Weekdays in Ordinary Time	✓	✓	✓	✓	✓	✓

✓ = permitted.

✗ = not permitted.

The table of rubrics inserted here governs when celebrations using the formularies from Ritual Masses, Masses for Various Needs and Occasions, Votive Masses, and Masses for the Dead are permitted within the liturgical year.

VI = Ritual Masses (General Instruction of the Roman Missal [hereafter, GIRM], no. 372). Masses for various needs and occasions and votive Masses, in cases of serious need or pastoral advantage, at the direction of the local Ordinary or with his permission (GIRM, no. 374).

V2 = Masses for various needs and occasions and votive Masses, in cases of serious need or pastoral advantage, at the discretion of the parish priest or the priest celebrant (GIRM, no. 376).

V3 = Masses for various needs and occasions and votive Masses chosen by the priest celebrant in favour of the devotion of the people (GIRM, nn. 373, 375).

DI = Funeral Mass (GIRM, no. 380).

D2 = Mass on the occasion of news of a death, final burial, or the first anniversary (GIRM, no. 381).

D3 = Daily Mass for the dead (GIRM, no. 381). When DI and D2 are not permitted, neither is D3.

(3) Funeral Mass

A Funeral Mass may be celebrated on any day, except Solemnities which are Holy Days of Obligation, Maundy Thursday, the Triduum, and the Sundays of Advent, Lent, and Eastertide.

(4) Prefaces of the Eucharistic Prayer

Solemnities, Feasts and certain other days are provided with Prefaces (either Proper or Common). These are indicated in the Calendar and are always used.

On Memorials either a seasonal Preface or an appropriate Preface of Saints may be used, according to the desire of the priest.

Prayers I and II for Reconciliation have their own Prefaces, but may be used with other appropriate Prefaces that refer to penance, e.g. the Prefaces of Lent.

Prayers I-IV for Use in Masses for Various Needs have their own Prefaces which may not be replaced.

(5) Choice of Eucharistic Prayer

Prayer I (The Roman Canon) may always be used, and particularly on days for which proper texts or insertions are provided; the feasts of apostles and saints mentioned in the Prayer; and on Sundays.

Prayer II is more appropriately used on weekdays and in special circumstances. Its own Preface may always be replaced by another. It is also suitable for a Mass for the Dead, with the optional formula for naming the deceased.

Prayer III is preferred for Sundays and feasts of the saints, who may be named within it. It also offers a formula for the dead, making it appropriate for occasions commemorating Christian Death.

Prayer IV is an integral text, with an invariable preface. It may only be used on Sundays and ferial days of Ordinary Time, when a Mass has no Proper Preface of its own.

Prayers I and II for Reconciliation and Prayers I-IV for Use in Masses for Various Needs may be used in association with the Votive and other Masses noted in the rubrics for each Prayer.

SECTION 7: LITURGICAL INFORMATION

Fulfilment of Obligation

The obligation of participating in the Mass is satisfied by assisting at Mass wherever it is celebrated in a Catholic rite, either on the Sunday or Holy Day itself or on the evening of the previous day. (Canon 1248.1)

Reception of the Eucharist a Second Time on the Same Day

It is permitted to receive Holy Communion twice on one day, provided this takes place during the celebration of Mass (Canon 917). This provision is to be observed except in the case of Viaticum for the dying.

Eucharistic Fast

Whoever is to receive the blessed Eucharist is to abstain for at least one hour before Holy Communion from all food and drink, with the sole exception of water and medicine (Canon 919.1).

A priest who, on the same day, celebrates Mass twice or three times may consume something before the second or third celebration, even though there is not an hour's interval (Canon 919.2).

The elderly, and those who are suffering from some illness, as well as those who care for them, may receive the blessed Eucharist even if within the preceding hour they have consumed something (Canon 919.3).

Abstinence

(1) Traditional Catholic devotions such as making the sign of the cross with care and reverence, praying the Angelus and saying a prayer before and after meals, are straightforward actions which both dedicate certain moments in our daily lives to Almighty God and demonstrate our love and trust in His goodness and providence. If these devotions have been lost or even forgotten, particularly in our homes and schools, we have much to gain from learning and living them again.

(2) Every Friday is set aside as a special day of penitence, as it is the day of the suffering and death of the Lord. It is important that all the faithful again be united in a common, identifiable act of Friday penance since the virtue of penitence is best acquired as part of a common resolve and witness. The law of the Church requires Catholics on Fridays to abstain from meat, or some other form of food, or to observe some other form of penance laid down by the Bishops' Conference. The Bishops have decided that this penance be fulfilled simply by abstaining from meat and by uniting this to prayer. Those who cannot or choose not to eat meat as part of their normal diet should abstain from some other food of which they regularly partake. This decision came into effect on Friday 16 September 2011.

(3) Re-emphasising the importance of penitence is but one of the responses the Bishops wish to make to the growing desire of people to deepen and give identity to the spiritual aspects of their lives. It is also clear that many of us forget our obligation to do penance on a Friday. On a Sunday our prayer is in thanksgiving to God for the new and eternal life brought to us by Christ's resurrection from the dead. On a Friday our prayer is in thanksgiving for the gift of the mortal life that we have been given; a life which Christ willingly sacrificed on the cross for our sake. A fitting prayer then, as part of our Friday penance, would be to ask Almighty God to turn away all threats to mortal life. The act of abstinence itself can be offered consciously as a prayer for life and in reparation for sins against life. It can also be put at the service of others if we

make a sacrifice and give the financial savings made from our abstention (or fasting) to charities which assist those who are poor or suffering. If we are unable to make that financial sacrifice, we can still perform a 'work of charity', an act of kindness and love to another person who is in need or suffering in some way.

(4) Canon 1251 states: 'Abstinence from eating meat or another food according to the prescriptions of the Conference of Bishops is to be observed on Fridays throughout the year unless they are solemnities; abstinence and fast are to be observed on Ash Wednesday and on the Friday of the Passion and Death of Our Lord Jesus Christ'.

Canon 1252 states: 'The law of abstinence binds those who have completed their fourteenth year. The law of fasting binds those who have attained their majority, until the beginning of their sixtieth year. Pastors of souls and parents are to ensure that even those who by reason of their age are not bound by the law of fasting and abstinence, are taught the true meaning of penance'.

Those under 14 years of age, the sick, the elderly and frail, pregnant women, seafarers, manual workers according to need, guests at a meal who cannot excuse themselves without giving great offence to their hosts or causing friction, and those in other situations of moral or physical impossibility are not required to observe abstention from meat; in other words, we should act prudently.

(5) The Holy See has noted that the 'gravity' of the obligation applies to our intention to observe penance as a regular and necessary part of our spiritual lives as a whole. Therefore, the 'gravity' of the obligation does not relate to observing the specific act of penance (abstaining from meat) prescribed by the Conference of Bishops. The 'gravity' of the obligation applies to the intention to do penance during the prescribed penitential days and seasons of the Church's year. Failure to abstain from meat on a particular Friday then would not constitute a sin.

KEY TO THE CALENDAR

RANKS OF CELEBRATION

There are three ranks of celebration: Solemnity, Feast, Memorial. These are indicated in the calendar by the typeface used, thus:

SOLEMNITY   FEAST   Memorial

ABBREVIATIONS

\+ indicates that attendance at Mass fulfils the Sunday or Holy Day obligation
Ps on the right of the page indicates the Week of the Psalter
§ indicates a reference to the Cycle of Prayer

ALTERNATIVE OR SHORT FORM READINGS

These are indicated within brackets, thus: *(Short form Gospel)*. If the readings on a Memorial are not taken from the weekday cycle, but from the readings suggested in Lectionary Volume II, alternatives or short forms are indicated thus: *(* Alternative Reading)*.

SECTION 7: LITURGICAL INFORMATION, KEY TO THE CALENDAR

CELEBRATION OF FIRST VESPERS

These are noted for Vigil Masses which have proper readings and/or prayers, for Solemnities and for Feasts falling on Sundays, which would otherwise not have First Vespers.

Solemnities and all Sundays other than Easter Day have First Vespers, unless these are impeded by Second Vespers of a higher-ranking Solemnity.

LITURGICAL COLOURS

B	Black	When the Saturday Mass of the Blessed Virgin Mary
G	Green	is celebrated in Ordinary Time, either White or Green
P	Purple	vestments may be used.
R	Red	When vestments of the appropriate colour are not
RP	Rose Pink	available, White may always be substituted.
W	White	

TABLE OF MOVEABLE FEASTS

	2023	2024	2025
Lectionary (Sunday/Weekday)	A/I	B/2	C/I
First Sunday of Advent	27 November 2022	3 December 2023	I December 2024
Nativity of the Lord	25 December	25 December	25 December
Epiphany	6 January	7 January	5 January
Ash Wednesday	22 February	14 February	5 March
Easter Sunday	9 April	31 March	20 April
Ascension	18 May	9 May	29 May
Pentecost	28 May	19 May	8 June
Corpus Christi	11 June	2 June	22 June
Ss Peter and Paul	29 June	30 June	29 June
Assumption BVM	15 August	15 August	15 August
All Saints	I November	I November	2 November
First Sunday of Advent	3 December	I December	30 November

- **Bold entries** denote Holydays of Obligation in England and Wales. The Epiphany, Ss Peter & Paul, the Assumption of the Blessed Virgin Mary and All Saints, falling on Saturday or Monday, are transferred to the Sunday.
- Table supplied by CBCEW Liturgy Office for England and Wales: **www.liturgyoffice.org.uk**

NOVEMBER/DECEMBER 2022

LECTIONARY FOR SUNDAYS: YEAR A

SEASON OF ADVENT

Advent has a twofold character: as a season to prepare for Christmas, when Christ's first coming to us is remembered; and as a season when that remembrance directs the mind and heart to await Christ's Second Coming at the end of time. Advent is thus a period for devout and joyful expectation.

The playing of the organ and other musical instruments, and the decoration of the altar with flowers should be done in a moderate manner, as is consonant with the character of the season, without anticipating the full joy of the Nativity of the Lord. The same moderation should be observed in the celebration of Matrimony. **Eucharistic Prayer 4 is not used in this season.**

NOVEMBER 2022

26 Sat evening	P	First Vespers (Divine Office Volume I)	
27 Sun	P	+ 1st SUNDAY OF ADVENT: *Creed, Advent Preface I (and on following days)* Mass & Office of the day	*Ps Week I*
28 Mon	P	Advent feria: *(Use Alternative 1st Reading)* Mass & Office of the day	
29 Tue	P	Advent feria: Mass & Office of the day	
30 Wed	R	ST ANDREW, Apostle, Patron of Scotland: *Gloria, Proper Readings, Preface I or II of Apostles* Mass & Office of the Feast	*National*

DECEMBER 2022

1 Thu	P	Advent feria: Mass & Office of the day	
2 Fri	P	Advent feria: Mass & Office of the day	*Friday abstinence*
3 Sat	W	St Francis Xavier, Priest: Mass & Office of the Memorial § Migrants' Day	
evening	P	First Vespers	

SECTION 7: LITURGICAL CALENDAR

DECEMBER 2022

4 Sun	P	+ 2nd SUNDAY OF ADVENT: *Ps Week 2*
		Creed, Advent Preface 1
		Mass & Office of the day
5 Mon	P	Advent feria: Mass & Office of the day
6 Tue	P	Advent feria: Mass & Office of the day *or*
	W	St Nicholas, Bishop: Mass & Office of the Memorial
7 Wed	W	St Ambrose, Bishop & Doctor:
		Mass & Office of the Memorial
evening	W	First Vespers
8 Thu	W	**THE IMMACULATE CONCEPTION OF THE BLESSED VIRGIN MARY, Patron of the Diocese:**
		Gloria, Proper Readings, Creed, Proper Preface
		Mass & Office of the Solemnity
9 Fri	P	Advent feria: Mass & Office of the day *or* *Friday abstinence*
	W	St Juan Diego Cuauhtlatoatzin: Mass & Office of the Memorial
10 Sat	P	Advent feria: Mass & Office of the day *or*
	W	Blessed Virgin Mary of Loreto; Mass & Office of the Memorial
evening	RP or P	First Vespers
11 Sun	RP or P	+ 3rd SUNDAY OF ADVENT (*Gaudete* Sunday): *Ps Week 3*
		Creed, Advent Preface 1
		Mass & Office of the day
12 Mon	P	Advent feria: Mass & Office of the day *or*
	W	Our Lady of Guadalupe: Mass & Office of the Memorial
13 Tue	R	St Lucy, Virgin & Martyr: Mass & Office of the Memorial
14 Wed	W	St John of the Cross, Priest & Doctor: Mass & Office of the Memorial
15 Thu	P	Advent feria: Mass & Office of the day
16 Fri	P	Advent feria: Mass & Office of the day *Friday abstinence*

Memorials which occur on days between 17 and 31 December may be commemorated at Mass by using the Collect of the saint in place of the Collect of the day. In the Office of Readings the proper hagiographical reading and responsory may be added after the

DECEMBER 2022

Patristic reading and responsory; the Collect of the saint concludes the office. At Lauds and Vespers the antiphon (proper or common) and Collect of the saint may be added after the Collect of the day. At Mass, proper texts and readings are given for the weekdays from 17-24 December, and these should be used instead of those indicated for the weekdays of the third or fourth week of Advent.

17 Sat	P	Advent feria:	*Friday abstinence*
		Advent Preface II (and on following days)	
		Mass & Office of 17 December	

evening	P	First Vespers: Magnificat antiphon of 17 December

18 Sun	P	+ 4th SUNDAY OF ADVENT:	*Ps Week 4*
		Creed, Advent Preface II	
		Mass of the day; Office of the day, with readings, also Benedictus & Magnificat antiphons of 18 December	
		(see Divine Office Vol I, page 125 ff)	
		§ Expectant Mothers	
		Announce Holy Day of Obligation	

19 Mon	P	Advent feria: Mass & Office of 19 December

20 Tue	P	Advent feria: Mass & Office of 20 December

21 Wed	P	Advent feria: Mass & Office of 21 December
		(Alternative 1st reading)
		(St Peter Canisius, Priest & Doctor)

22 Thu	P	Advent feria: Mass & Office of 22 December

23 Fri	P	Advent feria: Mass & Office of 23 December	*Friday abstinence*
		(St John of Kanty, Priest)	

24 Sat	P	Advent feria: Mass & Office of 24 December

SEASON OF CHRISTMAS

After the annual celebration of the Paschal Mystery there is no more ancient feast day for the Church than the recalling of the memory of the Nativity of the Lord and of the mysteries of his first appearing. **Eucharistic Prayer 4 is not used in this season.**

evening	W	First Vespers
	W	+ Proper Vigil Mass of Christmas precedes or follows
		Gloria, Proper Readings (Short form Gospel), Creed, (kneel at Incarnatus), a Preface of the Nativity & Communicantes in the Roman Canon

DECEMBER 2022

For pastoral reasons, readings at the following Christmas Masses may be chosen from among all those provided for the Solemnity.
It is appropriate that a Solemn Vigil be kept by celebrating the Office of Readings before the Mass during the Night. Compline is omitted by those attending that Mass.

W   **+ Mass during the Night**
Gloria, Proper Readings, Creed (kneel at Incarnatus), a Preface of the Nativity & Communicantes in the Roman Canon

25 Sun   **W**   **+ THE NATIVITY OF THE LORD (CHRISTMAS):**
Gloria, Proper Readings (Short form Gospel at Day Mass only), Creed (kneel at Incarnatus), a Preface of the Nativity & Communicantes in the Roman Canon
Mass & Office of the Solemnity
All priests may celebrate or concelebrate three Masses today, provided that they are celebrated at their proper time.

26 Mon   **R**   ST STEPHEN, The First Martyr:
Gloria, Proper Readings, a Preface of the Nativity & Communicantes in the Roman Canon
Mass, Lauds & Lesser Hours of St Stephen, Vespers of the Octave

   R   *(+ In parishes dedicated to ST STEPHEN, his Solemnity is observed: Gloria, 2nd Reading from the Common of Martyrs, Other Readings Proper, Creed, a Preface of the Nativity & Communicantes in the Roman Canon,* **Mass & Office of the Solemnity with Second Vespers)**

27 Tue   **W**   ST JOHN, Apostle & Evangelist:
Gloria, Proper Readings, a Preface of the Nativity & Communicantes in the Roman Canon
Mass, Lauds & Lesser Hours of St John, Vespers of the Octave

   W   *(In parishes dedicated to ST JOHN, his Solemnity is observed: Gloria, 1st Reading from the Proper of All Saints, Other Readings Proper, Creed, a Preface of the Nativity & Communicantes in the Roman Canon,* **Mass with First and Second Vespers of the Solemnity)**

28 Wed   **R**   THE HOLY INNOCENTS, Martyrs:
Gloria, Proper Readings, a Preface of the Nativity & Communicantes in the Roman Canon
Mass, Lauds & Lesser Hours of the Holy Innocents; Vespers of the Octave

29 Thu   **R**   ST THOMAS BECKET, Bishop & Martyr,   *National* Patron of the Parish Clergy:
Gloria, (Alternative Collect), Proper National Readings (Short form Gospel), a Preface of the Nativity & Communicantes in the Roman Canon
Mass, Lauds & Lesser Hours of St Thomas, Vespers of the Octave

DECEMBER 2022/JANUARY 2023

	R	*(In parishes dedicated to ST THOMAS BECKET, his Solemnity is observed:*
		Gloria, (Alternative Collect), 1st Reading from the Common of Martyrs, 2nd Reading & Gospel (Short form) from National Proper, Creed, a Preface of the Nativity & Communicantes *in the Roman Canon,* **Mass with First & Second Vespers of the Solemnity)**
30 Fri	W	**+ THE HOLY FAMILY OF JESUS,** *No Friday* **MARY AND JOSEPH:** *abstinence* *Gloria, 1st or 2nd Reading, Gospel of Year A, a Preface of the Nativity &* Communicantes *in the Roman Canon* **Mass & Office of the Feast**
31 Sat	W	**7th DAY IN THE OCTAVE OF CHRISTMAS:** *Gloria, a Preface of the Nativity &* Communicantes *in the Roman Canon* **Mass & Office of the Octave** (St Sylvester I, Pope)
evening	W	First Vespers

JANUARY 2023

1 Sun	W	**+ SOLEMNITY OF MARY, THE HOLY MOTHER OF GOD THE OCTAVE DAY OF THE NATIVITY OF THE LORD:** *Gloria, Proper Readings, Creed, Preface I of Blessed Virgin Mary &* Communicantes *in the Roman Canon* **Mass & Office of the Solemnity Announce Holy Day of Obligation**
		A Preface of the Nativity is used on weekdays of the Christmas season, unless other provision is made.
2 Mon	W	Ss Basil the Great and Gregory Nazianzen, *Ps Week 2* Bishops & Doctors: *Readings of 2 January* **Mass & Office of the Memorial**
3 Tue	W	Christmas feria: *First Collect, Readings of 3 January* **Mass & Office of the day** *or*
	W	**The Most Holy Name of Jesus: Mass & Office of the Memorial**
4 Wed	W	Christmas feria: *First Collect, Readings of 4 January* **Mass & Office of the day**

JANUARY 2023

5 Thu — W — Christmas feria:
First Collect, Readings of 5 January
Mass & Office of the day

evening — W — First Vespers
W — + Proper Vigil Mass of the Epiphany precedes or follows
Gloria, Epiphany Readings, Creed, Proper Preface & Communicantes of the Epiphany in the Roman Canon

6 Fri — W — **+ THE EPIPHANY OF THE LORD:**   *No Friday*
Gloria, Creed, Proper Preface & Communicantes   **abstinence**
of the Epiphany in the Roman Canon; an increased display of lights is recommended.
At today's Mass, after the Gospel, the announcement may be made of moveable feasts according to the formula given in the Roman Pontifical, on page 1247 of the Missale Romanum, editio typica tertia *and page 1505 of the Roman Missal.*
Mass & Office of the Solemnity

7 Sat — W — Christmas feria:
Second Collect, Readings of 7 January (Vol I, page 164), Preface of the Nativity or of the Epiphany
Mass & Office of the day *or*
W — St Raymond of Penyafort, Priest: **Mass & Office of the Memorial**

evening — W — First Vespers

8 Sun — W — + THE BAPTISM OF THE LORD:
Gloria, (Alternative Collect), 1st and 2nd Reading, Gospel of Year A, Creed, Proper Preface
Mass & Office of the Feast

The Season of Christmas ends.

ORDINARY TIME - BEFORE THE SEASON OF LENT
LECTIONARY FOR SUNDAYS: YEAR A
WEEKDAY LECTIONARY: YEAR I
Eucharistic Prayer 4 may be used until the Season of Lent
The choice of Masses which may be celebrated *ad lib* is shown in the Liturgical Information on page 294.
On ferial days in Ordinary Time the Office of a saint included for that day in the Roman Martyrology may be celebrated. Occasional Votive Offices are permitted, although care to observe the four-week cycle of the Office should be maintained.

9 Mon — G — feria, First Week of Year 1:   *Ps Week 1*
Mass ad lib; Office of the day

JANUARY 2023

10 Tue	G	feria: Mass ad lib; Office of the day
11 Wed	G	feria: Mass ad lib; Office of the day
12 Thu	G	feria: Mass ad lib; Office of the day *or*
	W	St Aelred of Rievaulx: *National*
		Mass & Office of the Memorial
13 Fri	G	feria: Mass ad lib; Office of the day *or* *Friday abstinence*
	W	St Hilary, Bishop & Doctor: Mass & Office of the Memorial
14 Sat	G	feria: Mass ad lib; Office of the day *or*
	W	Blessed Virgin Mary on Saturday: Mass & Office of the Memorial
evening	G	First Vespers
15 Sun	G	+ 2nd SUNDAY IN ORDINARY TIME: *Ps Week 2*
		Gloria, Creed, a Preface of Sundays in O.T.
		Mass & Office of the day
		§ Peace Day
16 Mon	G	feria, Second Week of Year1: Mass ad lib; Office of the day
17 Tue	W	St Anthony, Abbot: Mass & Office of the Memorial
		From 18-25 January the Octave of Prayer for Christian Unity takes place. A Mass for the Unity of Christians may be celebrated on any ferial day during the Octave.
18 Wed	G	feria: Mass ad lib; Office of the day
19 Thu	G	feria: Mass ad lib; Office of the day *or*
	W	St Wulstan, Bishop: *National*
		Mass & Office of the Memorial
20 Fri	G	feria: Mass ad lib; Office of the day *or* *Friday abstinence*
	R	St Fabian, Pope & Martyr: Mass & Office of the Memorial *or*
	R	St Sebastian, Martyr: Mass & Office of the Memorial
21 Sat	R	St Agnes, Virgin & Martyr:
		Mass & Office of the Memorial
evening	G	First Vespers

SECTION 7: LITURGICAL CALENDAR

JANUARY/FEBRUARY 2023

22 Sun	G	+ 3rd SUNDAY IN ORDINARY TIME *Ps Week 3* (OF THE WORD OF GOD): *Gloria, (Short form Gospel), Creed, a Preface of Sundays in O.T.* Mass & Office of the day § Openness to the Word of God
23 Mon	G	feria, Third Week of Year 1: Mass ad lib; Office of the day
24 Tue	W	St Francis de Sales, Bishop & Doctor: Mass & Office of the Memorial Anniversary of the Episcopal Ordination of Cardinal Vincent Nichols (1992). An intention may be included in the Universal Prayer and the Mass 'For the Bishop' (Roman Missal page 1306) may be celebrated on a subsequent ferial day.
25 Wed	W	THE CONVERSION OF ST PAUL THE APOSTLE: *Gloria, Proper Readings (Alternative 1st Reading), Preface 1 of Apostles* Mass & Office of the Feast
26 Thu	W	Ss Timothy and Titus, Bishops: *(Proper Alternative 1st Reading)* Mass & Office of the Memorial
27 Fri	G W	feria: Mass ad lib; Office of the day *or* *Friday abstinence* St Angela Merici, Virgin: Mass & Office of the Memorial
28 Sat	W	St Thomas Aquinas, Priest & Doctor: Mass & Office of the Memorial
evening	G	First Vespers
29 Sun	G	+ 4th SUNDAY IN ORDINARY TIME: *Ps Week 4* *Gloria, Creed, a Preface of Sundays in O.T.* Mass & Office of the day Announce Optional Racial Justice Collection
30 Mon	G	feria, Fourth Week of Year1: Mass ad lib; Office of the day
31 Tue	W	St John Bosco, Priest: Mass & Office of the Memorial

FEBRUARY 2023

1 Wed	G	feria: Mass ad lib; Office of the day

FEBRUARY 2023

2 Thu	W	**THE PRESENTATION OF THE LORD:**
		Blessing of candles (Alternative), with Procession or Solemn Entry, no Penitential Act, Gloria, 1st or 2nd Reading, (Short form Gospel), Proper Preface
		Mass & Office of the Feast

3 Fri	W	Ss Laurence, Dunstan and Theodore,	*Friday abstinence*
		Archbishops of Canterbury:	*Diocesan*
		see Diocesan Supplement Book or online	
		Mass & Office of the Memorial	
	R	*The blessing of St Blaise on throats may be given today*	

4 Sat	G	feria: Mass ad lib; Office of the day *or*
	W	Blessed Virgin Mary on Saturday: Mass & Office of the Memorial

evening	G	First Vespers

5 Sun	G	+ 5th SUNDAY IN ORDINARY TIME:	*Ps Week 1*
		Gloria, Creed, a Preface of Sundays in O.T.	
		Mass & Office of the day	
		§ Racial Justice	
		Racial Justice Collection	

6 Mon	R	St Paul Miki and Companions, Martyrs:
		Mass & Office of the Memorial

7 Tue	G	feria, Fifth Week of Year 1: Mass ad lib; Office of the day

8 Wed	G	feria: Mass ad lib; Office of the day *or*
	W	St Jerome Emiliani:
		(Short form Gospel)*
		Mass & Office of the Memorial *or*
	W	St Josephine Bakhita: Mass & Office of the Memorial
		§ Day for Victims of Trafficking and Those who Work to Combat it

9 Thu	G	feria: Mass ad lib; Office of the day

10 Fri	W	St Scholastica, Virgin:	*Friday abstinence*
		Mass & Office of the Memorial	

11 Sat	G	feria: Mass ad lib; Office of the day *or*
	W	Our Lady of Lourdes: Mass & Office of the Memorial *or*
	W	Blessed Virgin Mary on Saturday: Mass & Office of the Memorial
		§ World Day for the Sick

evening	G	First Vespers

FEBRUARY 2023

13 Sun	G	+ 6th SUNDAY IN ORDINARY TIME: *Ps Week 2*
		Gloria, (Short form Gospel), Creed, a Preface of Sundays in O.T.
		Mass & Office of the day

| 13 Mon | G | feria, Sixth Week of Year1: Mass ad lib; Office of the day |

14 Tue	W	SS CYRIL, Monk and METHODIUS, Bishop, *National*
		Patrons of Europe:
		Gloria, Proper Readings, Preface of Holy Pastors
		Mass & Office of the Feast
		§ Europe

| 15 Wed | G | feria: Mass ad lib; Office of the day |

| 16 Thu | G | feria: Mass ad lib; Office of the day |

17 Fri	G	feria: Mass ad lib; Office of the day *or* *Friday abstinence*
	W	The Seven Holy Founders of the Servite Order:
		Mass & Office of the Memorial

| 18 Sat | G | feria: Mass ad lib; Office of the day *or* |
| | W | Blessed Virgin Mary on Saturday: Mass & Office of the Memorial |

| | G | First Vespers |

19 Sun	G	+ 7th SUNDAY IN ORDINARY TIME: *Ps Week 3*
		Gloria, Creed, a Preface of Sundays in O.T.
		Mass & Office of the day
		Announce Ash Wednesday, Day of Fast & Abstinence
		Announce Mandatory Diocesan Lenten Alms Appeal

| 20 Mon | G | feria, Seventh Week of Year 1: Mass ad lib; office of the day |

| 21 Tue | G | feria: Mass ad lib; Office of the day *or* |
| | W | St Peter Damian, Bishop & Doctor: Mass & Office of the Memorial |

SEASON OF LENT

The season of Lent is a preparation for the celebration of Easter. The liturgy prepares the catechumens for the celebration of the Paschal Mystery by the various stages of Christian initiation; it also prepares the faithful, who recall their baptism and do penance in preparation for Easter.

Memorials which occur on a weekday may only be commemorated at Mass by using the Collect of the saint in place of the Collect of the day. In the Office of Readings the proper hagiographical reading and responsory may be added after the Patristic reading and responsory; the Collect of the saint concludes the office. At Lauds and Vespers the antiphon (proper or common) and Collect of the saint may be added after the Collect of the day. The *Alleluia* is always omitted, both in the Office and in Mass.

It is not permitted to adorn the altar with flowers, and the organ and other instruments may only be played for the purpose of sustaining the singing. An exception is made for *Laetare* Sunday, and for Solemnities and Feasts.

During the Lenten season the Apostles' Creed may appropriately be used as an alternative when the Creed is appointed to be said.

For the celebration of marriage, the parish priest should alert spouses to the need to take account of the particular penitential character of this season.

Eucharistic Prayer 4 is not used in this Season; Eucharistic Prayers for Reconciliation may appropriately be used during Lent.

On Ash Wednesday and the Sundays of Lent, the Prayer over the People is used, with the Invitation and prescribed Blessing Formula (Roman Missal, page 722); on other days of Lent the use of the Prayer and prescribed Blessing is optional.

(Divine Office Volume II)

22 Wed	P	**ASH WEDNESDAY:**	*Fast &*
		Penitential Act omitted, Blessing and distribution	*Abstinence*
		of ashes after the homily, Preface III or IV of Lent	**Ps Week 4**

The ashes, according to custom, are from branches blessed the previous year. The blessing and distribution of ashes may take place outside Mass, in a Liturgy of the Word after the homily; the celebration then concludes with the Universal Prayer, Blessing and Dismissal.

Mass & Office of the day; at Lauds Pss and Canticle of Friday, Week 3 may be used

On ferial days of the Lenten season one of the four Lenten prefaces is used, unless other provision is made

23 Thu	P	Lent feria: Mass & Office of the day	
		(St Polycarp, Bishop & Martyr)	
24 Fri	P	Lent feria: Mass & Office of the day	*Friday abstinence*
25 Sat	P	Lent feria: Mass & Office of the day	
in Cathedral		2.30pm Rite of Election	
evening	P	First Vespers	
26 Sun	P	+ 1st SUNDAY OF LENT:	*Ps Week 1*
		(Short form 2nd Reading), Creed, Preface of First Sunday of Lent	
		Mass & Office of the day	
		§ Candidates for the Sacraments	
		Announce Optional Lent Fast Day	

FEBRUARY/MARCH 2023

| 27 Mon | P | Lent feria: Mass & Office of the day | |
| | | (St Gregory of Narek, Abbot & Doctor) | |

| 28 Tue | P | Lent feria: Mass & Office of the day | |

MARCH 2023

1 Wed	W	ST DAVID, Bishop, Patron of Wales:	*National*
		Gloria, Proper National Readings, Preface of Holy Pastors	
		Mass & Office of the Feast	

| 2 Thu | P | Lent feria: Mass & Office of the day | |

3 Fri	P	Lent feria: Mass & Office of the day	*Friday abstinence*
		§ World Day of Prayer	
		§ Lent Fast Day	

| 4 Sat | P | Lent feria: Mass & Office of the day | |
| | | (St Casimir) | |

| evening | P | First Vespers | |

5 Sun	P	+ 2nd SUNDAY OF LENT:	*Ps Week 2*
		Creed, Preface of Second Sunday of Lent	
		Mass & Office of the day	
		§ Candidates for the Sacraments	
		Collect Lent Fast Day Offerings	

| 6 Mon | P | Lent feria: Mass & Office of the day | |

| 7 Tue | P | Lent feria: Mass & Office of the day | |
| | | (Ss Perpetua and Felicity, Martyrs) | |

| 8 Wed | P | Lent feria: Mass & Office of the day | |
| | | (St John of God, Religious) | |

| 9 Thu | P | Lent feria: Mass & Office of the day | |
| | | (St Frances of Rome, Religious) | |

| 10 Fri | P | Lent feria: Mass & Office of the day | *Friday abstinence* |

| 11 Sat | P | Lent feria: Mass & Office of the day | |

| evening | P | First Vespers | |

MARCH 2023			
12 Sun	P	+ 3rd SUNDAY OF LENT: *(Short form Gospel), Creed, Proper Preface* Mass & Office of the day RCIA - First Scrutiny: the Ritual Mass (pages 1177-9), (Short form Gospel), Proper Preface (pages 260-1) and Insertions in the Eucharistic Prayer. § Candidates for the Sacraments The Gospel of the Samaritan Woman may be repeated on a ferial day, with 1st Reading and Psalm as in year A of the Lectionary. The matching Preface and Communion should also be used.	*Ps Week 3*
13 Mon	P	Lent feria: Mass & Office of the day Anniversary of the Election of Pope Francis (2013). By decision of the Bishops' Conference, this is observed on the Solemnity of Ss Peter and Paul, Thursday 29 June.	
14 Tue	P	Lent feria: Mass & Office of the day	
15 Wed	P	Lent feria: Mass & Office of the day	
16 Thu	P	Lent feria: Mass & Office of the day	
17 Fri	W	ST PATRICK, Bishop, Patron of Ireland: *Gloria, Proper Readings, Preface of Holy Pastors* Mass & Office of the Feast	*National* *Friday abstinence*
18 Sat	P	Lent feria: Mass & Office of the day (St Cyril of Jerusalem, Bishop & Doctor) The Lenten discipline in the use of organ, other musical instruments and flowers does not apply to *Laetare* Sunday.	
evening	RP or P	First Vespers	
19 Sun	RP or P	+ 4th SUNDAY OF LENT (*Laetare* Sunday): *(Short form Gospel), Creed, Proper Preface* Mass & Office of the day RCIA - Second Scrutiny: the Ritual Mass (pages 1179-80) with Year A Readings, Proper Preface (pages 270-1), Insertions in the Eucharistic Prayer. § Candidates for the Sacraments	*Ps Week 4*

MARCH 2023

		The Gospel of the Man born Blind may be repeated on a ferial weekday, with 1st Reading and Psalm as in Year A of the Lectionary. The matching Preface and Communion Antiphon should also be used. The Alternative Readings (Vol I, page 287 ff) may also be used.	
20 Mon	W	**ST JOSEPH, Spouse of the Blessed Virgin Mary, Patron of the Diocese:** *Gloria, Proper Readings (Alternative Gospel), Creed, Preface of St Joseph* Mass & Office of the Solemnity	
21 Tue	P	Lent feria: Mass & Office of the day	
22 Wed	P	Lent feria: Mass & Office of the day	
23 Thu	P	Lent feria: Mass & Office of the day (St Turibius of Mogrovejo, Bishop)	
24 Fri	P	Lent feria: Mass & Office of the day	*Friday abstinence*
evening	W	First Vespers	*Abstinence ends*
25 Sat	W	**THE ANNUNCIATION OF THE LORD:** *Gloria, Proper Readings, Creed (kneel at Incarnatus), Proper Preface* Mass, Lauds & Lesser Hours of the Solemnity	
		The practice of covering crosses and images in the church may be observed. Crosses remain covered until the end of the celebration of the Lord's Passion on Good Friday; images until the beginning of the Easter Vigil.	
evening	P	First Vespers	
26 Sun	P	+ 5th SUNDAY OF LENT: *(Short form Gospel), Creed, Proper Preface* Mass & Office of the day RCIA - Third Scrutiny: the Ritual Mass (pages 1180-1) with Year A Readings, Proper Preface (pages 281-2) and Insertions in the Eucharistic Prayer. § Candidates for the Sacraments	*Ps Week 1*
		The Gospel of Lazarus may be used on a ferial weekday, with 1st Reading and Psalm as in Year A of the Lectionary. The matching Preface and Communion Antiphon should also be used. The Alternative Readings (Vol I, page 316 ff) may also be used.	

MARCH/APRIL 2023

27 Mon	P	Lent feria: *(Short form 1st Reading)* Mass & Office of the day
28 Tue	P	Lent feria: Mass & Office of the day
29 Wed	P	Lent feria: Mass & Office of the day
30 Thu	P	Lent feria: Mass & Office of the day
31 Fri	P	Lent feria: *Friday abstinence* *(Alternative Collect)* Mass & Office of the day

APRIL 2023

1 Sat	P	Lent feria: Mass & Office of the day

HOLY WEEK

In Holy Week the Church celebrates the mysteries of salvation accomplished by Christ in the last days of his earthly life, from his messianic entry into Jerusalem, until his blessed Passion and glorious Resurrection. Lent continues until Maundy Thursday.

evening	R	First Vespers
2 Sun	R	**+ PALM SUNDAY OF THE PASSION OF THE LORD:** *Ps Week 2* *Blessing of Palms (Alternative Blessing) and Procession or Solemn Entrance before the Principal Mass; the latter may be repeated or the Simple Entrance used before other Masses, Narrative of the Lord's Passion (Short form), Creed, Proper Preface* Mass & Office of the day § Candidates for the Sacraments Announce Good Friday, Day of Fast and Abstinence Announce Mandatory Holy See Good Friday collection
3 Mon	P	MONDAY OF HOLY WEEK: *Preface II of the Passion of the Lord* Mass & Office of the day
4 Tue	P	TUESDAY OF HOLY WEEK: *Preface II of the Passion of the Lord*
in Cathedral	W	12noon Chrism Mass Mass & Office of the day

APRIL 2023		
5 Wed	P	**WEDNESDAY OF HOLY WEEK:** *Preface II of the Passion of the Lord* Mass & Office of the day

THE PASCHAL TRIDUUM

In the Sacred Triduum, the Church solemnly celebrates the greatest mysteries of our redemption, keeping by means of special celebrations the memorial of her Lord, crucified, buried and risen.

The Paschal Fast should also be kept sacred. It is to be celebrated everywhere on the Friday of the Lord's Passion and, where appropriate, prolonged also through Holy Saturday as a way of coming, with spirit uplifted, to the joys of the Lord's Resurrection.

6 Thu	P	**MAUNDY THURSDAY:** Office of the day Vespers are not said by those attending the Evening Mass. *Holy Communion may be distributed to the faithful only during the Mass of the Lord's Supper. The sick, however, may receive Communion at any hour. The celebration of Mass without a congregation is prohibited.*
	W	**Evening Mass of the Lord's Supper:** *Gloria, during which bells are rung; the Washing of Feet may be carried out; Preface I of the Most Holy Eucharist and insertions in the Roman Canon. Procession & Reposition of the Blessed Sacrament take place if the Celebration of the Lord's Passion is to take place in the Church; watching before the Altar of Repose then follows with solemnity until midnight and may conclude with Compline II of Sunday.*
7 Fri	R	**GOOD FRIDAY:** Office of the day *Fast & Abstinence* It is highly appropriate that the Office of Readings and Lauds be celebrated solemnly with the people. Vespers are not said by those attending the Afternoon Liturgy. Compline II of Sunday may conclude the day. *Holy Communion is distributed to the faithful only during the Celebration of the Lord's Passion, but may be taken at any time to the sick who are unable to take part in this liturgy. Only the Sacraments of Penance and of the Anointing of the Sick may be celebrated.*
	R	**The Celebration of the Passion of the Lord:** *This takes place in the afternoon, at about 3pm (or at least not before noon and not after 9pm). (Alternative Opening Prayer, forms of Showing of the Cross)* Collection for the Holy Places
8 Sat	P	**HOLY SATURDAY:** Office of the day *Fast as desired* It is highly appropriate that the Office of Readings and Lauds be celebrated solemnly with the people. Vespers are of Holy Saturday. Compline (II of Sunday) is not said by those attending the Easter Vigil.

The Church abstains completely from the celebration of Mass. Holy Communion may only be given as Viaticum. Only the Sacraments of Penance and the Anointing of the Sick may be celebrated.

SEASON OF EASTER

Throughout the Easter season, the *Angelus* is replaced by *Regina Caeli*. The Apostles' Creed may appropriately be used as an alternative on days when the Creed is appointed to be said. Eucharistic Prayer 4 is not used in this Season.

at night	W	**+ The Easter Vigil in the Holy Night:**

The entire celebration of the Easter Vigil must take place during the night, so that it begins after nightfall and ends before daybreak. The celebration of a Mass without the rites of the Easter Vigil is not permitted. Multiple alternative texts for the Vigil.
Gloria, Year A Gospel, Preface I of Easter, Proper Insertions in the Roman Canon, Commemoration of the Baptised in the Eucharistic Prayer (pages 1183-4), double Alleluia added to the Dismissal

The Office of Readings is omitted by those who attend the Vigil.

The Paschal candle should be placed near the ambo or altar, and kept there for the whole Easter season until the end of Pentecost Sunday. It is lit for the more solemn liturgical celebrations during this time.

9 Sun	W	**+ EASTER SUNDAY OF THE RESURRECTION:**

Either: In place of the Penitential Act, Vidi aquam is sung and all are sprinkled with water blessed at the Vigil to recall their Baptism; in this case the Creed is used.
Or: If the Renewal of Baptismal Promises is desired, this takes place after the homily and the Creed is omitted.
(Alternative Entrance Antiphon), Gloria, (Alternative 2nd Reading, Alternative Gospel Readings of the Vigil or Easter Wednesday [latter Evening Mass only]), Sequence, Creed or Renewal of Baptismal Promises, Preface I of Easter, Proper Insertions in the Roman Canon, Commemoration of the Baptised in the Eucharistic Prayer (pages 1183-4), double Alleluia added to the Dismissal
Mass & Office of the Solemnity

10 Mon	W	**MONDAY WITHIN THE OCTAVE OF EASTER:**	Ps Week I

(Alternative Entrance Antiphon), Gloria, Sequence ad lib, Preface I of Easter, Proper Insertions in the Roman Canon, double Alleluia added to the Dismissal
Mass & Office of the Solemnity

APRIL 2023

11 Tue	W	**TUESDAY WITHIN THE OCTAVE OF EASTER:** *Gloria, Sequence ad lib, Preface 1 of Easter, Proper Insertions in the Roman* *Canon, double Alleluia added to the Dismissal* Mass & Office of the Solemnity
12 Wed	W	**WEDNESDAY WITHIN THE OCTAVE OF EASTER:** *Gloria, Sequence ad lib, Preface 1 of Easter, Proper Insertions in the Roman* *Canon, double Alleluia added to the Dismissal* Mass & Office of the Solemnity
13 Thu	W	**THURSDAY WITHIN THE OCTAVE OF EASTER:** *Gloria, Sequence ad lib, Preface 1 of Easter, Proper Insertions in the Roman* *Canon, double Alleluia added to the Dismissal* Mass & Office of the Solemnity
14 Fri	W	**FRIDAY WITHIN THE OCTAVE OF EASTER:** *No Friday abstinence* *Gloria, Sequence ad lib, Preface 1 of Easter, Proper Insertions in the Roman* *Canon, double Alleluia added to the Dismissal* Mass & Office of the Solemnity
15 Sat	W	**SATURDAY WITHIN THE OCTAVE OF EASTER:** *Gloria, Sequence ad lib, Preface 1 of Easter, Proper Insertions in the* *Roman Canon, double Alleluia added to the Dismissal* Mass & Office of the Solemnity
evening	W	First Vespers
16 Sun	W	**+ SECOND SUNDAY OF EASTER** *Ps Week 2* (or of DIVINE MERCY): *(Alternative Entrance Antiphon), Gloria, Sequence ad lib, Creed, Preface 1* *of Easter, Proper Insertions in the Roman Canon, double Alleluia added* *to the Dismissal* Mass & Office of the Solemnity
		Throughout the Easter season, particular attention should be paid to the mystagogical formation of the newly baptised. On ferial days of the Easter season one of the five Easter prefaces is said, unless other provision is made.
17 Mon	W	Easter feria: Mass & Office of the day
18 Tue	W	Easter feria: Mass & Office of the day
19 Wed	R	St Alphege, Bishop & Martyr: *National* see *Diocesan Supplement Book or online*

APRIL 2023			
		Mass & Office of the Memorial	
20 Thu	W	Easter feria: Mass & Office of the day	
21 Fri	W	Easter feria: Mass & Office of the day *or*	*Friday abstinence*
	W	St Anselm, Bishop & Doctor:	*National*
		Mass & Office of the Memorial	
22 Sat	W	Easter feria: Mass & Office of the day	
evening	W	First Vespers	
23 Sun	W	+ 3rd SUNDAY OF EASTER:	*Ps Week 3*
		Gloria, Creed, a Preface of Easter	
		Mass & Office of the day	
		Announce Mandatory Diocesan PTF Collection	
		§ Human Work	
24 Mon	R	**ST GEORGE, Martyr, Patron of England:** *National*	
		(Alternative Entrance Antiphon), Gloria, 1st Reading from National Proper	
		2nd from Common of Martyrs, Gospel from National Proper (Alternative	
		Reading), Creed, Preface I or II of Holy Martyrs	
		Mass & Office of the Solemnity	
25 Tue	R	ST MARK, Evangelist:	
		Gloria, Proper Readings, Preface II of Apostles	
		Mass, Lauds & Lesser Hours of the Feast	
26 Wed	W	Easter feria: Mass & Office of the day	
27 Thu	W	Easter feria: Mass & Office of the day	
28 Fri	W	Easter feria: Mass & Office of the day *or*	*Friday abstinence*
	R	St Peter Chanel, Priest & Martyr: Mass & Office of the Memorial *or*	
	W	St Louis M Grignion de Montfort, Priest:	
		Mass & Office of the Memorial	
29 Sat	W	ST CATHERINE OF SIENA, Virgin & Doctor,	*National*
		Patron of Europe:	
		Gloria, Proper Readings, Preface of Holy Virgins & Religious	
		Mass & Office of the Feast	
		§ Europe	
evening	W	First Vespers	

SECTION 7: LITURGICAL CALENDAR

APRIL/MAY 2023

30 Sun	W	+ 4th SUNDAY OF EASTER:	Ps Week 4
		Gloria, Creed, a Preface of Easter	
		Mass & Office of the Day	
		§ World Day of Prayer for Vocations	
		Collection for Priests' Training Fund	

MAY 2023

1 Mon	W	Easter feria:	
		Alternative Gospel Reading should be used	
		Mass & Office of the day *or*	
	W	St Joseph the Worker:	
		Proper Gospel Reading, Preface of St Joseph	
		Mass & Office of the Memorial	
		§ Human Work	
2 Tue	W	St Athanasius, Bishop & Doctor: Mass & Office of the Memorial	
3 Wed	R	SS PHILIP and JAMES, Apostles:	
		Gloria, Proper Readings, Preface I or II of Apostles	
		Mass & Office of the Feast	
4 Thu	R	THE ENGLISH MARTYRS:	*National*
		Gloria, Either the Readings for today's former Feast of the Beatified Martyrs or those for the former Feast of the Forty Martyrs on 25 October, given in the current editions of the Lectionary, may be used, Preface I or II of Holy Martyrs	
		Mass & Office of the Feast	
5 Fri	W	Easter feria: Mass & Office of the day	*Friday abstinence*
6 Sat	W	Easter feria: Mass & Office of the day	
evening	W	First Vespers	
7 Sun	W	+ 5th SUNDAY OF EASTER:	Ps Week 1
		Gloria, Creed, a Preface of Easter	
		Mass & Office of the day	
8 Mon	W	Easter feria: Mass & Office of the day	
9 Tue	W	Easter feria: Mass & Office of the day	
		§ Day of Prayer for the Victims and Survivors of Sexual Abuse	
10 Wed	W	Easter feria: Mass & Office of the day *or*	
	W	St John of Avila, Priest & Doctor: Mass & Office of the Memorial	

MAY 2023

11 Thu	W	Easter feria: Mass & Office of the day
12 Fri	W	Easter feria: Mass & Office of the day *or* *Friday abstinence*
	R	Ss Nereus and Achilleus, Martyrs: Mass & Office of the Memorial *or*
	R	St Pancras, Martyr: Mass & Office of the Memorial
13 Sat	W	Easter feria: Mass & Office of the day *or*
	W	Our Lady of Fatima: Mass & Office of the Memorial
evening	W	First Vespers
14 Sun	W	+ 6th SUNDAY OF EASTER: *Ps Week 2*
		Gloria, Creed, a Preface of Easter
		Mass & Office of the day
		Announce Mandatory Holy See CCN Collection
		Announce Holy Day of Obligation
15 Mon	W	Easter feria: Mass & Office of the day
16 Tue	W	Easter feria: Mass & Office of the day
17 Wed	W	Easter feria: Mass & Office of the day
evening	W	First Vespers
	W	+ Proper Vigil Mass of the Ascension precedes or follows
		Gloria, Ascension Readings, Creed, Preface 1 or II of the Ascension & Communicantes in the Roman Canon
18 Thu	W	+ **THE ASCENSION OF THE LORD:**
		Gloria, (Alternative Collect), (Alternative 2nd Reading), Creed, Preface 1 or II of the Ascension & Communicantes in the Roman Canon
		Mass & Office of the Solemnity
		On ferial days until Pentecost a preface of Easter or of the Ascension is used, unless other provision is made.
19 Fri	W	Easter feria: *Friday abstinence*
		1st Collect; St Dunstan having been commemorated on 3 February in Westminster, his National feast is not observed on this day
		Mass & Office of the day
20 Sat	W	Easter feria:
		1st Collect
		Mass & Office of the day *or*
	W	St Bernadine of Siena, Priest: Mass & Office of the Memorial

MAY 2023

evening	W	First Vespers

21 Sun — W

+ 7th SUNDAY OF EASTER: *Ps Week 3*
Gloria, Creed, a Preface of Easter or of the Ascension
Mass & Office of the day
§ World Communications Day
Collection for Catholic Communications Network
Anniversary of the Installation of Cardinal Vincent Nichols,
Eleventh Archbishop of Westminster (2009). An intention may be
included in the Universal Prayer.

22 Mon — W / W

Easter feria: Mass & office of the day *or*
St Rita of Cascia, Religious: Mass & Office of the Memorial

23 Tue — W

Easter feria: Mass & Office of the day

24 Wed — W

Easter feria: Mass & Office of the day

25 Thu — W

St Bede the Venerable, Priest & Doctor: *National*
Mass & Office of the Memorial

26 Fri — W

St Philip Neri, Priest: *Friday abstinence*
Mass & Office of the Memorial

27 Sat — W

ST AUGUSTINE OF CANTERBURY, Bishop: *National*
Gloria, Proper National Readings, Preface of Holy Pastors
Mass & Office of the Feast

The fifty days of the sacred season of Easter conclude with Pentecost
Sunday, when the Church recalls the gift of the Holy Spirit to the
Apostles, the beginnings of the Church, and the start of her mission to
all tongues and peoples and nations.

It is appropriate that the Vigil Mass of Pentecost be celebrated in the
extended form, using the readings and prayers to be found in the
liturgical books. This Mass, however, does not have a baptismal
character, as does the Easter Vigil, but instead is a celebration of more
intense prayer, after the example of the Apostles and disciples, who
together with Mary, the Mother of Jesus, were one in persevering
prayer, as they awaited the outpouring of the Holy Spirit.

evening — R / R

First Vespers
+ Proper Vigil Mass of Pentecost precedes, follows or incorporates
*Gloria, (Two Alternative Collects), (Choice of Old Testament Readings),
Creed, Proper Preface* & Communicantes *in the Roman Canon, double
Alleluia added to the Dismissal*

MAY 2023		

28 Sun   **R**   **+ PENTECOST SUNDAY**
Gloria, , Sequence, Creed, Proper Preface & Communicantes *in the Roman Canon, double* Alleluia *added to the Dismissal*
Mass & Office of the Solemnity
§ The Church

The Easter season ends. After today, the Paschal Candle is no longer kept in the sanctuary, but moved to the baptistry, where it is lit at baptisms. At funerals it is placed and lit near the coffin, to signify that Christian death is a true Passover.
From tomorrow, the recitation of the *Angelus* is resumed.

[R]   When Monday or Tuesday after Pentecost are days on which it is customary for the faithful to attend Mass, the Mass of Pentecost Sunday or the Votive Mass of the Holy Spirit may be used.

ORDINARY TIME - AFTER THE SEASON OF EASTER
The weeks of Ordinary Time celebrate no particular aspect of Christ. Instead, celebration is made of the mystery of Christ in all its fullness.

LECTIONARY FOR SUNDAYS: YEAR A
WEEKDAY LECTIONARY: YEAR 1
ORDINARY TIME: WEEK 8
(Divine Office Volume III)
Eucharistic Prayer 4 may be used in this Season.
The choice of Masses which may be celebrated *ad libitum* is shown in the Liturgical Information on page 294.
On ferial days in Ordinary Time the Office of a saint included for that day in the Roman Martyrology may be celebrated. Occasional Votive Offices are permitted, although care to observe the four-week cycle of the Office should be maintained.

29 Mon   **W**   The Blessed Virgin Mary, Mother of the Church: *Ps Week 4*
Readings of the ferial day or from the Common of the BVM
Mass & Office of the Memorial (Roman Missal, Votive Mass 10 B, page 1411 ff; Office *ad interim* from the Common of the BVM)

30 Tue   **G**   feria, Eighth Week of Year 1: Mass ad lib; Office of the day

31 Wed   **W**   THE VISITATION OF THE BLESSED VIRGIN MARY:
Gloria, Proper Readings (Alternative 1st Reading), Preface II of the Blessed Virgin Mary
Mass & Office of the Feast

JUNE 2023

1 Thu	W	**OUR LORD JESUS CHRIST** *National* **THE ETERNAL HIGH PRIEST:** *Gloria, Year A Readings, Preface of the Priesthood of Christ and of the Church [Roman Missal, page 324 ff]* Mass & Office of the Feast
2 Fri	G R	feria: Mass ad lib; Office of the day *or* *Friday abstinence* Ss Marcellinus and Peter, Martyrs: Mass & Office of the Memorial
3 Sat	R	St Charles Lwanga and Companions, Martyrs: Mass & Office of the Memorial
evening	W	First Vespers
4 Sun	W	**+ THE MOST HOLY TRINITY:** *Gloria, Creed, Proper Preface* Mass & Office of the Solemnity
5 Mon	R	St Boniface, Bishop & Martyr: *National* Mass & Office of the Memorial *Ps Week 1*
6 Tue	G W	feria, Ninth Week of Year 1: Mass ad lib; Office of the day *or* St Norbert, Bishop: Mass & Office of the Memorial
7 Wed	G	feria: Mass ad lib; Office of the day
8 Thu	G	feria: Mass ad lib; Office of the day
9 Fri	G W W	feria: Mass ad lib; Office of the day *or* *Friday abstinence* St Ephrem, Deacon & Doctor: Mass & Office of the Memorial *or* St Columba, Abbot: Mass & Office of the Memorial *National*
10 Sat	G W	feria: Mass ad lib; Office of the day *or* Blessed Virgin Mary on Saturday: Mass & Office of the Memorial
evening	W	First Vespers
11 Sun	W	**+ THE MOST HOLY BODY AND BLOOD** **OF CHRIST (CORPUS ET SANGUIS CHRISTI):** *Gloria, Sequence ad lib, Creed, Preface II of the Most Holy Eucharist (Preface I may be used)* Mass & Office of the Solemnity Announce Mandatory CBCEW Day for Life Collection

JUNE 2023			
12 Mon	G	feria, Tenth Week of Year 1: Mass ad lib; Office of the day	Ps Week 2
13 Tue	W	St Anthony of Padua, Priest & Doctor: Mass & Office of the Memorial	
14 Wed	G	feria: Mass ad lib; Office of the day	
15 Thu	G	feria: Mass ad lib; Office of the day	
evening	W	First Vespers	
16 Fri	W	**THE MOST SACRED HEART OF JESUS** **(Diocese consecrated to the** **Sacred Heart, 17 June 1873):** *Gloria, (Alternative Collect), Proper Readings, Creed, Proper Preface* Mass & Office of the Solemnity	*No Friday* *abstinence*
17 Sat	W	The Immaculate Heart of the Blessed Virgin Mary: *Proper Gospel, Preface I of the Blessed Virgin Mary* Mass & Office of the Memorial	
evening	G	First Vespers	
18 Sun	G	+ 11th SUNDAY IN ORDINARY TIME: *Gloria, Creed, a Preface of Sundays in O.T.* Mass & Office of the day § Day for Life Collection for Life	Ps Week 3
19 Mon	G W	feria, Eleventh Week of Year 1: Mass ad lib; Office of the day *or* St Romuald, Abbot: Mass & Office of the Memorial	
20 Tue	R	St Alban, Protomartyr: *Proper National Collect* Mass & Office of the Memorial	*Diocesan*
21 Wed	W	St Aloysius Gonzaga, Religious: Mass & Office of the Memorial	
22 Thu	R	SS JOHN FISHER, Bishop, and THOMAS MORE, Martyrs: *Gloria, (Alternative Collect), Proper National Readings, Preface I or II of* *Holy Martyrs* Mass & Office of the Feast § Those who suffer Persecution	*National*

JUNE 2023

23 Fri	G W	feria: Mass ad lib; Office of the day *or* St Etheldreda (Audrey), Virgin: Mass & Office of the Memorial	*Friday abstinence* *National*
evening	W W	First Vespers Proper Vigil Mass of the Nativity of St John the Baptist precedes or follows *Gloria, Proper Readings, Creed, Preface of St John the Baptist*	*Abstinence ends*
24 Sat	W	**THE NATIVITY OF ST JOHN THE BAPTIST:** *Gloria, Proper Readings, Creed, Preface of St John the Baptist* Mass & Office of the Solemnity, with Second Vespers and + Evening Mass	
25 Sun	G	+ 12th SUNDAY IN ORDINARY TIME: *Gloria, (Short form Gospel), Creed, a Preface of Sundays in O.T.* Mass & Office of the day Announce Holy Day of Obligation Announce Mandatory Holy See Collection for Peter's Pence	*Ps Week 4*
26 Mon	G	feria, Twelfth Week of Year 1: Mass ad lib; Office of the day	
evening in Cathedral	R	First Vespers	
27 Tue	R	St John Southworth, Priest & Martyr: *see Diocesan Supplement Book or online, (Short form 1st Reading)* Mass & Office of the Memorial	*Diocesan*
in Cathedral	R	+ **ST JOHN SOUTHWORTH,** **Priest & Martyr:** *Gloria, Readings all from the Common of Martyrs, Creed, Preface 1 of* *Holy Martyrs; see Diocesan Supplement Book or online* Mass & Office of the Solemnity	*Diocesan*
28 Wed	R	St Irenaeus, Bishop, Doctor & Martyr: Mass & Office of the Memorial	
evening	R R	First Vespers + Proper Vigil Mass of Ss Peter and Paul precedes or follows *Gloria, Proper Readings, Creed, Preface of Ss Peter and Paul*	
29 Thu	R	+ **SS PETER and PAUL, Apostles** **St Peter, Prince of Apostles, Patron of the Diocese:** *Gloria, Proper Readings, Creed, Preface of Ss Peter and Paul* Mass & Office of the Solemnity	

JUNE/JULY 2023

		The anniversary of the election of Pope Francis is observed today, by decision of the Bishops' Conference. A special intention for the Holy Father should be included in the Universal Prayer.	
30 Fri	G R	feria: Mass ad lib; Office of the day *or* The First Martyrs of Holy Roman Church: Mass & Office of the Memorial	*Friday abstinence*
in Cathedral	W	First Vespers	*Abstinence ends*

JULY 2023

1 Sat	W	DEDICATION OF THE CATHEDRAL (1910): *Diocesan* *Gloria, Common of the Dedication (Roman Missal page 1095), Readings from Common of the Dedication, Vol II, page 1392 ff* Mass & Office of the Feast	
in Cathedral	W	**DEDICATION OF THE CATHEDRAL (1910):** *Diocesan* *Gloria, Common of the Dedication (Roman Missal page 1091), Readings from Common of the Dedication Vol 2, page 1392 ff, Creed* Mass & Office of the Solemnity, with Second Vespers and + Evening Mass	
evening	G	First Vespers	
2 Sun	G	+ 13th SUNDAY IN ORDINARY TIME: *Ps Week 1* *Gloria, Creed, a Preface of Sundays in O.T.* Mass & Office of the day Collection for Peter's Pence Announce Mandatory CBCEW Collection for Stella Maris	
3 Mon	R	ST THOMAS, Apostle *Gloria, Proper readings, Preface I or II of Apostles* Mass & Office of the Feast	
4 Tue	G W	feria, Thirteenth Week of Year 1: Mass ad lib; Office of the day *or* St Elizabeth of Portugal: *(* Short form Gospel)* Mass & Office of the Memorial	
5 Wed	G W	feria: Mass ad lib; Office of the day *or* St Anthony Zaccaria, Priest: Mass & Office of the Memorial	
6 Thu	G R	feria: Mass ad lib; Office of the day *or* St Maria Goretti, Virgin & Martyr: Mass & Office of the Memorial	

SECTION 7: LITURGICAL CALENDAR

JULY 2023

7 Fri	G	feria: Mass ad lib; Office of the day	*Friday abstinence*
8 Sat	G W	feria: Mass ad lib; Office of the day *or* Blessed Virgin Mary on Saturday: Mass & Office of the Memorial	
evening	G	First Vespers	
9 Sun	G	+ 14th SUNDAY IN ORDINARY TIME: *Ps Week 2* *Gloria, (Alternative Psalm), Creed, a Preface of Sundays in O.T.* Mass & Office of the day § Sea Sunday Collection for Stella Maris	
10 Mon	G	feria, Fourteenth Week of Year 1: Mass ad lib; Office of the day	
11 Tue	W	ST BENEDICT, Abbot, Patron of Europe: *National* *Gloria, Proper Readings, Preface of Holy Pastors or* *Holy Virgins and Religious* Mass & Office of the Feast § Europe	
12 Wed	G	feria: Mass ad lib; Office of the day	
13 Thu	G W	feria: Mass ad lib; Office of the day *or* St Henry: Mass & Office of the Memorial	
14 Fri	G W	feria: Mass ad lib; Office of the day *or* *Friday abstinence* St Camillus de Lellis, Priest: Mass & Office of the Memorial	
15 Sat	W	St Bonaventure, Bishop & Doctor: Mass & Office of the Memorial	
evening	G	First Vespers	
16 Sun	G	+15th SUNDAY IN ORDINARY TIME: *Ps Week 3* *Gloria, Creed, a Preface of Sundays in O.T.* Mass & Office of the day	
17 Mon	G	feria, Fifteenth Week of Year 1; Mass ad lib; Office of the day	
18 Tue	G	feria: Mass ad lib; Office of the day	
19 Wed	G	feria: Mass ad lib; Office of the day	
20 Thu	G R	feria: Mass ad lib; Office of the day *or* St Apollinaris, Bishop & Martyr: Mass & Office of the Memorial	
21 Fri	G	feria: Mass ad lib; Office of the day *or* *Friday abstinence*	

JULY/AUGUST 2023

	W	St Lawrence of Brindisi, Priest & Doctor: Mass & Office of the Memorial
22 Sat	W	ST MARY MAGDALENE: *Gloria, Proper Readings (Alternative First), Proper Preface* Mass & Office of the Feast
evening	G	First Vespers
23 Sun	G	+ 16th SUNDAY IN ORDINARY TIME: *Ps Week 4* *Gloria, Creed, a Preface of Sundays in O.T.* Mass & Office of the day § Europe (St Bridget of Sweden)
24 Mon	G W	feria, Sixteenth Week of Year 1: Mass ad lib; Office of the day *or* St Sharbel Makhluf, Priest: Mass & Office of the Memorial
25 Tue	R	ST JAMES, Apostle: *Gloria, Proper Readings, Preface I or II of Apostles* Mass & Office of the day
26 Wed	W	Ss Joachim and Anne, Parents of the Blessed Virgin Mary: Mass & Office of the Memorial
27 Thu	G	feria: Mass ad lib; Office of the day
28 Fri	G	feria: Mass ad lib; Office of the day *Friday abstinence*
29 Sat	W	Ss Martha, Mary and Lazarus: *Proper Alternative Gospels* Mass & Office of the Memorial
evening	G	First Vespers
30 Sun	G	+17th SUNDAY IN ORDINARY TIME: *Ps Week 1* *Gloria, (Alternative Psalm), Creed, a Preface of Sundays in O.T.* Mass & Office of the day
31 Mon	W	St Ignatius of Loyola, Priest: Mass & Office of the Memorial

AUGUST 2023

1 Tue	W	St Alphonsus Liguori, Bishop & Doctor: Mass & Office of the Memorial

SECTION 7: LITURGICAL CALENDAR

AUGUST 2023

On 2nd August the plenary indulgence (the *Portiuncula*) may be acquired in minor basilicas, shrines and parish churches. Requirements: a devout visit to a church and the recitation there of the Lord's Prayer and Creed, in addition to sacramental confession, Holy Communion and prayer for the intentions of the Holy Father. This indulgence may be gained only once. The visit may be made from noon the previous day to midnight on the day itself.

2 Wed — G — feria: Mass ad lib; Office of the day *or*
W — **St Eusebius of Vercelli, Bishop: Mass & Office of the Memorial** *or*
W — **St Peter Julian Eymard, Priest: Mass & Office of the Memorial**

3 Thu — G — feria: Mass ad lib; Office of the day

4 Fri — W — **St John Vianney, Priest:** *Friday abstinence*
Mass & Office of the Memorial

5 Sat — G — feria: Mass ad lib; Office of the day *or*
W — **The Dedication of the Basilica of St Mary Major:**
Mass & Office of the Memorial *or*
W — **Blessed Virgin Mary on Saturday: Mass & Office of the Memorial**

evening — W — First Vespers

6 Sun — W — **+ THE TRANSFIGURATION OF THE LORD:**
Gloria, 1st and 2nd Readings, Year A Gospel, Creed, Proper Preface
Mass & Office of the Feast

7 Mon — G — feria, Eighteenth Week of Year 1: *Ps Week 2*
Mass ad lib; Office of the day *or*
R — **St Sixtus II, Pope, and Companions, Martyrs:**
Mass & Office of the Memorial *or*
W — **St Cajetan, Priest: Mass & Office of the Memorial**

8 Tue — W — **St Dominic, Priest: Mass & Office of the Memorial**

9 Wed — R — **ST TERESA BENEDICTA OF THE CROSS,** *National*
Virgin & Martyr, Patron of Europe:
Gloria, Proper Readings as in the Lectionary for St Cecilia (22 November), Preface I or II of Holy Martyrs
Mass & Office of the Feast
§ Europe

10 Thu — R — **ST LAWRENCE, Deacon & Martyr:**
Gloria, Proper Readings, Preface I or II of Holy Martyrs
Mass & Office of the Feast

AUGUST 2023

11 Fri	W	St Clare, Virgin: Mass & Office of the Memorial	*Friday abstinence*
12 Sat	G	feria: Mass ad lib; Office of the day *or*	
	W	St Jane Frances de Chantal, Religious:	
		[see Divine Office for 12 December, Vol I, p 33* ff]	
		Mass & Office of the Memorial *or*	
	W	Blessed Virgin Mary on Saturday: Mass & Office of the Memorial	
evening	G	First Vespers	
13 Sun	G	+ 19th SUNDAY IN ORDINARY TIME:	*Ps Week 3*
		Gloria, Creed, a Preface of Sundays in O.T.	
		Mass & Office of the day	
		Announce Holy Day of Obligation	
14 Mon	R	St Maximilian Mary Kolbe, Priest & Martyr:	
		Mass & Office of the Memorial	
evening	W	First Vespers	
	W	+ Proper Vigil Mass of the Assumption precedes or follows	
		Gloria, Proper Readings, Creed, Proper Preface	
15 Tue	W	**+ THE ASSUMPTION OF THE BLESSED VIRGIN MARY:**	
		(Alternative Entrance Antiphon), Gloria, Proper Readings, Creed, Proper Preface	
		Mass & Office of the Solemnity	
16 Wed	G	feria, Nineteenth Week of Year 1: Mass ad lib; Office of the day *or*	
	W	St Stephen of Hungary:	
		(* Short form Gospel)	
		Mass & Office of the Memorial	
17 Thu	G	feria: Mass ad lib; Office of the day	
18 Fri	G	feria: Mass ad lib; Office of the day	*Friday abstinence*
19 Sat	G	feria: Mass ad lib; Office of the day *or*	
	W	St John Eudes, Priest: Mass & Office of the Memorial *or*	
	W	Blessed Virgin Mary on Saturday: Mass & Office of the Memorial	
evening	G	First Vespers	
20 Sun	G	+ 20th SUNDAY IN ORDINARY TIME:	*Ps Week 4*
		Gloria, Creed, a Preface of Sundays in O.T.	
		Mass & Office of the day	

AUGUST 2023

21 Mon	W	St Pius X, Pope: Mass & Office of the Memorial
22 Tue	W	The Queenship of the Blessed Virgin Mary: *Preface I or II of the Blessed Virgin Mary* Mass & Office of the Memorial
23 Wed	G W	feria, Twentieth Week of Year 1: Mass ad lib; Office of the day *or* St Rose of Lima, Virgin: Mass & Office of the Memorial
24 Thu	R	ST BARTHOLOMEW, Apostle: *Gloria, Proper Readings, Preface I or II of Apostles* Mass & Office of the Feast
25 Fri	G W W	feria: Mass ad lib; Office of the day *or* *Friday abstinence* St Louis: Mass & Office of the Memorial *or* St Joseph Calasanz, Priest: *(* Short form 1st Reading)* Mass & Office of the Memorial
26 Sat	G W W	feria: Mass ad lib; Office of the day *or* Blessed Dominic of the Mother of God, Priest: *National* Mass & Office of the Memorial *or* Blessed Virgin Mary on Saturday: Mass & Office of the Memorial
evening	G	First Vespers
27 Sun	G	+ 21st SUNDAY IN ORDINARY TIME: *Ps Week 1* *Gloria, Creed, a Preface of Sundays in O.T.* Mass & Office of the day
28 Mon	W	St Augustine, Bishop & Doctor: Mass & Office of the Memorial
29 Tue	R	The Passion of St John the Baptist: *Proper Gospel, Preface of St John the Baptist* Mass & Office of the Memorial
30 Wed	G R	feria, Twenty-First Week of Year 1: Mass ad lib; Office of the day *or* Ss Margaret Clitherow, Anne Line and *National* Margaret Ward, Martyrs: Mass & Office of the Memorial
31 Thu	G W	feria: Mass ad lib; Office of the day *or* St Aidan, Bishop, and the Saints of Lindisfarne: *National* Mass & Office of the Memorial

SEPTEMBER 2023

SEPTEMBER 2023

1 Fri	G	feria: Mass ad lib; Office of the day	*Friday abstinence*
		Anniversary of the Death of Cardinal Cormac Murphy-O'Connor, 10th Archbishop of Westminster (2017)	
		§ World Day of Prayer for the Care of Creation	
2 Sat	G	feria: Mass ad lib; Office of the day *or*	
	W	Blessed Virgin Mary on Saturday: Mass & Office of the Memorial	
evening	G	First Vespers	
3 Sun	G	+ 22nd SUNDAY IN ORDINARY TIME:	*Ps Week 2*
		Gloria, Creed, a Preface of Sundays in O.T.	
		Mass & Office of the day	
		Announce Optional Catholic Education Service Collection	
4 Mon	G	feria, Twenty-Second Week of Year1:	
		Mass ad lib; Office of the day *or*	
	W	St Cuthbert, Bishop:	*National*
		Mass & Office of the Memorial	
5 Tue	G	feria: Mass ad lib; Office of the day	
6 Wed	G	feria: Mass ad lib; Office of the day	
7 Thu	G	feria: Mass ad lib; Office of the day	
8 Fri	W	THE NATIVITY OF THE BLESSED VIRGIN MARY: *Friday abstinence*	
		Gloria, (Alternative Proper 1st & Short form Gospel Readings), (Alternative Prayer over the Offerings), Preface I or II of the Blessed Virgin Mary	
		Mass & Office of the Feast	
9 Sat	G	feria: Mass ad lib; Office of the day *or*	
	W	St Peter Claver, Priest: Mass & Office of the Memorial *or*	
	W	Blessed Virgin Mary on Saturday: Mass & Office of the Memorial	
evening	G	First Vespers	
10 Sun	G	+ 23rd SUNDAY IN ORDINARY TIME:	*Ps Week 3*
		Gloria, Creed, a Preface of Sundays in O.T.	
		Mass & Office of the day	
		§ Education Sunday	
		Collection for Catholic Education Service	
		Announce Manadatory CBCEW *Evangelii Gaudium* Appeal Collection	

SEPTEMBER 2023

11 Mon	G	feria, Twenty-Third Week of Year 1: Mass ad lib; Office of the day
12 Tue	G	feria: Mass ad lib; Office of the day *or*
	W	The Most Holy Name of Mary: Mass & Office of the Memorial
13 Wed	W	St John Chrysostom, Bishop & Doctor: *(* Short form Gospel)* Mass & Office of the Memorial
14 Thu	R	**THE EXALTATION OF THE HOLY CROSS:** *Gloria, 1st or 2nd Reading, Preface of the Holy Cross (Preface I of the Passion of the Lord may be used)* Mass & Office of the Feast
15 Fri	W	Our Lady of Sorrows: *Friday abstinence* *Sequence ad lib, (Alternative Gospel Reading), Preface I or II of the Blessed Virgin Mary* Mass & Office of the Memorial
16 Sat	R	Ss Cornelius, Pope, and Cyprian, Bishop, Martyrs: Mass & Office of the Memorial
evening	G	First Vespers
17 Sun	G	+ 24th SUNDAY IN ORDINARY TIME: *Ps Week 4* *Gloria, Creed, a Preface of Sundays in O.T.* Mass & Office of the day Annual Mass Count – 1 § *Evangelii Gaudium* Day Collection for *Evangelii Gaudium* Appeal
18 Mon	G	feria, Twenty-Fourth Sunday of Year 1: Mass ad lib; Office of the day
19 Tue	G	feria: Mass ad lib; Office of the day *or*
	R	St Januarius, Bishop & Martyr: Mass & Office of the Memorial
20 Wed	R	St Andrew Kim Tae-gŏn, Priest, Paul Chŏng Ha-sang, and Companions, Martyrs: Mass & Office of the Memorial
21 Thu	R	**ST MATTHEW, Apostle & Evangelist:** *Gloria, Proper Readings, Preface I or II of Apostles* Mass & Office of the Feast
22 Fri	G	feria: Mass ad lib; Office of the day *Friday abstinence*

SEPTEMBER/OCTOBER 2023

23 Sat	W	St Pius of Pietrelcina, Priest: Mass & Office of the Memorial
evening	G	First Vespers
24 Sun	G	+ 25th SUNDAY IN ORDINARY TIME: *Ps Week 1* *Gloria, Creed, a Preface of Sundays in O.T.* Mass & Office of the day Annual Mass Count – 2 § The Harvest
25 Mon	G	feria, Twenty-Fifth Week of Year 1: Mass ad lib; Office of the day
26 Tue	G R	feria: Mass ad lib; Office of the day *or* Ss Cosmas and Damian, Martyrs: Mass & Office of the Memorial
27 Wed	W	St Vincent de Paul, Priest: Mass & Office of the Memorial
28 Thu	G R R	feria: Mass ad lib; Office of the day *or* St Wenceslaus, Martyr: Mass & Office of the Memorial *or* St Lawrence Ruiz and Companions, Martyrs: Mass & Office of the Memorial
29 Fri	W	SS MICHAEL, GABRIEL and RAPHAEL, *Friday abstinence* Archangels: *Gloria, Proper Readings (Alternative 1st Reading), Preface of the Angels* Mass & Office of the Feast
30 Sat	W	St Jerome, Priest & Doctor: Mass & Office of the Memorial
		The Rosary should be recommended to the faithful, and its nature and importance explained. A plenary indulgence may be gained by reciting five decades of the Rosary in church, as a family at home, as a religious community, or as a pious fraternity, or in general whenever several persons have gathered for a good purpose; in other circumstances a partial indulgence may be gained.
evening	G	First Vespers

OCTOBER 2023

| 1 Sun | G | + 26th SUNDAY IN ORDINARY TIME: *Ps Week 2*
Gloria, (Short form 2nd reading), Creed, a Preface of Sundays in O.T.
Mass & Office of the day
Annual Mass Count – 3
Announce Optional Harvest Fast Day Collection |

OCTOBER 2023

2 Mon	W	The Holy Guardian Angels
		Proper Gospel Reading, Preface of the Angels
		Mass & Office of the Memorial
3 Tue	G	feria: Mass ad lib; Office of the day
4 Wed	W	St Francis of Assisi: Mass & Office of the Memorial
5 Thu	G	feria: Mass ad lib; Office of the day *or*
	W	St Faustina Kowalska, Virgin: Mass & Office of the Memorial
6 Fri	G	feria: Mass ad lib; Office of the day *or* *Friday abstinence*
	W	St Bruno, Priest: Mass & Office of the Memorial
		§ Harvest Fast Day
7 Sat	W	Our Lady of the Rosary: Mass & Office of the Memorial
evening	G	First Vespers
8 Sun	G	+ 27th SUNDAY IN ORDINARY TIME: *Ps Week 3*
		Gloria, Creed, a Preface of Sundays in O.T.
		Mass & Office of the day
		Annual Mass Count - 4
		§ Week of Prayer for Prisoners and their Families
		Collect Harvest Fast Day Offerings
9 Mon	W	ST JOHN HENRY NEWMAN, Priest *National*
		Gloria, Proper Readings, Preface of Holy Pastors
		Mass & Office of the Feast
10 Tue	G	feria: Mass ad lib; Office of the day *or*
	W	St Paulinus of York, Bishop: *National*
		Mass & Office of the Memorial *or*
	R	St Denis, Bishop, and Companions, Martyrs:
		Mass & Office of the Memorial *or*
	W	St John Leonardi, Priest: Mass & Office of the Memorial
11 Wed	G	feria: Mass ad lib; Office of the day *or*
	W	St John XXIII, Pope: Mass & Office of the Memorial
12 Thu	G	feria: Mass ad lib; Office of the day *or*
	W	St Wilfrid, Bishop: Mass & Office of the Memorial *National*
in City of Westminster	W	First Vespers

OCTOBER 2023

13 Fri — W — ST EDWARD THE CONFESSOR, *Friday abstinence*
Patron of the Diocese: *Diocesan*
Gloria, Proper National Readings, Preface I or II of Saints; see Diocesan Supplement Book or online [also National Collect]
Mass & Office of the Feast

in City of Westminster — W — **ST EDWARD THE CONFESSOR, Patron of the Diocese and of the City of Westminster:** *No Friday abstinence Diocesan*
Gloria, Proper National Readings (1st from Common of Holy Men and Women), Creed, Preface I or II of Saints; see Diocesan Supplement Book or online [also National Collect]
Mass & Office of the Solemnity

14 Sat — G — feria: Mass ad lib; Office of the day *or*
R — St Callistus I, Pope & Martyr: Mass & Office of the Memorial *or*
W — Blessed Virgin Mary on Saturday: Mass & Office of the Memorial

evening — G — First Vespers

15 Sun — G — + 28th SUNDAY IN ORDINARY TIME: *Ps Week 4*
Gloria, (Short form Gospel) Creed, a Preface of Sundays in O.T.
Mass & Office of the day
Announce Mandatory Holy See World Mission Sunday Collection

16 Mon — G — feria, Twenty-Eighth Week of Year1: Mass ad lib; Office of the day

17 Tue — R — St Ignatius of Antioch, Bishop & Martyr:
Mass & Office of the Memorial

18 Wed — R — ST LUKE, Evangelist:
Gloria, Proper Readings, Preface II of Apostles
Mass & Office of the Feast

19 Thu — G — feria: Mass ad lib; Office of the day *or*
R — Ss John de Brébeuf and Isaac Jogues, Priests, and Companions, Martyrs: Mass & Office of the Memorial *or*
W — St Paul of the Cross, Priest: Mass & Office of the Memorial

20 Fri — G — feria: Mass ad lib; Office of the day *Friday abstinence*

21 Sat — G — feria: Mass ad lib; Office of the day *or*
W — Blessed Virgin Mary on Saturday: Mass & Office of the Memorial

evening — G — First Vespers

OCTOBER/NOVEMBER 2023

22 Sun	G	+ 29th SUNDAY IN ORDINARY TIME:	*Ps Week 1*
		Gloria, Creed, a Preface of Sundays in O.T.	
		Mass & Office of the day	
		§ World Mission Day (One Mass for the Evangelisation of Peoples is permitted today or on a subsequent ferial day)	
		Collection for World Mission Sunday	
23 Mon	G	feria, Twenty-Ninth Week of Year 1: Mass ad lib; Office of the day *or*	
	W	St John of Capistrano, Priest: Mass & Office of the Memorial	
24 Tue	G	feria: Mass ad lib; Office of the day *or*	
	W	St Anthony Mary Claret, Bishop: Mass & Office of the Memorial	
25 Wed	G	feria: Mass ad lib; Office of the day	
26 Thu	G	feria: Mass ad lib; Office of the day *or*	
	W	Ss Chad and Cedd, Bishops:	*National*
		Mass & Office of the Memorial	
27 Thu	G	feria: Mass ad lib; Office of the day	*Friday abstinence*
28 Sat	R	SS SIMON and JUDE, Apostles:	
		Gloria, Proper Readings, Preface I or II of Apostles	
		Mass & Office of the Feast	
evening	G	First Vespers	
29 Sun	G	+ 30th SUNDAY IN ORDINARY TIME	*Ps Week 2*
		Gloria, Creed, a Preface of Sundays in O.T.	
		Mass & Office of the day	
		Announce Holy Day of Obligation	
		Announce Mandatory Diocesan Sick and Retired Priests Collection	
30 Mon	G	feria, Thirtieth Week of Year 1: Mass ad lib; Office of the day	
31 Tue	G	feria: Mass ad lib; Office of the day	
	W	First Vespers	

NOVEMBER 2023

1 Wed	W	**+ ALL SAINTS:**
		Gloria, Proper Readings, Creed, Proper Preface
		Mass & Office of the Solemnity

NOVEMBER 2023

A plenary indulgence, applicable only to the souls in Purgatory, is granted to any of the faithful who (1) on one of the days from 1-8 November visit devoutly a cemetery or simply pray mentally for the dead; (2) on All Souls' Day visit a church or chapel with devotion and there recite the Our Father and the Creed.

A partial indulgence, applicable only to the souls in Purgatory, is granted to any of the faithful who (1) visit devoutly a cemetery or who simply pray mentally for the dead; (2) recite devoutly Lauds or Vespers of the Office of the Dead, or the invocation 'Eternal rest grant unto them, O Lord...'

2 Thu   P
or B

THE COMMEMORATION OF ALL THE FAITHFUL DEPARTED (ALL SOULS' DAY):
The altar is not decorated with flowers and the organ is used only to sustain the singing.
Mass & Office of the Dead
Readings selected from Masses for the Dead, a Preface for the Dead
All priests are permitted to say three Masses today, with an interval of time between one Mass and the next, and on condition that while one of the Masses may be applied in favour of any person, the second Mass should be applied for all the faithful departed, and the third for the intentions of the Holy Father.

3 Fri   G
W
W

feria: Mass ad lib; Office of the day *or*   *Friday abstinence*
St Martin de Porres, Religious: Mass & Office of the Memorial *or*
St Winifride, Virgin: Mass & Office of the Memorial *National*

4 Sat   W

St Charles Borromeo, Bishop:
Mass & Office of the Memorial

evening   G

First Vespers

5 Sun   G

+ 31st SUNDAY IN ORDINARY TIME: *Ps Week 3*
Gloria, Creed, a Preface of Sundays in O.T.
Mass & Office of the day
Collection for Sick and Retired Priests

6 Mon   G

feria, Thirty-First Week of Year 1: Mass ad lib; Office of the day

7 Tue   G
W

feria: Mass ad lib; Office of the day *or*
St Willibrord, Bishop: Mass & Office of the Memorial

8 Wed   G

feria: Mass ad lib; Office of the day

SECTION 7: LITURGICAL CALENDAR

NOVEMBER 2023

9 Thu	W	**THE DEDICATION OF THE LATERAN BASILICA:**
		(Alternative Entrance Antiphon), Gloria, (Alternative Collect), 1st or 2nd Reading, Proper Preface
		Mass & Office of the Feast

10 Fri	W	St Leo the Great, Pope & Doctor:	*Friday abstinence*
		Mass & Office of the Memorial	

11 Sat	W	St Martin of Tours, Bishop:
		Mass & Office of the Memorial

evening	G	First Vespers

12 Sun	G	+ 32nd SUNDAY IN ORDINARY TIME:	*Ps Week 4*
		Gloria, (Short form 2nd Reading), Creed, a Preface of Sundays in O.T.	
		Mass & Office of the day	
	P	+ One Requiem Mass permitted (REMEMBRANCE SUNDAY)	
	or B	*Readings selected from Masses for the Dead, Creed, a Preface for the Dead*	
		§ World Day of the Poor	

13 Mon	G	feria, Thirty-Second Week of Year 1: Mass ad lib; Office of the day

14 Tue	G	feria: Mass ad lib; Office of the day

15 Wed	G	feria: Mass ad lib; Office of the day *or*
	W	St Albert the Great, Bishop & Doctor:
		Mass & Office of the Memorial

16 Thu	W	St Edmund of Abingdon, Bishop:	*Diocesan*
		see Diocesan Supplement Book or online [also National Collect]	
		Mass & Office of the Memorial	

17 Fri	G	feria: Mass ad lib; Office of the day *or*	*Friday abstinence*
	W	St Hilda, Abbess:	*National*
		Mass & Office of the Memorial *or*	
	W	St Hugh of Lincoln, Bishop:	*National*
		Mass & Office of the Memorial *or*	
	W	St Elizabeth of Hungary, Religious	*National*
		Mass & Office of the Memorial	

18 Sat	G	feria: Mass ad lib; Office of the day *or*
	W	The Dedication of the Basilicas of Ss Peter and Paul, Apostles:
		Proper Readings, Preface I or II of Apostles
		Mass & Office of the Memorial *or*
	W	Blessed Virgin Mary on Saturday: Mass & Office of the Memorial

NOVEMBER 2023

evening	G	First Vespers
19 Sun	G	+ 33rd SUNDAY IN ORDINARY TIME *Ps Week 1* *Gloria, Creed, a Preface of Sundays in O.T.* Mass & Office of the day
20 Mon	G	feria, Thirty-Third Week of Year 1: Mass ad lib; Office of the day
21 Tue	W	The Presentation of the Blessed Virgin Mary: *Preface I or II of the Blessed Virgin Mary* Mass & Office of the Memorial
22 Wed	R	St Cecilia, Virgin & Martyr: Mass & Office of the Memorial
23 Thu	G R W	feria: Mass ad lib; Office of the day *or* St Clement I, Pope & Martyr: Mass & Office of the Memorial *or* St Columban, Abbot: Mass & Office of the Memorial
24 Fri	R	St Andrew Dũng-Lạc, Priest, *Friday abstinence* and Companions, Martyrs: Mass & Office of the Memorial
25 Sat	G R W	feria: Mass ad lib; Office of the day *or* St Catherine of Alexandria, Virgin & Martyr: Mass & Office of the Memorial *or* Blessed Virgin Mary on Saturday: Mass & Office of the Memorial
evening	W	First Vespers
26 Sun	W	**+ OUR LORD JESUS CHRIST, King of the Universe:** *Gloria, Creed, Proper Preface* Mass & Office of the Solemnity § Youth Day
27 Mon	G	feria, Thirty-Fourth Week of Year 1: Mass ad lib; Office of the day
28 Tue	G	feria: Mass ad lib; Office of the day
29 Wed	G	feria: Mass ad lib; Office of the day
30 Thu	R	ST ANDREW, Apostle, Patron of Scotland: *National* *Gloria, Proper Readings, Preface I or II of Apostles* Mass & Office of the Feast

DECEMBER 2023

DECEMBER 2023

I Fri	G	feria: Mass ad lib; Office of the day	*Friday abstinence*
2 Sat	G	feria: Mass ad lib; Office of the day *or*	
	W	Blessed Virgin Mary on Saturday: Mass & Office of the Memorial	

LECTIONARY FOR SUNDAYS: YEAR B

SEASON OF ADVENT

Advent has a two-fold character: as a season to prepare for Christmas, when Christ's first coming to us is remembered; and as a season when that remembrance directs the mind and heart to await Christ's coming at the end of time. Advent is thus a period for devout and joyful expectation.

The playing of the organ and other musical instruments, and the decoration of the altar with flowers should be done in a moderate manner, as is consonant with the character of the season, without anticipating the full joy of the Nativity of the Lord. The same moderation should be observed in the celebration of marriage. **Eucharistic Prayer 4 is not used in this Season.**

evening	P	First Vespers (Divine Office Volume I)	
3 Sun	P	+ Ist SUNDAY OF ADVENT	*Ps Week I*
		Creed, Advent Preface I (and on following days)	
		Mass & Office of the day	
		§ Migrants' Day	
4 Mon	P	Advent feria: Mass & Office of the day *or*	
	W	St John Damascene, Priest & Doctor:	
		Mass & Office of the Memorial	
5 Tue	P	Advent feria: Mass & Office of the day	
6 Wed	P	Advent feria: Mass & Office of the day *or*	
	W	St Nicholas, Bishop: Mass & Office of the Memorial	
7 Thu	W	St Ambrose, Bishop & Doctor: Mass & Office of the Memorial	
evening	W	First Vespers	
8 Fri	W	**THE IMMACULATE CONCEPTION**	*No Friday*
		OF THE BLESSED VIRGIN MARY,	*abstinence*
		Patron of the Diocese:	
		Gloria, Proper Readings, Creed, Proper Preface	
		Mass & Office of the Solemnity	

DECEMBER 2023

9 Sat	P	Advent feria: Mass & Office of the day *or*
	W	St Juan Diego Cuauhtlatoatzin: Mass & Office of the Memorial
evening	P	First Vespers
10 Sun	P	+ 2nd SUNDAY OF ADVENT: *Ps Week 2*
		Creed, Advent Preface I
		Mass & Office of the day
11 Mon	P	Advent feria: Mass & Office of the day *or*
	W	St Damasus I, Pope: Mass & Office of the Memorial
12 Tue	P	Advent feria: Mass & Office of the day *or*
	W	Our Lady of Guadalupe: Mass & Office of the Memorial
13 Wed	R	St Lucy, Virgin & Martyr:
		Mass & Office of the Memorial
14 Thu	W	St John of the Cross, Priest & Doctor:
		Mass & Office of the Memorial
15 Fri	P	Advent feria: Mass & Office of the day *Friday abstinence*
16 Sat	P	Advent feria: Mass & Office of the day

Memorials which occur on days between 17 and 31 December may be commemorated at Mass by using the Collect of the saint in place of the Collect of the day. In the Office of Readings the proper hagiographical reading and responsory may be added after the Patristic reading and responsory; the Collect of the saint concludes the office.

At Lauds and Vespers the antiphon (proper or common) and Collect of the saint may be added after the Collect of the day.

At Mass, proper texts and readings are given for the weekdays from 17-24 December, and these should be used instead of those indicated for the weekdays of the third or fourth week of Advent.

evening	RP or P	First Vespers
17 Sun	RP or P	+ 3rd SUNDAY OF ADVENT (*Gaudete* Sunday): *Ps Week 3*
		Creed, Advent Preface II (and on following days)
		Mass of the day; Office of the day, with Readings, also Benedictus & Magnificat antiphons of 17 December (see Divine Office, Vol 1, page 117 ff)
18 Mon	P	Advent feria: Mass & Office of 18 December
19 Tue	P	Advent feria: Mass & Office of 19 December

DECEMBER 2023

20 Wed	P	Advent feria: Mass & Office of 20 December
21 Thu	P	Advent feria: Mass & Office of 21 December *(Alternative 1st Reading)* (St Peter Canisius, Priest and Doctor)
22 Fri	P	Advent feria: Mass & Office of 22 December *Friday abstinence*
23 Sat	P	Advent feria: Mass & Office of 23 December (St John of Kanty, Priest)
evening	P	First Vespers: Magnificat antiphon of 23 December
24 Sun	P	+ 4th SUNDAY OF ADVENT: *Ps Week 4* *Creed, Advent Preface II* Morning Mass of the day; Lauds with Readings, also Benedictus antiphon of 24 December and Lesser Hours of the day (see Divine Office Vol I, page 173 ff) § Expectant Mothers Announce Holy Day of Obligation

SEASON OF CHRISTMAS

After the annual celebration of the Paschal Mystery there is no more ancient feast day for the Church than the recalling of the memory of the Nativity of the Lord and of the mysteries of his first appearing. Eucharistic Prayer 4 is not used in this season.

evening	W W	First Vespers + Proper Vigil Mass of Christmas precedes or follows *Gloria, Proper Readings (Short form Gospel), Creed, (kneel at Incarnatus), a Preface of the Nativity & Communicantes in the Roman Canon*

For pastoral reasons, readings at the following Christmas Masses may be chosen from among all those provided for the Solemnity. It is appropriate that a Solemn Vigil be kept by celebrating the Office of Readings before the Mass during the Night.
Compline is omitted by those attending that Mass.

	W	+ Mass during the Night *Gloria, Proper Readings, Creed (kneel at Incarnatus), a Preface of the Nativity & Communicantes in the Roman Canon*
25 Mon	W	**+ THE NATIVITY OF THE LORD (CHRISTMAS):** *Gloria, Proper Readings (Short form Gospel at Day Mass only), Creed (kneel at Incarnatus), a Preface of the Nativity & Communicantes in the Roman Canon*

DECEMBER 2023

Mass & Office of the Solemnity
All priests may celebrate or concelebrate three Masses today, provided that they are celebrated at their proper time.

26 Tue	R	**ST STEPHEN, The First Martyr:** *Gloria, Proper Readings, a Preface of the Nativity &* Communicantes *in the Roman Canon* Mass, Lauds & Lesser Hours of St Stephen, Vespers of the Octave
	R	*(In parishes dedicated to St Stephen his Solemnity is observed:* *Gloria, 2nd Reading from the Common of Martyrs, Other Readings Proper, Creed, a Preface of the Nativity &* Communicantes *in the Roman Canon,* **Mass & Office of the Solemnity with Second Vespers)**
27 Wed	W	**ST JOHN, Apostle & Evangelist:** *Gloria, Proper Readings, a Preface of the Nativity &* Communicantes *in the Roman Canon* Mass, Lauds & Lesser Hours of St John; Vespers of the Octave
	W	*(In parishes dedicated to St John the Evangelist, his Solemnity is observed:* *Gloria, 1st Reading from the Proper of All Saints, Other Readings Proper, Creed, a Preface of the Nativity &* Communicantes *in the Roman Canon,* **Mass with First and Second Vespers of the Solemnity)**
28 Thu	R	**THE HOLY INNOCENTS, Martyrs:** *Gloria, Proper Readings, a Preface of the Nativity &* Communicantes *in the Roman Canon* Mass, Lauds & Lesser Hours of the Holy Innocents; Vespers of the Octave
29 Fri	R	**ST THOMAS BECKET, Bishop & Martyr** *No Friday* **Patron of the Parish Clergy:** *abstinence* *Gloria, (Alternative Collect), Proper National Readings (Short form Gospel), a Preface of the Nativity and* Communicantes *in the Roman Canon* Mass, Lauds & Lesser Hours of St Thomas Becket; Vespers of the Octave
	R	*(In parishes dedicated to St Thomas his Solemnity is observed:* *Gloria, 1st Reading from the Common of Martyrs, Other Readings Proper, Creed, a Preface of the Nativity &* Communicantes *in the Roman Canon,* **Mass with First and Second Vespers of the Solemnity)**
30 Sat	W	**6th DAY IN THE OCTAVE OF CHRISTMAS:** *Gloria, a Preface of the Nativity &* Communicantes *in the Roman Canon* **Mass & Office of the Octave**

SECTION 7: LITURGICAL CALENDAR

DECEMBER 2023/JANUARY 2024

31 Sun	W	+ THE HOLY FAMILY OF JESUS, MARY AND JOSEPH: *Gloria, 1st and 2nd Readings, Gospel of Year B or ad lib Year B Readings,* *Creed, a Preface of the Nativity &* Communicantes *in the Roman Canon* **Mass & Office of the Feast** (St Sylvester I, Pope)
evening	W	First Vespers and + Evening Mass

JANUARY 2024

1 Mon	W	+ **SOLEMNITY OF MARY,** **THE HOLY MOTHER OF GOD** **THE OCTAVE DAY OF THE NATIVITY OF THE LORD:** *Gloria, Creed, Preface 1 of Blessed Virgin Mary &* Communicantes *in the* *Roman Canon* **Mass & Office of the Solemnity** **Announce Holy Day of Obligation**
		A Preface of the Nativity is used on weekdays of the Christmas season, unless other provision is made.
2 Tue	W	Ss Basil the Great and Gregory Nazianzen, *Ps Week 2* **Bishops & Doctors:** *Readings of 2 January* **Mass & Office of the Memorial**
3 Wed	W	Christmas feria: *First Collect, Readings of 3 January* **Mass & Office of the Day** or
	W	**The Most Holy Name of Jesus: Mass & Office of the Memorial**
4 Thu	W	Christmas feria: *First Collect, Readings of 4 January* **Mass & Office of the Day**
5 Fri	W	Christmas feria: *Friday abstinence* *First Collect, Readings of 5 January* **Mass & Office of the day**
6 Sat	W	Christmas feria: *First Collect, readings of 6 January* **Mass & Office of the day**
evening	W	First Vespers + Proper Vigil Mass of the Epiphany precedes or follows

JANUARY 2024

		Gloria, Epiphany Readings, Creed, Proper Preface & Communicantes *of the Epiphany in the Roman Canon*
7 Sun	W	**+ THE EPIPHANY OF THE LORD:** *Gloria, Creed, Proper Preface* & Communicantes *of the Epiphany in the Roman Canon; an increased display of lights is recommended.* *At today's Mass, after the Gospel, the announcement may be made of moveable feasts according to the formula given in the Roman Pontifical, on page 1247 of the* Missale Romanum, editio typica tertia *and page 1505 of the Roman Missal.* **Mass & Office of the Solemnity**
8 Mon	W	**THE BAPTISM OF THE LORD:** *Gloria, (Alternative Collect), 1st or 2nd Reading, Gospel of Year B or ad lib Year B Readings, Proper Preface* **Mass & Office of the Feast**

The Season of Christmas ends.

INDEX OF ADVERTISEMENTS

INDEX

Calendar 2023

JANUARY
S	M	T	W	T	F	S
1	2	3	4	5	6	7
8	9	10	11	12	13	14
15	16	17	18	19	20	21
22	23	24	25	26	27	28
29	30	31				

FEBRUARY
S	M	T	W	T	F	S
			1	2	3	4
5	6	7	8	9	10	11
12	13	14	15	16	17	18
19	20	21	22	23	24	25
26	27	28				

MARCH
S	M	T	W	T	F	S
			1	2	3	4
5	6	7	8	9	10	11
12	13	14	15	16	17	18
19	20	21	22	23	24	25
26	27	28	29	30	31	

APRIL
S	M	T	W	T	F	S
						1
2	3	4	5	6	7	8
9	10	11	12	13	14	15
16	17	18	19	20	21	22
23	24	25	26	27	28	29
30						

MAY
S	M	T	W	T	F	S
	1	2	3	4	5	6
7	8	9	10	11	12	13
14	15	16	17	18	19	20
21	22	23	24	25	26	27
28	29	30	31			

JUNE
S	M	T	W	T	F	S
				1	2	3
4	5	6	7	8	9	10
11	12	13	14	15	16	17
18	19	20	21	22	23	24
25	26	27	28	29	30	

JULY
S	M	T	W	T	F	S
						1
2	3	4	5	6	7	8
9	10	11	12	13	14	15
16	17	18	19	20	21	22
23	24	25	26	27	28	29
30	31					

AUGUST
S	M	T	W	T	F	S
		1	2	3	4	5
6	7	8	9	10	11	12
13	14	15	16	17	18	19
20	21	22	23	24	25	26
27	28	29	30	31		

SEPTEMBER
S	M	T	W	T	F	S
					1	2
3	4	5	6	7	8	9
10	11	12	13	14	15	16
17	18	19	20	21	22	23
24	25	26	27	28	29	30

OCTOBER
S	M	T	W	T	F	S
1	2	3	4	5	6	7
8	9	10	11	12	13	14
15	16	17	18	19	20	21
22	23	24	25	26	27	28
29	30	31				

NOVEMBER
S	M	T	W	T	F	S
			1	2	3	4
5	6	7	8	9	10	11
12	13	14	15	16	17	18
19	20	21	22	23	24	25
26	27	28	29	30		

DECEMBER
S	M	T	W	T	F	S
					1	2
3	4	5	6	7	8	9
10	11	12	13	14	15	16
17	18	19	20	21	22	23
24	25	26	27	28	29	30
31						